God and Intelligence
in Modern Philosophy

GOD AND INTELLIGENCE
IN MODERN PHILOSOPHY

A CRITICAL STUDY IN THE LIGHT OF
THE PHILOSOPHY OF SAINT THOMAS

BY

FULTON J. SHEEN, PH.D., D.D., LL.D.
AGRÉGÉ DE L'INSTITUT SUPÉRIEUR DE PHILOSOPHIE À
L'UNIVERSITÉ DE LOUVAIN

WITH AN INTRODUCTION BY

G.K. CHESTERTON

IVE Press

New York – 2009

Cover Design
© IVE Press

Cover Art

Text
© National Society for the Propagation of the Faith

Institute of the Incarnate Word, Inc.

Manufactured in the United States of America

113 East 117th Street
New York, NY 10035

Ph. (212) 534 5257
Fax (212) 534 5258

E-mail IVEPRESS@IVE.ORG
http:// www.ivepress.org

ISBN 978-1-933871-30-1

© Catalogued in the Library of Congress of the US.

Printed in the United States of America ∞

REGINAE SINE LABE ORIGINALI CONCEPTAE
QUAE DUM CREATOREM TERRAE
PARIT IN TERRIS INCARNATUM
RERUM RECREANDARUM FACTA EST PRINCIPIUM
HOC QUALECUMQUE EST OPUS
IN EIUSIDEM CREATORIS HONOREM EXARATUM
MILLE BENEFICIORUM MEMOR
EIUSDEM VIRGINIS PATROCINIO
DUM EXCOGITAT DUM SCRIBIT DUM RETRACTAT
IMPETRATORUM
DEDICAT AUCTOR INDIGNUS
ALTERI SI POSSIT NEMINI
LIBENTIORI ANIMO PLACITURUS

Introduction

In this book, as in the modern world generally, the Catholic Church comes forward as the one and only real Champion of Reason. There was indeed a hundred years ago a school of free-thinkers which attacked Rome by an appeal to reason. But most of the recent free-thinkers are, by their own account rather than by ours, falling from reason even more than from Rome. One of the best and the most brilliant of them, Mr. Bernard Shaw, said only the other day that he could never entirely agree with the Catholic Church because of its extreme rationalism. In this perception he is at least quite rational; that is, as we poor rationalists would say, he is quite right. The Church is larger than the world; and she rightly resisted the narrow rationalists who maintained that everything in all the world could be approached in exactly the same way that is used for particular material things in this world. But she never said those things were not to be approached, or that reason was not the proper way to approach them, or that anybody had any right to be unreasonable in approaching anything. She defends the wisdom of the world as the way of dealing with the world; she defends common sense and consistent thinking and the perception that two and two make four. And today she is alone in defending them.

I remember a romance of a rambling but rather interesting sort which came out in one of the strange and sensational series that used to be produced by the late W. T. Stead. It began with the incident of a modern sceptical heroine going into a confessional-box and telling the priest that she did not believe in his religion. He asked her what she did believe in and she said reflectively, "Well, I don't believe in the Bible, and I don't think I believe in the immortality of the soul, and I'm not sure that I believe in God," and so on. And the unmoved cleric replied, "I didn't ask you what you didn't believe, but what you do believe." "Well," said the lady, "I believe that two and two make four." "Very well then," said the priest, "live up to that."

That always struck me as a good story, though it was in a queer setting; but it has had a still more queer sequel. In those last days of the nineteenth century, the sceptical lady did make that quotation from the multiplication table assuming it to be a minimum which nobody could possibly help believing. Yet somewhere about the same time the typical prophet of that period, Ibsen, may have been writing the words: "Who knows that two and two do not make five in the fixed stars?"

One would have thought that in an age of such fine and finished rationalists, somebody would have been rational enough to answer him with the obvious question: "If you are not sure there are any fixed facts, how do you come to be sure there are any fixed stars?" The very existence of many fixed stars is only proved by mathematics; that is, it is made by making a million times over the assumption that two and two make four. But curiously enough I have never heard of this sort of rational reply made to a doubt like that of Ibsen's except by Roman Catholics. The mathematical formula may be the maximum of the lady's belief and the minimum of the priest's philosophy, but he is more ready to stand up for his philosophy than she is for her religion. That sort of lady today is running after every raving fad of mysticism and credulity so long as it is opposed to reason. She is following M. Coué who says it is better to call things better because they are worse. She is running after Mrs. Eddy because Mrs. Eddy denounces a toothache which does not exist for existing. She is running after Professor Einstein because he is credited with saying that straight lines are crooked, that parallel lines meet, and that a yard may measure more one way than another. She is running after the pragmatists because they have a proof that all proofs are worthless. She is running after the Eastern mystics because they are supposed to say that nothing is good because it is everything or else that everything is good because it is really nothing. But the little priest is still sitting in his confessional-box believing that two and two make four, and living up to that.

The question to which Dr. Sheen here applies the rational as opposed to the irrational method is the most tremendous question in the world; perhaps the only question in the world. For that reason I prefer to leave its intrinsic consideration to him;

and in these few words of introduction to deal with the method rather than the subject matter. The subject matter is the nature of God in so far as it can be apprehended at all by the nature of man. As Dr. Sheen points out, the intellectual purity of the problem itself is much confused nowadays by a sort of sentimental version of the divine dignity of man. As in every other modern matter, the people in question seize on the sentiment without the reason for it. There is nothing particular about the objective anthropoid in a hat that anybody could be actually forced to regard him as a sacred animal; like a sacred cat or a sacred crocodile. This sentiment is a sediment; it is the dregs of our dogma about a divine origin. They begin by bowing down to man as the image of God; and then forget the God and bow down to the graven image. Similarly, as he also points out, the question of yes and no is weakened with all that wearisome discussion about less and more, which has been made fashionable ever since the old fuss about Evolution. It is the view that Being is Becoming; or that God does not exist yet, but may be said to be living in hopes. The blasphemy is not ours. It is enough for us that our enemies have retreated from the territory of reason, on which they once claimed so many victories; and have fallen back upon the borderlands of myth and mysticism, like so many other barbarians with whom civilization is at war.

G. K. Chesterton.

July, 1925.

Preface

THIS book does not pretend to be exhaustive. The field which it covers is too vast and the literature of the subject too varied to admit of minute analysis. Its aim is rather to suggest solutions of modern problems in the light of the philosophy of St. Thomas. To this end it sets in contrast the modern and the Thomistic notions of God and Intelligence. The modern notions, particularly those drawn from contemporary English and American philosophy, are first exposed uncritically and objectively. Whatever disadvantages such a method may have, it certainly has the great advantage of allowing modern thought to state itself, both in its negative and in its positive position on, the problem in hand.

A critical appreciation of the modern doctrines on God and Intelligence follows upon this exposition. The development of the Thomistic doctrine is prompted in almost every case by the line of thought of our contemporaries. There is no purely positive treatment of traditional doctrines. All this is presupposed. This work is merely an emphasis of certain points of view which have an interest for contemporary thought. It presumes that the Scholastic notions of God, His Nature and His Intelligence, as well as the criteriological and ontological problems of knowledge, have been already treated. Hence there is no attempt made in the course of this book to treat traditional theodicy in its entirety. Should the reader desire to read a classic presentation of the traditional thought on God and Intelligence, he can peruse with profit *Dieu, son Existence et sa Nature*, by Fr. Garrigou-Lagrange, O.P. It may also be interesting to study another presentation in *L'Intellectualisme de St. Thomas*, by Pierre Rousselot, S.J.

The five arguments for the existence of God have not been treated, because they have been thoroughly dealt with by others, and also because contemporary philosophy calls rather for a treatment of their substitute notions, such as religious experience and hypothesis. Thus, while positive expositions of Scholastic doctrine look towards the traditional, this work looks rather to the solutions which traditional thought may bring to modern problems. *It seeks to make St. Thomas functional, not for a school, but for a world.* It is only accidentally that St. Thomas belongs to the thirteenth century. His thought is no more confined to that period of human history than is the multiplication table. Truth is eternal though its verbal expression be localized in time and space. If need makes actuality, then St. Thomas was never more actual than he is today. If actuality makes modernity, then St. Thomas is the prince of modern philosophers. If a progressive universe is a contemporary ideal, then the philosophy of St. Thomas is its greatest realization. Modern Idealism needs the complement of his realism; empiricism needs his transcendental principles; philosophical biologism his metaphysics; sociological morality his ethics; sentimentalism his theory of the intelligence; and the world needs the God he knew and loved and adored.

I wish to thank all those who have assisted in any way in the publication of this book. I acknowledge much indebtedness to Rt. Rev. Simon Deploige, Ph.D., LL.D., for his personal interest and kind encouragement. My deepest thanks are also due to Dr. Léon Noël, who not only suggested the problem but kindly inspired everything that is best in the treatment of it. I am also indebted to Dr. Nicholas Balthasar and Dr. A. Mansion for their valuable criticisms and suggestions; and to Dr. J. G. Vance, Vice-President of St. Edmund's College, Ware, England, for the characteristically kind way in which he assisted in the revision of the manuscript. I wish, too, to thank my former colleague Fr. Ronald Knox, M.A., and my esteemed friend Dr. Gerald B. Phelan, for their kind help, each in his own particular way; and also Rev. F. T. Bentley and Rev. M. G. E. Copplestone for their assistance in correcting the proofs.

F.J. SHEEN

Louvain, June 19, 1925.

CONTENTS

PART I

CHAPTER I:

The Problem

MODERN philosophy has seen the birth of a new notion of God. There is nothing of greater importance, as there could be nothing more ultimate. Even the very attitude of one man to another or of one nation to another varies with the conception of God. The outlook on the world changes the moment the outlook on God changes. And if we had intellectual vigour enough to ascend from effects to causes, we would explain political, economical and social phenomena less by credit sheets, balance of trade and reparations, than by our attitude towards God.

The new idea of God has not burst upon the world with the suddenness of a new star. It has had its antecedents dating back over half a century. New scientific notions, increased faith in the philosophy of progress, birth of new values and interpretations of life, love of novelty, dissolution of dogmas, each has contributed its share to bring it into being.

Now that it is born, it stands before the world, not so much as a modified notion, as a new creation. Though coming from the past, it differs from all that has appeared in the past. It is, as it were, one of the novelties of evolution; it differs from the old even more than Aphrodite differs from the sea from which she sprang. Its face is set in another direction. It brings man into greater prominence. It exalts him even to the extent of giving him a "vote in the cosmic councils of the world." It is, in a word, the "transfer of the seat of authority from God to man."

But what is this new notion of God? It is God in evolution. God *is* not. He *becomes.* In the beginning was not the Word, but in the beginning was *Movement.* From this movement God is born by successive creations. As the world progresses, He progresses; as the world acquires perfection, He acquires perfection. He is therefore not the Alpha or the Omega of things, for His destiny and perfection lie hidden in the final evolution of the universe.

Man is a necessary step in the evolution of God. The divine shows in him as well as in God. One day it will manifest itself completely. Just as man came from the beast, God will come from man. The perfectibility of man implies the manifestation of the divine. "Men will be like Gods."

It is the purpose of this work to examine this new notion of God. But this problem cannot be adequately treated apart from another problem which is intimately bound up with it. This other problem is the value of the intelligence. As men lost faith in the intelligence, they acquired faith in the God of becoming. The modern God was born the day the "beast intellectualism" was killed. The day the intelligence is reborn, the modern God will die. They cannot exist together; for one is the annihilation of the other.

But why the intimate relation between the two? Apart from the purely technical reason which centres round the analogical notion of Being, there are two general considerations which englobe all others. The first is drawn from the universe, the second from God.

There is in all things a first perfection in virtue of their own specific nature. Because the specific being of one thing is not the being of another thing, one thing lacks the perfection of another. By the very fact that a lark is a lark, it must lack the perfection of a sunset. The perfection of every creature, then, is only relatively perfect, because it is only a *part* of the whole perfection of the universe, which includes the perfection of all particular things, just as one instrument in an orchestra is a part of the whole perfection of the harmony which issues from it.

To remedy this imperfection, by which one nature excludes the perfection of another nature, there has been given to some created things another perfection, namely, the *intellect*, in virtue of which it can know all things and possess within itself the perfection of other things, so that *the perfection of the whole universe can exist in it.* Man's ultimate end, according to Aristotle, consists in this knowledge of the order and cause of the universe; and for the Christian it consists in the beatific vision of God; for "what is there which may not be seen in seeing Him who sees all things?"[1]

The intellect, then, is the perfection of the universe because it can sum up all creation within itself. In doing this, it becomes the articulate spokesman of the universe and the great bond between brute matter and Infinite Spirit.

What happens, then, when a philosophy rejects the intellect? It breaks the link between the world and God, denies a hymn of divine praise to the Creator, and knocks the world into an unintelligible pluralism.

There is yet another reason for the close relation of God and the intellect. Its point of departure is the fact that man is the image of God. "The nature of an image requires likeness in species; thus the image of the king exists in the son: or, at least in some specific accident, and chiefly in the shape; thus we speak of a man's image in copper. Whence Hilary says pointedly that *an image is of the same species.*

"Now it is manifest that specific likeness follows the ultimate difference. But some things are like God first and most commonly because they *exist*; secondly, because they *live*; and thirdly, because they *know* or *understand*; and these last, as Augustine says, approach so near to God in likeness, that among all creatures nothing comes nearer to Him. It is clear, therefore,

---

*All citations have been taken without modification from Longmans, Green and Co.'s publication of Fulton Sheen's "God and Intelligence," (New York, 1938).

[1] *De Veritate*, q. 2 art. 2. (References to St. Thomas throughout this work are given without mentioning his name.) It is the Vives edition which is used, except for the *Summa*, when the Leonine edition is used. Cajetan (1468-1534), one of the most illustrious commentators on the works of St. Thomas, develops the above notion technically in his commentary on *Summa Theol.*, I q. 53 art. 3.

that intellectual creatures alone, properly speaking, are made to God's image."[2]

"Since man is said to be to the image of God by reason of his intellectual nature, he is the most nearly like God according to that in which he can best imitate God in his intellectual nature. Now the intellectual nature imitates God chiefly in this, that God understands and loves Himself. Wherefore we see that the image of God is in men ... inasmuch as man possesses a natural aptitude for understanding and loving God; and this aptitude consists in the very nature of the mind, which is common to all men."[3]

What results from this image of God in man, in virtue of his intellect? This conclusion: that, intensively and collectively considered, the *human intelligence is more perfect than all other visible creation*, because in it, as in no other creature, is found the capacity for the highest good, viz. God.[4] Being spiritual, and capable of possessing the visible universe within it in a spiritual way, it is already in potency for a knowledge of God, who is the Supreme Good—a capacity which soon passes into act through reasoning on the visible things of the universe which reveal the invisible God. gathering the invisible via the visible

Without the intelligence the universe lacks its perfection as without it man lacks his. Without it man ceases to be, not only the crown of visible creation, but even the image of God. We are like God inasmuch as we have an intellect; we are like beasts inasmuch as we have flesh. The denial of the intelligence is a denial of an infinitely perfect God, as a denial of an infinitely perfect God is a denial of the intelligence. The two problems are inseparable.

But why study this problem in the light of the philosophy of St. Thomas?

---

[2] I q. 93 art. 2 c.

[3] I q. 93 art. 4 c. The image of God may be in man in a second and third way, both of which are proper to the supernatural order, viz. inasmuch as man habitually knows and loves God, and this image consists in the conformity of grace; and inasmuch as man loves God perfectly, and this image consists in the likeness of glory. Hence a threefold image of creation, re-creation and likeness. The first is in all men, the second only in the just and the third only in the blessed in heaven.

[4] I q. 93 art. 2 ad 3. "Id autem in quo creatura rationalis excedit alias creaturas est intellectus."—I q. 93 art. 6 c.

One reason, and that negative, certainly is the self-confessed bankruptcy of modern thought.[5] No philosophical congress is complete today without a lecture on the confusion amid philosophers. The world is full of thinking, but there is no agreement in thought. There are philosophers, but there is no philosophy. There are "distinguished men but no man; big heads but no head. Heads of schools without schools, leaders without followers, societies without members."[6] Spencerian thought has been buried in the grave of the Unknowable; the history of Pragmatism is now being written as an exaggerated reaction against Idealism. Italian Neo-idealism has dissolved philosophy into history and melted reality into mind; Bergsonian *becoming* is decaying, and a sort of philosophical *biologism* remains as its heritage. The hurry, the fever, the restlessness, the excitement which blind us to the divine in things leave nothing but a philosophy of action for men of action. ... "Men are suffering from the fever of violent emotion, and so they make a philosophy of it."[7]

It is not Neo-Thomism which is criticizing modern thought. It is modern thinkers. Those who have most contributed to philosophical chaos are now assuming a pessimistic outlook for the philosophical future which they have helped to create. Testimonies of modern thinkers are abundant on this point. Speaking of his contemporaries, George Santayana writes in his own excellent style: "There is much life in some of them. I like their water-coloured sketches of self-consciousness, their rebellious egotisms, their fervid reforms of phraseology; their peep-holes through which some very small parts of things may be seen very clearly; they have lively wits, but they seem to me like children playing blind-man's-buff; they are keenly excited at not knowing where they are. They are really here, in the common natural world, where there is nothing in particular to threaten or

[5] The word *modern* throughout this work is used not to designate a period of time but a state of mind. It is not chronological but descriptive, and applies particularly to all forms of philosophy which believe in *modernizing* the conception of God to keep pace either with the advance of science or with the needs of the age.

[6] Dr. LUDWIG STEIN, *Die philosophischen Strömungen der Gegenwart.* Translation by Maitra (1918), p. 7.

[7] S. RADHAKRISHNAN, *The Reign of Religion in Contemporary Philosophy* (1922), pp. 41, 46.

allure them, and they have only to remove their philosophical bandages to see where they are."[8]

Professor Lovejoy remarks: "What the public wants most from its philosophers is an experience of initiation; what it is initiated into is often a matter of secondary importance. Men delight in being ushered past the guarded portals, in finding themselves in dim and awful precincts of thought unknown to the natural man, in experiencing the hushed moment of revelation and in gazing upon strange symbols of which none can tell just what they symbolize."[9]

But where turn for sanity? Professor A. E. Taylor has given his answer. "If philosophy," he says, "is ever to execute her supreme task, she will need to take into more serious account, not only the work of the exact sciences, but the teachings of the great masters of life ... For us it means that it is high time philosophy ceased to treat the great Christian theologians as credulous persons whose convictions need not be taken seriously ... If we are to be philosophers in earnest we cannot afford to have any path which may lead to the heart of life's mystery blocked for us by placards bearing the labels 'reactionary,' 'unmodern' and their likes. That what is most modern must be best is a superstition which it is strange to find in a really educated man. A philosopher at any rate should be able to endure the charge of being 'unmodern' with fortitude ... Abelard and Saint Thomas very likely would have failed as advertising agents, company promoters or editors of sensational daily papers. But it may well be that both are better fitted than Lord Northcliffe ... to tell us whether God is or what God is.

"In short, if we mean to be philosophical our main concern will be that our beliefs should be true; we shall care very little

---

[8] *Soliloquies in England and Later Soliloquies*, p. 210.

[9] *The Practical Tendencies of Bergsonism*, p. 2. *Cf.* RALPH BARTON PERRY, *Recent Philosophical Tendencies*, pp. 20, 22. "Modern philosophers have a message for the age, and that is the declaration of independence from the claims of the intellect. They pat the plain man on the back, and give him a philosophy which would justify his beliefs about the world. They tell him, we do not force on you any scheme of metaphysics, but give you only a method or a way of dealing with things, and you are free to fasten the system to any system of values. They fix no standpoints and profess no theory. They are philosophical anarchists doubting all thought and believing all facts."—S. RADHAKRISHNAN, *The Reign of Religion in Contemporary Philosophy* (1922), p. 46.

whether they happen to be popular with the intellectual 'proletarians' of the moment, and if we can get back to truth we shall not mind having to go back a long way after it."[10]

This opinion is becoming more general. There is even now a decided willingness to turn to *philosophia perennis*, and the long tradition of common sense. Over twenty-five years ago, when Neo-Thomism was born, it met with violent opposition. Rudolf Eucken wrote his *Thomas von Aquino und Kant, ein Kampf zweier Welten*, denouncing the menace of the new philosophy. In 1924, at the Philosophical Congress of Naples, the distinguished Neo-Thomist, Fr. Gemelli, occupied a platform with Professor A. Liebert of the Kantgesellschaft: the latter to recognize in the philosophy of St. Thomas a complement to critical philosophy; the former to show the necessity of such a complement.

In other words, the time is at hand when modern philosophy, not only because of its own confessed bankruptcy, but also because of the inherent merits of the *philosophia perennis*, must take definite cognizance of the thought of St. Thomas. This brings us to the positive side of the philosophy of the Angelic Doctor, namely, the fact that he is the first of modern philosophers, as M. Étienne Gilson of the University of Paris has put it. "He is the first, not because he has created the principles and invented the attitude in which we live, nor because all the directions of thought by which the thirteenth century prepared the modern epoch were concentrated in his works; but because he is the first occidental of whom the thought is neither enslaved to dogma nor to a system."[11]

But there is yet another reason why the philosophy of St. Thomas is particularly useful at this moment. What are the two great problems with which modern philosophy is struggling? Are they not the immanence of God in the universe and the subjectivity of thought? All religion hangs on the first and all

[10] *Recent Developments in European Thought*, p. 48. *Cf. St. Thomas as a Philosopher*, same author: "But if we are not all of us professed Thomists, we are all, I believe, agreed to recognize in St. Thomas one of the great master-philosophers of human history, whose thought is part of the permanent inheritance of civilized Europeans, and whose influence is still living and salutary" (p. 1).

[11] ÉTIENNE GILSON, *Études de Philosophie médiévale* (1921), preface, p. V.

science on the second. The divine and the human are in the balance with these two problems.

But there is no philosophical system in existence which so completely and thoroughly treats and solves these questions as the Thomistic. In recent years deep students have taken out of St. Thomas the fundamental principles which underlie his whole work. One of them is the real distinction between essence and existence; the other is the doctrine of realism in knowledge. The first has been called the "fundamental truth of Christian philosophy;"[12] the second the "corner-stone of philosophical reconstruction."[13] Both of these fundamental principles are the solutions of the two vexed problems of modern thought.

If solution of modern problems is a recommendation for a philosophy which, in the strict sense, is neither ancient nor modern, but *ultra-modern*,[14] then the philosophy of St. Thomas is pre-eminently suitable to modern times. It is *ultra-modern*, because it is spiritual and is not subject to decrepitude and death. "By its universality, it overflows infinitely, in the past as in the future, the limits of the present moment; it does not oppose itself to modern systems, as the past to that which is actually given, but as something perennial to something momentary. *Anti-modern* against the errors of the present time, it is *ultra-modern* for all truths enveloped in the time to come."[15]

Intellectual restoration is the condition of economic and political restoration. Intellectual values are needed more than "cosmic imaginings," and God is needed more than "a new idea of God." If we look to the foundations, the superstructure will take care of itself. Thomistic Intellectualism is the remedy against anarchy of ideas, riot of philosophical systems and breakdown of spiritual forces. "The Intelligence is life and the greatest thing there is in life."[16] This Thomistic principle is at once an expression of the ideal of modern philosophy and the very preventative against its decay.

---

[12] N. DEL PRADO, *De Veritate Fundamentali philosophiae Christianae* (1911).

[13] LÉON NOËL, *Saint Thomas et la Pensée moderne* (1925), p. 12.

[14] JACQUES MARITAIN, *Antimoderne* (1922), p. 16. M. Maritain was at one time a disciple of M. Bergson, and at present is one of the leaders of the Thomistic restoration in France.

[15] JACQUES MARITAIN, *Antimoderne* (1922), p. 16.

[16] *Contra Gentes*, lib. 4 c. I I.

This work is divided into two parts. The first is an exposition without criticism of the modern grievances against an intellectualist philosophy along with its attacks on any intellectual knowledge of God and the substitute notion—the God of becoming. The second part is a critical examination of the modern doctrines of the intelligence and God in the light of the philosophy of St. Thomas.

CHAPTER II:

The modern attack on the intelligence

(A) Considered as a faculty

WHAT is the purpose of the intellect? Is it the faculty of the divine, the transcender of the contingent, the plaything of the contemplative, or is it merely a primitive tool used crudely by men for want of a better instrument? Does not science itself demonstrate the truth of the latter alternative? At what age do we fix the appearance of man on earth? Is it not at the time when he manufactured tools and arms? The old quarry of Moulin-Quignon is the remotest scientific evidence we have of this fact. Man first showed intelligence in manufacturing tools ... further than this we know nothing about intelligence on this earth. Though it be a long stretch from this day and age to the quarry of Moulin-Quignon, is it not true that even today we find men still making and utilizing instruments, not exclusively instruments of necessity, it is true, but those of luxury and comfort? "If therefore we could strip ourselves of all pride, and if, in order to define our species, we hold strictly to that which history and prehistory present us as the constant character of man and intelligence, we would not say perhaps *Homo sapiens*, but *Homo Faber*."[17] "Speculation is a luxury, action is a necessity."[18]

To the latter the intelligence is destined. It is the great right arm of mechanics, but, being practical, it is alien to the needs of the thinker. It exists solely for human needs and is limited by them.[19] It serves man for a time in his upward march of

---

[17] HENRI BERGSON, *L'Évolution Créatrice*, 21st edition, p. 151.

[18] Ibid., p. 47.

[19] J.B. BAILLIE, *Studies in Human Nature*, pp. 36, 149. WILLIAM KINGSLAND, *Our Infinite Life* (1922), p. 187. "So strong is the bent of the intellect towards matter...etc."—H.

evolution, but sooner or later it is destined to be replaced by a faculty of the spirit. As men get out of the practical the intelligence ceases to have value for them. Its "imperialism of principle and mechanism of means"[20] stamp it as geometric and rigid. Everything which is evil is to be attributed to the intelligence, not only in the field of philosophy, but in that of politics and economics. Even the defeat of the German army, it has been said, was due to its intellectualism.[21] In any case its practical character excludes it from philosophy. To some other faculty than the intelligence the philosopher must make his appeal.

(B) Attack on the Intelligence considered in its Operation

If the *purpose* of the intellect as a *faculty* has been exaggerated in the past, it would seem true also that *the value of its operations* has been grossly misrepresented. Here a few elementary facts may help to fix the misrepresentations.

The three operations of the intellect are, it will be recalled, apprehension, judgment and reasoning.

Apprehension is the act by which the intelligence sees or perceives something without affirming or denying it.

Judgment is the act of the mind by which it unites in affirming and separates in denying certain predicates of a given subject; *e.g.* Peter is mortal or Peter is not a quadruped.

Reasoning is the act of the mind by which it passes from a truth already known to another truth not previously known.

WILDON CAR., Litt.D., *The Philosophy of Change*, p. 176. For the intelligence considered as a unifier of discordant knowledge, see GEORGE SHANN, *Evolution of Knowledge* (1922), p. 94. For the intelligence considered as the faculty of cataloguing all things under one of four possible relations, see J. C. THOMAS, D.Sc., *Life, Mind and Knowledge* (1921), p. 66. The relations, according to this writer, are: (1) the relation of a sense impression to previous ones as to whether it is like or different; (2) relative disposition of objects and events in space; (3) the relative order and sequence in time; (4) their physical descent or parentage, *i.e.* out of what collocation of condition and forces did they emerge, and to what changes in time can they give birth?

[20] PAUL GEMAHLING, *Le Procès de l'Intelligence.*

[21] Ibid. (1922), p. 22

(a) Abstraction

The absurdity of abstraction is said to be evident, once its process has been explained. According to the modern conception, abstraction may be represented as either additive or subtractive. Additive abstraction is the consideration of the elements which are to be found common in phenomena without any regard for their differences. "It is essentially a human production; it is obtained by considering some special aspect in which certain experiences resemble one another, as mentally isolated from the aspects in which they differ."[22] The additive abstractive process, thus understood, applied to any army passing in review would be the consideration of the most common element in it—the uniform, for example. The poverty of the abstractive process, then, is immediately revealed in the scantiness of the knowledge it gives us.

In the words of Professor Stout, "Abstraction is the name given to the method by which the universal is found, that method being, we are told, to leave out what is different in the particular instances compared and to add together what they possess in common. If we look at the actual procedure of thought, we do not find this account confirmed. Gold, silver, copper and lead differ in colour, brilliancy, weight and density, but their universal which we call metal is not found on comparison by simply leaving out these differences without compensation."[23] "Life does not proceed by the association and addition of elements."[24] Abstraction at bottom is therefore essentially unlifelike.

Besides the *additive* abstraction there is also the *subtractive* abstraction of which Taine spoke. Here the mind considers the common elements not directly but indirectly. The additive abstraction adds the common notes, the subtractive abstraction

---

[22] GEORGE SHANN, *The Evolution of Knowledge* (1922), p. 54; also chap. III.

[23] STOUT, "Nature of Universals," *Mind* (April 1922). p. 189. For Professor Stout, the universal is "distributive unity of a class."

[24] *L'Évolution Créatrice*, p. 97. "La blancheur d'un lis n'est pas la blancheur d'une nappe de neige."—H. BERGSON, *Matière et Mémoire*, p. 171. "If we are asked how we arrive at the description of an apple, for example, assuming now the apple as part of the already accepted world of real things to which we react, we should naturally say that we note by the abstracting eye the redness of the apple, the taste, the shape, and ignoring the fact that these are embodied in a particular existential form, we hold them before the mind in their own right just as characters."—A. W. ROGERS, *What is Truth?* (1922), p. 62.

strips off common notes. It is the concave side of additive abstraction. It may be represented as a "peeling process."

Imagine an essence in the centre of an onion by which it is intelligible. In order to get to the essence the onion must be peeled, each peel corresponding to an individuating note.

"The botanist who wishes to describe the artichoke describes the stem, the root, and the leaves. The metaphysician eliminates all that and studies the rest. This manner of procedure, exposed in this form, seems absurd; it is, however, that of the metaphysicians. When it is a question of living beings, they eliminate all the physico-chemical phenomena. This elimination made, they suppose that there still remains something." [25]

If the poverty of the intellectual method be revealed in the mere consideration of its abstractive process, its complete

---

[25] DELBERT, *La Science et la Réalité*, p. 117.

"L'Intelligence d'après lui (conceptualisme) resout l'unité superficielle de l'individu en qualités diverses, dont chacune, *isolée* de l'individu qui la limitait, devient par là même, représentative d'un genre."—*Matière et Mémoire*, p. 171.

"We begin with the whole continuous given reality; in order to deal with it, we have to analyse it, to isolate the elements with which we are to deal. This isolation must of course remove those elements from their setting in the rest of reality...we may presumably remove the lack of sunshine during the summers 1912 and 1913 from its relation of simultaneity with Mr. Asquith's Premiership without affecting its nature at all in any other respect ... The point which I wish to emphasize in this connection is that there are some relations whose removals make no difference to the related term other than the removal itself."—WILLIAM TEMPLE, *Mens Creatrix* (1923), pp. 73-78.

The American philosopher William James has delivered himself of a critique of conceptual knowledge, but has openly confessed it to be Bergsonian in character. He has dedicated Chapter VI of *Pluralism* to his French colleague's attacks. M. Bergson, he writes, made him more bold in his anti-intellectualism (*Pluralistic Universe*, p. 212). And in the letter of congratulations which Professor James sent to M. Bergson on the occasion of the publication of his *L'Évolution Créatrice*, we find the following: "O my Bergson, you are a magician...to me at present the vital achievement of the book is that it inflicts an irremediable death-wound upon Intellectualism. It can never resuscitate....But the beast has its death-wound now, and the manner in which you have inflicted it (internal versus *temps d'arrêt*) is masterly in the extreme. I feel that at bottom you and I are fighting the same fight, you a commander, and I in the ranks ... I am so enthusiastic as to have said only two days ago ... I thank heaven that I have lived to this date ... that I have witnessed the Russo-Japanese War, and seen Bergson's new book appear ... the two great modern turning-points in history and thought."—(*Letters*, vol. ii pp. 290-4.) Two days after he wrote this letter, he sent another to Doctor Schiller of Oxford, who also shares his views, as the letter indicates: "But have you read Bergson's new book? It seems to me that nothing is important in comparison with that divine apparition; all our positions, real time, a growing world, asserted magisterially, and the beast intellectualism killed absolutely dead."—(Ibid., vol. ii p. 290.)

uselessness is said to be revealed in the idea or the concept which it gives us.

In most recent years the attack on the concept has become less marked, it now being accepted as a foregone conclusion that it has been proved worthless. There is no use in beating a dead dog. Whatever philosophical criticism is given today is in greater part a repetition of that made by the great French Academician Henri Bergson. It is under his leadership that the intellectualist position has met its severest attacks, and it is round his arguments that all modern anti-intellectualists rally. Not only to his anti-intellectualism but also to his positive doctrine English philosophy is profoundly indebted. The greater portion of English and American philosophy which has appeared in recent years is Bergsonian in inspiration. In giving the critique of M. Bergson we are giving one which is original, forceful and sincere.

(b) Concept

The general criticism of the concept, under which fall all particular criticisms, is that the concept is "naturally unsuited for life."[26]

It is unsuited for life, for three reasons:—

1. It substitutes a symbol for reality.
2. It solidifies movement.
3. It breaks up what is continuous and successive.

1. The primary condition that a concept must fulfil, if it is to be suited for life, is that it give reality itself and not a mere symbol of reality. Life deals with realities and not with figures, with substances and not with shadows. But a concept gives merely figures, shadows and symbols, and is consequently unsuited for the purposes of life. At best it gives us merely "a rubric under which we write all living beings,"[27] or a "frame in which we place an infinity of objects one alongside the other."[28] The concept "man," for example, is such a scheme under which all the individual men in the world are grouped. It has the advantage of

[26] *L'Évolution Créatrice*, p. 179.
[27] Ibid., p. 28.
[28] Ibid., p. 162.

extension, it is true, but it reveals nothing about the nature of the reality. It lacks comprehension, and in lacking that it fails to attain reality.[29] The mind in the face of reality merely stamps out a ticket or gives a receipt which is valuable for all objects of that class, but this ticket or receipt is in no way representative of reality. It is a mere symbol or a *sucédané* that is no longer remembered as such.[30]

In generating concepts the mind "generates signs, institutes relations and analogies, substitutes its representations and its disconnected language, for the direct voice of all simple things."[31] Concepts give us a "world of representations as in a cage of glazed glass, where we are in contact with products of industry, *artificiata*, very much as in a museum, where, under the pretext of a lesson on things in themselves, we know the field of wheat only by a dry straw glued to a pasteboard along with other dead samples."[32] To accept this symbol or substitute, the *sucédané* of the real, as the real itself is no less foolish, according to M. Blondel, than for a young lover, in the presence of his fiancée, to continue to look at her photograph instead of looking on her.[33]

And furthermore, if the concept is a mere substitute for reality there is necessarily an unbridgable distance between mind and object. How can the subject ever know the object if a mere rubric or frame or symbol insists on putting itself between the two? It would seem, therefore, from the mere consideration of the concept considered in itself, that the intelligence is characterized, as M. Bergson has told us, by a natural unfitness for life.

2. *It solidifies movement.*—The first characteristic of life is movement. So fundamental is this characteristic that immobility is often taken as the first apparent sign of death. Not only is the

[29] Ibid., p. 162.

[30] M. BLONDEL, *Le Procès de l'Intelligence*, p. 228.

[31] M. BLONDEL, *Le Procès de l' Intelligence*, p. 231. *Cf. L'Évolution Créatrice*, p.97.

[32] Ibid., p. 237.

"The danger of this conception (stratification of sedimentary ideas) is that when a new problem presents itself to the thought, or a new reality presents itself to be studied, there is the irresistible temptation for it, in place of laboriously creating the original method or concept which is necessary for the reality, to try to seek in the old arsenal of ready-made ideas that which can dispense it from this intellectual effort."—Ibid., p. 20.

[33] Ibid., p. 243.

individual life in movement, but the whole universe with it, whether it be organically or biologically considered. Evolution is in the background of all modern science.

What does the intellect do in the face of movement? First of all, to seize movement it must break it up, by taking snapshots of it. The multitudinous photographs which are quickly run through a moving-picture machine introduce an extrinsic and impersonal movement, but in themselves they are not photographs of the movement. Neither is the concept expressive of movement, but merely snapshots of it. While it is busy at this work, life which is fluid is passing away all the time.[34]

Then, again, to represent movement it must fall back on a juxtaposition of these snapshots as is done in the moving-picture machine. It represents the becoming as a "series of states, of which each one is homogeneous with itself and consequently does not change." Life is liquid, abstraction is solid. One therefore cannot represent the other. The Humpty Dumpty that fell from the wall, with the help of all the king's horses and all the king's men could never be put together again. So neither can life be constructed in its liquid wholeness, once it has been solidified by thought. "Out of no amount of discreteness can you manufacture the concrete."[35]

In virtue of this tendency to solidify, which is proper to the intelligence, it remains incapable of ever seizing novelty and creation. "Our intelligence is satisfied with a consequence determined in function of determined antecedents, or means determined in function of determined end." But novelty and creation have no antecedents. The intelligence, therefore, remains incapable of ever grasping them.[36]

Furthermore, since all life is in evolution, and since an eternal *devenir* is at the bottom of all things, is not the intelligence itself a mere emanation of this evolution, and just a product of its

---

[34] *L'Évolution Créatrice*, pp. 323-55. "Life appears to intellectual apprehension as an extension, as a succession of states."—H. WILDON CARR, Litt.D., *The Philosophy of Change* (1912), p. 29. Concepts enable us " to catch hold as it were of certain positions of our changeful stream of presentations."—C. H. RICHARDSON, *Supremacy of Spirit*, p.19.

[35] W. JAMES, *Pluralistic Universe*, p. 253. "Concepts are merely a limit and a mean zone to the total superior life."—*Le Procès de l'Intelligence*, article of PAUL ARCHAMBAULT, p. 20.

[36] *L'Évolution Créatrice*, pp. 177-8.

process? To say, therefore, that the intelligence can grasp evolution is to say the part can grasp the whole ... and obviously this is absurd.[37]

3. *It breaks up what is continuous and successive.*—The universe is a continuum; it is an organic whole; its growth is biological, not crystalline. The senses reveal this continuity. If we but run our fingers over a surface, we are in contact with it continuously. But what does the intelligence do in the face of this continuity? It breaks up the continuous into discrete parts. It represents time by a constant, instead of representing it as a continuous succession or flux.[38]

This analytic static character of the intelligence is due to its very nature. From the moment it came from the hands of nature, it was destined for inorganic solids.[39] It can better handle reality for its practical uses by splitting it up, and for this reason it has been the ideal faculty for mechanics. Every division of matter into independent bodies of absolute determined shapes is artificial.[40] This the intelligence does of necessity.

The conclusion which contemporary thought draws from this critique is that the intelligence is smitten by a general incapacity to understand life. It gives only dead conceptual symbols instead of living realities; it reveals the dynamic as static, the concrete as abstract, the fluid as a solid, and the living as inert. Following it, we are "brought to ease only in the discontinuous, the immobile and death."[41]

An additional word about judgment and reasoning may be desirable.

The elements which enter into a judgment are concepts. But the concepts, according to the findings of contemporary thought, are not representative of the real—but mere substitutes for it.

---

[37] Ibid., Introd., p. 2. "Our intellect takes views of movement, frames it and moulds it in rigid concepts, but lets the movement itself escape."—H. WILDON CARR, *The Philosophy of Change*, p. 36. "Intellect is only a function of life, not life itself."—WILLIAM KINGSLAND, *Our Infinite Life* (1922). "The nature of our intellect is to know reality in the static form we call matter, and not in the flowing form we call life."—The *Philosophy of Change*, p.176.

[38] *L'Évolution Créatrice*, p. 10.

[39] Ibid., p. 167.

[40] H. BERGSON, *Matière et Mémoire.*

[41] *L'Évolution Créatrice*, p. 179.

The judgment, then, will share the shortcoming of its elements and fail in like manner to reach reality.[42]

The consequence is that we will henceforth be less interested in the truth of judgments than in their value. The fundamental importance of this philosophy of value will be clearly seen in our treatment of religious experience.[43]

The third operation of the mind is reasoning, by which the mind passes from the known to the unknown truth. But what is reasoning but the combination of concepts and judgments? Both of these, according to the modern position, are inadequate for life. Reasoning based on them must then of necessity be worthless. Mr. Bertrand Russell tells us that "reason and analysis are blind gates leading to the morass of illusion."[44]

So far the first headlong attack upon the reasoning powers. We turn to pass rapidly in review some of the philosophies that have contributed to the anti-intellectualist assault by disparaging all proof, and by discarding truth.

A philosophy without proofs is what is wanted for men of action who "propose something and do not want to be restrained by the necessity of giving reasons for it."[45] "It would seem that knowledge concerning the universe as a whole is not to be obtained by metaphysics, and that the proposed proofs, that, in virtue of the laws of logic, such and such things must exist and such and such others cannot, are not capable of surviving careful scrutiny."[46] "We find an assumption that was the soul of Scholasticism, the assumption, namely, that anything that is necessary in the way of belief must be susceptible of articulate proof, as rampant as it ever was, in the religious agnosticism of today; and we find it, moreover, blossoming out into corollaries, as for instance that to believe anything without such proof is to

---

[42] Ibid., pp. 330-32.

[43] "At the present time philosophy is carried on more explicitly in terms of value than at any previous time."—A. SETH PRINGLE-PATTISON, LL.D., D.C.L., *The Idea of God* (2nd edition), p. 39.

[44] *Mysticism and Logic* (1918), p. 9.

[45] RALPH BARTON PERRY, *Present Conflict of Ideals*, p. 296.

[46] BERTRAND RUSSELL, M.A., F.R.S., *Problems of Philosophy*, p. 221.

be unscientific, and that to be unscientific is the lowest depth to which a man can fall."[47]

Professor James, thanks to the influence of M. Henri Bergson, came to emancipate himself completely from all logic. "For my part, I have found myself compelled to *give up logic*, fairly, squarely and irrevocably. It has an imperishable use in human life, but that use is not to make us acquainted with the essential nature of reality ... Reality, life, experience, concreteness, immediacy, use what word you will, exceeds our logic, overflows and surrounds it." Vision, then, and not proof is the supreme way of attaining truth. "A man's vision is the great fact about him. Who cares for Carlyle's reason, or Schopenhauer's or Spinoza's? Philosophy is the expression of man's most intimate character, and all definitions of the universe are but the deliberately adopted reactions of human character upon it ... Philosophy is only a matter of passionate vision rather than of logic—logic only finding reasons for the vision afterwards."[48] "Emotional congeniality and social prestige" precede it.[49] Demonstration attaches itself to consistency. But consistency is an attribute of the intellectualist position. Proofs therefore must be made less exacting. "Abstract consistency," Dr. Bradley tells us, "is a superstitious idolatry;"[50] and when speaking of the subject of religion and the need of logic and consistency in treating of its subject-matter, he asks, "Is there any need for us to avoid self-contradiction?"[51] Sir Henry Jones would not go so far, but he would stop at contraries. "We cannot rest in contradiction, but we can be content with opposites."[52] What all philosophy up to this time has called contradiction, is now really only a choice of things more or less satisfactory. Not merely in theory, but in the very act of philosophizing itself, the fundamental principles of thought are removed from their lofty and absolute position and

[47] W. JAMES, Preface to PAULSEN'S *Introduction to Philosophy.*

[48] *Pluralistic Universe*, pp. 212-14, p. 20, p. 176.

[49] JOHN DEWEY, *Reconstruction in Philosophy* (1920), p. 20.

[50] F. BRADLEY, *Essays in Truth and Reality*, p. 445

[51] Ibid., p. 430.

[52] *A Faith that Enquires*, p. 317. He admits, however, that we are all consistent. The difficulty a philosopher will have in objecting to Bradley is made quite clear by himself: "If you are willing to be inconsistent you cannot be refuted."—*Truth and Reality*, p. 235.

made something relative and changing.[53] Thus in the free philosophy of vision, loosened from the strait jackets of Intellectualism, we must not be shocked to find such statements as this: "The contradiction of a conation co-existing with fruition must be realized."[54] The modern mind is not long in choosing between the "apparent discord of healthy moral sentiment" and the artificial moral symmetry of a philosophic system.[55]

Not only will consistency and logic cease to be the ideal of modern thought, but even truth itself will cease to be the ideal. Professor Radhakrishnan in enumerating the characteristics of modern thought points this out as important: "Now we do not care," he writes, "to ascertain whether an opinion is true or false, but only whether it is life-furthering, life-preserving. We start with a certain view of life, think of a few things as necessary to it, and conclude that they are true and objective ... Impulse to knowledge and love of truth cease to be the motives of philosophy, and some moral ideas or religious prejudices which we wish to defend even at the cost of consistency take their place."[56]

So true is this, that one of the modern thinkers explicitly states that the condition upon which you accept his conclusion is that you cease to use the criterion of truth. "No one is likely to content himself with the doctrine which I advocate, if he believes there is no truth except the truth which is self-consistent and ultimate."[57] Truth is not an end of dialectics; it is merely a "preliminary means to other vital satisfactions."[58] "There is no reason to set up a peculiar process of verification for the satisfying of an intellectual interest, different in kind from the

[53] F. C. S. SCHILLER, *Humanism*, p. 188. "The trained Scholastic, if you are so ill advised as to enter into argument with him, will break down all your miserable modern criticisms of Saint Thomas and will prove to you logically the existence of all his medieval entities. You remain speechless and unconvinced. For his entities no matter how logical will not fit in with our modern view, and in spite of logic we can no longer get from them any sense of reality."—PRATT, *Religious Consciousness*, p. 199.

[54] B. BOSANQUET, *Individuality and Value*, Appendix, p. 248. "See the reasoning process by which a transition is made through contradictories, thanks to the magic word 'nevertheless.'"—A. SETH PRINGLE PATTISON, *The Idea of God*, p. 317.

[55] T. B. BAILLIE, *Studies in Human Nature* (1921), p. 10.

[56] *The Reign of Religion in Contemporary Philosophy*, p. 13.

[57] F. BRADLEY, *Essays on Truth and Reality*, p. 437.

[58] W. JAMES, *Pragmatism*.

rest, superior in dignity and autocratic in authority. For there is no pure intellect."[59] M. le Roy goes even further than his English colleague: "It is not a question of being right or wrong. It is a mark of great coarseness to wish to be right ... It is a testimony of a great want of culture."[60] Even the source of Truth itself is to be suspected of being polluted. We are bound to conclude, one recent author tells us, "that in the cosmic ordering of human life the Spirit of the world must have something else to do than to be reasonable as we count reasonableness. It is possible that not reasonableness but dramatic completeness may be the chief unifying quality of man's life."[61] If the term "truth" is to be retained it is merely to mean that which "works well," or the "satisfyingness of a conclusion," or its "cash value in terms of particular experience."[62]

Briefly, Intellectualism, according to the modern doctrine, is an enemy of life. It is cold, inert, unsympathetic. Its symbol is the "cold and perfect image of Minerva at the top of the Parthenon, the serenity of whose visage expresses all the certitudes, and the folds of whose marble robes have all the symmetric rigidity of the syllogism—those tranquil Roman ways of the intelligence."[63]

The science of metaphysics, which has reared itself upon these lifeless foundations, must therefore cease to claim a worth for itself. "It must always take in its final form an idiosyncrasy"[64] and in its final form it is "a work of imagination superimposed upon other works of the imagination," or, in the well-known words of Dr. Bradley, the "science of giving bad reasons for what we believe on instinct."[65]

Intellectualism is consequently a highly defective philosophical method; it is a "besetting sin,"[66] even "the very original sin of thought,"[67] and a "beast."[68] Imagination is superior to the

---

[59] F. C. S. SCHILLER, *Studies in Humanism*, p. 7.
[60] *Revue de Philosophie* (1906), vol. ii. p. 417.
[61] J. B. BAILLIE, *Studies in Human Nature*, p. 11.
[62] W. JAMES, *Varieties of Religious Experience*, p. 448, p. 443.
[63] GAETAN BERNOVILLE, *Minerva ou Belphégor* (1921), p. 153.
[64] F. C. S. SCHILLER, *Studies in Humanism*, p. 18.
[65] *Appearance and Reality*, p. xiv
[66] W. JAMES, Preface to PAULSEN'S *Introduction to Philosophy.*
[67] H. BERGSON, *Matière et Mémoire.*
[68] *Letters of William James*, vol. ii. p. 296.

intellect, and this for no less than sixteen reasons.[69] Aesthetics surpasses it as a clue to reality; the artistic vision of Apollo is superior to the logic of Socrates, "Marguerite is worth more than Aristotle."[70] Belphegor is superior to Minerva.[71]

> 'But yesterday the word of reason might
> Have stood against the world; now lies it there,
> And none so poor to do it reverence.'

[69] D. W. FAWCETT, *Divine Imagining.*
[70] Ibid., p. 213.
[71] GAETAN BERNOVILLE, *Minerva ou Belphégor* (1921).

CHAPTER III:

REJECTION OF THE DEMONSTRABILITY OF GOD'S EXISTENCE, AND SOME NEW APPROACHES

IT follows from the preceding train of thought that the "theism of philosophical research in which the idea of God is arrived at by a process of reflective thought must give way to the theism of religious consciousness for which God is in some way an immediate object."[72] The system which, "starting with the intellectual standpoint, moves along with the intellectual action of man," must give way to the other which "begins from the standpoint of religion and moves along with the religious and spiritual experience."[73]

Contemporary thought is practically unanimous upon this point. In 1904 Professor James Pratt sent to William James a list of questions on the subject of religious belief. In answer to the question, "Why do you believe in God? Is it from argument?" the Harvard Professor answered, "Emphatically No."[74] All arguments for the existence of God he regarded as illusory.[75] In his work on Religious Experience he made his answer clearer: "Can the existence of God be proven? No. The book of Job went over this whole matter once for all and definitely. Ratiocination is a relatively superficial and unreal path to the

---

[72] W. R. SORLEY, *Moral Values and the Idea of God* (2nd edition, 1921), p. 302.

Cf. R. ALFRED HOERNLÉ, *Studies in Contemporary Metaphysics* (1921), p. 294; G. FONSEGRIVE, *L'Évolution des Idées* (1921), p. 218; S. ALEXANDER, *Space, Time and Deity* (1922), vol. II. p. 343.

[73] W. N. CLARKE, *An Outline of Christian Theology*, p. 155.

[74] *Letters of William James*, vol. ii. p. 213. "Not by the intellect can we enter into this absolute, this inner sanctum of life."—W. KINGSLAND, *Our Infinite Life* (1922), p. 187.

[75] E. BOUTROUX, *Science and Religion* (Eng. trans.), p. 318.

Deity. I will lay my hand upon my mouth, I have heard of Thee by the hearing of the ear, but now my eye seeth Thee." Then in his own graphic style he goes on to tell us what has happened to the proofs: "That vast literature of proofs for God's existence drawn from the order of nature, which a century ago seemed to be so overwhelmingly convincing, today does little more than to gather dust in libraries, for the simple reason that our generation has ceased to believe in a kind of a God that must be argued for. The arguments for God's existence have stood for hundreds of years with the waves of unbelieving criticism breaking against them, never totally destroying them in the ears of the faithful, but on the whole slowly and surely washing away the mortar from between their joints."[76]

Modern philosophy is so convinced of the uselessness of the proofs of God's existence that it has ceased to give reasons for ignoring them. It is in possession of the fact, and that is quite sufficient. For this reason one looks in vain in the most recent theistic literature for a sound criticism of the proofs. They "have long since passed the critical stage in which critical minds find them convincing, and they are gradually approaching the stage in which men gradually cease to find them interesting."[77] The Inaugural Address on Philosophy at the University of Edinburgh in 1919, which summarized contemporary thought, gave its witness to the general opinion of the impossibility of proving "by dialectical arguments the existence of God."[78] Professor Alexander in his Gifford Lectures asserted the fact that "no one now is convinced by the traditional arguments of the existence of God."[79] Mr. William L. Davidson, in his work, *Recent Theistic Discussion*, declares it to be "*obvious* that God's existence cannot in any sense of the term be proven;"[80] while Dr. Carr in his *Theory of Monads* is no less emphatic: "I maintain that it is not the cosmological or teleological or any other logical argument from

[76] *Varieties of Religious Experience*, pp. 448, 74, 171. *Cf.* C. A. BECKWITH, *The Idea of God* (1923), p. 171.

[77] W. R. SORLEY, *Moral Values and the Idea of God*, p. 299.

[78] NORMAN KEMP SMITH, p. 28.

[79] *Space, Time and Deity*, vol. ii. p. 343. *Cf.* Rev. J. H. BEIBITZ, M.A., *Belief, Faith and Proof* (London, 1922).

[80] p. 30; italics ours.

which has sprung our idea of God."[81] Manifestly "the proofs have fallen on evil times."[82] While there is thus the widest difference of opinion, there is a curious unanimity as to the needlessness of all the demonstrative methods of the intellect in the domain of religious phenomena.[83] Any one who should attempt to revive them in a really philosophical work would be looked upon with the same suspicion as a scientist who would seek to revive the four element theory of the ancients. A member of the Aristotelian Society of England has put them beyond hope. "We cannot hope," he writes, "by intellectually seeking to find out God."[84] At present, then, the proofs have merely a historical interest. The very word "proofs" is written in quotation marks to indicate that a value has been attributed to them which they really do not possess.[85] The opinion among contemporary thinkers on this matter is unanimous. There are not to be found "so intellectually poor to do reverence to the 'proofs' for the existence of God."[86] "To the modern mind these 'proofs,' when presented in their traditional garb, stalk about with the unsubstantiality of ghosts.

'They were mighty, but they vanished,
Names are all they left behind them.'"[87]

The reason for the rejection of the proofs is distinct from the fact of their rejection. But the fact has become so much stressed that little attention is given to the reason. The argument most often given, strangely enough, is the argument from authority—to wit, the great Kantian tradition. The critique which Kant directed against the proofs is accepted as final and absolute. "The fatal defects all these (traditional arguments) have, it is almost universally conceded, been clearly expressed once for all by Kant."[88] "The bare fact that all idealists since Kant felt

---

[81] *Space, Time and Deity*, vol. ii. p. 115.

[82] W. R. THOMSON, B.D., *The Christian Idea of God* (1919), p. 177.

[83] Sir HENRY JONES, *A Faith that Enquires* (1922), p. 48.

[84] JAMES WARD, *Proceedings of the Aristotelian Society*, "In the Beginning..." (vol. xx., 1920, p. 7). Professor JAMES says they are "absolutely hopeless."—*Religious Experience*, p. 455. *Cf.* H. G. WELLS, *God the Invisible King*, p.24.

[85] W. R. THOMSON, *op. cit.*, p. 6.

[86] Ibid. *Cf.* Jos. A. LEIGHTON, Ph.D., LL.D., *Man and the Cosmos* (1922), p.555.

[87] C. A. BECKWITH, *The Idea of God*, p. 111.

[88] JAMES WARD, *Pluralism and Theism* (2nd edition, 1920), p.406.

entitled to scant or neglect them, shows they are not solid enough to serve as religion's all-sufficient foundation."[89] More to him than to any one else this "changed attitude" toward the proofs must be traced.[90] Through his efforts they have been discredited[91] and have lost all their interest.[92]

Another idea urged against the proofs is their peculiar reference to the problem of religion. Some regard them as worthless through being so intimately bound up with religion; while others find them worthless because they are not sufficiently bound to religion. Professor Hoernlé, for example, repudiates the proofs because of their uselessness when "divorced from their basis in religion;"[93] while Professor Sorley discards them because they have always been associated with religion.[94]

The Modern Substitutues for the Intellectual Proof

I. Religious Experience

"This depreciation of proofs in modern thinking, or at any rate the tacit agreement to leave them in the background,"[95] opens the way to substitutes for the rational procedure, the most popular of which is religious experience. The validity of this approach to God passes almost unquestioned. Its general acceptance has been taken as one of the most striking phenomena in modern thought.[96] To it all schools of philosophy make their appeal, whether they be Disillusionists, Symbolists, Idealists or Progressionists.[97] In fact, there is scarce one single

---

[89] *Varieties of Religious Experience*, p. 437.

[90] W. R. SORLEY, *Moral Values and the Idea of God*, p. 299.

[91] "Kant's great achievement lies in having demonstrated that the whole force of 'proofs' depends upon the famous ontological argument."—A. E. TAYLOR, M.A. (Oxon.), D.Litt., *Elements of Metaphysics* (9th edition, 1923), p.400.

[92] W. R. THOMSON, *Christian Idea of God*, p. 177.

[93] *Op. cit.*

[94] *Op. cit. Cf.* Rev. J. H. BEIBITZ, M.A., *Belief, Faith and Proof* (1922), pp. 12-14; C. A. BECKWITH, *Idea of God*, p. 112

[95] W. R. THOMSON, *The Christian Idea of God*, p. 178.

[96] ALFRED HOERNLÉ, *Studies in Contemporary Metaphysics*, p. 294.

[97] R. B. PERRY, "Contemporary Philosophy of Religion," *Harvard Theol. Review*, vol. vii.

philosophical system in contemporary thought which has disputed its validity. It is so generally admitted as to be accepted as a "presupposition;"[98] it is a recognized measure of philosophical conclusions,[99] and strong enough to stand all pragmatic tests.[100] It is even "the basis of the necessity of thought which posits the idea of God."[101] In fact, "the man who demands a reality more solid than religious consciousness knows not what he seeks."[102] "Modern religion bases its knowledge of God entirely upon experience; it has encountered God. It does not argue about God. It relates."[103]

But while religious experience as the "revealer of the Ultimate Reality"[104] is the accepted way of attaining to God, the question of the nature of this "experience" is quite distinct from the fact of its existence. The method is widely used, but there is much indefiniteness about its nature. All admit, however, that it is essentially non-intellectual.

Religious experience, properly so called, is a certain experience of God in the heart of man, thanks to which God is attained without a reasoning process and with a certitude stronger than that attaching to scientific truth. Professor James, who has done so much to further this philosophy, has defined "religious experience" as "any moment of life that brings the reality of spiritual things more home to me."[105] "In Mystical Experience the believer is continuous to his own consciousness, at any rate, with a wider self from which saving experiences flow in." Those who have those experiences cannot be moved from them by logic, or science or persuasion.[106]

---

no.3, July 1914.

[98] R. F. COLLINWOOD, *Religion and Philosophy* (1916), p. 3.

[99] C. C. WEBB, "The God of Professor Alexander," *Church Quarterly Review*, vol. xviii. no.186 (January 1922), p. 352.

[100] EUGENE W. LYMANN, Experience of God in Modern Life (1919).

[101] L. P. JACKS, *Religious Perplexities* (1922), p. 65.

[102] F. H. BRADLEY, *Appearance and Reality*, p. 449. *Cf.* A. SETH PRINGLE-PATTISON, *The Idea of God*, p. 220; C. C. WEBB, *Divine Personality and Human Life*, vol. i. p. 481.

[103] H. G. WELLS, *God the Invisible King*, p. 24.

[104] W. L. DAVIDSON, *Recent Theistic Discussion* (1921), p. 138.

[105] *Letters*, vol. ii. p. 215. K. B. BAMFIELD, *On Values* (1922), p. 62; Rev. A. CALDECOTT, D.D., "Emotional Argument applied to Immortality," p. 41, in *Lectures on Immortality*, edited by W. R. Matthews, M.A., B.D.

[106] *Pluralistic Universe*, pp. 307-8. *Cf. La Valeur de l'Expérience religieuse* (Paris, 1908).

Professor Alexander has given religious experience a more determined significance by calling it instinct. "When we ask how we come by the cognition of God," he writes, "we must answer that, as with love and hate and appetite and aversion, it is because the world itself provokes in us a certain specific response which makes us aware, no matter in how primitive a form, of God." This religious appetite or instinct is comparable to our appetite for food and drink, "which, though it does not make its object, discovers it."[107]

II. *Intuition.*

Religious experience and intuition have this in common: both deny the necessity of reason in attaining a knowledge of God. They differ, however, in this: religious experience is in space and time; intuition is sometimes said to be outside space and time, except time in the sense of *durée.* The experience seizes facts after they have sprung forth from their source or *after* their evolution. Intuition seizes them in the very process of their evolution.[108] Religious experience is destined for action. It seeks only a value for the present age or the present cosmic need. Intuition, on the other hand, looks not toward the active but rather to the contemplative. It seeks not the exterior but the interior.[109]

Intuition transcends the intellect, which is accused of distorting reality and cutting it up into lifeless fragments. "Life appears to intellectual apprehension as an extension, as a succession of states. In intuition we see the reality as fluid, as unfixed, before it is congealed into concepts, before even it is perceived in space and time." It enables us to "apprehend reality

---

[107] *Space, Time and Deity*, vol. ii. pp. 352, 374, 382, 385. See CYRIL E. HUDSON, *Recent Psychology and the Christian Religion* (1923), p. 62: Application of Freudianism to religion. The essential difference between an instinct and a sentiment is that, in the instinct the connexion between the cognitive and the conative dispositions is innate, while in the sentiment the connexion is acquired through individual experience."—McDOUGAL, Preface to *Social Psychology.*

[108] Intuition s'agit "d'une connaissance par le dedans, qui les saisit (les faits) dans leur jaillissement même au lieu de les prendre une fois jaillis, qui creuserait ainsi au-dessous de l'espace et du temps spatialisé."—*L'Évolution Créatrice*, p. 390.

[109] "Tandis que l'intelligence traite toutes choses mécaniquement l'instinct procède, si l'on peut parler ainsi, organiquement, s'il s'intériorisait en connaissance au lieu de s'extérioriser en action, si nous savons l'interroger et s'il pouvait répondre il nous livrerait les secrets les plus intimes de la vie."—Ibid., p.179.

at its source, as it flows, before it takes the bend, before it obeys the bias which the intellect imposes."[110] In intuition the seer and the seen become one in an ineffable experience of unity. Intuitional experience gives the whole of things; the knower plunges into the flux of reality and becomes one with it. It transports us into the very heart of the real, whether that real be a rose, a duration in time or God Himself. It is a kind of intellectual sympathy by which one sets oneself in the interior of an object in order to coincide with the very reality of that object, with its uniqueness, with that in it, consequently, which cannot be expressed.[111]

If intuition or "real knowledge" transcends discursive thought, it is not alone in doing so. In other systems imagination enjoys superiority over any of the discursive approaches to God.[112] "Imagination comes most nearly to the surface as that phase of my psychical life, imagination narrowly so called, which, pervasive phase though it be, the psychologist contrasts with other phases. In this quarter we glimpse that 'psychical form of spontaneous generation,' that becoming *ex nihilo*, which is the work of real novelty and figures so largely in my account of creative evolution."[113] "Imagination transcends thought in that it makes us aware of the limitations of thought. And how do we define imagination? We fail utterly in attempts at definition."[114]

---

[110] H. WILDON CARR, Litt.D., *The Philosophy of Change* (1912), p. 29, p. 202. *Cf. Theory of Monads*, same author, p. 117.

[111] *L'Évolution Créatrice*, pp. 170, 197, 210, 211, 216, 259. "Instinct is wonderful. But intuition is far more so, for it is the power of direct spiritual insight into the reason of things, which is acquired neither by knowledge nor by experience, and which is therefore superior to both."—J. GURNHILL, *Christian Philosophy* (1921), p. 31. See J. H. TUCKWELL, *Religion and Reality* (1915), p. 297.

An interesting theory compounded of St. Thomas and Bergson has recently been expounded by the author of *L'Action*, M. Maurice Blondel. In *Le Procès de l'Intelligence* he distinguishes two kinds of knowledge. First, the notional knowledge, that is, the knowledge by concepts, which gives merely *artificiata* and substitutes for reality, and extrinsic affirmation without ever penetrating the intrinsic nature of being. This knowledge prepares the way for the more perfect kind, namely, the real knowledge, a knowledge ... *cognitionem per unionem et caritatem*, "dialectically prepared by all the trials and proofs of passion and action." *Nam amor est magis unitivus quam notio*, une union qui tend à réaliser le voeu suprême de toutes les facultés de notre être et du plan divin *ut unum sint*."—pp. 238, 242, 267, 269.

[112] DOUGLAS FAWCETT, *Imaginism and the World Process*, chap. I.

[113] Ibid., *Mind* (April 1922), vol. xxi. no.122.

[114] F. C. CONSTABLE, M.A., "The Meaning of Consciousness," *Quest*, 1921, quoted by D. Fawcett.

III. Faith, Hypothesis

More recent literature on theodicy seems to indicate the growing popularity of faith as an approach to God. Of course, faith must not here be understood in the traditional sense as meaning the submission of the intellect and the will to a revealed doctrine on account of the authority of God revealing. For our contemporaries, the foundation of faith is not of the intellectual order. It is an effort of the mind to explain its sentiment and to disengage God from some 'felt contact.' Faith is a sum of possibilities or a hypothesis to be confirmed, or else the practical acceptance of some hypothesis which appears more apt than others to satisfy our needs, tendencies and hopes. At its root there lies a distinction between knowing and believing. Hence, although we cannot know God rationally, we can nevertheless believe in Him.

One of the recent Gifford Lecturers, Sir Henry Jones, has called "A Faith that Enquires" a faith that stands the test of an inquiring intelligence. "We approach the facts of life with a preconception, favourable or unfavourable, of the existence and the nature of God, which is the result, not so much of external observation as of reflexion upon our own nature and needs. Hence our religious faith or scepticism has the same ultimate use and character as a scientific hypothesis, and its validity must be tested in the same way."[115] Simply because we find certain instances in which our laws do not apparently seem to be verified, we must not deny their existence. "Not proven is not disproven."[116] "The religious hypothesis, like all others, is never finally proved, it is always and everywhere in the act of being proved. It is the one thing that is being done through creation. It is the experiment—the Grand Perhaps of the Universe."[117] The Universe thus becomes a great spiritual laboratory and the experimental test of the Grand Perhaps. Beliefs are no longer dogmas, but truths which the Church "challenges the unbelieving world to put to the test, and to the hardest test it can find even

[115] p. 213.
[116] p. 216.
[117] p. 103.

among the worst intricacies of the pathetic tragedies of human life."[118]

Religious faith is like the test of an invention, and in no wise like the arguments for or against a theory. It consists in observing "how it works."[119] "Our faith beforehand in an uncertified result is the *only thing that makes the result come true.* Suppose, for instance, that you are climbing a mountain, and have worked yourself into a position from which the only escape is by a terrible leap. Have faith that you can successfully make it and your feet are nerved to its accomplishment. But mistrust yourself, and think of all the sweet things you have heard the scientists say of *maybes*, and you will hesitate so long that at last, all unstrung and trembling, and launching yourself in a moment of despair, you roll into the abyss. In such a case (and it belongs to an enormous class), the part of wisdom as well as of courage is to *believe what is in the line of your needs*, for only by such belief is the need fulfilled. Refuse to believe, and you shall indeed be right, for you shall irretrievably perish. But believe, and again you shall be right, for you shall save yourself. You make one or two of the possible universes true by your trust or mistrust—both universes having been only *maybes* in this particular before you contributed your act."[120] With reference, then, to the problem of God, "we must bear in mind the fact that God is a hypothesis characteristic of the religious view of the world, and that, like every other hypothesis, it should help to explain the facts to which it is relevant."[121]

---

[118] pp.104-5.

[119] pp. 85, 86. Note the similarity between this and Dr. Schiller's words: "The presuppositions of scientific knowledge and religious faith are the same. So, too, is the mode of verification by experience. The assumptions which work, *i.e.* which approve themselves by ministering to human interests, purpose and objects of desires are 'verified' and accepted as 'true.'"—F. C. S. SCHILLER, *Studies in Humanism* (1906), p. 362.

[120] W. JAMES, *The Will to Believe*, p. 59. See F. C. S. SCHILLER, *Studies in Humanism*, p. 357; WILLIAM JAMES, *Pragmatism*, p. 146.

[121] RAY WOOD CELLARS, Ph.D., *The Next Step in Religion* (1918), p. 160.

"The five arguments for the Divine Existence ... afford us the means of applying Theism as a working hypothesis to large classes of facts; and if this furnishes a better explanation of them than any other hypothesis, we have every right to assert its truth."—J .H. BEIBITZ, M.A., *Belief, Faith and Proof* (1922), p. 16, p. 19.

"Faith is a venture; it begins as the resolution to stand or fall by the noblest hypothesis."—Dean INGE, "Can the New Idealism dispense with Mysticism?" *Proceedings of the Aristotelian Society* (1923), p. 180. "For better or for worse I acknowledge God," etc. "I acknowledge also God, Who is, I contend, beyond disproof."—L. MORGAN, *Emergent*

At this moment the notion of God as a hypothesis is no more popular in English philosophy than in the German. After a delay of many years H. Vaihinger finally brought out in 1912 his *Philosophie des Als-Ob*, which is the inspiration of much of the more recent German philosophy. The author disclaims any affiliation with Pragmatism. "An idea whose theoretical truth or incorrectness, and therewith its falsity, is admitted, is not for that reason practically valueless and useless, for such an idea, in spite of its theoretical nullity, may have great practical importance."[122] The work is, if we are to believe the author, a fulfillment of the prophecy Kant made in 1797 that in one hundred years his philosophy would be appreciated and understood. The basis of the thought is fiction, and not hypothesis. The two are not the same. Hypothesis looks to reality and from reality receives its verification. Fiction, on the contrary, proceeds as if the thing existed. Fiction is merely an auxiliary construction, a circuitous approach, a scaffolding afterwards to be demolished, while the hypothesis looks forward to being definitely established. The former is artificial, the latter is natural. The fiction seeks to invent, the hypothesis to discover.

Evolution (Gifford Lectures), pp. 36, 61, 173. See A. SETH PRINGLE-PATTISON, *Idea of Immortality* (1922), pp. 196-7; L. P. JACKS, *Religious Perplexities*, p. 6; A. K. ROGERS, *What is Truth* (1923), p. 166.

"Divine guidance must be postulated if we are to maintain the three great values—knowledge, love, beauty." God is a "presupposition of all these beauties."—ARTHUR J. BALFOUR, *Theism and Thought* (Gifford Lectures, 1922-3), pp. 248, 251.

[122] English translation by E. K. Ogden (1924), p. viii. The original title is "Die Philosophie des als ob: System der theoretischen, praktischen und religiösen Fiktionen der Menschheit auf Grund eines idealistischen Positivismus" (1st edition, Berlin, 1911).

"Die Hypothese geht stets auf die Wirklichkeit ... sie unterwirft sich der Probe auf ihre Wirklichkeit und verlangt schliesslich Verifikation."—Ibid., cap. 21, pp.143-4. For distinction between the two, *Cf.* p. 148.

This theory applied to Metaphysics, Relativity, Psychology, Physics, Religion and God. See W. VAIHINGER and RAYMOND SCHMIDT, *Annalen der Philosophie* (Leipzig, 1922), Zweiter Band; PAUL SPECHERBAUM, *Das Vaihingeasche Als Ob* (1922), pp. 77, 78, 79; Dr. WALTER STRAUCH, *Die Philosophie des Als Ob und die Hauptsache leihsten Probleme der Rechtswissenschaft* (1923), p. 13; Dr. JOHANNES WEGENER, *Die Christliche Religion als Religion des Als Ob* (1923).

"Dieser praktische Gottesglaube bedeutet so viel wie; leben als ob es ein höchstes Wesen gäbe, dem man Rechenschaft schuldig ist, obschon man weiss, dass es ein solches Wesen nicht geht."—H. SCHOLZ, *Annalen der Philosophie* (Dritter Band, Leipzig): "Die Religionsphilosophie des Als Ob," pp. 2, 29.

Thus we have some idea of the main substitutes for intelligence. In our next chapter we shall attempt a more detailed analysis.

CHAPTER IV:

THE CHARACTERISTICS OF THE MODERN NON-INTELLECTUAL APPROACH TO GOD

THE explicit nature of these substitutes, particularly of religious experience, which is the most common, becomes clearer when contrasted with the intellectual proofs. Reactions are always more intelligible when compared with that from which they have reacted. A threefold aspect of the reaction may be noted in the matter under consideration.

1. The intellectual approach began with the *world*—not the world of internal experience but the external world of movement, contingency, varied perfections, efficient causality and finality. Its point of departure was extra-mental. The source of its proofs was in the open air. In reacting against this so-called indirect method, the modern approach placed itself not in the external world but in *self*—the world of internal experience. It goes to God, not through the world, but through the ego.

2. The intellectual approach was through the reasoning process built on the world of reality. Between the apprehension of the external world and of God there intervened necessarily a logical process; the bridge between the two was built by the reasoning mind. God was not given in the world. He had to be sought by means of the world. The reaction against intellectualism naturally insisted on a non-logical process. A God that we had to argue for was not worth having, James contended. Instead of being *mediately* known, God is said to be *immediately* known; instead of being known by *reason*, He is known by intuition or by the heart, as the great organ of immediacy and spontaneity.

3. The third difference consists in the values attributed to the respective approaches. For the intellectualist the value of the knowledge obtained by reasoning is determined *independently of self*. As it began independently of self in proving the existence of God, by taking its point of departure in the world, so would it let its conclusions be determined independently of self. The modern approach, on the contrary, taking its point of departure in the self concludes in function of that *self rather than in function of the object*. The knowledge of God is thus symbolic and extrinsic rather than real and intrinsic.

1. Self is the Starting Point of the Approach to God

Erdmann is the authority for the statement that this very characteristic is one of the predominant traits of modern philosophy.[123] "During the last fifty years men have been learning to find God within rather than without."[124] The God that is found from "without" is a "sterile God," because "you have to go to the world which he created to get an inkling of his actual character."[125] "God has no meaning to us out of relation to our own lives or to spirits resembling ourselves in their finite grasp and infinite reach; and, in the nature of the case, we have positively no grounds for positing his existence outside of that reference." God and self are not two independent facts. To maintain this is to lose "our hold upon the experienced fact, which is the existence of the one in the other and through the other."[126] To put this fact in the first person, it may be said that "I experience in *myself*, in a manner which none other can teach me, the truth of the affirmation that God is."[127]

What could be more intimately related to self than Imagination, which Mr. Fawcett tells us is the ideal approach for

[123] *History of Philosophy*, vol. ii. p. 2; G. FONSEGRIVE, *L'Évolution des Idées*, p. 218.
[124] CH. F. D'ARCY, "God and the Struggle for Existence:" Essay in *Love and Omnipotence*, p. 17.
[125] W. JAMES, *Varieties of Religious Experience*, pp. 498-9.
[126] A. SETH PRINGLE-PATTISON, *The Idea of God*, p. 254.
[127] K. B. BAMFIELD, *On Values* (1922), p. 62.

those who have been disheartened by a metaphysics of the Intellect?[128] If, however, instead of using the Imagination to attain contact with the Divine Reality, we use Desire, the *self* is the same starting-point. Desire is essentially personal. Its objects appear before it, not because the world has been a provocative cause of them, but because Desire is the cause of objects (nature, Spirit and God) appearing before the mind. "Mind's knowledge of things must be conceived to proceed from her own nature; it being by her own activity alone that any of these beings ever appear to her."[129]

Dr. Carr has not departed from the method of his contemporaries, even though his manner of expression be different. The God concept, he says, is a result of the mind-body unity, which is enlarged into a conception of universal activity. "In the moment of experience, mind and body are not two things but one. It would be impossible even to make the distinction, were experience confined to the actual, without outlook on the past and on the future. When we consider universal activity in the same mode in which we conceive our individual activity, then we have the idea of God ... It is the intuition of this unity which is the basis of the necessity of the thought which posits the idea of God."[130] From the mere fact "that we are conscious of having had personal experience of the Divine Reality, we know properly that God exists."[131] As H. G. Wells has put it in his own charming style, there is within us "an undoubting immediate sense of God."[132]

To seek after God apart from ourselves is as useless, we are told, as for a dog to chase his own tail. "The Hound of Heaven is on his own trail, and the vestige still lures the scent of a foregone conclusion."[133] The Kingdom of God is within us, and God Himself can be found therein, it would seem, if we would but distil Him out. We do not need to prove Him. He is not to

[128] D. W. FAWCETT, *Divine Imaginism and the World Process* (passim).

[129] K. J. SPALDING, *Desire and Reason*, pp. 16, 12, 211.

[130] H. WILDON CARR, *Theory of Monads*, pp. 117, 119.

[131] DOUGLAS C. MACINTOSH, Ph.D., *Theology as an Empirical Science*, p.91.

[132] *God the Invisible King.*

[133] B. J. BLOOD, *Dedicatory Words of Pluriverse. Cf.* J. LINDSAY, *Great Philosophical Problems* (1922), pp. 156-7; MAY SINCLAIR, *The New Idealism*, pp. 213, 314; J. LEIGHTON, *Man and the Cosmos*, p. 550; J. LINDSAY, *A Philosophical Study of Theistic Idealism*, p. 97.

be found amid the thunder and lightning of Sinai, but is in the very intimacies of our own experience.

2. *God is Known Non-Rationally*

Not by the use of affective feeling alone do we begin with the self as a starting-point in theodicy. The Cartesian argument from the idea of infinity and the Anselmian ontological argument, as also that of the Rosminian school, began also from within. A difference between them is this: their self was the intellectual and not the affective. Modern philosophers, on the contrary, while beginning with self, deny the necessity of reason to prove the existence of God. This would necessarily follow from their avowed anti-intellectualism, did they not further assure us of the uselessness of reasoning. Intellectualism gave God only *mediately*—that is, through a reasoning process built on the world. Modern systems, on the contrary, give God *immediately* and concomitantly with the affective state. God is in no case the result of an inference.[134] No longer will philosophy, in these days of labour-saving devices, use the old-fashioned way of mounting to God through reasoning. There is no necessity to go outside us nor to reason on what is inside us. Why laboriously climb up Jacob's ladder to heaven when we can bring heaven and its God down into our very hearts? God is not external to us, but we have a "consciousness of Him in principle and communicating Himself to us."[135]

The insistence on the immediacy and directness by which God is attained within the self leads naturally to a diminished interest in the problem of the existence of God. Once it is admitted that God is given immediately, the problem of God's existence ceases to be. Contemporary philosophy has been logical in its deductions from its premises on this point. It has

---

[134] JOSEPH A. LEIGHTON, *Man and the Cosmos*, p. 550; W. JAMES, *Varieties of Religious Experience*, p. 502. "He is not something inferred, but given in direct contact and apprehension."—BARON VON HÜGEL, *Essays and Addresses in the Philosophy of Religion* (1921).

[135] J. LINDSAY, *A Philosophical Study of Theistic Idealism*, p. 97; *Great Philosophical Problems* (1922), p. 225.

consequently insisted that the important point of theodicy is not the existence but the nature of God. "What may in a sense be doubted is not God's existence, but God's nature."[136] The reason is obvious: "ultimately our only credence of the existence of anything must be our consciousness of it ... Thus the religious consciousness is the sufficient evidence of the existence of its object ... So far as we mean by God no more than the object of this religious consciousness, the existence of God is not really doubtful at all."[137] "In other words, the existence of the object as real is implied in the actual existence of the want. Just as in the case of hunger on the lower or animal side of our nature, hunger as a want obviously could not originate save in a living organism whose very existence depends on its being nourished by food, and therefore presupposes the real existence of the object food, so, in the higher or spiritual side of our being, the actual fact of the need of God, laid deep in the human constitution, implies that God *is*, as both originating and as satisfying it."[138] "Men have never believed in God only after they have proved His existence; on the contrary, they were certain they had experienced God before they sought for the rational meaning or the ground of that experience."[139]

But what is the exact nature of the substitutes for the old discursive approach to God? It may be an intuition, and this is "a direct apprehension of a reality which is non-intellectual, and non-intellectual means that it is neither a perception nor a conception, nor an object of reason, all of which are intellectual forms."[140] Or, it may be described as a "sensation," "feeling," "instinct," "emotion," all of the psychological or the biological order, or as a "sthenic affection, an excitement of the cheerful, expansive, dynamogenic order which, like any tonic, freshens our vital powers ... The name of 'faith state,' by which Professor

---

[136] ALFRED HOERNLË, *Studies in Contemporary Metaphysics*, p. 297.

[137] C. WEBB, *Problems in the Relation of God and Man*, pp. 143, 145. "Aber im Gefühle der Andacht entwickelt uns sich davon sehr fest und sicher eine positive Erkenntnis, wenn schon eine völlig wir nicht unaussprechliche. Und wenn schon wir nicht sagen können was Gott sei, können wir doch fühlen."—OTTO, *Kantische Freische Religionsphilosophie* (Tübingen, 1909), p. 111 ff.

[138] W. L. DAVIDSON, *Recent Theistic Discussion*, pp. 29-30.

[139] C. A. BECKWITH, *The Idea of God*, p. 112.

[140] H. WILDON CARR, *op. cit.*

Leuba designates it, is a good one."[141] Its essentially non-intellectual character may be brought out by comparing it with a bar of iron without touch or sight, and which, "without any representative faculty whatever, might nevertheless be strongly endowed with an inner capacity for magnetic feeling; and as if, through various arousals of its magnetism by magnets coming and going in its neighbourhood, it might be consciously determined to different attitudes and tendencies. Such a bar of iron could never give you an outward description of the agencies that had the power of stirring it so strongly, yet of their presence, and of their significance for life, it would be intensely aware through every fibre of its being."[142] Just as the iron bar is incapable of any intellectual justification of its polarization, so, too, are we incapable of demonstrating how God comes into us. The fact is, He is there, and He is there non-intellectually, and is just as real as "the thrust of a sword or an embrace."[143]

Mr. Fawcett has vaguely but beautifully described this affective approach as a "psychical form of spontaneous generation."[144] The Imagination creates its own life and its own objects, just as Desire creates its own objects; it generates them spontaneously within itself, and needs no recourse to a principle outside itself. The religious impulse which gives us God, without a syllogism based on a block-universe, is to be identified with an impulse of life; it is biological and belongs to all the orders. Even the animals have a religious sense.[145]

In the psychological order this religious experience may be defined as a "special instance of a *perception in a complex*." Just as we have an intuitive awareness of our own existence in conscious experience, and of the existence of physical objects in sense experience, so in religious experience at its best "the religious subject is aware, in an empirical intuition, of religious dependence which proves to be a Source of Religious Deliverance."[146] The conscious person, by the extension or expansion of his

---

[141] W. JAMES, *Varieties of Religious Experience*, p. 505.
[142] Ibid., p. 55.
[143] H. G. WELLS, *God the Invisible King*.
[144] "Imaginism and the World Process," *Mind* (April 1922), p. 160.
[145] JAMES HENRY TUCKWELL, *Religion and Reality* (1915), p. 55.
[146] D. C. MACINTOSH, *Theology as an Empirical Science*, chap. vi. p. 91.

consciousness, is made "continuous with a wider self through which saving experiences come."[147]

"Religious experience" means essentially an "emotion," or a "feeling,"[148] or better still a "*sense of reality, a feeling of objective presence, a perception* of what we might call *something there*, more deep and more general than any of the special and particular senses" by which the current psychology supposes existent realities to be originally revealed.[149]

Now it may be asked, is this "consciousness," this "feeling," this "sthenic affection" a special way of knowing, or a special emotion for a particular object. There are some who are inclined to think it distinct from other psychological experiences. Professor Laird asks: "Indeed, why should we deny that religious experience, and particularly mystical experience, is fundamentally a new way of knowing?" [150] Without admitting a special organ for such experiences, it seems that Professor Alexander is of this opinion. "However many other elements," he writes, "gather around it and swell the full tide of religious sentiment, its essential constituent is something with a unique flavour of its own, corresponding to its specific object, and *is distinct from other emotions, and its apprehension of its object distinct from other kinds of apprehension.*"[151] If, then, there be such a thing as a special emotion for religion, it follows that "our knowledge of God, the Great Universal, is a consciousness of Him which is not of a kind with our knowledge of matters of fact—a consciousness not definable in the ordinary way or sense."[152]

This attribution of a "special consciousness" or "special emotion" or "way of knowing" is not general among contemporary philosophers. James does not admit any such special emotion for religion,[153] and for the most part he has been the inspiration of his contemporaries on this very matter.

---

[147] *Varieties of Religious Experience*, p. 515.
[148] S. ALEXANDER, *Space, Time and Deity*, vol. ii. p. 373.
[149] *Varieties of Religious Experience*, p. 58.
[150] *A Study in Realism* (1920), p. 211.
[151] *Space, Time and Deity*, vol. ii.. p. 402, p. 377; italics ours.
[152] JAMES LINDSAY, *Philosophical System of Theistic Idealism* (1917), p. 97.
[153] *Varieties of Religious Experience*, pp. 28-9.

Of greater importance is the particular value of the intellect in the modern philosophy of experience. Admittedly it does not hold the first place; but does it hold a place at all? The answer is faintly affirmative. While the basis is non-intellectual, its explanation may be and often is intellectual. "What metaphysical knowledge or inquiry does, is only to bring such immediate knowledge to greater conceptual clearness."[154] What, then, is the meaning of the proofs for the existence of God? They have, according to our contemporaries, no absolute value. Professor Hoernlé answers that they are "but a making plain what, in a sense, is there and possessed by us all the time, but that, for all its presence, we may fail securely to grasp or clearly discern."[155] "Reason with its guiding logic seems a secondary creation advantaging only finite sentients, miserably supplied with direct or immediate knowledge, who have to infer."[156] "The unreasoned and immediate assurance is the deep thing in us; the reasoned argument is but a surface exhibition. Instinct leads; intelligence does but follow ... Our passions and our mystical intuitions fix our beliefs beforehand." The "element of feeling" in religion is habilitated only by "subordinating its intellectual part. Individuality is founded on feeling and the recesses of feeling; the darker, blinder strata of character are the only places in the world in which we catch real fact in the making."[157]

The author of the voluminous *Space, Time and Deity* is in perfect accord with his contemporaries in the view that feeling is of primary and intellect of secondary importance. "Religious feeling itself," he writes, "suggests the notion of God which when elaborated by reflexion is discovered to be that of the world big with deity." ... "It is the feeling or emotion which images the object, not the idea which induces the emotion." But if God is

[154] JAMES LINDSAY, *Great Philosophical Problems*, p. 225.

[155] R. F. ALFRED HOERNLÉ, M.A., *Matter, Life, Mind, God.*

[156] D.W. FAWCETT, *Divine Imagining*, p. 155.

[157] *Varieties of Religious Experience*, pp. 74, 436, 501. "There is need for a religious belief founded otherwise than on metaphysics, and a metaphysics able in some sense to justify that creed seems to be what is required to fulfil our wishes."—F. H. BRADLEY, *Essays on Truth and Reality*, p. 446. "Philosophy comes from religion. It is first religion which puts us in relation with the whole."—C. C. WEBB, *Philosophy and the Christian Religion* (Inaugural Address, Oxford, 4th May 1920), p. 12. "Intellect we shall put in its proper place as complementary to the subjective life of the Spirit."—WILLIAM KINGSLAND, *Our Infinite Life* (1922), p. 189. See J. R. BAILLIE, *Studies in Human Nature*, p. 165.

given by mere feeling, why is it that not every one believes in the existence of God? The answer is interesting: "A man may be partially or wholly deity-blind, as he is stone-deaf ... he may lack the emotional suggestibility of deity:"[158] hence his unresponsiveness.

Both in the chronological and in the logical order reflective development of the religious experience is of secondary and minor importance. There is unanimity on this point. Dogmas are merely the "buildings-out performed by the intellect into which feeling originally supplied the hint."[159] A recent work on the Psychology of Religion has enumerated in their order the elements producing belief. The first element is the traditional one—effects of training and suggestion in childhood. The second element is of experiences harmonizing with beliefs: (*a*) a natural factor—the experience of beauty and the harmony of the world; (*b*) a moral factor—the experience of moral conflict; (*c*) an affective factor—interior religious experience. The third and last element is rational—an intellectual justification of beliefs.[160] These psychological interpretations are in perfect accord with the modern contempt for dogmas, which are of course intellectual in nature. They are in no sense the necessary development of religious consciousness, and religion is better without them.[161]

3. The Nature of God is not the Object of the Non-Intellectual Experience, but God as related to us

The discarded traditional approach to the existence of God began with the external world and allowed its conclusions to be determined by the reasoning process, independently of the self.

The modern approach, on the contrary, maintains that the old method fails to take account of our own selves. The aim of

158 *Space, Time and Deity*, vol. ii. pp. 378, 375, 377.

159 *Varieties of Religious Experience*, p. 431.

160 ROBERT H. THOULESS, M.A., *An Introduction to the Psychology of Religion* (Cambridge, 1923). Jastrow says the elements are (1) emotion, (2) convention, (3) reason.

161 BERTRAND RUSSELL, *Free Man's Religion.*

experience is not so much to attain God as He is in Himself, but as He is related to us. The determinant of the validity of the experience is not the object, but the experiencing subject. Experience alone constitutes its own object, and it expresses it necessarily in terms of experience itself. God is therefore to be designated in ways that are extrinsic to Himself, but intrinsic to us.[162]

The object of faith comes not from the outside but the inside the object of desire does likewise, and their value is determined by the experience which produced them. It is quite true, therefore, to say that "at the present time philosophy is carried on more explicity in terms of value than at any previous time."[163] The great concern of our contemporaries is "the absolute validity of the practical idea," and by a "practical idea" is meant one "which has to do with life as it launches itself on the great venture of living."[164] The end of the science which treats of God is "the enterprise of considering the place and the value of religion as an experience and attitude of universal humanity."[165] In every case God as related to man is the object of the experience; whether or not the proofs, intellectual or affective, prove God's existence, matters but little; the values which these proofs symbolize still remain unchanged.[166]

There is no need to appeal to an object outside of the experiencing subject to test the validity of the experiences. "Religion as a matter of experience is held to be witness to its own validity. The experience itself is the final court of appeal, and its authority is supposed to be higher and more unerring than that of any logic."[167] "The emotional attitude is non-intellectual, and carries its own assurance in its own state and its warrant in the complete satisfaction which the emotion supplies. The spontaneity of the existence and the fullness of individuality which the emotion supplies are the sole and sufficient guarantee of their certainty and of the sincerity of experience."[168] The same

162 A. SETH PRINGLE-PATTISON, *The Idea of God*, pp. 334-45.
163 Ibid., p. 39.
164 W. R. THOMSON, *The Christian Idea of God*, p. 165.
165 JOSEPH A. LEIGHTON, Ph.D., D.D., *Man and the Cosmos*, p. 555.
166 C. A. BECKWITH, *The Idea of God*, p. 119, p. 112.
167 Sir HENRY JONES, *A Faith that Enquires*, p. 84.
168 J. B. BAILLIE, *Studies in Human Nature*, p. 164.

criterion is to be used in judging God as a hypothesis. "If there are certain forms of religious faith, certain hypotheses, which deepen the meaning of natural facts, which amplify and extend the suggestiveness of the natural sciences, and, so far from traversing their findings, accept and invite them; and if in the world of human conduct they dignify human character, add reach and sanity to man's aims, construct and consolidate human society, elevate and secure the life of man and make for peace and mutual helpfulness amongst the nations ...; if, in a word, a form of religious faith or hypothesis *works* in these ways, then indeed is the proof of its validity strong; stronger than the proof of any other hypothesis, because wider and deeper."[169] This verification of hypothesis is not of the conceptual order,[170] being, as it is, "a spiritual attitude of welcome which we assume towards what we make to be a truth."[171]

This is not the first time in history that philosophy has maintained that God is to be designated by purely extrinsic denominations. Kant designated God by purely extrinsic denominations founded on the postulate of the moral law; in this case, however, the conclusions were confined to purely philosophical speculation. With the modern thinkers God is designated by extrinsic denominations founded on what is practical and pragmatic.[172]

What, then, is the nature of these extrinsic denominations? If God is to be interpreted in terms of experience rather than in terms of knowledge, how interpret experience? This is one of the important problems in the modern philosophy of religion.[173] In its broadest lines religious experience will be interpreted according to philosophical systems. Pragmatism and Idealism, Empiricism and Platonism will interpret experience according to their own systems, and will consequently lead to divergent results.

---

[169] Sir HENRY JONES, *A Faith that Enquires*, p. 104. "The test of religious faith lies in the kind of behaviour that it inspires and controls, and in the contribution it makes to human well-being."—Ibid., p. 96. *Cf.* RICHARD MÜLLER, *Persönlichkeit and Weltanschauung* (Leipzig, 1919). Also ERIC S. WATERHOUSE, D.D., M.A., *The Philosophy of Religious Experience* (London, 1923), p. 196.

[170] W. JAMES, *The Will to Believe*, pp. 65-74.

[171] F. C. S. SCHILLER, M.A., D.Sc., *Problems of Belief*, p. 14.

[172] M. CHOSSAT, art. "Dieu," *Dictionnaire de Théologie Catholique.*

[173] W. R. THOMSON, *The Christian Idea of God*, p. 6.

Ernest Troeltsch of Heidelberg, speaking of the Empirical and the Platonic interpretations, writes: "The one view inclines to monism and pantheism, the other to untiring activity and living interaction between God and the soul."[174] Another writer declares that the Idealistic interpretation ends in an "Ultimate Being in which all problems are solved and all contradictions resolved, and it reduces the finite world which is the nearest concern of struggling, toiling humanity to an unintelligible puppet-show." Pragmatism, on the contrary, finds a finite God in its interpretation of experience. The conceptions of Pragmatism "show the modern-age emphasis upon volition, control, reconstruction, scientific method, and the democratic faith that the individual counts, even in the largest concerns, can be taken up as significant factors of religious consciousness."[175]

There is yet another broader interpretation of religious experience, in which all systems agree. Modern systems yield a threefold general interpretation of religious experience

(1) According to the needs of the individual.

(2) According to the spirit of the age.

(3) According to the evolution of the world.

(1) According to the Needs of the Individual

In the last analysis, experience is not of systems, but of individuals. The Idealist has experience, not as one Idealist in common with others, but rather as an individual. The Empiricist likewise has not the same experience as his Empirical friend across the sea, but rather his own individual experience. Ultimately, one of the principal determinants of religious experience is that of the individual needs. The God of the Intellectualist was the *God-proved-by-reason-to-be-existent.* Such a God is too far from our needs, it is contended. Hence the *God-I-feel-I-can-use* is of much greater value. "The gods we stand by are the gods we need and can use."[176] Hence it follows that,

---

[174] "Empiricism and Platonism in the Philosophy of Religion," *Harvard Theological Review*, vol. v. no. 4, p. 418.

[175] CLARENCE H. HAMILTON, *Journal of Religion* (Nov. 1921), vol. i. no. 6, pp. 618, 622.

[176] *Varieties of Religious Experience*, p. 331. *Cf.* F. H. BRADLEY, *Essays in Truth and Reality*, p. 431.

although we cannot prove the existence of God, it does not mean that God has lost all His value. The idea may be "theoretically worthless," it is quite true, but it still has a "regulative use."[177] Individual need is to be the judge of God. "The voice of human experience within us, judging and condemning all gods that stand athwart the pathway along which it feels to be advancing," is the measure by which individuals prefer certain gods at one time and certain gods at another.[178] Professor Leuba writes: "The truth of the matter can be put this way: God is not known, He is used—sometimes as a meat-purveyor, sometimes as moral support, sometimes as friend, sometimes as object of love. If He proves Himself useful, the religious consciousness asks for no more than this. Does God really exist? How does He exist? What is He? are so many irrelevant questions. Not God but life, more life, a larger, richer, more satisfying life, is, in the last analysis, the end of religion. The love of life, at any and every level of development, is the religious impulse."[179]

(2) Interpretation According to the Spirit of the Age

Times change, and God should change with them—not merely the expression of our belief in the Deity, but even our very notion of the Deity itself. Just as we have discarded the old phaeton of our grandfathers, why should we not discard the "grandfather notion" of God? We believe in conveyances just as our grandfathers did, but not the same kind. We believe in God, too, but not the same kind of a God. "Because Abraham or Paul saw God clearly through windows of ancient architecture, we insist upon looking through the windows, whether or not we see the vision. We insist on keeping our windows open toward Jerusalem when they ought to be open upon the life of today."[180]

A Professor of Theology in the University of Chicago has enumerated eighteen reasons why we should have a new idea of

---

[177] J. WARD, *Pluralism and Theism*, p. 230. William James, once asked the question, "Do you believe in God because you have experienced His Presence?" answered, "No, but rather because I need it, so that it must be true."—*Letters of W. James*, vol. ii. p. 213.

[178] *Varieties of Religious Experience*, pp. 329-30.

[179] "The Contents of Religious Consciousness," *Monist*, xi. p. 536. Quoted by JAMES, *Varieties of Religious Experience*.

[180] H. A. YOUTZ, *Enlarging Conception of God*, p. 28. *Cf.* SALEM G. BLAND, *The New Christianity* (1920), p. 120.

God. Among these eighteen are: thought has changed in all subjects in the last fifty years; the scientific spirit approaches reality today through observation and experience, whereas the old notion of God was formulated in a non-scientific way; the old notion of God was that of a Creator, and today the world knows we cannot prove the absolute origin of the universe. Furthermore, present-day use of the Scriptures is gradually unfolding the Man-idea; authority has shifted from the external to the internal; the radical distinction between the natural and the supernatural order is denied; history has proved a new idea of God; fusion of Semitic and Aryan thought; new studies on Jesus Christ; psychology of religion; dynamic doctrine of reality, experience, ethicized theology, literary interest in the idea of God; new social emphasis, *i.e.* the attempt to make the Gospel real in settlement work; influence of the War; revision of arguments for the existence of God; and finally, the new notion of the Trinity—all of these make it imperative to conclude that the "traditional idea is inadequate; men are no longer content to have a God at second-hand."[181] The same conclusion has been reached by another writer who antedates this work by a few years, but does not advance nearly the same number of reasons.[182]

So important is this chronological measure of God by which He is made to "fit the urgent needs of the world's present outreach and endeavours,"[183] that its value must be reckoned independently of any evidence.[184] If a man at the present time finds it impossible to accept the traditional notion of God, a philosopher will be found to whittle it down.[185] If a new theory appears on the philosophical horizon, the notion of God or His attributes is made to fit this theory so as to suit better the "thought of the age."[186] We must keep up to the minute with our God as we do with our scientific and philosophical theories and modes of thought. Similarly there is an increasing insistence on a

---

[181] C. A. BECKWITH, *The Idea of God*: "Reasons for the New Idea," pp. 5-38. Quotation, p. 65.

[182] EDMUND H. REEMAN, *Do we need a New Idea of God?* (1918).

[183] Ibid., p. 90.

[184] *Varieties of Religious Experience*, p. 328.

[185] BERTRAND RUSSELL, "Essence of Religion," *Hibbert Journal*, vol. ix. no. 41, p. 50.

[186] C. C. WEBB, "The God of Professor Alexander," *Church Quarterly Review*, vol. xliii. no. 186 (January 1922), p. 335.

new idea of God to suit democracy as a form of government. The War gave us the shibboleth, "Make the world safe for democracy:" the philosopher echoed, "Make God safe for democracy." "Recent political and social developments, which make men increasingly impatient of masters, prepare them also to reject God, who rules simply by Divine right."[187] "There are many also who feel that the great democratic uprising of the world cannot be without its effect upon our thought of God, and who are finding it increasingly difficult to reconcile the oligarchic and monarchical elements that predominate in our common God-ideas with modern democratic urge and impulse."[188] The modern man is all-powerful. "Man's life, man's world, are man's achievement. He is mastering the oceans, the deserts, the land and the air." There is no place for tyrants in such a universe where man is so powerful, and the time is coming with the advent of the "new era of democracy" when there will be none—either "political, economic or religious."[189] Away, then, with the "bickering monopolist who will have no other Gods but Me," the author of the *History of the World* tells us.[190] The "higher man" of today, in the face of the rising tide of democracy, will not tolerate that "old-fashioned theism" with its "exalted monarch."[191]

Professor A. C. McGiffert, in an address to the students of the Andover Theological Seminary, enumerated the conditions on which God will be accepted "in these days of growing democracy."[192] The War has done much to scrap both monarchies and monarchical gods. Such notions of God as the King of kings and the Ruler of rulers were shaped under the influence of courts and thrones, and for that reason are unacceptable in this day and age.[193] The modern man will measure a God for himself—one to suit his own government; and that God we are assured will not and "must not be an

[187] D. W. FAWCETT, *Divine Imagining*, p. 222.

[188] E. H. REEMAN, *Do we need a New Idea of God?*, p. 10. *Cf.* CHARLES GORE, D.D., *Belief in God* (1921), p. 22.

[189] A. EUSTACE HAYDON, "Theological Trend of Pragmatism," *American Journal of Theology*, vol. xxii. no. 4, p. 411.

[190] H. G. WELLS, *God the Invisible King*, p. 7.

[191] W. JAMES, *Pragmatism*, p. 70. *Cf.* G. H. HOWISON, *Limits of Evolution*, pp. 253-5.

[192] "Christianity and Democracy," *Harvard Theological Review*, vol. xii. no. 1 (January 1919), p. 49.

[193] E. H. REEMAN, *Do we need a New Idea of God?*, p. 69.

irresponsible autocrat to whom men are but puppets and for whose glory they exist."[194] Keeping in mind this modern tendency to democratize and modernize God, we are better prepared for the shock that Professor Sellars gives us in his *Next Step in Religion*: "Paul's God was an Oriental monarch; to the modern he is a cad."[195]

For the Americans, if we are to believe a writer in the *Journal of Religion*, God will be measured to fit the Idealized Common Will of the United States;[196] or else, according to another, will be made the "presiding genius or President of the Great Cosmic Commonwealth."[197]

(3) Interpretation in Terms of Evolution

The same spirit which prompts people to measure God by modern democracy prompts them also to measure Him by more recent science. Among the scientific hypotheses which have gained favour in the last century, that of evolution ranks foremost. "Doubtless the greatest dissolvent in contemporary thought of old questions, the greatest precipitant of old methods, new intentions, new problems, is the one effected by the scientific revolution that found its climax in the *Origin of Species*."[198] There is hardly a philosophy of religion which has not re-interpreted the nature of God in accordance with evolution. This will be made clear in the following chapter, where the modern notion of God is treated. "Slowly but surely the idea of evolution is undermining the foundations of orthodox Christian theology. For a static conception of the universe was the cement on which those foundations were laid; and as the idea of evolution makes headway and the static conception falls into disrepute, the foundations of the orthodox theology, which have long shown signs of instability, will become more and more

---

[194] A. C. MCGIFFERT, *Christianity and Democracy*, p. 49.

[195] p. 162 ff.

[196] ED. S. AMES, "Validity of the Idea of God," *Journal of Religion*, vol. i. no. 5 (September 1921).

[197] EDMOND G. HOLMES, M.A., *Cosmic Commonwealth* (1920), p. 5. *Cf.* R. A. WOODS, "Democracy a New Unfolding of Human Power," in *Studies in Philosophy and Psychology* (1906).

[198] JOHN DEWEY, *Influence of Darwinism in Philosophy* (1910), p. 20.

unstable, and at last, in the fullness of time, the whole structure will totter and fall."

"When I say that the idea of evolution is undermining the foundations of orthodox theology, I mean first and foremost that it is tending to revolutionize our conception of God. The change from a static to a dynamic view of things, from the category of *esse* to the category of *fieri*, is bound to have its effect. For the Creator of Being and the Source (and Goal) of Becoming are, as concepts, at opposite poles of human thought."[199]

---

[199] EDMOND G. HOLMES, M.A., "The Idea of Evolution and the Idea of God," *Hibbert Journal*, vol. xxi. no. 2 (January 1923), p. 227.

CHAPTER V:

THE MODERN IDEA OF GOD

IT is not without some misgiving that we begin here a sketch of the modern idea of God. The protests, the descriptions and the dissatisfaction with the traditional notion of God are often made up of "hard sayings." We quote them, however, to throw light on the new notions. But we do so with a regret which has been very well expressed by Professor Ralph Barton Perry of Harvard University. "No one," he says, "has taken the name of the Lord his God in vain so frequently and so unconcernedly as the philosopher. While philosophers dispute, believers witness with dismay the apparent dissolution, not only of God, but of immortality, freedom, marriage and democracy as well. I wish that philosophy, for technical purposes, might speak a language of its own, and settle the dispute in the vernacular that does not arrest the attention of the community. If this were possible, philosophy would be better entitled to the full benefit of that immunity from direct social responsibility which is most conducive to clear seeing and right thinking."[200]

There is much unanimity among modem philosophers concerning the necessity of a new idea of God. The old notion of God must give way to a new one to suit the needs of the twentieth century. "The worst God of all," it has been said, "is the God of the older Christian theology: God the Father, the creator of evil, who in His all-power and all-knowledge deliberately plans a cruel universe bristling with traps for His creatures. The older theology thought of God as spending every moment of His eternity in eaves-dropping and spying on immoral man, haunting every bedroom and listening to every obscene story, and equally observant of the murderer with his bloody

---

[200] *Present Philosophical Tendencies* (1912), p. 22.

chopper and the child with its fingers in the jam."[201] "Recent political and social developments, which make men increasingly impatient of masters, prepare them also to reject God who rules simply by Divine right."[202] A God of this kind—omnipotent and monarchical—"leaves us cold ... Who has not had sometimes the feeling that it was a little unfair for the omnipotent and omniscient God to judge human beings created by Him, apart from their own choice, in a state of comparative ignorance and weakness?"[203] "If I thought there was an omnipotent God who looked down on battles and deaths and all the waste and horror of this war—able to prevent these things—doing them to amuse himself, I would spit in his empty face."[204]

The old notion of creation, too, as applied to God must be done away with and be included "in the same circle of ideas as the waving of a magician's wand."[205] It has "no place in serious thinking nor in genuine religion," it being the "product of a childish fancy," and lacks "sweep and infinity enough to meet the requirements of even the illiterate natives of India. The vaster vistas which scientific evolutionism has opened, and the rising tide of social democratic ideas, have changed the type of our imagination, and the older monarchical theism is obsolete or obsolescent. The place of the divine in the world must be organic and intimate. An external creator and his institutions may still be verbally confessed at church in formulas that linger by

---

[201] MAY SINCLAIR, *The New Idealism*, pp. 304-5.

[202] D. W. FAWCETT, *Divine Imagining*, p. 222.

[203] LUCIUS HOPKINS MILLER, *Bergson and Religion* (1916), pp. 124-5.

[204] H. G. WELLS, *Mr. Britling Sees it Through*, p. 397. "I cannot believe it, and if I could I do not think I would have much use for such a God anyway."—E. H. REEMAN, *Do we need a New Idea of God?*, p. 20. "The socialized human being looks with natural scepticism upon any proposition to the effect that there is a wholly good God."—W. E. HOCKING, Ph.D., *Human Nature and its Re-making*, p. 393.

See J .WARD, *Pluralism and Theism*, p. 244. Dr. RASHDALL, *Moral Values and the Idea of God* (2nd edition, 1921), p. 484; "Personality, Human and Divine," in *Personal Idealism*, p. 391; *Doctrine and Development*, p. 8; R. H. DÓTTERER, Ph.D., "Doctrine of the Finite God in Modem War-Time Thought," *Hibbert Journal*, vol. xvi. no. 3, pp. 418-21; W. JAMES, *Varieties of Religious Experience*, pp. 131, 525; *Pluralistic Universe*, p. 310; J. MCTAGGART, *Some Dogmas of Religion*, p. 277; W. R. SORLEY, *Philosophy and Religion*, p. 82; *Theory of Good and Evil*, p. 237; F. H. BRADLEY, *Essays in Truth and Reality*, p. 432; BERNARD BOSANQUET, *Individuality and Destiny*, pp. 248-51; W.M.THORNBURN, "Omnipotence and Personality," *Mind* (April 1920), series 114, p. 163; F. C. S. SCHILLER, "Omnipotence," *Proceedings of the Aristotelian Society*, pp. 264-7; G. H. HOWISON, *Limits of Evolution* (2nd edition), pp. 359, 360, 422.

[205] A. SETA PRINGLE-PATTISON, *The Idea of God in the Light of Recent Philosophy*, p. 303.

their inertia, but the life is out of them; we avoid dwelling on them, the sincere heart of us is elsewhere."[206] "Whatever sort of being God may be, we know that He is nevermore that mere external inventor of contrivances intended to manifest His glory in which our great-grandfathers took such satisfaction; though just how we know this, we cannot possibly make clear by words either to others or to ourselves."[207]

But this is so much rhetoric. It would be unjust to limit the grievances of modern philosophers to such statements. There seem to be two complaints against the traditional notion which cannot well be passed over.[208] The first of these is that God is static. The second, that He is aloof from the world's needs and desires.

1. God is Static

By a static God is meant a rigid, immutable God, "existing in solitary bliss and perfection."[209] "That helplessness which a fixed and static perfection implies, that eternally immobile substance with which theology in the past has identified its perfect God, must give way" to the notion of the non-static, which "involves the rejection of the idea of God as perfect in the sense that He is unchangeable. It looks obvious that what is perfect cannot change except for the worse. But even were that true, it does not justify us in saying that the impossibility of change or its absence is either a feature or a condition of perfection. Changelessness may be a ruinous condition. It is evidently a conception that is totally inapplicable to life in every form and at every stage. Life is constant self-creation. We are in some ways and in some degrees

---

[206] W. JAMES, *Pluralistic Universe*, pp. 29, 30, 119. H. A. OVERSTREET, *God as the Common Will*, p. 155. F. C. S. SCHILLER, *Riddles of the Sphinx*, p. 354 ff. J. MCTAGGART, *Some Dogmas of Religion*, pp. 243-5.

[207] W. JAMES, *Varieties of Religious Experience*, p. 14.

[208] The doctrine of the finite God, which had so much vogue immediately after the War, the basis of which was the problem of evil, now seems to be a thing of the past. There area few voices still crying in the wilderness, but they are lost in the din of cries for the evolving and growing God.

[209] A. SETA PRINGLE-PATTISON, *The Idea of God in the Light of Contemporary Philosophy* (2nd edition), p. 411.

new beings every day; for the past constantly enters in us and becomes a part of us. The instant that process stops, death ensues: death *is* the stopping of a process. But it is also the substitution of another: decay sets in. As a matter of fact, neither in the world of dead objects nor in the world of living beings can we find anything but process." But if this be so, God can in no sense be static and changeless. Such a notion of Him seems to contradict the very facts of daily experience.[210]

2. *God is Aloof from the World's Needs*

If God is static and the world is progressive, it follows that He is little interested in this world of ours. "It is highly important, therefore, for religious thinking—and for philosophic thinking also—to rid itself of a transcendence which seeks to magnify God's greatness by separating Him from the world, placing Him at a distance from it and making Him self-sufficient and complete without it."[211] "Instead of a Divine Being who dwells aloof from the world-process and can only look on at it, seeing that it is already statically perfect,"[212] God must be a "God in the dirt." "The prince of darkness may be a gentleman, as we are told he is; but whatever the God of heaven and earth is, He surely can be no gentleman. His menial services are needed in the dust of our human trials, even more than His dignity is needed in the empyrean."[213] "He who is a king and not a marionette cannot beg off from the duties of his station."[214] "Benevolent he must be, but benevolent despotism becomes God no more than man."[215] The old attributes which were shaped under monarchies

[210] Sir HENRY JONES, *A Faith that Enquires*, pp. 302, 359. *Cf.* EDMOND G. HOLMES, *Dying Lights and Dawning* (1924), p. 23. Also B. H. STREETER, "The Spirit" in *Collection of Essays*. A. SETA PRINGLE-PATTISON, art. "Immanence and Transcendence," Ibid., pp. 6, 16.

[211] Ibid., p. 13.

[212] Sir HENRY JONES, *A Faith that Enquires*, p. 356.

[213] W. JAMES, *Pragmatism*, p. 72.

[214] R. W. SELLARS, *The Next Step in Religion*, p. 159.

[215] A.C. MCGIFFERT, *Harvard Theological Review*, vol. xii. no. 1, p. 49. God must "be shorn of the word omnipotence, in order that He may become less awe-inspiring, perhaps less mysterious, less removed from us and all our possibilities ... Omnipotence divides Him by an inseparable gulf from us."—FRANCIS HOWE JOHNSON, *God in Evolution*, p. 91.

Cf. S. ALEXANDER, *Space, Time and Deity*, vol. ii. p. 390.

are useless today. They are nothing but "the shuffling and matching of pedantic dictionary adjectives, aloof from morals, aloof from human needs, something that might be worked out from the mere word God by one of those logical machines of wood and brass which recent ingenuity has contrived, as well as by a man of flesh and blood ... instead of bread we have a stone; instead of a fish a serpent."[216]

But if the traditional notion of God is insufficient for modern minds, because its God is static, and consequently gives man no genuine cooperation in the cosmic struggle, what kind of God will meet modern requirements? The answer is simple: God in evolution.[217]

So far the general negative criticism of the traditional doctrine of God. We now pass to some specific and constructive views of individual philosophers. They are chosen as representatives of different outstanding schools.

God according to Professor S. Alexander

It has been thought for some time that the era of new systems of philosophy had closed, and that the future held merely the task of adapting them to science and classifying them.[218] Professor Alexander of Manchester has arisen to protest that novelty is not yet ended in philosophy. In 1914, in a paper read before the British Academy, he said, "I have the conviction, which I cannot here defend, that there is only one matrix from which all qualities come." The Gifford Lectures of 1916-18 were the realization of his conviction. These lectures, published in two large volumes, entitled *Space, Time and Deity*, though new in their content, yet have something in common with contemporary philosophy, viz. the insistence on progress and evolution.[219]

Professor Alexander tells us that the stuff from which all things are made is Space-Time. Space-Time is motion in itself

---

[216] W. JAMES, *Varieties of Religious Experience*, pp. 446-7; *Pragmatism*, p. 120.

[217] EDMOND G. HOLMES, *Dying Lights and Dawning*, p. 4. "This solidarity, ante-mundane figure is the residuum of a primitive and pictorial fashion of thinking."—A. SETH PRINGLE-PATTISON, *The Idea of God*, p. 304.

[218] L. NOËL, "Le Système de M. Alexander," *Revue Néo-Scolastique*, no. 94. (Mai 1922), p. 240 ff.

[219] As well as the fact that he joins Croce and Bergson as time-philosophers.

without the motion of a body.[220] Space and Time are not distinct; they cannot exist separately. Time is the soul of Space-Time; Space is the body of Space-Time. Spinoza had extension and thought as the attributes of his one ultimate reality. Professor Alexander's theory retains extension as Space, but changes thought into Time. This is not to imply that his theory is in any way a copy of Spinoza's; the resemblance extends no further.

From Space-Time all things come. In the course of evolution it breaks itself up into various existents, all of which are retained in the all-embracing stuff of Space-Time. Therefore any portion of Space-Time possesses qualities common to the other existents generated within the universe of Space-Time. The fundamental pervasive features of these existents are the categories—except quality. Quality is distinct; it varies with the kingdom in which it appears—*i.e.* the kingdom of matter, life or mind. The quality of each of these is in part identical with a lower level; *e.g.* life has similarity with matter, and mind with life. The relation of the higher to the lower quality is that of mind to its neural basis. It is the soul of that which is below. Thus life is the soul of the body, which is matter; and mind is the soul of the body, which is life; just as in the great Space-Time, Time is the soul and Space is the body of Space-Time.

Now, what place has God in such a system? Some critics have thought that God was introduced only as a "ceremonious bow" or as a "point of honour" in respect for the terms of the Gifford Lectures.[221] But Professor Alexander denies this imputation, and insists that his book on God is not mere comedy to complete the three preceding tragic books. He assures us that he is "very serious."[222]

[220] "That which is proximately fundamental is an event-particle. An event-particle is the limiting case of a motion. There is also a motion-quality which is just pure motion. Motion does not imply anything which moves. It is anterior to things. Space-Time is abstraction from motions. The event-particle is half way between Space and Time."—*Space, Time and Deity*, vol. i. pp. 321, 329 ff.

[221] C. C. WEBB, "Space, Time and Deity," *Church Quarterly Review*, vol xliii. no. 186 (January 1922). *Cf. Mind*, new series 117 (January 1921).

[222] "Some Explanations," an article written by Professor Alexander in *Mind* (October 1921, new series 120), in answer to Mr. Broad's invitation of January 1921, in *Mind*, to make some of his doctrines more explicit.

In discussing theodicy, Professor Alexander draws a distinction between Deity and God. Deity is a quality; God is a Being.

(a) Deity.—As stated above, within the all-embracing stuff of Space-Time the universe exhibits, in its emergence in time, successive levels of finite existence, each with its characteristic empirical quality. At one end of these is undifferentiated Space-Time; at the other end progressive value. Among the three principal qualities the highest known to us at present is mind or consciousness. Deity is the next higher empirical quality to the highest we know. This is true throughout all the levels of existence.

Deity . . .	. E
Mind . . .	. D
Life . . .	. C
Matter . .	. B
Empirical configurations of Space-Time .	. A

A, B, C, D represent the various levels of existence in the process of Space-Time Evolution. Now, by definition, deity is the next higher quality to the one yet evolved. When, therefore, the "growing world" is at A, deity is at B. When the growing world is at B, deity is at C. When the world reaches C, deity has moved ahead to D. Now in our present state we have reached D, and deity is at E. Deity, then, is always the quality just in front of us. Very tantalizingly it runs ahead of us, like a shadow pursued. Deity is therefore a "variable quality, and as the world grows in time, deity changes with it."[223] Professor Alexander does not wish to say that matter in some way thinks or forecasts life. This it is incapable of doing. Only mind can do that. He merely wishes to say that if we could think ourselves back into the material existence, we should feel ourselves (though matter would be the highest that we know) "swept on in the movement of Time ... there would still be that restless movement of Time which is not the mere turning of a squirrel in its cage, but the nisus towards a

[223] Vol. ii. p. 348.

higher birth."[224] But how this "experience" would take place in the "material soul" would require a power of description of "greater capacity" than Professor Alexander admits he has. It is to be noted that man alone does not know deity, nor does deity exist alone for him. It arises at each level of existence, whether it be the mere indistinct configurations of Space-Time, or matter or life.

What is the nature of deity? Deity is not mere mind or spirit like ourselves, any more than life is mere matter, or mind mere matter and life. We therefore cannot tell what deity is, except that it is not pure mind.

(b) What is God? God is the Being who possesses the quality of deity. "God is the whole world as possessing the quality of deity."[225] Just as Time is the soul and Space is the body of Space-Time, so is the whole world the "body" of God, and deity is His "mind."

But deity may be possessed in two ways, either ideally or actually; and according as it is possessed, an actual and an ideal God will result. What is the difference between the actual and the ideal God? It is a difference of existence. One *is*; the other *becomes*. "God as actually possessing deity does not exist, but is an ideal, is always becoming; but God as the whole universe tending towards deity does exist."[226] "As an actual existent, God is the infinite world with its nisus towards deity."[227]

God is therefore the universe striving towards deity. Now, suppose it attains deity. Would we then have a God possessing infinite deity? A realized and accomplished God? No, says Professor Alexander, because if infinite deity did exist, "God would cease to be infinite God," and He would break up into a series of finite Gods or "angels" who would be a higher race of creatures than ourselves, with a God further on. Infinite deity implies an infinite world striving after deity. In this sense God is infinite. But the attainment of the deity makes deity finite. Far back in the dim past, when there were only mere configurations

---

[224] Ibid.

[225] Vol. ii. p. 353.

[226] S. ALEXANDER, "Some Explanations," *Mind* (October 1921, new series 120) p. 428.

[227] Vol. ii. p. 353.

of Space-Time, the universe was straining toward the infinite mind. For that level of existents deity was matter; but when the nisus reached matter, the deity became life; when the nisus reached life, the deity became mind; now we are striving toward the deity, and when we attain it, it will dissolve as an emotional state into a mere "finite God or angel." Our search will have been in vain.

"God, as an actual existent, is always becoming deity but never attains it. He is the ideal God in embryo. The ideal, when fulfilled, ceases to be God, and yet it gives shape and character to our conception of the actual God, and always tends to usurp its place in our fancy."[228] The essence of God, if we may so speak, is a nisus—a striving towards deity. He is in the process of evolution and not outside it; for He is the "whole universe with a nisus towards deity."[229] His perfection increases as the universe increases. His being increases in like manner. His perfection, if He will ever possess it, is to be placed at the term of the evolutionary process rather than at the beginning. He is the unattainable Omega of Space-Time.

God according to Professor Pringle-Pattison

The conception of God given us by Professor Pringle-Pattison centres round his view of the whole universe. He finds that all the opposition between facts and values, between science and religion, knowledge and faith, has passed into philosophy through Kant and Hume, who insisted on the fatal separation of the subject knowing and the object known. The problem is how to bridge this chasm between the "finished world" and the "independent knower equipped from heaven knows where with a peculiar set of faculties."[230] The problem is solved, according to the Professor, by substituting biological for mechanical categories. This substitution destroys all opposition between subject and object. "Man is organic to the universe and the universe is organic to man."[231] The universe has developed man

[228] Ibid., p. 365.

[229] Ibid., p. 362.

[230] *The Idea of God in the Light of Recent Philosophy* (Gifford Lectures of 1912-13), 2nd edition, 1920, p. 112.

[231] p. 177.

for its own self-expression. This is the goal to which Nature is always working, namely, "the development of an organ by which she may become conscious of herself and enter into the joy of her own being."[232]

This oneness of the universe, then, has solved the problem of the object and subject relation. Secondary qualities are not something apart and separated from reality; they are one with it. Values and reality are not separated, for the same reason; they are organic in nature. Neither are God and nature separated, for there is something organic between God and man and God and the world. To maintain that God and man are two independent facts is to lose hold "upon the experienced fact, which is the *existence of one in the other and through the other*."[233] "The true revelation of the divine must be sought, therefore, as I have contended, in the systematic structure of finite experience as a whole."[234]

The traditional idea of God, then, must be profoundly transformed, for "the traditional idea, to a large extent an inheritance of philosophy from theology, may be not unfairly described as a fusion of the primitive monarchical ideal with Aristotle's conception of the Eternal Thinker."[235] The new conception of God, then, which will be more in keeping with our times will not be the God of Aristotle—"a God standing outside the world's process." "There is much left out of such a conception." The life of such a God would be one of "heartless ease, troubled by nothing."[236]

The new notion will avoid two extremes: first, that of a "purely immanent view of the Divine as equivalent to sheer Pantheism, in which no distinction whatever is drawn between God and nature;" and secondly, that of the "transcendence which is equivalent to Deism, and which, according to this author, is

[232] p. 114.
[233] p. 254: italics ours.
[234] *The Idea of God in the Light of Recent Philosophy* (Gifford Lectures of 1912-13), 2nd edition, 1920, p. 220.
[235] p. 407.
[236] p. 408-9.

exemplified in the rigid Monotheism of the Jewish people and in Mahommedanism."[237]

What follows is important. "In the present connexion it may be suggested that the transcendence which must be retained, and which is intelligible, refers to a distinction of value or of quality, not to the ontological separateness of one being from another."[238] God and the universe are organic one to another. They both have existed eternally. Creation is therefore an eternal act. It is an eternal process of communication, the "infinite in and through the finite, the finite in and through the infinite."[239]

"God, therefore, is not purely immanent, nor is He purely transcendent. There is only one phrase which expresses what He really is, namely, 'organic with the universe.' He becomes an abstraction if separated from the universe of His manifestation, just as the finite subjects have no independent subsistence outside of the Universal Life, which mediates itself to them in a world of objects. We may conceive God as an experience in which the universe is felt and apprehended as an ultimately harmonious whole; and we must, of course, distinguish between such an infinite experience and the experience of ourselves and other finite persons. But we have no right to treat either out of relation to the other."[240]

In conclusion, God is "not an Absolute living in solitary bliss and perfection, but a God who lives in the perpetual giving of Himself, who shares the life of His finite creatures, bearing in and with them the whole burden of their finiteness, their sinful wanderings and sorrows, and the suffering without which they cannot be made perfect ... The Omnipotence of God will mean neither the tawdry trappings of regal pomp nor the irresistible might of a physical force. The Divine omnipotence consists in the all-compelling power of goodness and love to enlighten the grossest darkness and to melt the hardest heart … And thus for a

---

[237] "Immanence and Transcendence," in *The Spirit*, pp. 4, 11; *The Idea of God* (2nd edition), p. 221.

[238] Ibid., p. 255.

[239] Ibid., pp. 315, 414. "The whole meaning of Creation is seen to be the origination of conscious spirits; for to them alone can God reveal Himself, and from them alone can He obtain a response. There is, in strictness, no creation, no finite universe at all, till spirits are created."—"Immanence and Transcendence," in *The Spirit*, p. 17.

[240] *The Idea of God*, p. 314.

metaphysic which has emancipated itself from physical categories, the ultimate conception of God is not that of a pre-existent Creator, but, as it is for religion, that of the eternal 'Redeemer of the world.' This perpetual process is the very life of God, in which, besides the effort and the pain, He tastes, we must believe, the joy of victory won."[241]

God according to Mr. Douglas Fawcett

In order that contemporary philosophy might descend to the full depths of an anti-intellectual and consequently of any affective philosophy, it was necessary that some one should herald the power of the imagination. Bergson had exalted intuition and sympathetic fusion with the external world; Ward exalted faith; James and a host of others maintained the dignity of immediate "experience;" but no one had poetry enough in him to propose imagination as the clue to philosophical solutions. Mr. Douglas Fawcett has recently come to fill the want in his work *The Divine Imagining.* He assures us that it is intended for "disillusioned metaphysicians."

Professor Mackenzie, after a somewhat unfavourable criticism of this work in *Mind*,[242] later comes to correct his criticism. "I now regard Mr. Fawcett's work as considerably more important than I at first perceived. It seems at least, if nothing else, to be the necessary supplement to such an account as that of Professor Alexander."[243]

The world, according to Mr. Fawcett, is not so much the result of rational design as the adventure of the imagination. Imagination, or rather the "Divine Imagining, in its modes and transformations, is the sole ground of reality."[244] The process by which this ultimate reality works itself out is that of Creative Evolution, which is "an aspect of the Divine Imagining." In the words of the author, this source is to be explained as follows: "Ultimate reality is best viewed as imaginal; as conscious activity (consciring), which, as embodied in content, resembles most

[241] Ibid., pp. 411, 412; "Immanence and Transcendence," in *The Spirit*, pp. 11, 13.

[242] April 1922.

[243] *Mind* (October 1922).

[244] DOUGLAS FAWCETT, "Imaginism and the World Process," *Mind*, vol. xxxi. no. 122 (April 1922), p. 154.

nearly that human experience which we call imaginary, conservative and creative, reproductive and productive … Reason which may have set up an Absolute is an instance of secondary creation such as subserves the living … but which has no standing in reality at large such as could be called cosmic … The universe interpreted according to the analogy of Reason yields the Hegelian or *Rational Idea*; interpreted according to that of imagining, the *Imaginal Idea* or Divine Imagining. But while the former solution cannot be stretched so as to cover all the facts of experience, the imaginal embraces them, as a sequel could show, readily enough."[245]

The question now presents itself: is the Divine Imaginal, the source of all reality, to be identified with God? Mr. Fawcett has no hesitation in answering that "God must not be equated with the Divine Imaginal, which shows *alike in Him* in the opposition with which He contends, and perhaps indefinitely many other Gods."[246] He is rather within the content whole of the Divine Imaginal. By evolution "He buds off from the Divine Imagining."[247] He is a member of the great society of sentients, and in fact, as "the Great Sentient God might be called the child of the Divine Imagining."[248] He is, therefore, a product of the evolutionary process—not coming only at the end in the fashion of Professor Alexander's God, but developing even from the beginning.[249] "He began to be with the slow coalescence of the superior sentients of a world system. But when? Considering the history of my present life, I find that my appearance as a conscious individual began long after the first stage of the formation of my body. And it might be urged that God arose similarly long after the origin of this changing world system of content, which is His Body." Mr. Fawcett then confesses he cannot solve the problem. "Our private imagining, as we might say, is not adequate to cosmic imagining, and modesty enjoins reticence."[250]

[245] Ibid., p. 158-68.
[246] Ibid., p. 168.
[247] DOUGLAS FAWCETT, *The Divine Imagining* (1921), p. 218.
[248] Ibid., p. 219.
[249] J. MACKENZIE, Note, *Mind* (October 1922).
[250] *The Divine Imagining*, p. 223.

The process of its development is best expressed in the words of the author: "Like the risen Osiris, who, after an interval of struggle, suffering and defeat, died that he might live again in glory, the Divine Imaginal descends into imperfection and conflict, and re-arises; is redeemed and redeems itself as a conscious God. And since God is a society of finite sentients and finite sentients are each and all evolved, the evolution of God is seen to be the compensation for that corruption of eternity in which the world process began."[251]

This closes our rapid summary of the doctrine of three individual philosophers. To see how characteristic they are of contemporary ideas, we add a few descriptions drawn from many diverse sources.

God may be described as a "perfect process," a phrase Sir Henry Jones has used. But this seems to be a contradiction. "It looks obvious that what is perfect cannot change except for the worse," and "it does not seem easy to justify the conception of the Divine Being as moving from perfection to perfection. Compared with the latter stage, the earlier manifestly comes to appear to be defective and imperfect. A movement from perfection to perfection looks like a logical impossibility. Every present, when it arrives, seems to condemn what went before as at least a partial failure." But this is merely apparent. "At stage *A*, may not *a* be perfection? And at stage *B*, may not *b* acquire that character? Is it quite certain that there are static limits to the indwelling perfections of the Divine nature, or indeed to anything that develops? What is admirable in a grown-up man can be repellent in a child …"

"To me," continues Sir Henry Jones, "the idea of God as the *perfect in process*, as a movement from splendour to splendour in the spiritual world, as an eternal achievement and never-resting realization of the ideals of goodness in human history, is endlessly more attractive, and, I believe, more consistent with our experience in the present world-process, than a being eternally contemplating his own perfections."[252]

---

251 Ibid., p. 221.

252 *A Faith that Enquires*, pp. 358-60.

"If a figure may represent him," Mr. Wells tells us, "it must be the figure of a beautiful youth already brave and wise, but hardly come to his strength. He should stand lightly on his feet in the morning time, eager to go forward, as though he had but newly arisen to a day that was still but a promise; he should bear a sword, that clean discriminating weapon. His eyes should be bright as swords; his lips should fall apart with eagerness for the great adventure before him, and he should be in very fresh and golden harness, reflecting the rising sun. Death should still hang like mists and cloud-banks and shadows in the valleys of the wide landscape about him. There should be dew upon the threads of gossamer and little leaves and blades of turf at his feet."[253] Such is the modern God.

The same notion is put forward by Professor Rogers. "I think," he writes, "it may be regarded as the natural demand of human nature that the future should open up real accessions of good, and that a place should therefore be provided for novelty and growth in this ultimate universe. It is true that heaven has mostly been conceived in terms of rest. But in such a doctrine a note of weariness and relaxation is evident which, though excusable as a reaction against a life of toil which men are now forced to undergo, ought plainly not to be allowed to settle our final religious convictions; and I think that it does not, in fact, represent the best religious insight. As we know the good in human terms, it is bound up everywhere with activity and change; and it is difficult, and probably impossible, to conceive of it concretely when change has been eliminated … I see no reason to deny to God the same progressive enjoyment of changing values which is needed to constitute value itself in the long run. This, no doubt, involves with each step a growth in knowledge also … God's consciousness of what is still to come may be, I think, as ours is, no consciousness of an actual eternity, but only of an absence of finality in any values at any time achieved."[254]

---

[253] *God the Invisible King*, p. 67.

[254] *What is Truth?*, pp. 174, 175, 176, 180. *Cf. Emergent Evolution* of Professor L. MORGAN, for whom God is the "ultimate Source on which emergent evolution ultimately depends" (p. 36, 52, 116). Despite this dependence, God is "the Nisus directive of the course of events" (p. 34), or the "Nisus in Causality manifested in all natural events" (p. 301). "But unless we also intuitively enjoy His activity within us, feeling that we are in *a measure one with Him in substance*, we can have no immediate knowledge of Causality or of

The modern notion of God is on all sides that of an evolving God, who is either tending toward deity, budding off from the Divine Imaginal in one of the world systems, or else organic with a progressing world. He *is* not: He is *becoming.* His life is evolving with the cosmic order and is "developing through the cooperative contributions (conscious and unconscious) of all creatures."[255] He is, therefore, helped by us,[256] and without us would for ever remain unachieved.[257] He "needs not our prayers, our incense or the easy homage of our lips, but our brain, our blood, our will, our life."[258] Ay, more than this, "God Himself, in short, may draw vital strength and *increase of very being* from our fidelity."[259]

God as source of our existence and of emergent evolution" (p. 301).

255 H. A. OVERSTREET, "God and the Common Will," *Hibbert Journal,* vol. xiii. no. 1 (October 1914), p. 155.

256 H. G. WELLS, *God the Invisible King,* p. 67.

257 A. C. MCGIFFERT, "Christianity and Democracy," *Harvard Theological Review,* vol. xii. No. 1, p. 49.

258 E. H. REEMAN, *Do we need a New Idea of God?*, pp. 24-28.

259 WILLIAM JAMES, *Is Life worth Living?*, p. 28; italics ours. This statement of James is a more or less philosophical expression of a note which he sent to Dr. Schiller, in which, by means of a story, he ridiculed a God who was not a growing God in a growing world. "Lecturing to my class, he (Höffding) told against the Absolutists an anecdote of an 'American' child who asked his mother if God made the world in six days. 'Yes.' 'The whole of it?' 'Yes.' 'Then it is finished, all done?' 'Yes.' 'Then in what business now is God?' If he tells it at Oxford you must reply 'Sitting for his portrait to Royce, Bradley, and Taylor.'"—*Letters of William James,* vol. ii. p. 26. F. HOWES JOHNSON, *God in Evolution.*

PART II

CHAPTER I:

ANTI-INTELLECTUALISM

THE spirit of modern thought, whatever else it may be, is anti-intellectual. All the operations of the intellect from abstraction to reason have undergone a rigorous criticism, and even the faculty of the intellect itself has not been spared.[260] Professor Perry summarizes this modern spirit in these words: "Psychology speaking for emotion and instinct has reduced intellect to impotence over life; metaphors have subordinated it to the will. Bergson and his followers have charged it with falsehood; while with Pragmatists and Instrumentalists it has sunk so low that it is dressed in livery and sent to live in the servants' quarters."[261]

What is the origin of this anti-intellectualism? What reasons have prompted a general and unmerciful assault on the intelligence? To begin with, there is a confusion of the intellect and reason. In the traditional doctrine of intellectualism the difference is as follows: the intelligence apprehends in a simple way an intelligible truth; reason moves from the known to the

---

[260] "Distrust of the intellect is the characteristic note of recent philosophy. Today we have nothing else than contempt for the tribe of thinkers. Instead of reason philosophers we have faith philosophers. It has become the fashion to idealize impulse over reason, sentiment over thought, and to denounce all system-making."—R. F. RADHAKRISHNAN, *The Reign of Religion in Contemporary Philosophy*, p. 42.

[261] "The Integrity of the Intellect," *Harvard Theological Review* (July 1920), vol. xiii. no. 3, p. 221. *Cf.* Professor ALIOTTA, *The Idealistic Reaction against Science*; English trans. McCaskill, Introd., p. XV: "One of the essential characteristics of contemporary thought is undoubtedly the reaction from intellectualism in all its forms."

unknown.[262] They are related as "generation" to "esse," as circumference of a circle to the centre.[263] The Intelligence does not explain; it does not reason; it grasps. It sees an intelligible object as the eye sees a sensible object. Reason, on the contrary, is related to the intelligence as movement is related to rest; as acquiring a thing is related to having a thing. They are not, however, two distinct faculties, but merely two different modes of operation of the one faculty.

What does intelligence mean to modern thinkers? It means reason—that laborious, mediate approach to reality. What reason is for the Scholastic, intellect is for the contemporary. What intellect is for the Scholastic, intuition, instinct, imagination and experience are for the others. There is more than a mere confusion of terminology here. Rather there is a failure to appreciate the real worth of the intelligence; and because of this, numerous substitutes have been devised to fill the void. The confusion is well illustrated in the works of M. Bergson, who has been the inspiration of much anti-intellectualism among his contemporaries.

In his first work, *Essai sur les Données Immédiates*,[264] he makes a study of the measurement of sensation, and declares all measurement of sensation to be symbolic. Direct measurement is impossible because sensations have no extensive quantity, and because intensive quantity is a subterfuge. Indirectly, however, we measure sensations by spatial symbolism, inasmuch as a function of life is to handle objects. Life is wholly ordained to action, and habits acquired by the life of action produce natural, spontaneous reduction of reality to spatialized form, *e.g.* language.

---

262 "Intelligere enim est simpliciter veritatem intelligibilem apprehendere; ratiocinari autem est procedere de uno intellecto ad aliud ad veritatem cognoscendam."—I q. 79 art. 8; I-II q. 93 art. 4; 3 d. 4 q. art. 1 ad 5; *C. G.*, lib. 4 c. 11.

"Aliquis intelligere dicitur quod interius in ipsa rei essentiam veritatem quodammodo legit; ratio vero discursum quemdam designat, quod ex uno in aliquid cognoscendum anima humana pertingit vel pervenit."—*De Veritate*, q. 15 art. 1; *Post. Analy.*, lib. 1 art. 1.

263 "Et sic motus comparatur ad quietem, et ut principium et ut ad terminum; ita et ratio comparatur ad intellectum ut motus ad quietem et ut generatio ad esse."—*De Veritate*, q. 15 art. 1. "Intelligere enim dicit nihil aliud quam simplicem intuitivam intellectus in id quod sibi est praesens intelligibile."—3 d. 4 q. art. 5.

264 21st edition (1921).

The conclusion is, then, that there is more in consciousness than the spatial symbol can represent. Hence there must be in us a double ego. First the superficial ego, which is an ensemble of habits all related to *space*, as well as words destined to be exchanged with others. This ego reacts automatically in practice, and upon a given stimulus the reaction is previsible; *e.g.* recalling of a man's name on seeing his face. Besides this superficial ego, there is the profound ego which basks in the freedom of the contingent, the qualitative and the heterogeneous fusion of all reality in pure duration. If the thought is not lucid, it is at least that of M. Bergson.

Here is the first Bergsonian confusion of the intellect and reason. For M. Bergson the superficial ego is reason or *intelligence*, and the profound ego is intuition. What he really should have said, if he had the distinction well in mind, was that the superficial ego is reason and the profound ego is the intelligence. But from this initial misunderstanding the confusion continues in all his subsequent works, with the result that the intelligence is finally rejected as the "original sin of all thought."

In his next work, *Matière et Mémoire*,[265] he analyses the idea of consciousness. In mind he finds two currents, one tending toward action, the other tending toward reverie. The first is concerned with resemblances, and is adapted to present action; the second is concerned with differences. The first current, which is perception, becomes synonymous with intelligence; the second current, memory, which is a virtuality without any relation to action, becomes synonymous with intuition. Again the same confusion.

In his well-known *L'Évolution Créatrice*,[266] that which was but dimly hinted at in the superficial and the profound ego, perception and the memory, now becomes clear and transparent. The superficial ego and perception were in the two first works destined for action. In *L'Évolution Créatrice* it is the intelligence which is destined for action. The profound ego and memory were destined for reverie, for immediacy, for pure *durée*; and these

[265] 17th edition (1921).
[266] 25th edition (1921).

now become intuition. The confusion still remains; intelligence is taken for reason, and reason for intelligence.

Looking at the works of M. Bergson from this point of view, it is quite true to say that logically *L'Évolution Créatrice* was the first of his works, although it appeared last in point of view of time. The ideas of this latter work were really the inspiration of all the others.

The successors of M. Bergson and his contemporaries have fallen into the same confusion. Throughout the whole realm of philosophy the intelligence is understood as reason and criticized as such; faith, desire, instinct, sympathetic intuition, imagination, and a host of other substitutes which give immediacy in knowledge, come in to replace the discarded "intelligence."[267]

What the contemporaries are attacking, then, is not intelligence, for intelligence is the immediate and intuitive knowledge after which they are seeking under the forms of desire, experience, "sympathetic intuition" and the like. The attack is really directed against reason and against the *Scientific Intellectualism of the last century, and in no way against the Scholastic or the traditional doctrine of the intellect.* The traditional doctrine of the intelligence is beyond their attack, either because it is unknown, or because it has been wrongly identified with the false Scientific Intellectualism of the nineteenth century. The history of this philosophy is so well known that it suffices merely to recall it briefly.

The growth of modern philosophy is not organic. It grows not from within like a living organism, but from without like a crystal. It grows on contradictions. Swinging always between the two extremes, it passes precipitately from one extreme to the other. Traditional thought, on the contrary, which is the philosophy of a school and not of individuals, grows and expands by the development of first principles. It remains in the mean,

[267] J. B. BAILLIE, *Studies in Human Nature* (p. 36): "The Intellect is a 'specialization of the life of the mind.'" Among the Idealists, Croce opposes philosophy and science. One is theoretical, the other is practical. The concept of the former possesses universality and concreteness; the latter, which is a pseudo-concept, lacks both universality and concreteness—*e.g.* mathematics lacks concreteness—; biology lacks universality. The first is intuition; the second is reason. What Croce wants is immediacy and directness; reason for him equals science.

and would fall into error only if it moved toward the extremes. The *Ethics* of Aristotle, for example, avoided the extreme rigorism of the Stoics and the extreme liberalism of the Epicureans. The *Metaphysics* of Aristotle avoided the static philosophy of Parmenides and the dynamic philosophy of Heraclitus. By necessity, in every error there is a half-truth; every philosophical and theological error is either an exaggeration or an under-emphasis. No system of thought is bad *in se*—nothing is. *Ens et verum convertuntur.*

The origin of modern anti-intellectualism is to be found in a reaction to another system of thought with an over-emphasized reason. And perhaps in a decade or two, in perfect accordance with its principle of growth by contradictions, we shall have another philosophy which will be the philosophy of the static and the philosophy of reason. It is bound to come unless modern thought really takes over the biological growth to which it is so devoted, and begins to grow from within rather than from without.

Scientific Intellectualism took as its inspiration a form of degenerate Cartesianism. Descartes took as his rule of method, to accept only those things which could not be doubted. In this spirit Scientific Intellectualism, misunderstanding Descartes, sought to make war on all that the mind could not comprehend. Intelligence would now be the plaything of man, and in a much more fantastic way than with the decadent Scholastics of the fourteenth and fifteenth centuries. Outside the truths catalogued by science and found by reason there was said to be no truth. Its postulates were, first, that nothing is unknowable or mysterious. Everything can be explained by reason and by science. The discovery of electro-magnetism and thermodynamics renewed physics; chemistry took on a new birth. Le Verrier discovered in his workroom with a pen in his hands the stars which the observers found in the heavens with a telescope; Pasteur threw new lights on the origin of life; Champollion deciphered the hieroglyphics. Man was gradually solving the problems of the universe. Religion, the "faith-states," were gradually crumbling.

The second postulate was that of Determinism. Everything in the universe is determined by fixed and unalterable laws. In virtue of this determinism the universe could be studied scientifically. Vice and virtue do not exist; they are products, like vitriol and sugar. Man is a *théorème en marche*. He is a part of nature and subject to its determined laws.[268]

The philosopher of Scientific Intellectualism was Comte. According to his Positivistic system, all phenomena are to be regarded as subject to invariable natural laws. There are laws; we have merely to discover them. After we have discovered these laws, we must group them together in categories and reduce them to the smallest possible number. Philosophy, then, is not a search for causes, because causes are beyond experience. Philosophy is merely the analysis of the circumstances of experience. Look at the facts. Get the laws from the facts. Nothing can be known outside of the facts, or outside of the positive sciences. Outside of facts and laws there is nothing. Science knows no limits.

If facts are supreme, what is not a fact is an illusion. Substance, cause, metaphysics, principles and the like are illusions. The metaphysical stage of man is merely an intermediary stage between the age of fable and mythology, which for Comte is theology, and the age of science, which is the age of Positivism. Metaphysics existed merely to give verbal formulae to the images of the imagination, substituting, for example, a *vis dormitiva* for the "Sandman."[269]

Kant and Comte—Positivism and Criticism—agreed that nothing outside the phenomenal sciences can be known with certainty. They repose on indisputable facts. Kant and Comte, however, differed on the limits of science. Kant went further

---

[268] G. FONSEGRIVE, *L'Évolution des Idées dans la France contemporaine*, chap. III.

[269] AUGUSTE COMTE, *Cours de Philosophic Positive* (5th ed., 1892), t. 1, chap. XIV. pp. 2, 3, 4, 11ff. In France, Taine and Renan were gradually "explaining away all religion," thanks to the power of reason and of science. Nothing could escape the advances of science. M. Berthelot in the introduction to his *Les Origines de l'Alchimie* writes: "The world today is without mystery." Renan, following the same inspiration, declared that what we mean by God is merely the mind becoming conscious of its nature. "Reason is the God we seek." Taine reduced human nature to a product of the "race, the environment and the moment," and at the end of his *Philosophes français* showed that all the events of the world depend upon an "eternal axiom pronounced at the beginning of time." Even in literature the sovereignty of fact dominated. The method of Comte was to observe facts, suppose and verify. Zola did this in his novels. He invented personages and invented circumstances, then placed them together and watched the reaction, which would be just as rigorous and determined as the reaction of hydrogen and ogygen to an electric spark. His personages were a mere collection of observations. There is no moral struggle—everything is physiological.

than Comte. For Kant, what pure reason could not demonstrate the practical reason might postulate. What Comte relegated to the metaphysical and theological age of evolution, Kant referred to the much more dignified practical reason.

Proud of its own reason, convinced that nothing was beyond its power, such a spirit was destined for a fall and for a reaction. The reaction came, as it always comes in moments of satiety; but unfortunately, instead of reconstructing reason, it destroyed it altogether, and fell into a furious anti-intellectualism.

What, then, is modern anti-intellectualism? Is it an attack upon the faculty *of the intelligence, or is it an attack upon a state of mind?* Unquestionably it is an attack upon a state of mind which sought to glorify reason—not the reason of the Scholastics, for there was a prejudice against that; not the reason of Descartes, for that had degenerated in his successors; but the reason of Positivists—a Scientific Intellectualism which exaggerated its powers even to the denial of limits of knowledge.

Professor Aliotta, speaking of the reaction against this Scientific Intellectualism, writes: "The mind of man, which could not rest content with a simple transference of results attained by the methods of the natural sciences to the realm of philosophy, and was reluctant to stay its steps on the threshold of the Unknowable, sought within itself other and deeper activities which should throw open the portals of mystery. Art, moral life and religious belief were called upon to fill the void left by scientific knowledge; and the reaction went so far as to extend to the human intellect itself as a whole a distrust which should have been confined to *scientific naturalism and its claims to be able to comprehend the infinite riches of mind and nature within a few mechanical formulas*."[270]

The reaction to Scientific Intellectualism was threefold—religious, philosophical and scientific. The religious reaction was based on a desire to save the eternal verities. Just as Kant saw his ideals crumbling under the attacks of Hume and sought to save them by the help of the practical reason, so too, now, many who

[270] *The Idealistic Reaction against Science*, translated into English by Agnes McCaskill, Introd. p. XV. GEORGE FONSEGRIVE, *L'Évolution des Idées dans a France contemporaine* (1921), pp. 108-71.

are eager for the security of religious truths, seeing them battered and broken by science, seek to save them by appealing to some non-rational element. They make the mistake that Kant made before them. Instead of examining the value of the attack made on them, they take flight, hiding themselves in faith, tradition and infused ideas. Not until the time of Leo XIII and his encyclical, *Aeterni Patris,* did the defenders of religious truths turn the weapon of genuine intellectualism against their adversaries.

Among the religious reactions were Traditionalism,[271] Fideism,[272] and Ontologism,[273] making their appeals respectively to tradition, faith and infused ideas.

While those interested in the eternal verities were reacting on the basis of faith, tradition and innate ideas, the less religiously interested thinkers reacted on more purely philosophical grounds. Those who began the reaction were close enough to Scientific Intellectualism to see its defects; they had heard of the ideals of "Scientism" and had seen its feeble realizations; they had seen the ravages of an Intellectualism which set no limits to the powers of reason and which left no room for the things of eternity. *Sub specie scientiae,* and not *sub specie aeternitatis,* was its unique point of view.

Instead of correcting the abuse and putting reason in its due place and asserting its limits, they left it altogether, and set up the substitute of will, mystical experience and sense experience.

But the reaction is not yet complete even in Empiric Criticism. Professor Aliotta writes: "The concept of pure experience, the functional relation, the stable dependence of elements are remnants of the old intellectualism. We must go

---

[271] DE BONALD, *Sur un dernier ouvrage de M. l'Abbé de La Mennais,* t. 1, p. 645. LA MENNAIS, *Recherches philosophiques,* pp. 62, 68, 69; *Essai sur l'Indifférence,* pp. 203-4.

[272] BAUTAIN, *Philosophie du Christianisme*; UBAGHS, *Logicae seu Philosophiae rationalis elementa;* A. BONNETTY, *Annales de Philosophie chrétienne* (1830-55), *passim.*

[273] DENZINGER, *Propositions of Rosmini* (Nos. 1891-1930). It is worth remarking that outside the circles of common-sense philosophy there is today a resort to the same tentatives to reconstruct belief in God, as there was in the last half of the nineteenth century. In both cases there is a reaction from the intellect: in the former because reason was anti-religious; at the present time because reason is powerless. The effect in both cases is the same—an appeal to non-rational elements: then faith, tradition and innate ideas; now faith, instinct, imagination, desire, etc. The same fault is at the bottom of both. Both need an *Aeterni Patris*—one to convince them of the limits of scientific reason, the other to convince them of the powers of speculative reason.

further and deny all and every permanent relation, and form of conceptual reflection, if we would attain to that deeper experience which abstract formulae have falsified and impoverished."[274]

The Complete Reaction against Intellectualism

A real attack against "Scientism" had to come from science itself in order to strike at the foundations. Its weapons must be the findings of science, and not dark, cavernous subjective states, practical reasons and traditions. The credit for making just such an attack must be given to the eminent French scientist, Emil Boutroux, who in his work *La Contingence des Lois de la Nature* dealt the first real telling blow against his predecessors in the field of science.

Scientific theories are in reality only conventions—they are expressions of the habits of nature. Laws are only provisional because they are symbolic. They are only the expression of functional relations. The aim of science, therefore, is no longer to find the natural laws that exist in the objective reality; for these laws are evolving as science evolves.[275] The search for the external necessity in the world is not the ideal of the scientist; rather it is to manufacture the truth. Scientific hypotheses are merely *devices of the mind* used to explain the world in a simple fashion without recourse to experience. While hypotheses are pure conventions, M. Poincaré does not admit that they are caprices. Because they are useful, they have a quality which a whim does not always possess.

From this brief *exposé* of modern science the following conclusions may be drawn:—

(1) A characteristic of modern science is the increasing stress on the importance of mathematics. Mathematics is the best expression of the functional relations of measures. It is what may be called a "mixed science," a science formally mathematical to

[274] *The Idealistic Reaction against Science*, p. 89.

[275] LUCIEN POINCARÉ, *La Physique moderne: son Évolution* (1920), chap. 1.

which the physical data furnishes the matter.[276] Einstein, for example, took time out of the province of physics and placed it in the field of mathematics; and so much so, that his theory is not wholly intelligible except in mathematical language.[277]

(2) A second characteristic of modern science is insistence upon intuition, and the contribution of mind to matter. Science has passed from being merely a passive revelation of external reality to the interpretation. It now adds something over and above the phenomena, and something which the phenomena themselves cannot give.[278] There is an opposition between the brute fact and the scientific fact, as Poincaré has put it, or between the brute fact and the theoretical interpretation of Duhem. Mind gives something which matter does not give. In other words, there is intuition in science.

(3) Scientific theories are but mere instruments and tools without any permanent value. The formulae of science are not true, they are merely useful and convenient. They serve for a time, and sooner or later are supplanted by new and other formulae. They are relative, therefore, to the advance and the convenience of science.

Such is the attitude of the modern scientist toward his subject-matter. It is far different from the old notion of science, particularly that of ancient physics. It is different because it is more limited. In a certain sense it seems to be a recognition of the contingency and the want of necessity that is in the pure empirical order.

But what is the outlook of philosophy on this new scientific spirit? There are three possible points of view open to it. Philosophy might have ignored it altogether and gone on speculating about material things without ever looking in the direction of science. Or it might have entered into a full consideration of the findings of science and rendered an appreciation of their conclusions in the light of the more

[276] JACQUES MARITAIN, *Theonas*, p. 79.

[277] LUCIEN FABRE, *Les Théories d'Einstein* (Paris, 1922), p. 23.

[278] "La seule réalité objective, ce sont les rapports des choses. Ces rapports ne sauraient être conçus en dehors de l'esprit qui les conçoit ou qui les sent ... Dire qu'il y a autre chose que la pensée, c'est une affirmation qui ne peut avoir de sens."—POINCARÉ, *La Valeur de la Science*, chap. XI.

universal principles of philosophy. Lastly, it might have taken up an attitude of subordination, in which philosophy steps down from its high throne as the mistress of sciences, and, instead of availing itself of the conclusions of science, becomes its servant. This latter attitude has been that of modern philosophy. Modern philosophy is a lyric poet of science.

By the *principle of lyricism* is meant that, immediately upon the discovery of any important theory in one science, modern philosophy applies it to its own field whether it is applicable or not. Instead of making scientific discoveries its minister, it ministers unto them. Descartes' philosophy was born of an excessive devotion to the new physics and astronomy of his time. When Newton discovered the laws of gravitation, Kant sought to give philosophy the same certainty that Newton gave physics and thus escape the empiricism of Hume. Comte gave the world a new sociology, and philosophy began to turn itself into sociology. Darwin described the origin of species by evolution; philosophy lyricized Darwin and evolutionized everything—even God. Nietzsche lyricized the principle of the conservation of energy in his *Eternal Return*.[279]

---

[279] An excellent example of the modern philosophical craze of lyricism is seen in the new Relativity-Worship. The eminent scientist Einstein, as well as his genuinely scientific followers, has denied that the theory of relativity has philosophical implications, being, as it is, merely "an analysis of the physical conceptions of time and space" (*Nature*, 17th February 1921, p. 781). "What philosophy has to recognize in scientific relativity is simply an increased degree of accuracy due to the greater exactitude of physical concepts; which means, again, that little, if indeed anything, truly metaphysical is in the question at all ... Change in standpoint once more gives no change in the actual."—J. E. TURNER, "Scientific Relativity," *Mind* (January 1922), no. 121.

"The theory is not, in its nature or in its standards, essentially different from the other physical theories; it deals with experimental results and theoretical deductions which naturally arose from them."—A. S. EDDINGTON, *Mind* (October 1920), no. 116, p. 415.

"I would emphasize, then, that the theory of relativity of time and space is essentially a physical theory like the atomic theory of matter, or the electromagnetic theory of light; and it does not overstep the natural domain of physics."—Ibid., p. 416.

Despite the fact that the theory is physical, there are not wanting those who would make it metaphysical or criteriological. The laws and theories of matter thus become the laws and theories of spirit. See A. N. WHITEHEAD, *The Principles of Relativity, with application to Physical Sciences.* The first part of this work is epistemological. See also B. BOSANQUET, *The Meeting of Extremes in Contemporary Philosophy*; A. ALIOTTA, *La Teoria di Einstein e le mutevoli prospettive del mondo*; THOMAS GREENWOOD, "Einstein and Idealism," *Mind*, vol. xxxi. p. 205; Lord HALDANE, *Reign of Relativity*; H. WILDON CARR, Litt.D., *The General Principle of Relativity in its Philosophical and Historical Aspects*; A. RABB, *The Absolute Relations of Time and Space*; R. AINSCOUGH, "Some Remarks on Relativity," *Mind* (October 1922), vol. xxxi. p. 489.

This process of lyricism is more rampant today than it ever was. We have just noted above the conclusions of modern science—conclusions which strictly and properly belong to the study of the empirical as empirical. But no sooner have these scientific notions been advanced than a group of philosophers march forward to lyricize them—to apply the methods and conclusions of a science of one order to that of an entirely different order. In a general and broad way the lyricism may be represented as follows:

(1) EMPIRICAL SCIENCE

Formulae are convenient; they are not true—but useful.

Philosophical Lyricism.

(a) Philosophical principles, God, eternal verities are useful. Their truth is to be determined by their usefulness. *Pragmatism.*[280]

(b) Pure thought in philosophy and pure formulae in science are fictions. Man is the measure of truth. *Humanism.*[281]

(c) The value of the idea, as the value of the scientific hypothesis or formula, is determined by its instrumental or functional efficacy. *Instrumentalism.*[282]

(2) EMPIRICAL SCIENCE

Mathematics gives the best expression of the coordination of physical laws which experience makes known to us. Thus space and time in the Einstein theory are made intelligible through mathematics.

Philosophical Lyricism.

(a) Deification of space and time as ultimates, either in combination or singly. S. Alexander, *Space, Time and Deity.* M. Bergson, *L'Évolution Créatrice.* B. Croce, *The Philosophy of the Spirit.*

(b) Mathematical rendering of logic. Logic and mathematics are identical. The common ground of the two is eight indefinable notions and twenty undemonstrable principles.[283]

---

[280] W. JAMES.

[281] F. C. S. SCHILLER.

[282] J. DEWEY, *Studies in Logical Theories.*

[283] B. RUSSELL, *The Principles of Mathematics* (Cambridge, 1901). *Cf.* A. N. WHITEHEAD, *A Treatise on Universal Algebra*; PADOA, *La Logique déductive dans sa dernière phase de développement* (1912); LOUIS ROUGIER, *La Structure des théories déductives* (1921).

(3) EMPIRICAL SCIENCE

Laws add something to fact. Scientific hypothesis is nature interpreted by mind. The pure fact is quantity; the interpreted fact is quality. There is intuition in science.

Philosophical Lyricism.

Philosophy is the science of the qualitative. Intuition gives the qualitative, intelligence gives the practical quantitative fact. Quantity is repetition, quality a creation. Quantity is determination, quality is liberty. Quantity is previsible, quality is novelty.[284]

Three conclusions disengage themselves from this brief review of modern philosophy. First, modern anti-intellectualism is in great part a lyricism of the scientific reaction to the exaggerated Scientific Intellectualism of last century, and is not due to a recognized failure of the intelligence to serve speculative needs. Mechanism was made identical with the intellect—an equation which should never have been made—and in reacting against mechanism the intellect fell into disrepute.

Secondly, the reaction against intellectualism is really not a criticism of a *faculty*, but of a *state of mind*. An intelligence accidentally mutilated and blinded by the Positivist and Mechanicist schools has been confounded with the precious intelligence which God has given to man when He formed him in His image and likeness.

Thirdly, the whole anti-intellectualist position is a confusion between reason and intellect. 'Scientism' was a deification of reason, not of intellect. When this reason, which had exaggerated confidence in its own powers, had been proved unsound, the modern philosopher was satisfied that he had destroyed the

[284] This lyricism is particularly manifest in the works of M. Bergson. The contents of the three works may be outlined as follows:—

(1) *Essai sur les données immédiates.*

Superficial Ego= Quantity =Space= Intelligence.
Profound Ego=Quality= Time= Intuition.

(2) *Matière et Mémoire.*

Habitual Memory =Quantity=Space = Intelligence.
Pure Memory= Quality =Time= Intuition.

(3) *L'Évolution Créatrice.*

Intelligence=Quantity=Space=Homogeneity.
Intuition=Quality =Time= Heterogeneity.

intellect. The proposed substitutes for the "beast intellect" have therefore no right to existence. They are merely substitutes for a distorted reason. The intellect in its true nature has never been considered throughout this whole wave of thought which has so wrongly styled itself Anti-Intellectualist. It is not anti-intellectualist: it is anti-rationalist.

CHAPTER II:

THE THOMISTIC ANSWER TO THE IDEALS OF MODERN PHILOSOPHY

THOUGH the expression of philosophical systems be diverse, there runs through all of them a common current. The Spirit of the Times is one, though its expression be multiple. The negative goal towards which modern philosophy is striving is manifestly non-intellectual. This aspect we have already examined historically. The *positive* ideals of twentieth-century thinking remain to be examined. These ideals are said to be novel and new-born. They may have had distant antecedents, but they themselves are said never to have existed before. They are begotten chiefly by new advances in science and by a new outlook on the facts of experience. Such being the case, it is presumed that there can be no possible reconciliation between a philosophy which was begotten when science was alchemy, and a philosophy born of the newest and latest discoveries of the century. What fellowship could there be between light and darkness? Is not Scholastic philosophy the philosophy of the Dark Ages? "Can anything of good come from Nazareth?"

On the face of it, the modern prejudice against Scholasticism seems to rest on a solid foundation. It is quite true that St. Thomas did not have such scientists as Bateson, Duhem, Poincaré and others to lay the experimental foundations of his philosophy. It is also true that the Aristotelian physics and astronomy upon which he relied have since been discarded. But after all, were Aristotle and the Angelic Doctor less capable of interpreting the findings of science according to firmly established and self-evident principles than are the philosophers of today? The point of great importance is not the experience on which they had to draw, but the *interpretation* of it. A Conceptual Realist like St. Thomas, working on the ordinary and evident facts of daily experience, is certainly more capable of interpreting them than is an extreme idealist, even though the latter work on the "facts" of modern science.

In the last analysis, however, the only way of determining whether or not Scholastic philosophy is radically opposed to the ideals of modern philosophy, is to compare the two. In following this method we shall examine, first, the ideals of modern philosophy with particular reference to the supposed new ideals of scientific infiltration. Then we shall propose a Thomistic appreciation of these ideals, and in doing so we shall show—

First, that Thomistic philosophy better realizes the ideals of modern philosophy than does modern philosophy itself.

Secondly, in refusing to accept the Thomistic ideals modern philosophy is illogical and false to its own ideals.

The Ideals of Modern Philosophy

What are the ideals of modern philosophy?

The ideals which best correspond to the progress of science and the new spirit of the age are threefold:—

(1) *Philosophy must be an expression of life and a penetration into life.* "The application of science to increase, if not the richness, at any rate the fulness and complexity of life"[285] must be an ideal. Any system which can give a fuller measure of life, which can attain a more sympathetic and intimate communion with it, is the philosophy which can claim acceptance in this age. "Life, more life, richer, more satisfying life" is the goal of philosophy.[286] In pursuit of this ideal, "sympathetic intuitions," "religious experiences," "desires," "instincts" and "imaginings" have been proposed. Through these means a more intense fellowship and union with life have been promised.

---

[285] G. H. LANGLEY, "Interpretation of Religious Experience," *Hibbert Journal*, vol. xxii. no. 4, p. 649.

[286] JAMES LEUBA, "The Contents of Religious Consciousness," *Monist*, vol. xi. p. 536. Quoted by W. JAMES in *Varieties of Religious Experience*.

Scholastic philosophy is imagined to be the barrier that stands in the way of progress towards "life." It is presumed to be a philosophy of the static; a sort of card-index system of thought, in which everything is rigorously catalogued, and from which the spontaneous is rigorously excluded. It is said to be the philosophy of the inert and the lifeless, and the constantly recurring objection to it is that "it is characterized by a great incapacity for life."

(2) *The second ideal is that philosophy must express life in its continuity and Progressiveness.* "Progressiveness must be taken seriously. Change and progress must be signs of reality and not of imperfection."[287]

It is here that contemporary thought insists on the application of science to philosophy. The dominating hypothesis of these latter years is that of evolution, which manifests life in its gradual unfolding, from its lowest even to its highest manifestations. Lamarck, Darwin, Wallace and their successors have emphasized the evolution of life in biology. Tyndall, Huxley, Spencer, James, Dr. Schiller, M. Le Roy, M. Bergson, Professor Perry, and Dr. Shaun and a host of others have done the same for philosophy. If biology showed life to be progressive in its manifestations, why should not philosophy, which is the ultimate science of life, reveal life as a continuity?

Scholastic philosophy antedates modern biology. It is consequently suspected of being incapable of expressing the continuity and the evolution of life. Both through ignorance and through misunderstanding of its principles, it has become identified with a philosophy of the "block-universe" where all life is cut up into genus and species and into water-tight compartments which allow not the least co-penetration. The intellect, which it glorifies, is said to distort this life, to solidify and to break up the continuity of life and to falsify the life it proposes to interpret correctly. Mechanical concepts give only substitutes for life, and are even "the cause of death itself," as M. Bergson tells us. Instead of showing life in movement, it presents merely some juxtaposed snapshots, which are but poor

[287] G. H. LANGLEY, "Interpretation of Religious Experience," *Hibbert Journal*, vol. xxii. no.4, p. 649.

substitutes. The ideal philosophy must represent the fluid, the progressive, the continuous, and in the eyes of the moderns the *philosophia perennis* has failed to do this; hence the multitude of substitutes.

(3) *In the third place, philosophy should not only reveal life as continuous and progressive and fluid, but it should also reveal it as a process of unification.* This ideal is a consequence of the modern leaning toward biological interpretation. If there is evolution, then the present moment of evolution is the sum of all the previous moments, and the present phase is the sum of previous phases. In accordance with these biological theories, philosophy, it is said, should reveal how man sums up the various stages of evolution which have preceded him. The Culture-Epoch theory of Professor Hall is an obeisance to this ideal. According to this philosophy of education the child reveals in his play and in his growth the whole evolution of the race. In the realm of knowledge, man in his cognitive process should recapitulate and unify the cognitive processes below him. Thus M. Bergson makes his intuition a "glorified instinct" and a disinterested intelligence.[288] Intuition is said to be higher than both, and it recapitulates both. The process of unification is carried still further in the modern doctrines of Pantheism, in which God and the world become so unified as to be considered organically one with the other, so that "we experience one in and through the other."

Such are the three ideals of modern philosophy—the expression of life, in its continuity and in its unity. Every year brings forth new systems which better meet these ideals, and in all them the *philosophia perennis* is dismissed with the magic formula that "it is characterized by a great incapacity for life."

It is our contention that these ideals are not new; they are not the fruit of recent scientific discoveries, and they are not the new-born offspring of the nineteenth and the twentieth centuries. The principles themselves are metaphysical, not biological. Hence they are capable of being possessed by an age less

[288] It is thus that Bergson in the Introduction to his *Matière et Mémoire* professes a respectable duality as regards the theory of knowledge, but the body of the book is a most open confession of profound unity—the monism of becoming.

rigorously scientific than our own. *Furthermore, these ideals of modern, philosophy are better guaranteed by the philosophy of St. Thomas than by modern philosophy.*

To this end we shall show that the modern desire for a philosophy of life is best realized by the Thomistic principle: "the more immanent the activity, the higher the life."[289]

The second ideal, that philosophy must reveal itself as fluid, as continuous and progressive, is best secured by the principle that a "superior nature in its lowest perfection touches an inferior nature in its highest perfection;"[290] or, to put it dynamically: "movement decreases as the nature becomes more perfect."[291]

The third ideal, that life must be expressed as a unit and as a recapitulation of what has gone before, is best realized by the third Scholastic principle, that "that which is divided in inferior beings is united in superior beings," or "what is plural in the lower kingdoms is singular in the higher."[292]

These notions we shall apply to the various kingdoms to which modern philosophers, and particularly M. Bergson and Professor Alexander, have applied them—the mineral, vegetable, animal and rational; and in the angelic together with Professor Alexander, who goes one step further than M. Bergson. But in applying the principles to these kingdoms we are not doing so after the example of these and other modern thinkers, but after the application made in part by Aristotle, Dionysius, St. Gregory the Great, and in full by St. Thomas in the fourth book of the *Contra Gentes.* The exposition in the chapter which follows is little more than a translation of that remarkable chapter, which is to be numbered among the most beautifully synthetic pages St.

---

[289] "Quanto aliqua nature est altior, tanto id quod ex ea emanat magis est intimum."—*C. G.*, lib.4 c. 11.

[290] "Natura superior in suo infimo contingit naturam inferiorem ejus supremo."—*C. G.*, lib. 2 c. 91; DYONYSIUS, *Div. Nomin.*, c. 7. "Fines primorum iunguntur principiis secundorum."—ST. THOMAS in *Div. Nom.*, c. 7, lect. IV.

[291] ARISTOTLE, *De Coelo*, c 2.

[292] "Quanto aliquid est superius tanto habeat virtutem magis unitam, et ad plura se extendentem."—I q. 57 art. 2.

"These three principles have been called the three laws of the metaphysical light."—R. P. E. HUGON, *La Lumière et la Foi*, p.17. We acknowledge indebtedness to this work as the inspiration of this chapter.

Thomas has written, and deserves to be considered as well one of the finest pages in the whole realm of philosophy.

First Principle

The more Immanent the Activity, the Higher the Life.

Here we aim to show that intelligence is life inasmuch as it possesses the greatest immanent activity.

What is life? To take it in its most simple and elementary manifestation, it is movement; "that which moves itself." So reconciled have we become to this elementary manifestation, that our first impulse is to attribute death to anything which should be active and is not. An animal lying quietly in the sunshine gives the appearance of being lifeless as long as it is inactive. As soon as it acts, we attribute life to it. The term "life" is taken from these external appearances and applied to the nature to which it belongs.[293]

Life, then, in its simplest expression is activity. Activity, however, is twofold.[294] It is either transitive or immanent. So true is this distinction, that our very language has preserved the reality of it. A verb expresses action. A transitive verb is one that needs an object to complete it; an intransitive verb or immanent verb requires no object to complete it; it is completed within itself. A transitive action is one whose term of activity is always outside the agent, and which acts not for its own perfection but for the perfection of a thing distinct from itself: fire, for example. An immanent action, on the contrary, has its term within the agent itself, and acts for its own perfection, and not for the perfection of something outside itself: volition, for example.

---

[293] I q. 18 art. 2 c., II-II q. 3 art. 2 ad 1.

[294] *Metaphysics*, bk. 6, lect. 2; I q. 14 art. 2, and q. 18 art. 3 ad 1; II-II q.179 art. 1; III 35 q. 1 art. 1; I q. 119 art. 1 ad 2; *C. G.*, lib. 1, c. 97. See FRAGNAS, *Concepto de la Vida en sus manifestaciones segun la doctrine de S. Tomas* (1902); CL. BAEUMKER, *Über den Begriff des Lebens in der Scholastik*, p. 504 ff.; Cardinal MERCIER, *La dèfinition philosophique de la vie* (Louvain, 1898); A. GEMELLI, *L' Enigma della vita* (Firenze, 1914); Dr. MARTIN GRAB MANN, *Die Idee des Lebens in der Theologie des Hl. Thomas von Aquin* (Paderborn, 1922).

To which of these two activities does life essentially belong? Not to the transitive action as such, although many forms of life do possess transitive action. Beings possess life only in proportion to their immanent activity, and "the more immanent the activity, the higher the life."

PLANT LIFE.

The vegetable kingdom is the first of the kingdoms to manifest life. It merits this title in virtue of its immanent activity. Its immanent activity is the process by which it grows, thanks to the elements it takes up from the kingdom below it. It grows immanently by intussusception, not outwardly like a crystal. Its action is the lowest form of the three immanent activities which belong to organic life—movement of execution, movement of form and movement toward an end.[295] It has not a movement of form by which it can move from place to place. Neither has it the movement toward an end, by which it can choose means to a certain end or even an end in itself. Its end is determined. It possesses merely the movement of execution—the immanent activity of the vegetable soul. The body living by the immanent principle is the object of the vegetative soul. Its operation is threefold: one, by which it acquires being, and to this is ordained the *generative* potency; a second, by which the body *acquires* its due quantity, and to this is ordained the *augmentative* powers; a third, by which the body is *kept* in being and in its due quantity, and to this is ordained the *nutritive* powers. In the terms of modern biology, its immanent activity is the anabolic and the katabolic processes—the internal movement of increase and decrease.

Though there is immanent activity in the vegetable kingdom, and consequently life, there is at the same time much imperfection mingled with it. First, the materials which enter into the perfection of the vegetable kingdom are drawn from the outside—air, light, heat, phosphates and so forth. Secondly, the

[295] "Post inanimata vero corpora, proximum locum tenent plantae in quibus jam emanatio ex interiori procedit, in quantum scilicet humor plantae intraneus in semen convertitur et illud semen terrae mandatum crescit in plantam."—*C. G.*, lib. 4 c 2.

"Jam ergo hic primus gradus vitae invenitur; nam viventia sunt quae seipsa movent ad agendum, illa vero quae non nisi exteriora movere possunt, omnino sunt vita carentia; in plantis vero hoc indicium vitae est quod id quod in ipsis est movet aliquam formam."—*C. G.*, lib. 4 c. 2.

fruit of its existence is continued apart from the parent. Though the oak, for example, continues its own existence in the acorn, it does so in another individual. There is consequently much transitive activity mingled with the immanent activity in the vegetable kingdom. There is imperfection at both ends; a want of perfect immanence in its Alpha and Omega.[296]

THE ANIMAL KINGDOM.

Animal life is superior to plant life in virtue of a double immanent activity which it adds to plant life—the immanence of locomotion and the immanence of sensibility.

To the movement of execution which is possessed by plant life it adds the movement of form—locomotion. Its movement is not something imposed on it by nature, as it is on plants. It is determinable by the animal itself—that is, according to its sense knowledge.

For St. Thomas these two go hand in hand. We shall quote here his own words as a revelation of his deep penetration into the order and the laws of the sensible universe: "The more perfect the senses, the more perfect is the movement. Those things which have only the sense of touch move themselves by a motion of expansion and contraction, like the oyster, for example, whose motion surpasses but little that of the plants. Those things, however, which have a perfect sensitive power not only move themselves to know things immediately near or conjoined to them, but even move themselves by a progressive movement to things at a distance."[297] The relation, then, is direct between the perfection of sense knowledge and the perfection of locomotion.

---

[296] "Est tamen vita plantarum imperfecta, quia, emanatio in eis licet ab interiori procedat, tamen paulatim ab interioribus exiens quod emanat, finaliter omnino extrinsecum invenitur; humor enim arboris primo ab arbore egrediens fit flos et tandem fructus ab arboris cortice discretus, sed ei colligatus; perfecto autem fructu, omnino ab abore separatur, et, in terram cadens, sementina virtute producit aliam plantam. Si quis etiam diligenter consideret, primum hujus emanationis principium ab exteriori sumitur; nam humor intrinsecus arboris per radicem a terra sumitur de qua planta suscipit nutrimentum."—*C. G.*, lib. 4 c. 2.

"Plantae autem non cognoscunt propter suam materialitatem."—I q. 14 art. 1.

"Cause igitur quare non sentiunt (plantae) est quia non est in illis illa proportio quae requiritur ad sentiendum."—*De Anima*, lib. 2 lect. 24.

[297] I q. 18 art. 3 c.

In addition to the immanence of locomotion, animals possess the immanence of sensible knowledge. Animals reveal the first evidence of knowledge in the scale of beings. Thanks to their sensitive knowledge, they can possess immanently the lower orders in another way than the purely biological one. The plant which the animal sees, the water which the animal drinks, are possessed by it not only physiologically but also sensibly. There is a certain spiritual possession of the particular objects of sense knowledge in addition to the material possession. In virtue of this cognitive immanence the animal can justly be said to possess more life than plants.[298]

Though the animal possesses the immanence of locomotion and the immanence of sense knowledge, though it has a movement of form as well as a movement of execution, it nevertheless lacks perfect life for the reason that it lacks perfect immanent activity. It can never reflect upon itself. The term of its immanent activity is never within itself, but outside itself. In every case it is the good or the useful apprehended by the senses. As in the plant, the term of its generation is a being distinct from itself both in nature and operation. The end is always *ad extra*.[299]

Still another sign of its imperfection and want of perfect life is that it lacks the *movement of end*. It cannot choose an end for itself other than that imposed on it by nature. This end imposed is determined by instinct. Hence it is that all larks build their nests in the same way. Sense knowledge, then, is not the key to the perfect and richer life. For the same reason instinct cannot be the route to that life. We must seek the solution in other fields. Let us see if intelligence gives the answer.

[298] "Ultra plantarum vero vitam, altior gradus vitae invenitur quae est secundum animam sensitivam, cujus emanatio propria, etsi ab exteriori incipiat, in interiori tamen terminatur; et quanto emanatio magis incesserit, tanto magis ad intima devenitur, sensibile enim exterius formam suam exterioribus sensibus ingerit, a quibus procedit in imaginationem, et ulterius in memoriae thesaurum."—*C. G.*, lib. 4 c. 2.

[299] "In quolibet tamen hujus emanationis processu, principium et terminus pertinent ad diversa; non enim aliqua potentia sensitiva in seipsum reflectitur. Est ergo hic gradus vitae tanto altior quam vita plantarum, quanto operatio hujus vitae magis in intimis continetur; non tamen est omnino vita perfecta, quum emanatio semper fiat ex uno in alterum."—Ibid.

Intelligence—Human, Angelic, Divine

The Human Intelligence.

Man's title as "king of the universe" and "paragon of animals" is due to some faculty which he possesses in common with spiritual beings and not with corporeal beings. That faculty is the *intellect.* Thanks to it, man is ranged with angels and with God; for all possess in varying degrees of perfection that great power which Aristotle calls *life* and which the Angelic Doctor calls the "most perfect thing in life."[300] The intelligence, as human, stands the lowest among the three grades of intellectual beings. In relation, however, to the lower kingdoms it is far superior.

The human intellect reveals a greater immanence of action than is found in any of the lower kingdoms. Its life is therefore more nearly perfect.

First, the act of the intelligence remains in the intelligence itself. It is not an action passing to something extrinsic to it, as heat passes to a surrounding body.[301] The term of the intellectual act is not a *symbol* of the external object, as we shall see in a following chapter; it is the object itself possessed intentionally by the mind.[302] It is due precisely to this immanent possession of the object that the soul can reflect and know itself.[303]

---

300 "Intelligere, vita quaedam est, et est perfectissimum quod est in vita."—*Metaphysics*, lib. 12 lect. 8.

"It is the degree of immanence which distinguishes knowing from non-knowing things."—I q. 14 art. 1.

301 "Intelligere non est actio progrediens ad aliquid extrinsecum, sed manet in operante."—I q. 14 art. 4 c.

"Motus vel operatio cognitivae partis perficitur in ipsa mente."—*De Veritate*, q. 10 art. 9 c.; *De Pot.*, q. 9 art. 9; *C. G.*, lib. 1 c. 53; JOHN OF SAINT THOMAS, *De Sacra Trinitate*, q. 27 disp. 12 art. 5.

302 "Sed manet in ipso intelligence et habet relationem ad rem quae intelligitur ex eo quod species praedicta quae est principium intellectualis operationis ut forma est similitudo illius."—*C. G.*, lib. 1 c. 53.

"Species qua intellectus intelligit est similitudo rei intellectae."—SYLVESTER FERRARIENSIS in *C. G.*, 1 c. 53 i.

303 I q. 87 art. 1; A. GARDEIL, *Mélanges Thomistes*, "La Perception de l'âme par elle-même," p. 219 ff. "Est igitur supremus et perfectus gradus vitae qui est secundum intellectum, nam intellectus in seipsum reflectitur, et seipsum intelligere potest ... nam intellectus humanus, etsi seipsum cognoscere posit..."—*C. G.*, lib. 4 c. 2.

Secondly, the term of the intellectual operation remains in the intellect as *its act and as its perfection.* The animal kingdom by the act of generation perfects the existence of its species in the sense that it continues its existence in its progeny. The intellect, on the contrary, perfects its own existence immanently, as the term of its generation is in itself and not outside itself.[304]

How classify this immanent operation of the intelligence? To which of the ten categories of Aristotle does it belong? Does it belong to *quality* or to *action*? The answer of one of the recognized interpreters of the Angelic Doctor is that it belongs to the category of *quality*, which has the force of action. It does not belong *primarily* to the category of *action*, because action implies two elements, one of which cannot be applied to the intellectual operation. One of the elements of action is potentiality—progress towards a term—and this is an imperfection. The other element is actuality, which is the power of producing a term. The first element is wanting to the operation of the intelligence. The perfection of the act of knowing is not in the production of the term but in its contemplation. The production itself looks to the concept, but the act of knowledge terminates in the thing. The immanent activity does not demand that a term be produced; nevertheless, it can have one. This being so, it is ranked more properly under the category of *quality* than under that of action.[305]

[304] "Intellectum est perfectio intelligentis secundum speciem intelligibilem quam habet in intellectu."—I. q. 57 art.1 ad 1. CAJETAN in I q. 14 art. 4 no. 3.

[305] "Sed veritas est quod Thomistae, illam operationem, quam ponunt qualitatem, quia actio immanens est, dicunt esse qualitatem, quod eminenter habet vim actionis; non quia sit actio per modum viae et motus, quod est imperfectio; sed per modum actus secundi, quod est actualitas et perfectio, et sic habet id quod perfectionis et actualitatis est in actione; sicque habet vim ad producendum terminum quantum ad id quod virtutis et actualitatis est in producendo, non autem habet id quod potentialitatis et motus seu imperfectionis est in actione. Et sic actiones immanentes ex suo conceptu et ratione non postulant habere terminum predictum sed possunt tamen habere."—JOHN OF SAINT THOMAS, *De Sacra Trinit.*, q. 27 disp. 12 art. 5 n. 6, 7; *C. G.*, lib. 1 c. 100.

"In actionibus ubi non est motus non relinquitur aliud, quam habitudo principii ad principatum se producit ad suum principium."—2 d. 41 art. 1 ad 2.

"Ista operatio propter seipsam quaeritur, non propter aliquem terminum, nam etiamsi producatur aliquis terminus, v.g. verbum, adhuc perfectio intelligendi non est in productione talis termini, sed in contemplatione in verbo jam producto, ergo operatio immanens non se habet per modum medii et viae qua aliquis terminus acquiritur, sed potius ipsa est ultima actualitas, quam intendit operans, et sic non est de genere actionis praedicamentalis ... quia non quaeritur propter terminum causandum, sed propter suam actualitatem."—JOHN OF SAINT THOMAS, *Phil. Nat.*, t. 2 q. 14 art. 3; also t. 3 q. 2 art. 1.

"Actus immanentis sunt virtualiter actiones, licet formaliter sint qualitatis."—Ibid., q.

Though the human intelligence can glory in a more perfect life than that of plants or animals, or even the sensitive and instinctive knowledge of man; though the fecundity of that divine faculty, as Aristotle calls it, generates a term which is more intimately united with its spiritual progenitor than form is united to matter,—is it altogether free from imperfection? Does it possess that perfect immanent activity which alone belongs to the rich and perfect and satisfying life?

The very fact that the intelligence is dependent on the world of sensible phenomena for the materials of its operation is sufficient indication of its want of perfect immanence. The mind is a *tabula rasa*; without sense experience it does not function.[306] It is only in potency to the intelligibility which is in things. Just as the plant depends upon the mineral kingdom for the materials of its plant life; just as the animal depends on the mineral kingdom and the vegetable kingdom for the materials of its animal life,—so too does the intellectual life of man depend on the materials of sensible experience. Just as prime matter is in potency to natural things, so is our intellect in potency to intelligible things. Both need to be perfected. The form is the perfection of one, the intelligible species is the perfection of the other.[307] Furthermore, close as the union between the intellect and its term may be, there is still wanting a perfect identity. The external object which is possessed by the intellect is possessed intentionally—that is, by *information*. There is a distinction between the intellect and its species. If, however, the immanence were perfect, there would be identity.[308] Add to this another limitation of the human intelligence, namely, the fact that it is *measured*. Just as the movement of form and the movement towards an end determine plant life and constitute its measure; just as the movement towards an end by instinct determines animals and constitutes their measure,—so, too, in man there is something which

14 art. 3.

[306] "Intellectus humanus etsi seipsum cognoscere possit, tamen primum suae cognitionis initium ab extrinseco sumit; quia non est intelligere sine phantasmate."—*C. G.*, lib. 4 c. 2.

[307] I q. 14 art. 2 ad 3.

[308] "Similiter etiam quod intellectus perficiatur ab intelligibili vel assimiletur ei, hoc convenit intellectui quandoque est in potentia, quia per hoc quod est in potentia, differet ab intelligibili, et assimilatur ei per speciem intelligibilem quae est similitudo rei intellectae et perficitur per ipsam, sicut potentia per actum."—I q. 14 art. 2 ad 2.

determines and measures him. This measure in the speculative order is the first principle of thought, and in the practical order is the ultimate end. Though these measures in relation to the lower orders constitute the liberty and the glory of man, they are, in relation to the higher order, a mark of imperfection and dependence.

Angelic Intelligence.

If there is continuity in the universe, it is fitting that there should be intelligent beings without bodies, which are called angels.

It is to be regretted that many treatises on the intelligence omit entirely a consideration of angelic intelligence. Because angelology is properly the field of speculative theology, it does not follow that it has no place in philosophy. Angels belong to the hierarchy of beings; they are the highest created beings in the universe. Fitting in the universal order of things, and particularly in the order of intelligence, they cannot be passed over without disturbing the equilibrium of the whole. The existence of angels is proved by revelation, and reason itself, arguing from the due perfection of the universe, concludes the fitness of their existence. The perfection of the universe consists in an ascending scale of likeness on the part of creatures to God. Now, we know that God creates by intelligence and will. If, therefore, the effect is perfectly similar to the cause, there should be purely intellectual beings. If they possessed a body, they would be determined to a particular mode of being which would be at variance with the object of the intellect—universal being. The perfection of the universe therefore demands the existence of purely intellectual beings whom we call angels.[309]

At this point all consideration of life in a biological sense is left behind, but life under the consideration of immanent activity is still retained. Every living being has a certain immanent activity which is essential to it and without which it cannot exist. For separated substances like angels the essential immanent act is a purely intellectual one; they have no other operation.[310] Unlike

[309] I q. 50 art. 1 c.

[310] "Omnis substantia vivens habet aliquam operationem vitae in actu ex sua natura

the human intelligence, they are always in act. Therein is the first mark of higher immanence than the immanence manifested by our intelligence. We are in essential potency to natural knowledge before learning it. The angels, however, are only in accidental potency to natural knowledge; they have knowledge, but they may not always be considering it.[311] This being so, much of the imperfection which was found in the human intelligence is done away with. We are radically and fundamentally in potency to knowledge; the angel only accidentally. Our intellect may be likened to a tablet on which nothing is written; the angelic intellect, on the contrary, may be likened to a tablet already written upon, or to a mirror in which is reflected the reason of things.[312] It is worth noting at this point two details which will be considered more fully in the next chapter: first, the fact that a body is not absolutely necessary for intelligence as intelligence;[313] and secondly, that since angels are pure intellectual beings, they have no need of either an active or a passive intellect.[314]

A consideration, not only of the nature of the angelic intelligence, but also of the source of its knowledge, reveals an increasing immanence as compared with that of human intelligence. Our knowledge comes from the material universe; angelic knowledge comes from God. Our knowledge is acquired; angelic knowledge is infused. The manner in which a thing is naturally perfected follows the natural mode of its being. Our soul naturally is united to a body. Its intellectual perfection is effected, therefore, through the body—by sense experience. If

quae inest ei semper, licet aliae quandoque insint ei in potentia, sicut animalia semper nutriuntur, licet non semper sentiant. Substantiae autem separatae sunt substantiae viventes ut ex praemissis patet; nec habent aliam operationem vitae nisi intelligere. Oportet igitur quod ex sua natura sint intelligentes actu semper."—*C. G.*, lib. 2 c. 97.

"Perfectior igitur est intellectualis vita in angelis, in quibus intellectus ad sui cognitionem non procedit ex aliquo exteriori, sed per se cognoscit seipsum."—*C. G.*, lib. 4 c. 11.

311 I q. 58 art. 1 c. Angels, however, are in essential potency to knowledge by revelation; but never as regards knowledge by vision of the Word. The distinction which the Angelic Doctor makes between the natural and the supernatural knowledge of angels is seen at once.

312 "Intellectus noster comparatur tabulae in qua nihil est scriptum; intellectus autem angeli tabulae depictae, vel speculo in quo rerum rationes resplendit."—*De Veritate*, q. 8 art. 9.

313 "The very fact that the intellect is above sense is a reasonable proof that there are some incorporeal things comprehensible by the intellect alone."—I q. 51 art. 1.

314 I q. 54 art. 4 c.

this were not so, the body would be useless. The angels, however, have no conjunction with a body. Hence their intelligence is perfected without sense knowledge received through a body, or, in other words, it is perfected by an intellectual influx from God.[315] The power of the human intelligence is not complete naturally; it is progressive in its perfection. We advance in age and wisdom. The angelic intelligence, on the contrary, is naturally complete, owing to the infused ideas which it receives from God.[316] Our intelligence may be likened to an empty vase which can be filled by our own industry; the angelic intelligence is the vase already filled. It receives its knowledge at the same moment that it receives its intellectual nature.[317]

God, as the object of knowledge, is not possessed as immanently by man as by an angel. The idea which we have of God is not a similitude drawn from Him immediately, but is in part taken from the visible things of the world. It may be likened to a knowledge of an object which we see reflected in a mirror. The angel, however, knows God by a certain similitude, just as we know a stone by its similitude which appears in the eye.[318] The similitude produced in the angelic intelligence has God as its source and cause, just as the stone is the proximate source of its similitude in the eye.

The immanent activity of the angel is manifestly higher than that of animals or man. Its life is therefore more perfect. Yet it lacks something which would give it the perfect immanence which is the characteristic of perfect life. The very fact that their

---

[315] I q. 55 art. 2 c, and I q. 108 art. 1.

[316] "Potentia vero intellectiva in substantiis spiritualibus superioribus, id est in angelis, *naturaliter* completa est per species intelligibiles in quantum habent species intelligibiles connaturales ad omnia intelligenda quae naturaliter cognoscere possunt."—I q. 55 art. 2 c.

[317] "Et ideo suam perfectionem intelligibilem consequuntur effluxum, quo a Deo species rerum cognitarum acceperunt simul cum intellectuali natura."—I q. 55 art. 2 c.; I q. 56 art. 2 c.

"Non autem accipit cognitionem earum a rebus materialibus sed per species actu intelligibiles rerum sibi connaturales, rerum materialium notitiam habet."—I q. 57 art. 1 ad 3; *C. G.*, lib. 2 c. 96; *De Veritate*, q. 8 art. 9.

[318] "Alio modo per praesentiam suae similitudinis in potentia cognoscitiva sicut lapis videtur in oculo ... Cognitio autem qua angelus per sua naturalia cognoscit Deum ... similatur illi cognitioni, qua videtur res per speciem ab ea acceptam."—I q. 56 art. 3 c.

It must be noted that the angel does not see God by essence through this similitude, because no created similitude is sufficient to represent the divine essence.

ideas are infused, and that they have been given to them by God Himself, is quite sufficient to stamp them with some imperfection. It constitutes their measure. Though the term of their activity is immanent, it is not their substance.[319] The equation, being=knowing, cannot be made of angels.[320] Like all other creatures, there is a kind of composition in them which stamps them as imperfect.

From the lowest form of mineral to the highest species of angel there is, then, an increasing immanence manifested, and with each increase of immanence there is realized a more perfect nature. But at the same time there is something measured throughout this whole scale of beings. The plant is measured by its form, the animal by its instinct or end, and man by the first principles of his speculative and practical intellect, and angels by the ideas which they receive from God. The ultimate perfection of life is not reserved for any of these creatures.

Divine Intelligence.

The modern philosopher asks: "Where is the richer, fuller and more satisfying life?" The Angelic Doctor asks the same question in the *Summa*, in these words, "Is God Life?" The answer of the Angelic Doctor is as follows: Life is immanent activity; it is the power to move oneself, in contradistinction to being moved by another. The more perfectly, therefore, immanent activity belongs to anything, the more perfectly does it possess life.

In the Divine Intelligence being and knowing are identical. That which the Divine Intelligence possesses is not determined by anything extrinsic to itself, as we shall prove. Possessing perfect immanent activity, God therefore possesses Perfect Life.[321] God is Life.

When, therefore, it is said that God is Life, something more than a mere metaphor is implied. He is Life in such a true and real sense that He merits being called, in the words of St.

[319] I q. 54 art. 1 c.

[320] Ibid., art. 2.

"Nondum tamen ad ultimam perfectionem vita ipsorum (angelorum) pertingit quia, licet intentio intellecta sit eis omnino intrinseca, non tamen ipsa intentio intellecta est eorum substantia, quia non est item in eis intelligere et esse."—*C. G.*, lib. 4 c. 11.

[321] "Utrum Deo conveniat vita."—I q. 18 art. 3.

Augustine, the "Life of all Life."[322] The fundamental and ultimate reason why God is Life is that He is the Supreme Intelligence. "That thing whose nature is its act of understanding, and which, in what it naturally possesses, is in no way determined by another, is the supreme life. Hence it is that Aristotle in the Twelfth Book of his *Metaphysics*, after having shown that God is intelligence, concludes that He has the most perfect and eternal life, because *His Intellect is the most perfect and always in act.*" [323]

Such is the Scholastic answer to the philosophical search for life. If our search is for the Ultimate and the Perfect Life, then that Life is the Eternal, Omnipotent and Living God. "The richer, fuller and more satisfying life" is not in any evolving Space-Time, or Divinal Imagining or Eternal Becoming. These fictions do not possess life; they are merely in the process of attaining it. The having is more than the acquiring; the being is more than the becoming. If we are sincere in our search for the most perfect life, we must rest in the intelligence. Inasmuch as its activity is immanent, it is life itself. There is therefore no question whether or not the intelligence is adapted to life. *It is life.*

Modern philosophy, then, in refusing to accept the intelligence has been untrue to its ideals and its principles. It insists on a devotion to the spirit of the age and the conclusions of modern science, biology in particular. But modern biology explains life by an immanent principle. Consistency demands that life in all its manifestations be measured by the immanence of its activity. A rigorous application of this principle, it has been demonstrated, leads to the intelligence, and ultimately to the Divine Intelligence, which is identical with the Being of God. Pleading on the one hand for a philosophy in keeping with

---

[322] "Tu es vita vitarum."—*P. L.*, t. XXXII. "Conf." III. 6, col. 687, pp. 21-28.

[323] I q. 18 art. 3 c. "Ultima igitur perfectio vitae competit Deo, in quo non est aliud intelligere et aliud esse."—*C. G.*, lib. 4 c. 2.

"Vivere Dei est ejus intelligere. In Deo autem est idem intellectus, et quod intelligitur, et ipsum intelligere ejus. Unde quidquid est in Deo ut intellectum, est ipsum vivere vel vita ejus. Unde cum omnia quae facta sunt a Deo, sunt in ipso ut intellecta, sequitur quod omnia in ipso sunt ipsa vita divina."—I q. 18 art. 4 c.

"Sicut Deus est ipsum suum esse et suum intelligere, ita ejus suum vivere. Et propter hoc, sic vivet, quod non habet vivendi principium."—I q. 18 art. 3 ad 2; *Meta.*, lib. 12 lect. 8.

See Dr. MARTIN GRABMANN, *Die Idee des Lebens in der Theologie des Hl. Thomas von Aquin* (Paderborn, 1922), pp. 9-46.

science, and on the other for a philosophy which is out of harmony with science, many of our modern thinkers manifest an infidelity to their ideals. The philosophy of the Angelic Doctor, on the contrary, applies his principle throughout the whole gamut of existence from the plant up to God Himself. If the world is intelligible and orderly, the principles should be orderly. What is true in one order should not be false in another. If life is immanent activity in biology, it cannot be transitive activity in Space-Time, or a Divinal Imaginal or a Finite God. In adopting a mode of knowledge which is transitive, modern anti-intellectualists have been getting away from the heart of life. It may therefore be said to be "characterized by a great incapacity for life."

Second Principle

Modern philosophy, affected in part by biology, has greatly insisted on the necessity and continuity of the universe. The Scholastic system is reproached and rejected for having failed to show fluidity in the universe. Its proofs are said to be valid only on the hypothesis that the universe is split up into "blocks" or compartments. The ideal of contemporary thinking is to get away as far as possible from this so-called lifeless universe, and to express the continuity of the universe which the hypothesis of evolution has so wonderfully revealed to us.

The ideal of modern philosophy is legitimate. It is also the ideal of common-sense philosophy. The only difference is that the latter did not have to wait for biology to reveal progress in the universe; reason saw its necessity. The Scholastic principle of progress and continuity is metaphysical, not biological. It applies to all the kingdoms of the universe, and with greater applicability and logic than any of the modern applications.

The continuity and fluidity of the universe may be viewed either statically or dynamically. Statically, the continuity is revealed in the unfolding of the principle: "a higher nature in its lowest perfection touches a lower nature in its highest perfection." Dynamically, the same conclusion is revealed in the application of the principle, "the more perfect the nature, the less the movement."

The first principle, "Natura superior in suo infimo contigit naturam inferiorem in ejus supremo," is taken from the Fourth Book of *Divinis Nominibus* of Dionysius, and is used frequently throughout the works of the Angelic Doctor to prove the organic nature of the universe,[324] and the manner in which all things contribute to its beauty. In its application, the principle is best seen in his Commentary on the *De Anima* of Aristotle. Here we shall content ourselves with a brief indication of its general outline.

Passing over the close biological resemblances to be found between the highly developed plant and the lowest stage of animal life, and interesting ourselves purely in the philosophical side, we find the highest development of the plant life to be its immanent activity of generation, growth and nutrition, which are the functions of the vegetable soul. It is just at this point that the animal life joins the plant life. The lowest operations of the animal life are the operations of the vegetable soul. Thus there is a communion between plant and animal life. The highest perfection of animal life, in its turn, is its power to know through the senses. This perfection marks it off distinctly from the lower order, and is also the bond which unites it to the order above it, namely, the human intelligence. The phantasm is common to both animal and man, but it differs in each according to the respective differentiations of being. According to its real being it is sensible, according to its *esse relucentiae* it is intelligible.[325] Thus, what is highest in a lower order touches the lowest in a higher order. The lowest perfection of man, in relation to the order just below him, is sense knowledge. It is as necessary for his cognitional existence as the vegetative soul is for his animal existence. Instead of being cut off from the animal, man enjoys a fellowship with the perfection of animal existence. He continues in a certain sense that which constitutes the glory of the animal.[326]

---

[324] ST. THOMAS, *De Divinis Nominibus*, c. 7 lect. 4; *C. G.*, lib. 2 c. 91, 3 d. 27 q. 3 c.; I q. 57 art. 2; CAJETAN in I q. 79 art. 3 XII. "Fines primorum iunguntur principiis secundum."—DYONYSIUS, *De Divinis Nominibus*, 7 lect. iv.

[325] CAJETAN in I q. 79 art. 3 XII.

[326] The continuity of instinct, which is a sort of discernment (but a discernment determined by natural impulse) may be worked out in the same way with the gift of

So intimate and so close is this relationship between animal perfection and the human species, that it may truly be said that in the operation of the human intelligence the two are never separated. The Angelic Doctor, rejecting the doctrine of imageless thought, holds that there is a constant reversion to phantasms on the part of the intelligence. This one notion shows what a complete stranger he is to a rigid "block universe" in which there is neither continuity nor progress between the various orders.

But, to carry the principle further—what is the highest perfection of the human intelligence? It is a kind of intellectual perception and intuition by which it seizes essences, and truth in judgments. This intuition is feeble, as a following chapter will demonstrate, but it is nevertheless the link between it and the next highest order of the intelligence, namely, the angelic. All angelic knowledge is by intuition; it does not abstract, as the human mind does; it does not reason, as we do; *it sees.* Its whole intellectual life is an intuition. The principle of continuity and progress of the universe thus finds its application in a domain which far transcends the purely material order.

There are, in the angelic order alone, a progress and a continuity of perfection which greatly exceed those which are manifested in the material universe. The details of this gradual progress from the species of angel which stands next to the man, and the species of angel which is nearest to God, are beyond the privilege of our earthly knowledge. Revelation, however, has given us a peep into this mysterious and wonderful hierarchy of orders, and the Angelic Doctor, working on these data, has thrown much light on the application of our principle. There are three hierarchies of angels, and three choirs in each hierarchy, making a total of nine choirs. Each choir, from the lowest, that of guardian angels, to the highest, the Seraphim, has a continuity, one with another, by reason of the intellectual illumination which they receive. Each angel transmits to the angel immediately inferior the knowledge which it receives from above. It does not

---

discernment of man, which is based on particular propositions. *Cf.* also CAJETAN, I q. 55 art. 2 XIV: "Constat autem quod supremum in ordine sensibilium est esse imaginabile, quia est spiritualissimum intelligibilitate; et quod infimum in ordine intelligibili, est concurrere ad speciem intelligibilem educendum de potentia ad actum."

transmit this illumination in its fullness and perfection, but according to the capacity of the lower intelligence, just as a learned scientist does not transmit principles of science to his intellectual inferiors without examples. This transmission of illumination from the higher to the lower choirs, according to their intelligence, is the very reason of the continuity of the nine choirs, and of the ordination by which the highest perfection of one choir is linked with the lowest perfection of the superior choir.

No creature, however perfect, by the mere fact of its inherent imperfection can fill the gap between itself and God. This does not forbid a more perfect participation of the divine perfections by one creature rather than another. The highest order of intellectual creatures is the Seraphim, who, because of their more perfect knowledge of God, have a more perfect love of Him. Their very name signifies flame and light and love. This is their highest perfection.

There is not a continuity between creatures and God in the possession of *being*, in the pantheistic sense, but there is a continuity of order and an analogical possession of being. The universe is not a juxtaposition of indifferently related genus and species, as ill-advised opponents of common-sense philosophy would have us believe. It is a harmonious *crescendo* of perfections from the lowest minerals up to God—a hymn to the Creator.

Even this brief narration of the continuity in the intellectual order alone is sufficient to stress its importance. The intelligence is the key to the communion of the human and the angelic and the divine. From God, who is the source of intellectual light, knowledge descends progressively through the three hierarchies and nine choirs of angels, and finally to man himself, who in his turn not only seizes the intelligibility which is multiplied in the sensible (thanks to all things being the material realizations of the Eternal Ideas of God), but even projects his own intelligibility into matter under the form of finality. It becomes feebler as it grows in distance from its source, just as the rays and the heat of the sun become enfeebled as they are removed further from their source. But this is only a proof that the progressive orders of perfections which are found in creatures find their own reason and perfection in God.

Modern philosophy, in rejecting the intelligence, has rejected the cornerstone of the whole edifice of continuity and progress in the universe. *In ideal*, it has given man an angelic intelligence, and thus has broken continuity with the lower orders; *in fact*, it has given man a degenerate sense knowledge, and has broken continuity with the higher orders. Pleading for continuity and progress, and insisting on the application of biological hypotheses to metaphysics, it has in the end denied the possibility of continuity, by rejecting the intelligence. Scholasticism, on the contrary, did not have to wait for modern biology to reveal continuity and progress in the universe. For it, biological discoveries were confirmations, not revelations. They merely proved in a lower order what reason has already verified in the higher orders. The criticism which the *philosophia perennis* would urge against a philosophy which breaks down the continuity and the progress of the universe by rejecting the intelligence, would be precisely this, that it is a "philosophy of the 'block universe.'"

Third Principle

A third and legitimate ideal of modern philosophy is to explain life, not only according to its progressiveness and continuity, but also as a process of unification. Applying biological conclusions throughout the whole field of philosophy, modern writers have concluded that the present stage of evolution sums up all the previous stages; that the moral ideas of man are heritages of his animal existence, and that religion is a legacy of our primal fear of brute nature.

It has been too readily presumed by this class of thinkers that common-sense philosophy has been a complete and total stranger to any such philosophy of unification. Yet St. Thomas throughout the whole of his *Summa* is constantly recurring to the principle of unification that runs through the universe. But he is not in perfect accord with those who have broken away from the tradition of his school. For him the principle of unification is valid only on condition that there is no subordination of the higher to the lower order. It is this precisely which constitutes the modern principle. Which of the two is the more legitimate, we shall have occasion presently to examine.

"There is such an order in things, that the more perfect the nature, the greater is its unifying power and the more universal is its object."[327] Such is the Thomistic principle. As a matter of fact, the vegetable kingdom bears out its truth. The vegetable kingdom is higher than the mineral kingdom, as life is higher than matter. Those things which are disparate in the mineral kingdom, such as hydrogen, oxygen, phosphates, chlorides and the like, the plant unifies through its threefold operation. In going down to the lower kingdom for the materials which it unifies in order to carry on its own existence, it does not destroy them. Rather it utilizes them, and endows them with a mode of existence which they did not possess before. It ennobles and perfects them.

The animal kingdom verifies the principles with still greater clearness. Here, there is not a single process of unification, but a double one: the physiological and the cognitive. Physiologically, it unites the mineral and the vegetable kingdoms through the operations of nutrition. Endowed with a sensitive soul, the animal can possess these two lower kingdoms within itself by an act of sense knowledge. This possession and unification is far nobler than the other, for it possesses them in an ennobled way without at the same time altering their own mode of existence. "To possess a thing not materially but formally, which is the definition of knowledge, is the noblest manner of having or possessing it."[328] The cow, in consuming the prairie flower, unifies it within itself by destroying the proper existence of the flower; but in possessing it formally by an act of sense knowledge it unifies it within itself without destroying the proper existence of the flower.

In considering man, let us omit the physiological considerations in order to consider only those which are related to the act of knowledge. The faculties of the soul are ranged in a hierarchy according to the universality of their objects. The

[327] "Hoc enim rerum ordo habet, quod quanto aliquid est superius, tanto habet virtutem magis unitam et ad plura se extendentem."—I q. 57 art. 2 c.

"Quanto enim potentia est altior, tanto respicit universalius objectum."—I q. 78 art. 1.

[328] *In causis*, I 18.

higher the faculty, the more universal is its object. The lowest faculty is that of the vegetative soul, whose object is the body to which it is united. The sensitive faculty has a more universal object, and has a greater unifying power, inasmuch as its object is not the sensible body to which it is united, but the totality of sensible bodies. The disparate knowledge of the five senses is unified by a "general or common sense." This sense knows all that the five senses know, and even something which the external senses cannot know—for example, the difference between whiteness and sweetness.[329]

But man has a higher power of unification than that of the common sense. In virtue of his intellectual faculty, he seizes not only sensible bodies in general, as does the sensitive faculty, but being in all its universality.[330] All that is disparate and separate in the world of sense he can unite in the world of his intelligence; all the particular experiences of his sensitive nature he can unify in a law; all that exists, on earth, above the earth and under the earth he can unite under the analogical notion of being. Aristotle has rightly called man a *microcosm*; for in him all the lower kingdoms are united, and even the higher by negation and analogy.

Besides unifying, recapitulating and utilizing what is of a lower order, man in addition elevates it. In possessing immanently and formally all the lower kingdoms, man continues their existence, in a very ennobled way. He so elevates the lower kingdoms that it may be said in a certain sense that man is the mineral that blooms, the plant that feels, the animal that speaks. It is his nature to be the concerted harmony, living and permanent, of all these various lives.

This recapitulating power of the human intelligence is not absolutely the same in all men. Even the human intelligence admits of various degrees. The mental power of some men is greater than that of others. The trained mind can see more in one idea or one principle than the unschooled can see in many. The Angelic Doctor, for example, saw many more conclusions in

---

[329] "Sicut in ipso homine patet quod sensus communis, qui est superior quam sensus proprius, licet sit unica potentia, omnia cognoscit quae quinque sensibus exterioribus cognoscuntur, et quaedam alia quae nullus sensus exterior cognoscit, scilicet, differentiam albi et dulcis."—I q. 57 art. 2 c.; *C. G.*, lib. 2 c. 100.

[330] I q. 77 art. 4, and q. 78 art. 1 c.

the one principle that "nothing moves unless it is moved by another" than the generality of philosophers and theologians. This variability of unifying power is borne out by the fact that multiplied examples and figures of the imagination are necessary to communicate to a pupil that which the teacher sees in a single principle. Similarly, our intellect being imperfect, we cannot represent the perfection of God by a single idea, but must use diverse and multiplied conceptions—Goodness, Truth, Omnipotence and the like. If, however, our intellect were perfect, we could represent God by one single idea, just as the Verbum, the Second Person of the Blessed Trinity, is the perfect image and splendour of the Father.[331]

The principle, "the higher the nature, the greater is the power of unifying," has an even greater application in the angelic kingdom. What is separated in the lower orders is united in the higher; what is plural in the lower orders is singular in the higher. As we approach God we approach unity and perfection; as we descend from God we descend into multiplicity and imperfection. The human species has a two-fold principle of knowledge—that of sense and that of the intellect. Just as it unites into the "common sense" the findings of the five disparate senses of the sensible order, so, too, do the angelic species unite the findings of the sense and intellect which is common to man. Man knows by sense and intellect; the angel by intellect alone.[332]

The single principle of knowledge for the angels is the intelligence which is enriched with infused ideas from God. These infused ideas are far richer than our ideas; they unify that which is disparate in our knowledge. Our conceptual knowledge does not reveal all the particular determinations of a certain idea, but the angelic intelligence does. It sees all the possible realizations of an idea.[333] In the idea of man it sees all the

[331] "Similiter etiam intellectus noster secundum diversas conceptiones repraesentat divinam perfectionem, quia una quaeque imperfecta est; si enim perfecta esset, esset una tantum, sicut est unum tantum Verbum intellectus Divini."—*De Veritate*, q. 2 art. 1 c.

[332] "Anima autem humana est inferior in ordine naturae quam substantia separata. Ipsa autem cognoscitiva est universalium per duo principia, scilicet per sensum et intellectum. Substantia igitur separata, quae est altior cognoscit utrumque altiori modo per unum principium, scilicet per intellectum."—*De Veritate*, q. 2 art. 7 ad 4; q. 10 art. 5 ad 5; *C. G.*, lib. 2 c. 100. *De Veritate*, q. 2 art. 7 ad 4; q. 10 art. 5 ad 5.

[333] "Cognitio mentis angelicae est universalior quam cognitio mentis humanae, quia ad plura se extendit paucioribus mediis utens, et tamen est efficacior ad singularia

particular men of the universe. The same is true of judgments. Composite things the angel knows simply; mobile things the angel knows immovably; material things the angel knows immaterially.[334] All material things pre-exist in the angels more simply and immaterially than they exist in themselves, but more multiplied and imperfectly than they exist in God.[335]

Though this possession of innate ideas is common to all the angels, all do not possess the same ideas. This is the foundation of their distinction. God has more richly endowed some angels than others. As beings more closely approach God, the more perfect they become. As angels more nearly approximate the perfection of God, they possess fewer ideas. The angel of the lowest species has many more ideas than the angel of the higher species, but the latter has a far richer intelligence. As a man in a tower sees more of the city than a man in the street, so, too, does the superior angel, with a few rich and universal ideas, see more in them than an inferior angel sees in multiplied ideas. The superior angels know with lesser movement than the inferior. In a word, the superiority of angels increases as the number of their ideas decreases.[336] Though there be an infinity of degrees of graduated perfection, inasmuch as every angel is a distinct species, we can distinguish three principal grades of knowledge. The angels of the first hierarchy are turned directly towards God; they know intelligible essences inasmuch as they proceed directly from God. This hierarchy of angels, in the words of Dionysius, is in the "very vestibule of the divinity." The second hierarchy of angels knows the intelligible essences in the universal causes of creation—that is, in a plurality of objects. The third hierarchy considers them in their determination to particular effects—that is, in a multiplicity of objects equal to the number of created beings.[337]

---

cognoscenda."—*De Veritate*, q. 10 art. 5 ad 6.

[334] "Composita simpliciter et mobilia immobiliter et materialia immaterialiter."—I q. 58 art. 4.

[335] "Sic igitur omnia materialia in ipsis angelis praeexistunt simplicius quidem et immaterialius quam in ipsis rebus; multiplicius autem et imperfectius quam in Deo."—I q. 57 art. 1.

[336] *De Veritate*, q. 8 art. 10 c.; I q. 55 art. 3 c.

[337] I q. 108 art. 1 and art. 6. Each of the hierarchies is divided into three choirs, thus making nine choirs in all. See iv. d. 48 q. 4 art 3 c.

Though there is a progress toward unity and recapitulation of knowledge through the whole sphere of creation, no creature manifests a perfect recapitulation. Even the highest Seraphim has an idea which is distinct from its essence. The plenitude of intelligibility is found only in that Being in whom Knowing and Being are identical. The object of God's knowledge is a unique object which unites within itself all the multiplied knowledge of His creatures. He alone who stands at the summit of all things possesses all things within Himself according to the simplicity of His Being.[338] As in the physical order concentrated power is greater than dispersed power, so, too, in the intellectual order the intelligence which unifies all things is greater than the intelligence which knows them only disparately and disjointly. The higher the intellect, the more perfect it is; the more perfect it is, the more unified it is.[339]

The mere fact of having an intelligence is not a simple perfection, therefore. Rather, it is to know all things as one and yet without confusion, and by a knowledge which is identical with ones being.[340] In God alone is found this absolute perfection. Every idea is apprehended according to the intelligent being in whom it resides. In God intelligence and essence are the same. The intelligence is consequently in act with the intelligible, and hence in God the supreme knowledge and the supreme intelligibility join one another. He knows Himself perfectly.[341]

Man has different kinds of knowledge according to the different objects of his knowledge.

He has *intelligence* as regards the knowledge of principles; he has *science* as regards the knowledge of conclusions; he has *wisdom* according as he knows the highest cause; he has *counsel* or *prudence*

---

[338] "Et ideo in Deo, sicut in summo rerum vertice, omnia supersubstantialiter praeexistunt secundum ipsum suum simplex esse."—I q. 57 art. 3.

[339] "Quanto intellectus est superior, tanto est perfectior; quanto autem perfectior, tanto unitior, ut sic liceat loqui, eo quod virtus unites major est seipsa dispersa."—CAJETAN in I q. 55 art. 3 vi.

"Our intellect, since it knows God from creatures, in order to understand God, forms conceptions proportional to the perfections flowing from God to creatures, which perfections pre-exist in God united and simply, whereas in creatures they are received, divided and multiplied."—I q. 13 art. 4 c.

[340] "Non solum intelligere est perfectio simpliciter, sed etiam omnia per unum."—SAINT ANSELM, *Monol.* xv.;quoted in CAJETAN in I q. 55 art. 3 vi.

[341] *De Veritate*, q. 2 art. 2; *C. G.*, lib. 1 c. 47; I q. 14 art. 3 c.

according as he knows what is to be done. But God knows all there is by one single act of knowledge.[342]

Knowledge is not a quality in God, nor a habit, but a substance and an act.[343]

The object which God knows by Himself and immediately, is Himself. It is evident that in order to know immediately an object other than Himself, God ought to turn Himself from the immediate object, which is Himself, to another object. But this other object cannot be inferior to Himself, otherwise God would be imperfect. How, then, does God know other things?

In this way. "It is manifest that He perfectly understands Himself: otherwise His existence would not be perfect, since His existence is His act of understanding. Now, if anything is perfectly known, it follows of necessity that its power is perfectly known. But the power of anything can be perfectly known only by knowing to what its power extends. Since, therefore, the Divine power extends to other things by the very fact that it is the first effective cause of all things, as is clear from the aforesaid (q. 2 art 3), God must necessarily know things other than Himself. And this appears still more plainly if we add that the very existence of the first effective cause, viz. God, is His own act of understanding. Hence, whatever effects pre-exist in God, as in the first cause, must be in His act of understanding, and all things must be in Him, according to an intelligible mode; for everything which is in another is in it according to the mode of that in which it is.

"Now, in order to know how God knows things other than Himself, we must consider that a thing is known in two ways: in itself, and in another. A thing is known in itself when it is known by the proper species adequate to the knowable object: as when the eye sees a man through the image of a man. A thing is seen in another through the image of that which contains it: as when a part is seen in the whole by the image of the whole; or when a man is seen in a mirror by the image in a mirror, or by any other mode by which one thing is seen in another.

---

[342] I q. 14 art. 1 ad 2.

[343] I q 14 art 1 ad 1. "Inquantum Deus cognoscit suam essentiam ut sic imitabilem a tali creatura cognoscit eam ut propiam rationem et ideam hujus creaturae."—I q. 15 art 2.

"So we say that God sees Himself in Himself, because He sees through His essence; and He sees *other things not in themselves, but in Himself*: inasmuch as His essence contains the similitude of things other than Himself."[344]

"So far, therefore, as God knows His essence as capable of such imitation by any creature, He knows it as the type and idea of that creature; and in like manner as regards other creatures."[345]

In God, as in the cause, exists everything that is to be found in things.[346] All things that are in the world are but participation of this Divine and Perfect Knowledge. Everything that is multiple in the universe is simple in Him and without confusion; everything that is disparate in the universe is united in Him, for in Him all things exist, not according to their own material or participated existence, but according to His own Perfect Being. His knowledge is anterior to the material existence of things; it is not dependent on them. They are not the measure of His intelligence; rather they are measured by it.

The universe is a great pyramid at the base of which stand the lower kingdoms which are deprived of that God-like intelligence. As this pyramid tapers to a point, the intelligence grows in increasing perfection, uniting more within itself with less effort and movement. As the general sense of man unites the disparate five senses, so do ideas unite disparate sensations by giving the very reason of their being. As the intelligence unites the sense, so does the angel unite both sense and intellect. As the highest species of angels unites the ideas of the inferior species, so does God unite within Himself all things as Cause and Creator.

---

[344] I q. 14 art 5. " Intellectus autem divinus nulla alia specie intelligit quam essentia sua. Sed tamen essentia sua est similitudo omnium rerum. Per hoc ergo sequitur quod conceptio intellectus divini, prout seipsum intelligit, quae est Verbum ipsius, non solum sit similitudo ipsius Dei intellecti, sed etiam omnium quorum est divina essentia similitudo. Sic ergo per unam speciem intelligibilem, quae est divina essentia, et per unam intentionem intellectam, quae est verbum divinum, multa possunt a Deo intelligi."—*C. G.*, lib. 1 c. 53.

[345] I q. 15 art. 2. "God sees the effects of created causes in the causes themselves, much better than we can; but still not in such a manner that the knowledge of the effects is caused in Him by the knowledge of created causes, as is the case with us."—I q. 14 art. 8 ad 3.

[346] "Superius habet similitudinem cum inferiori ut sol cum igne. Et per hunt etiam modum in Deo est similitudo omnium, et quantum ad formam et quantum ad materiam, inquantum in ipso praeexistit ut in causa quidquid in rebus invenitur."—I q. 57 art. 2 ad 2.

If, therefore, philosophy would find the "richer, fuller and more satisfying life;" if it would find and express that life as continuous and fluid; if it would also reveal any stage of life as a recapitulation of all that has gone before,—it must accept the intelligence. There is no question as to whether or not it is suited for life. IT IS LIFE. It is the supreme and perfect kind of life. It is the only title a being has to permanence. *Da mihi intellectum, et vivam*, cried the Psalmist. "Give me intelligence, and I will live." Organic life is only the feeblest participation in the Divine Life. It is only the shadow of the substance.

Without the intelligence there can be no continuity and no fluidity in the universe. What the heart is to man, that intelligence is, and even more, to the universe. Discard the Intelligence and you create a gap in the universe that no instinct or imaginal can fill. The gradual progress of kingdoms, evolution, if we choose to call it such, becomes impossible. There is progress until man is reached; then there is retrogression. Recognize the intelligence and you have a harmonious progression of perfections reaching even to God Himself. Posit intelligence, and evolution becomes intelligible; deny it, and it becomes absurd.

In like manner, the recapitulation which evolution seems to demand becomes impossible without the intelligence. The pyramid of unification breaks in the middle unless there is given a spiritual faculty which can contain, without destroying, the disparate faculties of animal life. By no other title than that of his intelligence is man the spokesman of the universe. By no other way is it given to man to carry the whole universe back again to its God. Without intelligence the bond between God and the material universe is merely one of causality. With intelligence standing between these two orders the bond is one of knowledge and love.

The recognition of intelligence is the key to the problems of philosophy. Between those who accept and those who reject it there is an almost unbridgable abyss. The extremes are as life and death. M. Bergson has called the intelligence "death;" the Angelic Doctor calls it the "supreme and perfect kind of life." James has called it a "beast," because it destroys and tears reality to pieces; Aristotle has called it "divine," because it apprehends without destroying. Dr. Schiller has said it prevents us from gathering the golden apples in the garden of the Hesperides; St. Thomas declares it reveals to us the distinction between the Dead Sea apples and the tree of the fruit of life, and thus leads us into the very garden of pleasure, for it leads us to God Himself.

Intrinsically, intelligence is a perfection that transcends all the visible things of the universe. It is greater than the sun and the moon; greater than plants and animals and all the material productions of man; and this because it is capable of knowing and desiring the supreme and ultimate Good—God.[347]

[347] "Universum est perfectius in bonitate quam intellectualis creatura extensive et diffusive, sed intensive et collective similitudo divinae perfectionis magis invenitur in intellectuali creatura, quae est capax summi boni."—I q. 93 art. 2 ad 3.

"Hoc excelluit in homine, quia Deus ad imaginem suam hominem fecit, propter hoc quod dedit ei mentem intellectualem qua praestat pecoribus."—ST. AUGUSTUNE, 6 *Gen.*, *c.* 12.

CHAPTER III:

CRITICAL APPRECIATION OF THE MODERN OBJECTIONS AGAINST INTELLIGENCE

IN the criticism of the intelligence made by modern philosophers, abstraction has been made to appear as the outcome of man's evolution. As man developed from the lower forms to the higher, he found himself under the necessity of handling matter for practical and scientific purposes. Being "tool-making" by nature, abstraction developed in him to fit experience into convenient moulds of action. Conceptual knowledge, thus represented by M. Bergson, is a development from below and in response to new needs, and is an essentially imperfect operation.

For St. Thomas the reason of conceptual knowledge is just the contrary. We must keep in mind, he insists, that human intelligence is not the unique nor the perfect form of intelligence. When Averroes made intelligibility *in se* equal human comprehensibility, he said a "ridiculous thing."[348] The human intelligence is only one of the forms of the intelligence, and that the lowest form, as has been shown. Man is the only intellectual being with a body. The very fact that the more perfect intellectual being has no body proves that the intelligence does not of itself require a body. Human intelligence does require a body, it is true, but *not because the body is the organism by which the intellect functions. Rather it is because human intellect operates on material things.* "The body is necessary for the action of the intellect," says St. Thomas, "not as its organ of action, but on the part of the

[348] *Metaphysics*, bk. 2 lect. 1.

object; for the phantasm is to the intellect what colour is to the sight."[349]

The higher forms are the angelic and the divine. Man strictly speaking is not intellectual; he is rational. Rationality is a quality proper to the animal genus, and is not to be attributed either to God or to angels.[350] The Divine and the angelic intelligence being free from matter, are much more powerful than our own; for matter is the reason of unintelligibility. Human intelligence united with an animal organism must operate on matter. It is therefore natural for it to use phantasms.[351] But at the same time, being intelligence and thus serving as the link between the world of matter and that of spirit, man participates in a finite way in the light which makes all things intelligible, namely, the Light of God. This Light has been given to intellectual creatures in a graduated way, those which are more near to God participating in it more fully than those at a greater distance. If our intelligence, as it is naturally constituted on this earth, could receive the light that is given to angels, we would have no further need of sense knowledge, nor would we have any further need of abstraction.[352] The angels see more in their ideas than we see in ours, because the light of their intelligence is greater. Light is that which manifests anything according to the faculty of vision. In an extended sense it signifies a manifestation in the order of knowledge.[353] The human soul in the natural order has received only a small endowment of this light.[354] Thanks to this light, however, which operates in one way through the active intellect,

[349] I q. 75 art. 2 ad 3.

[350] "Rationale est differentia animalis et Deo non convenit nec angelis."—I d. 25 q. 1 art. 1 ad 4. PIERRE ROUSSELOT, *L'Intellectualisme de Saint-Thomas* (Paris, 1908), art. 1.

[351] "Et similiter naturale est anime quod indigeat phantasmatibus ad intelligendum; ex quo tamen sequitur quod diminuatur in intelligendo a substantiis superioribus."—*De Spirit. Creat.*, q. 1 art. 2 ad 7.

[352] "Si vero sit aliquis intellectus a rebus cognitionem non accipiens, universale ab eo cognitum non erit abstractum a rebus, sed quodammodo ante res praeexistens; vel secundum ordinem causae sicut universales rerum rationes sunt in Verbo Dei; vel saltem ordine naturae sicut universales rationes rerum sunt in intellectu angelico."—I q. 55 art. 3 ad 1; II-II q. 171 art. 3.

[353] "Primo quidem est institutum ad significandum id quod facit manifestationem in sensu visus; postmodum autem extensum est ad significandum omne illud quod facit manifestationem secundum quamcumque cognitionem."—I q. 67 art. 1 c.

[354] "Illa lux vera illuminat sicut causa universalis, a qua anima humana participat quamdam particularem virtutem."—I q. 79 art. 4 ad 1.

we are able to seize the *ratio* of things.[355] Abstraction, then, is a necessity in virtue of the weakness of the intellectual light in us.

To say that our intellect lacks the light of God and angels—a light which reveals the particular in the universal and the individuals in the species, and the defect of which must be supplied by abstraction—is equivalent to saying that abstraction *is an imperfection.* And this is precisely the common-sense notion. Common-sense philosophy has not defended abstraction because it has regarded it as a perfection; it has merely insisted on its necessity as a result of our present condition on earth. It is universally admitted that it is an imperfection; the Angelic Doctor explicitly calls it such. In his treatise on Spiritual Creatures he writes: "*Abstraction is an imperfection of the intellectual operation.*"[356] The light of man's intelligence is like the twilight compared to that of God and angels, and hence his intellectual vision is obscure.

Abstraction, then, from the ontological point of view, is not a development from a lower form in response to human needs. *It is not our nearness to the beast which makes it necessary: it is our distance from God. Knowledge is not a push from below, but a gift from above.* Being more perfect than the lower forms, man cannot come nor develop from them; for the more perfect cannot come from the less perfect.[357] Abstraction has not been formed in an Eternal "Devenir" because man became a tool-maker; it has been given by an Eternal Light because that Light is the destiny of man. It is an imperfection, but it is an imperfection with a promise, and its promise is the Light, the Life and the Love—God Himself.

Among the generality of modern thinkers, abstraction is represented either as a work of addition or as a work of subtraction: as addition, in that it considers some special aspect in which certain experiences resemble one another, as mentally

---

[355] "Intellectus agens est illuminare intelligibilia in potentia in quantum per abstractionem facit ea intelligibilia in actu."—I q. 54 art. 4 ad 2.

[356] "Abstractio accidit intellectuali operationi, et pertinet ad imperfectionem ipsius, ut ex his quae sunt intelligibilia in potentia, scientiam capiat; sicut est de imperfectione visus vespertilionis, quod necesse habeat videre in obscuro."—*De Spirit. Creat.*, q. 1 art. 5.

"Cognitio perfecta non habetur per medium universale, quia non est efficax ad cognitionem omnium propriam."—II d. 3 q. 3 art. 2 ad 3.

[357] "Imperfecta autem a perfectis sumunt originem et non e converso."—*De Spirit. Creat.*, 1 art. 1 ad 25; I q. 7 art. 5 c.

isolated from the aspects in which they differ.[358] It is subtractive in that it strips off little by little the differences in certain common experiences, until the general is discovered.

In both of these cases abstraction functions only after several experiences of objects which have something in common.

What is to be thought of this notion? Abstraction, in the true sense of the word, does not require a variety of experiences from which the common element is abstracted. One experience only—that is, one object—is sufficient to form an intelligible species. The idea of metal can be formed from one experience of gold, and is not necessarily dependent on our experiences of silver and brass and iron, as Mr. Stout implies. One triangle is sufficient to form the concept of a triangle. Furthermore, if we find what is common in many experiences we imply that that which is common to each is there previously to our finding it.

St. Thomas, in speaking of abstraction, uses the singular form, implying thereby that it is not necessarily from a multitude of experiences that we draw the intelligible species. It is from the particular, and not from the common factor among particular objects, that we make our abstraction. When seeking the essence of an object, the intelligence is satisfied with one material thing and does not need many material things except accidentally.[359]

A comparison between sense "abstraction" and intellectual abstraction also makes this clear.

"Whatever two things are intimately united one to the other, one can be known without the other. One apple is sufficient in order that the eye may consider the colour, without any consideration of the odour ... So likewise the intellect can

---

[358] GEORGE B. SHANN, *The Evolution of Knowledge* (1922), p. 54; and chap. III. *Cf.* STOUT, "The Nature of Universals," *Mind*, p. 189. "Pour abstraire utilement il faut déjà savoir généraliser," H. BERGSON, *De Matière et Memoire*, p. 170: see chap. II. of this work.

[359] "Abstrahere universale a particulari ... sicut hominis, lapidis, equi."—I q. 85 art. 1 ad 1.

"Abstrahet intellectus universale a particulari."—3 *De Anima.*

"Humanitas quae intelligitur non est nisi in hoc vel illo homine."—I q. 85 art. 2 ad 2.

"Objectum intellectus nostri secundum praesentem statum est quidditas *rei materialis.*"—I q. 85 art. 8 c.

"Speculator naturam universalem in *particulari* existentem."—I q. 84 art. 7 c.

"Ipsa natura cui accidit intelligi, non est nisi in *singularibus.*"—I q. 85 art. 2 ad 2.

"Natura in singularibus habet multiplex esse secundum diversitatem singularium."—*De Ente et Essentia*, c. 4.

consider some form without the individual notes of that form."[360] Two apples are not necessary in order that we may consider in one case the colour of the apple and in another its odour. So likewise one metallic substance is sufficient in which to consider the essence of metal, without any reference to its individuating notes.

But neither of these arguments goes to the root of the question. They are merely introductions to the main argument, which is this. Abstraction, as we shall show, abstracts the form from the individual phantasm presented by sense knowledge. But each individual object has its own *form.* Socrates has the form of man as well as Aristotle; Napoleon has it as well as Washington. That which makes each one a *man* is in him individually as well as it is in a thousand men. *If it were not so, he would not be a man.* If human nature belonged only to many men—as something common to them all—we would never say that Socrates or Plato has a human nature.[361] Humanity is proper to man as man.[362] The universal by its very nature can be in many things, but of course does not necessarily *inhere* in many things. There are certain universals which actively and *sub se* contain one singular—for example, the sun and the moon.[363] Now, if a certain community among various experiences were essential for an intelligible species, we would never have an idea of the sun or the moon, but merely an image of it. So true is this fact, viz. that the nature of a thing is in one thing as well as in many, that St. Thomas has said that so far as the *object known* is concerned no

---

[360] "Nihil prohibet duorum ad invicem conjunctorum unum intelligi absque eo quod intelligatur aliud. Sicut visus apprehendit colorem, absque hoc quod apprehendat odorem ... unde intellectus potest intelligere aliquam formam absque individuantibus principiis."—3 *De Anima*, lect. 8.

"De ratione autem hujus naturae est, quod in aliquo individuo existat; quod non est absque materia corporali; sicut de ratione naturae lapidis est, quod sit in hoc lapide; et de ratione naturae equi est quod sit in hoc equo."—I q. 84 art. 7 c.

[361] " Si enim pluralitas esset de ratione ejus numquam posset esse una."—*De Ente et Essentia*, c. 4.

[362] "Hoc nomen humanitas non continet in sua significatione nisi quod est *hominis* inquantum homo."—Ibid., c. 3.

[363] "Universale est quod natum est pluribus inesse, non autem quod pluribus inest; quia quaedam universalia sunt quae non continent sub se nisi unum singulare, sicut sol et luna."—*Metaphysics*, lib. 7 c. 13.

one intellect can know the same thing better than another intellect, otherwise it would not know the thing as it is.[364]

The modern notion of abstraction as addition represents it as proceeding by synthesis. The root of the modern error on this subject is that its theories of knowledge begin at the wrong end. Modern thinkers consider the universals as posterior to the singulars, while the Scholastics consider the universal as prior to singulars.[365] Multiplicity and plurality increase as we descend in the order of perfection. The particulars should therefore be posterior in the ontological order to the universals. The parts of a definition are never prior to the whole.[366] The perfect must precede the imperfect. It is because each thing is the realization of an idea in the mind of God that it is intelligible, and that it can be known. The idea that the architect has of a house precedes the idea which is found materialized in the house itself.[367]

Keeping in mind that the term intelligence is not restricted to human intelligence, but extends even to the angelic and the divine, let us see the effect of the modern theory of abstraction in these other intellectual realms. If intellectual knowledge came only from the addition or the subtraction of individual experiences, then God and angels would never know unless they drew their knowledge from sense experience. Angels know the individuals only through their ideas. In the ideas which they have received from God they see the particular realizations. The Supreme Being who is the cause of all things, and who has made all things according to His Eternal Ideas, sees all things in His essence, even down to the minutest particulars of His creation. He knows them in His essence and not in their material manifestations. If divine ideas ontologically depended on the

---

364 "Ex parts rei intellectae—et sic non potest unus eamdem rem magis intelligere quam alius; quia si intelligeret eam aliter eam *esse quam sit*, vel melius vel peius falleretur et non intelligeret." But from the part of the one knowing there may be a difference—I q. 85 art. 7 c.

365 "Universalia sunt priora singularibus, licet in cognitione sensitiva accidit e converso. Ibi enim singularia sunt priora."—*Metaphysics*, lib. 5 lect. 13.

"Universae non est idem communi, differunt enim quia commune de se non determinat ad id quod communicator pluribus sed idem numero vel non; sed universale hoc determinat quia numquam idem numero est in pluribus."—1 d. 19 q. 4 art. 2 ad 2.

366 *Metaphysics*, lib. 7 lect. 9.

367 "A forma quae est in anima nostra procedit forma quae est in artificialibus; in naturalibus autem est e contrario."—Ibid., lib. 7 lect. 6.

particulars, then the unit would depend on the multiple, the perfect on the imperfect, the intelligible on the sensible, the cause on the effect. Such a theory stands the world on its head, and, instead of explaining it, renders it unintelligible.

It has been shown that abstraction is not the separation of differences in a variety of similar experiences; for one particular contains the nature of the thing just as much as a multiplicity of the same particulars. But may it not be that abstraction is a *separation of the individual notes*, *the stripping off of the particular differences* in order that the intelligible may appear? Here there is an approach to the exact nature of the abstraction mingled with the confusion of the accidental with the substantial. It is to be regretted that some writers, anxious to popularize the great masters of Scholastic thought, and bent more on studying second-hand than primary sources, have defined abstraction as the "stripping off of individual notes so as to arrive at the nature or the essence of a thing." Such an explanation is not absolutely false, but it prepares the way for a misunderstanding. It implies that the stripping off of the individual notes is a real positive exspoliation, whereas *de facto* it is merely something negative.[368] In abstracting the form from the phantasm, the individual notes are disregarded, and the stripping off of the individual notes is not the cause of the form appearing. The individual notes (as Cajetan says) do not appear under the light of the active intellect. Hence the *nature* presented in the phantasm is used, though not its individual notes.[369] The form is abstracted from the matter, and the form is not the result of the stripping off of individual notes.[370] In this figure let A represent the form and B the

[368] *Cf.* CAJETAN in I q. 85 art. 1

[369] "Quae abstrahere nihil aliud est in production speciei quam uti ipsis phantasmatibus quoad naturam repraesentatam et *non* quoad individuale."—CAJETAN in I q. 85 art. 2 IX.

[370] "Cognoscere vero id quod est in material est abstrahere formam a material individuali, quam repraesentant phantasmata."—I q. 85 art. 1 c.

"Abstraction is not falsehood. For the intellect to abstract things which are not really abstract from one another, does not involve falsehood, as clearly appears in the case of the senses. If the intellect is said to be false when it understands a thing otherwise than it is, that is so if the word *otherwise* refers to the thing understood, for the intellect is false when it understands a thing otherwise than it is; and so the intellect would be false if it abstracted the species of a stone from its matter in such a way as to regard the species as not existing in matter, as Plato held. But it is not so if the word '*otherwise*' be taken as referring to the one who understands. For it is quite true that the mode of understanding

individuating matter, and let the composite of A and B equal the thing.

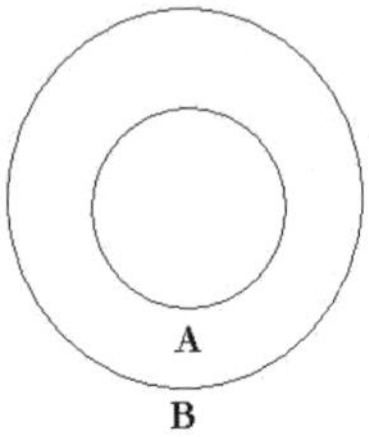

Abstraction in the strict sense of the term is not the stripping off of B to come to A after the manner in which we peel an onion to come to its centre. Abstraction is rather the illumination of the intelligibility in A which moves the active intellect without any consideration of B. The illumination of the phantasm reveals, not everything which is in it, as we have said, but only its nature. In revealing the intelligibility without the matter, the matter is neglected, and thus it is that the form is separated from its individuating notes.[371] The X-ray, to which the light of the active intellect may be compared, shines on the hand and reveals the bones without the skin.

St. Thomas explains this process in these words: "Not only does the active intellect throw light on the phantasm: it does more; by its own power it abstracts the intelligible species from the phantasm. It throws light on the phantasm, because, just as the sensitive part acquires a greater power by its conjunction with the intellectual part, so by the power of the active intellect the phantasms are made more fit for the abstraction therefrom of intelligible intentions. Furthermore, the active intellect abstracts the intelligible species from the phantasm, inasmuch as by the power of the active intellect we are able to disregard the conditions of individuality, and to take into our consideration the

in one who understands is not the same as the mode of a thing in existing: since the thing understood is immaterially in the one who understands, according to the mode of the intellect, and not materially, according to the mode of the material thing."—I q. 85 art. 1 ad 1.

[371] "Ea vero quae sunt in sensibilibus abstrahit intellectus, non quidem intelligens ea esse *separata*, sed *separatim* vel seorsum intelligens."—3 *De Anima*, lect. 12

specific nature, the image of which informs the passive intellect."[372]

Abstraction, therefore, is *not* "the consideration of some special aspect in which certain experiences resemble one another as mentally isolated from the aspects in which they differ;"[373] it does not mean "to leave" out what is different in particular instances compared, and to add together what they possess in common;[374] it is not "the association and addition of elements,"[375] nor the "isolation of *qualities* of an individual in order to make that *quality* representative of a genus,"[376] but it is the extraction by an illuminative act of what is intelligible in things—their ratio.[377]

This brings us to the objection of the "block universe," according to which the world is split up into rigid categories. But remark that up to this point the *universal*[378] has not been considered as universal. The reason for this is that by direct and spontaneous abstraction the *ratio* or intelligibility in things is revealed *as such*, and *independently* of its existence in this individual

---

[372] I q. 85 art. 1 ad 4.

[373] GEORGE SHANN, *The Evolution of Knowledge* (1922), p. 54.

[374] STOUT, "The Nature of Universals," *Mind* (April 1922), p. 189.

[375] *L'Évolution Créatrice*, p. 97.

[376] *Matière et Mémoire*, p. 171.

[377] Professor STOUT, it will be recalled (Part I. chap. ii.), considers the universal as the "distributive unity of a class." Of such a notion the author of *Relativity, Logic and Mysticism* has this to say: "Granted that the distributive unity of a class or kind is an ultimate and unanalysable type of unity, how would the fact help us in determining that (say) a particular thing, *a*, is a member or instance of the class *A*? In order to determine that *a* belongs to class *A*, I must somehow or other have knowledge of what it is that constitutes the class *A*. I cannot fall back on the ordinary supposition that the class is constituted by a character common to all the members, because to say that particular things share in a common character is, *ex hypothesi*, to say that each of them has a character which is a particular instance of a class of characters. How then do I obtain knowledge of a class of characters? Professor Stout's answer would appear to be that such knowledge is obtained immediately and directly through a mere inspection of some of its instances. Qualities and relations belong, he says, to classes just because they are qualities and relations. Characters *as such* are instances of universals, and this fact is just what makes so plausible the false statement that they are themselves universals. But how can they be recognized to be instances without that of which they are instances being, in some way, already known? And if a universal is the distributive unity of a class, how can such knowledge be obtained save by becoming aware of the various members of which the class is formed?"—G. DAWES HICKS, *Proceedings of the Aristotelian Society*, 13th to 16th July (1923).

[378] Here the term *universal* is used, not as the equivalent of *essence* or *nature*, but as the *essence* or *nature* applicable to a number of individual objects; e.g. *man* as applicable to Peter, Paul and John. *Cf.* I q. 85 art. 2 ad 2.

or in a thousand. Neither plurality nor individuality is the concern of the mind at the moment of direct abstraction.[379] For exactly the same reason the *ratio* or *essence* as it is known in the first moment of abstraction is known neither as genus nor as species. Rather, what is revealed is the *foundation* of universality, of genus and species, but not the universal itself as realizable in the individuals. This being clear, the charge brought against the Scholastic position by James and others, that the abstraction gives only a world of genus and species, is contrary to the true nature of abstraction.

It is only by another act of the mind that the universality of the idea is revealed; this second act of the mind is the act of reflection.

But why the two operations? Have they a real title to existence? Most certainly. Man is a composite of body and soul. Man knows by both sense and intellect.[380] Without a body or without matter, man would never need the reflective process; without a spiritual and intellectual soul, he could never have direct abstraction. The double process is necessary, then, because man is composed of body and soul.

The *idea*, in the sense of being a genus or species, *i.e. a universal*, in the sense of being applicable to many things, is due to this reflex act of the mind by which it turns back on the concept obtained by abstraction. In virtue of this relation determined by the reflex act, the essence becomes endowed with a double

---

[379] "Ideo si quaeratur utrum ista natura possit dici una vel plures, neutrum concedendum est; quia utrumque est extra intellectum ejus et utrumque potest sibi accidere."—*De Ente et Essentia*, c. 3.

[380] "Relinquitur ergo quod ratio speciei accidat naturae humanae secundum illud esse quod habet in intellectu. Ipsa enim natura habet esse in intellectu abstractum ab omnibus individuantibus, et habet rationem uniformem ad omnia individua quae sunt extra animam, prout essentialiter est imago omnium et inducens in cognitionem omnium, in quantum sunt homines, et ex hoc quod talem relationem habet ad omnia individua intellectus adinvenit rationem speciei."—*De Ente et Essentia*, c. 4.

Cf. I q. 76 art. 2 ad 3; I q. 85 art. 3 ad 4; I q. 86 art. 1. *De Veritate*, q. 2 art. 4 ad 2; Ibid., q. 10 art. 5 c. et ad 1, 2, 3. *C. G.*, lib. 2 c. 74 and c. 79. JOHN OF ST. THOMAS, *Logica*, t. 1 p. 2 q. 4 ad 1.

"Non proprie loquendo sensus aut intellectus cognoscunt sed home per utrumque."—*De Veritate*, q. 2 art. 6 ad 3. "Sed tames per quamdam reflexionem redit etiam in cognitionem ipsius phantasmatis, dum considerat naturam actus sui."—Ibid., q. 2 art. 6 c. "Similitudo speciei existens in intellectu humano non sufficit ad cognoscenda plura singularia; et propter hoc intellectui adjuncti sunt sensus, quibus singularia accipiunt."—Quod. 7 art. 3.

character: first, that of unity, inasmuch as the essence is one; secondly, multiplicity, because applicable to many things, at least in a confused way.

Universals, whether genus, species or the like, are not productions of the mind, as the *ratio* or essence is not a production of the mind. They are the fruit of a contact with sensible reality.[381] Instead, therefore, of abstraction being a cutting-up process, it is true rather to say that the sense and the sensible images are responsible for breaking up reality. The modern philosophers, therefore, in rejecting abstraction for having cut up the world, should rather have rejected the senses. If we had no senses, and if there were no matter, we would have no such problem as the multiplicibility of the nature indicated by the universals. We would see all the possible individual realizations in the idea itself, as does the angel. Our knowledge would then be much higher than it is now.

Another criticism opponents have urged against the intellect is that its knowledge is imperfect. It gives only the general, not the particular. It knows the rose in its universal elements, but not its colour, size, environment and particular beauty.

All this is quite true. The intellect does not see the particular. *But our senses do.*[382] That is the purpose of our senses. And the intellect, by conversion to phantasms and by reflection, can turn back upon the individuals and apply the universal idea to them. Why criticize the intellect for a function which is supplied by that which is its *necessary accompaniment* in our present stage of existence, namely, the senses? Such a criticism of the intellect is equivalent to forswearing the use of knives because we cannot

---

[381] "Intellectui respondet aliquid in re dupliciter. Uno modo *immediate*, quando videlicet intellectus concipit formam rei alicujus extra animam existentis, ut hominis vel lapidis. Alio modo *mediate* quando videlicet aliquid sequitur actum intelligendi, et intellectus reflexus supra ipsum considerat illud. Unde res respondet illi considerationi intellectus mediate, id est mediante intelligentia rei: verbi gratia, intellectus intelligit naturam animalis in homine, in equo, et multis aliis speciebus: ex hoc sequitur quod intelligit eam ut genus. Huic intellectui quo intellectus intelligit genus, non respondet aliqua res extra immediate quae sit genus; sed intelligentiae, ex qua consequitur ista intentio, respondet aliqua res."—*De Pot.*, q. 1 art. 1 ad 10.

[382] "Particulare autem apprehendimus per sensum et imaginationem."—I q. 84 art. 7.

"Contingentia prout sunt contingentia cognoscuntur directe quidem a sensu, indirecte autem ab intellectu."—I q. 86 art. 3 c.

sew with them. We have a needle for sewing and a knife for cutting, and one does not exclude the other.

And what is more, though the intellect does not seize the particular directly, but indirectly, it nevertheless possesses a knowledge of the thing higher than pure sense-perception.[383] "For the sensible image in sense is the likeness of only one individual thing, and can give the knowledge of only one individual. But the intelligible species of our intellect is the likeness of the thing as regards its specific nature, which is participable by infinite particulars: hence our intellect by the help of the intelligible species of 'man' in a certain way knows infinite men—not, however, as distinguished from each other, but as communicating in the nature of the species; and the reason is that the intelligible species of our intellect is the likeness of man, not as to the individual principles, but as to the principles of the species."[384] "As our intellect is infinite in power, so does it know the infinite. For its power is indeed infinite, inasmuch as it is not terminated by corporeal matter."[385] A knowledge of the *ratio* of

[383] "In re apprehensa per sensum intellectus multa cognoscit, quae sensus percipere non potest."—I q. 78 art. 4 ad 4; I q. 84 art. 6 ad 3; II-II q. 12 art. 4.

[384] I q. 14 art. 12 c. "On the other hand, the Divine essence, whereby the Divine intellect understands, is a sufficient likeness of all things that are, or can be, not only as regards the universal principles, but also as regards the principles proper to each one. Hence it follows that the knowledge of God extends to infinite things, even as distinct from each other."—Ibid.

"Una ratio lapidis in omnibus."—*De Spirit. Creat.*, q. 1 art. 2 ad 1.

"Intellectus per speciem rei formatus, intelligendo format in seipso quandam intentionem rei intellectae quae est ratio ipsius, quam significat definitio."—*C. G.*, lib. 1 c. 53.

"Quantum ad id quod rations est, *universalia sunt entia* quam particularia...quanto vero ad naturalem subsistentiam particularia magis sunt entia."—*Post. Anal.*, lib. 1 lect. 37.

"Anima intellectiva cognoscit rem aliquam in sua nature absolute, puta lapidis, inquantum est lapis absolute."—I q. 75 art. 5.

"Habet rationem uniformem ad omnia individua, quae sunt extra animam prout essentialiter est imago omnium."—*De Ente et Essentia*, c. 4.

[385] I q. 86 art. 2 ad 4. When it is said that the intellect knows the *ratio* or *quiddity* of things by intellectual abstraction, it must not be imagined that the *ratio* is extracted mechanically and understood perfectly. "Aliud se intelligere quidditatem rei; aliud ad modum quidditatis." The intellect does not always know the thing as it is in itself, but, *ad modum quidditatis*, because from its mode it is forced to penetrate the interior of a thing. This quiddity is called the proper object of the intellect. *Cf.* 3 *De Anima*, lect. XI.; II-II q. 8 art. 1. Our knowledge proceeds from the general to the particular: it becomes more perfect (I q. 85 art. 3). Hence "the essential differences between things are frequently unknown" (*De Pot.*, q. 9 art. 2 ad 5).

"Qui scit aliquid in universale scit illud indistincte ... tum est scientia completa in actu quando pervenitur per resolutionem ad distinctam cognitionem principiorum et

the triangle is worth more than its sense knowledge. A knowledge applicable to all times is worth more than a knowledge limited to this particular moment; a knowledge indefinitely reproducible is worth more than a knowledge of singularity.

This remark brings us more into the heart of the problem of the value of conceptual knowledge. At the outset we run counter to the attacks made on the concept by M. Blondel, M. Bergson and a host of other thinkers, for whom the concept is either a mere "effigy" or else an "impoverished" sensation. The first argument urged against it, is that it is merely a symbol of reality and not reality itself.[386] M. Bergson has called it a "rubric under which we write all living beings." M. Blondel has called it *artificiata.*

The presumption at the bottom of these and similar critiques is that the concept does not reveal *reality*, but merely gives a substitute for it. Such criticism applies to Cartesianism as well as to some of its decadent antecedents, but in no way does it apply to the Thomistic doctrine. It applies also to modern idealism, but is foreign to the thought of the *philosophia perennis.*

Thomistic thought has always maintained, and always will maintain under the penalty of being false to common sense, that by the concept we attain, *not to a picture of reality, but to the reality itself.* This doctrine has been called by Dr. Noel the "corner-stone of the critical reconstruction of philosophy."[387] St. Thomas has given a whole article to the problem of the idea, asking whether it is *that which we see*, or *that by which we see.* He first shows the false conclusions which follow from the theory that with the idea we remain with an effigy of things and do not attain to the thing itself: namely, "every science would be concerned, not with the objects outside the soul, but only with the ideas in the soul;" and secondly, it would lead to a degenerate pragmatism which maintains that whatever seems is true.

---

elementorum."—*Phy.*, lib. 1 lect. 1; 2 d. 3 q. 3 art. 2 ad 3.

What is attained in a confused way, at least, is that by which anything is understood, *i.e.* the first subject of existence and action, without which the intellect could not think of the thing.

Cf. JACQUES MARITAIN, *Éléments de Philosophie*, vol. i. pp. 139-148.

386 See Part I. chap. II.

387 *Saint-Thomas et la Pensée moderne*, *loc. cit.*

Passing to the constructive side, the Angelic Doctor continues: "There is a twofold action" *(Meta.*, ix. did. viii. 8): "one remains in the agent—for instance, to see and to understand; another passes into an external object—for instance, to heat and to cut; and each of these actions proceeds in virtue of some form. And as the form, from which proceeds an act tending to something external, is the likeness of the object of the action, as heat in the heater is the likeness of the thing heated; so the form, from which proceeds an action remaining in the agent, is the likeness of the object. Hence that by which the sight sees is the likeness of the visible thing; and the likeness of the thing understood, that is, the idea, is the *form by which* the intellect understands. But since the intellect reflects upon itself, by such reflection it understands both its own act of intelligence and the idea by which it understands. Thus the *idea is that which is understood secondarily*; but that *which is understood primarily is the object, of which the idea is a likeness.*"[388]

"That which is known by the intellectual vision are the *things themselves and not their images or effigies.*"[389] "*The stone is that which is known*, *and not the idea of the stone*, except indirectly by the act of reflection when the intellect turns back upon itself, otherwise our knowledge would be only of ideas instead of things."[390]

The idea, then, is not *that which* we see; it is that *by which* we see. The difference between these two notions sums up the fundamental difference which separates modern idealism in all its forms from Thomistic realism. The idea is not a substitute for

[388] I q. 85 art. 2 c.

[389] "Ipsa cognita per intellectualem visionem sunt res ipsae et non rerum imagines."—*De Veritate*, q. 5 art. 1 c.

"Id vero quod intelligitur est *ipsa ratio* rerum existentium extra animam, sicut etiam et res extra animam existentes visu corporali videntur."—*C. G.*, lib. 2 c. 75.

[390] "Lapis est id quod intelligitur, non autem species lapidis, nisi per reflexionem intellectus supra seipsum, alioquin scientiae non essent de rebus; sed de speciebus intelligibilibus."—I q. 76 art. 2 ad 4.

"Objectum intellectus est ipsa rei essentia, quamvis essentiam rei cognoscat per ejus similitudinem, sicut *per medium cognoscendi.*"—*De Veritate*, q. 10 art. 4 ad 1; *C. G.*, lib. 1 c. 46; lib. 2 c. 73, 75 and 98; lib. 3 c. 49.

"Intellectio enim qua lapis intelligitur ad lapidem terminatur."—Sylvester in *C. G.*, lib. 1 c. 53, 1.

"Sed in ipso immediate res cognita attingitur."—JOHN OF SAINT THOMAS, *Phil. Nat.*, t. 3 q. 5 art. 1.

CAJETAN in *S.*, I q. 85 art. 2. *Cf.* P. CORDOVANI, "Oggettività e transcendenza" in "S. Tommaso d'Aquino," *Rivista di Filosofia Neo-Scolastica* (Luglio-Agosto, 1924), p. 241 ff.

reality, nor is it a museum of samples, as M. Blondel would have us believe; nor is it a *rubric* under which we catalogue an object, as M. Bergson believes it to be. It is neither a portrait nor an instrumental sign like a medal which is first known before making known. It is a *sign*, the like of which does not exist in the material world of bodies—that is, a *formal sign*, the nature of which is to signify and to make known before being itself known by reflection.[391]

The problem of knowledge posited in these words: How can we be sure that the idea corresponds with the reality? does not exist for St. Thomas. There can be no question of correspondence when there is presence or identity. "It is the real immediately which I know. But a something beyond thought is unthinkable, it is said. But the real is not something beyond thought. It is independent and presented. Whether I welcome it or refuse it, my love or my hate can never alter or change it. Whether it pleases me to say so or to believe it, there will never be another truth for me than that which expresses it."[392] There is no problem of correspondence since there is no error where there is identity. The abstractive intuition of essence is without error. Error can exist only where there is composition, and here there is no composition.[393] The fault of modern idealism is to make the idea a *closed object* instead of an *open relation*, and to rest in the consideration of a photograph of a thing instead of the thing photographed. "A representation which is not the representation of anything is, at the same time and under the same formal relation, relative and non-relative."[394]

The idea is never the direct object of the knowledge of the intellect, but only the indirect. It is only by another act, a reflex one, that the intellect attains the idea. The thing is always known before the idea of the thing.[395] Because the idea terminates in the

---

[391] JACQUES MARITAIN, "L'Intelligence d'après M. Maurice Blondel," *Revue de Philosophie*, July-August 1923. *Cf. Réflexions sur l'Intelligence* (1924), p.33.

[392] LÉON NOËL, *op. cit.*

[393] "Objectum intellectuale est quod quid est, circa quod non errat, sicut neque sensus circa proprium sensibile."—I q. 57 art. 1 ad 2.

[394] GARRIGOU-LAGRANGE, *Dieu: Son existence et sa nature*, p. 138; I q. 85 art. 2 c.; I q. 76 art. 2 ad 4.

[395] "Veritas est in intellectu sicut consequens actum intellectus, et sicut cognita per intellectum; *consequitur* namque intellectus operationem, secundum quod judicium intellectus est de re secundum quod est; *cognoscitur* autem ab intellectu secundum quod

essence of the thing known, and the thing known is in the sense order, it must not be imagined that the idea has no necessary or universal value. The idea by reflex abstraction is still universal, so far as the *manner of knowing the thing* is concerned—namely, stripped of matter which prevents its communicability—but not formally universal, as regards the *nature represented.*[396] For the thing outside the mind is singular according to its mode of being, but is universal according to its nature.

If the intellect seizes the reality of the thing under its *ratio*, what is the difference between the *ratio* existing in the mind and the *ratio* existing in reality? What is the difference between the *ratio* of man existing in the mind and the *ratio* of man existing in Peter? Observe that the question is merely the difference of *ratio*, and not the difference between the universal and the particular.

So far as the *ratio* of the thing is concerned, there is no difference, whether it be apprehended by the mind or existent outside of the mind. The *ratio is* the essence, and the essence is the same in both; otherwise there would be no identity and no true knowledge.

But if the *ratio is* the same in both, is there no difference between them? The *ratio* has a different mode outside the mind from that which it has in the mind. Outside the mind its mode of existence is material and individual. In the mind it is without these material and individuating notes. It exists intentionally in the soul, and its term is this same object effectively known.

St. Thomas says: "The nature of the thing which is known is truly outside the mind, but it has not the same mode of being outside the mind as it has when it is known."[397] The ideas are not more excellent than the things, so far as their manner of representation is concerned, but they are more noble as regards the mode of their being.[398]

intellectus reflectitur supra actum suum, non solum secundum quod cognoscit actum suum sed secundum quod cognoscit proportionem ejus ad rem: quod quidem cognosci non potest, nisi cognoscatur natura principii activi quod est ipse intellectus in cujus natura est ut rebus conformetur."—*De Veritate*, q. 1 art. 9.

[396] "Ipsa natura, cui accidit vel intelligi, vel abstrahi, vel intentio universalitatis, non est nisi in singularibus. Sed hoc ipsum quod est intelligi, vel abstrahi, vel intentio universalitatis est in intellectu."—I q. 85 art. 2 ad 2. *De Ente et Essentia*, c. 4.

[397] I q. 56 art. 2 ad 4.

[398] "Species autem intellectus nostri non sunt excellentiores rebus ipsis quantum ad

In the material universe there is nothing exactly parallel to *intentional being.* Knowledge is an assimilation. But assimilation proceeds according to the nature of the one assimilating. In the physiological process of assimilation it is not necessary that the plant life continue the same mode of existence in the animal tissue as it did in its external environment. It is merely sufficient that the chemical constituents remain the same. "The essences of material things are in the human intellect, as a thing known in the one knowing, and not according to their real mode of being, as the intellect *does not apprehend things according to their mode of being,* that is, according to their materiality, *but according to its mode of being.*"[399] The ultimate reason of intentional being in the intellect is to supply the deficiencies of the natural being.[400] Thus they are enabled to acquire a mode of perfection which is not theirs by nature. It is thanks to this gift that man can sum up all creation within himself and give glory to God in the name of all visible creation.

The intellect, then, according to its *entitative being* (that is, the being of its own nature, in virtue of which it possesses immanent activity) is terminated by the idea, but according to its *intentional* being terminates in the thing known.[401] "Knowledge requires a double union: firstly, a union in entitative being, by which the subject is put in contact with the thing; then a union by which one becomes the other, which accomplishes itself in intentional being. Thus it is necessary that our intellect be determined by an accident which affects it in its entitative being, in order that it receive in itself the intentional being, and that the act of knowing be produced."[402] The idea, therefore is both subjective and objective, but under different relations. It is subjective as regards its entitative being, but objective as regards its intentional being; subjective as regards its being, and objective as regards its value.

---

repraesentationem, licet sint excellentiores ad modum essendi."—*De Veritate*, q. 8 art. 10.

[399] I q. 51 art. 1 ad 2; q. 50 art. 2 c.; q. 57 art. 1 ad 2.

[400] *De Veritate*, q. 2 art. 2.

[401] "Haec est perfectio cognoscentis inquantum est cognoscens; quia secundum hoc a cognoscente aliquid cognoscitur quod ipsum cognitum aliquo modo est apud cognoscentem, et ideo in 3 *De Anima*, dicitur anima esse quodammodo omnia, quia nata est omnia cognoscere. Et secundum hunc modum possibile est ut in una re totius universi perfectio existat."—*De Veritate*, q. 2 art. 2.

[402] JACQUES MARITAIN, *op. cit.*, p. 63.

Another illusion regarding the intellect which needs to be dissipated is that of the relation of the idea and the image. In his Oxford lecture on the Perception of Change, M. Bergson committed himself to the same confusion which reigns among his contemporaries, declaring the idea to be nothing more than a subtilized, or emaciated or impoverished sensation.[403]

It is owing to this confusion that a pure empiricist philosophy has taken such deep root in our day, just as it was owing to this same confusion in the past that a similar philosophy was formed. The Angelic Doctor, passing the history of Greek philosophy in review, has this to say, which is so apt for the moment: "Certain ancient philosophers, ignoring the power of the intellect, and not distinguishing between sense and intellect, thought there was nothing in the world except that which could be apprehended either by the senses or by the imagination. And because only bodies fall under the sensible faculties, they thought only bodies existed, as the philosopher says in his 4th Physics (text 52 and 57)."[404]

The difference between the two is clear cut and well defined. First, the image becomes more perfect as it possesses more details: the idea, on the contrary, becomes more perfect as it gets away from details. My *image* of the table is more perfect as it contains the details of its size, weight, colour, its surroundings, the books and papers which are upon it, and so forth. My *idea* of a table, on the contrary, is more perfect as it loses these details, and becomes so dispossessed of them that it can apply the notion to every table in the universe. *The image tends in the direction of material determination; the idea in the direction of material indetermination.* One goes in one direction, the other in the other. It is quite impossible, therefore, that one should ever "dissolve" into the other; for by their very nature they are different.

Among other important differences, St. Thomas points out this: a sense may be damaged by a sensible object which is too powerful for the senses. A terrific explosion renders men deaf; an intensely bright light renders them blind. The intellect, on the contrary, is never corrupted nor damaged by the excellence of its

403 p. 7
404 I q. 50 art 1 c.

object. The idea of virtue, of justice, of force, of faith, hope or charity, has never been so strong for our intelligence as to cripple it.[405] The idea of God even is not too strong for it. And what is more—and this is a further difference—not only do the intelligible ideas fail to corrupt our intellectual powers, but they even render them more capable of seeing other intelligible objects. He who knows greater things is better able to know the lesser things. Thanks to the knowledge of a principle of mathematics, for example, the mathematician will see a multitude of conclusions which the untrained mathematician would fail to see after many elaborate and multiplied examples. The principle of act and potency which Aristotle and the Angelic Doctor understood so well, instead of blinding their intelligence by its force, enabled them more clearly to see the necessity of an *Actus purus—God.*

A more fundamental difference—that, indeed, which underlies all others—is that the ratio contains the *ratio entis* of that which it represents, while the common image contains only the juxtaposed notes which make a thing known, but which never render the notes intelligible. Psychology, for example, characterizes man as reasonable, free, religious, sociable and the like. That which makes man *man* is not his sociability, his liberty and so forth, but rather his *rationality.*[406] All the other notes flow from this one, and are intelligible only in virtue of it. Without the idea there is only mechanical juxtaposition of qualities. This is one of the defects of modern anti-intellectualism. It rejects the intellect because it "cuts up reality into morsels," and at the same time falls into that very error by denying a difference in kind between concepts and images.[407]

A modern philosopher who has understood this necessary distinction is Dr. W. Tudor Jones. "No other conclusion is possible," he writes, "but that the human mind has been so

[405] "Sensus corrumpitur ab excellenti sensibili. Intellectus autem non corrumpitur ab excellentia intelligibilis; quinimmo qui intelligit majora potest melius postmodum minora intelligere. Est igitur alia virtus sensitiva et intellectiva."—*C. G.*, lib. 2 c. 66.

[406] GARRIGOU-LAGRANGE, *Sens commun* (3rd edition) p. 47. "Licet autem in cognitione sensitiva posit esse similitudo rei cognitae, non tamen *rationem* hujus similitudinis cognoscere ad sensum pertinet, sed solum ad intellectum."—*Metaphysics*, lib. 6 lect. 6.

[407] For a clear and detailed account of the difference between sensation and idea, see J. G. VANCE, Ph.D., M.A., *Reality and Truth* (1917), pp.146-59.

formed as to discover, conserve and further realities which are conceptual in their nature, and which, indeed, belong to another kind of sphere or dimension than the whole physical realm ... We are living in two kinds of worlds. We have all the time to start with the sensuous world, and have also to pass to the conceptual world, for it is in this conceptual world that the physical world finds its meaning, value and significance ... The first world without the second merely means the knowing of the letters of a language without being able to put them together into words and propositions. The second kind of world without the first means attempting to carry water in a bucket without a bottom to it."[408] Dr. Carr, as well, has seen the impossibility of dissolving concepts into images, or even subtilizing images into concepts. "Concepts are universals as distinct from particulars ... every attempt of the mind to discover the reality implied in our experience supposes the use of concepts, *and these concepts ... are totally different in kind from percepts.*"[409]

The second general criticism against conceptual knowledge was that it solidified movement. The concepts enable us to "grasp hold of certain portions of the changeful stream of reality,"[410] by taking "photographs of reality" and "substituting movement by some practical equivalent;"[411] but they do not grasp movement.

The intellect, it is said, cannot seize movement. If not, how did an Intellectualist such as Aristotle or St. Thomas know movement? How did they describe movement, not only in its sensible manifestations, not only in the enumeration of its kinds, but in the determination of *the very reason of movement*, in the doctrine of act and potency? If the intellect cannot know movement, how did the Angelic Doctor succeed in dividing the principal part of his *Summa* into the double movement of creatures—their procession from God and their procession back to God? Certainly a philosophy of the intellect, which has

---

[408] *Metaphysics of Life and Death* (1923), pp. 99, 100, 104. "If the general were nothing more than a sum of the particular, no progress could have been possible in the mind's interpretation of external things, or of itself and its contents" (p. 86).

[409] *A Theory of Monads* (1922), p. 285 ff.

[410] C. A. RICHARDSON, *The Supremacy of Spirit* (1922), p. 19.

[411] H. BERGSON, *L'Évolution Créatrice*, pp. 169, 323-53.

explained the goodness of all natural things by their tendency and movement to their ultimate end, is no stranger to movement.

Of course, this much must be conceded to the later critics. If the modern philosopher means that the *Eternel devenir* which is the ground of all things cannot be seized by the intelligence, he is perfectly within the bounds of common sense, for nothing is more unintelligible than an eternal becoming without a thing that becomes.

If, however, we mean movement as manifested about us in the real world of sense reality, and in particular local motion, it is very true that the intelligence cannot seize it as the senses do. The senses see it in all particular determinations, whereas the intellect does not. But from this it does not follow that the intelligence solidifies movement in seizing it, or that it takes a photograph of it. What the intelligence seizes is the *ratio* of the movement, and this is more profoundly *movement* in its very essence and nature than any knowledge by sense or sympathetic intuition. To seize the *ratio* of movement is not to solidify movement; rather it is to grasp it in all its fullness. The relation of act and potency which is grasped by the intelligence is so profoundly movement itself, that it can be applied to every movement in the universe from a gift of grace to the dropping of a leaf. If the intelligence grasped only a photograph of reality, it could not apply that photograph to all reality, any more than the photograph of one individual suffices for every man in the universe. What has been said above bears repetition: the *fact* that the intelligence seizes and grasps *movement as movement* is the greatest refutation of its imagined impossibility of doing so.

Another similar criticism is that the intellect through its conceptual knowledge breaks up the continuity in nature.[412] The intelligence can represent only the discontinuous, while life itself is continuous. Hence its unfitness for life.

The assumption at the base of this objection is that all reality is monistic and continuous, and that "every division of matter into independent bodies with absolutely determined limits is an artificial division."[413]

---

[412] See Part I. chap. II.

[413] HENRI BERGSON, *Matière et Mémoire*, p. 218.

There is pluralism in the universe as well as continuity. The intellect does not put pluralism there, but it finds it there. The continuity which is in the universe no other power than the intellect can perceive. It seizes the continuity of all orders, from the mineral up to the highest choir of angels, by seizing the *reason of the continuity*, namely, the differentiations of essences in the *unity of being*. There is no continuity intelligible but the continuity of being, and being is the object of the intellect and the intellect alone. Furthermore, does not the abiding consciousness which the mind has of itself and of its own continuity refute *by fact* any theoretical denial of the capacity of the intellect to grasp the continuous? The whole Bergsonian criticism is based on the false assumption that the intellectual elements are *external* and *foreign* to the real. "Without doubt the snapshots are exterior to the object photographed." But what does this metaphor mean? Does it mean that our ideas, the intellectual determinations by which we know the elements of a thing, are exterior to the thing analysed, or that they are of another order entirely? That the idea is of another order than the thing known is cheerfully granted. But it is not that which the Bergsonian metaphor seeks to prove; it is rather to make us believe that *in themselves* the elements of analysis are of an entirely different order from the thing analysed, and are exterior to it. Here the metaphor of a snapshot loses its value; for it is no longer a question of photography, but of the thing photographed. Is the Parthenon exterior to Athens and a part of Athens, or only a fragmentary symbol, because a photographic image of the Parthenon, which we see in Paris, for example, is exterior to Athens?[414]

Descending into the order of nature and accidents, the intellect cannot even here be said to break up the continuity of an object, for "those things which are in the sensible order the intellect abstracts, not by knowing them as *separated* from all materiality, but separately."[415] "And it is not necessary that those things which are distinguished according to the intellect be

[414] JACQUES MARITAIN, *La Philosophie Bergsonienne* (1914), pp. 49-50.

[415] "Ea vero quae sunt in sensibilibus abstrahit intellectus non quidem intelligens ea esse separata, sed separatim, vel seorsum intelligens."—*De Anima*, lib. 3 lect. 12.

"Non necesse est ut ea quae intellectus separatim intelligit, separatim esse habeant in rerum natura."—Opus xv., *De Angelorum Natura*.

"Oportet quod universalis conceptio applicetur ad particularia."—*C. G.*, lib. 2 c.48.

distinct among things, because the intellect does not apprehend things according to their mode of being, but according *to its mode.*"[416]

This last point touches the vital spot of anti-intellectualism and its substitute—intuition. When modern philosophy speaks of knowing movement as it is in its material reality, and continuity as it is in its material reality, it returns to the ancient philosophy of Empedocles, who insisted that like is known by like. Fire is known by fire, water by water, air by air, and earth by earth; such was the old doctrine.[417] The new is that *becoming* is *known by becoming* and *continuity by continuity*, for the ground of all things is becoming.

The idea, which is the bond between matter and spirit, is suppressed. The result is a juxtaposition, but not knowledge. It was just to avoid this fusion of one angel with another that St. Thomas saw the necessity of positing ideas in angels. If one angel knew another angel without a likeness there would be absorption, and knowledge never depends upon absorption.

Apart from this fact that "intuition" in the modern sense does away with the idea, it also inverts the order between the knower and the thing known. Instead of knowing the rose by a cognitive assimilation in the mind of the knower, modern sympathetic intuition assimilates the mind to the rose and becomes one with it and lives sympathetically with it.

But such perversion is extremely ill-becoming for a philosophy which deifies evolution and continuity in the universe. Plants assimilate minerals, but not *vice versa.* Why should there be a perversion in the cognitive order? Why should we be one with the rose instead of the rose one with us? In the physiological order it means that we never eat our dinner, but we are eaten by it.[418]

The intelligence being a spiritual faculty, has no designs against the material universe other than to reveal its intimate nature. It is not destined merely for the practical, as is wrongly

---

[416] I q. 3 art. 3 ad 1.

[417] "Sic autem intellectus non recipit formam, alioquin verificaretur opinio Empedoclis qui posuit quod terram terra cognoscimus et ignem igne."—I q. 50 art. 2 ad 2.

[418] "Intellectus non apprehendit res secundum modum rerum, sed secundum modum suum."—I q. 50 art. 2 c.

assumed by the anti-intellectualists, but also and principally for the spiritual. Abstraction and conceptual knowledge in general are in no way due to the necessity of handling the practical, but rather due to the inability of our mind to handle the spiritual as it is in its material expression. The intellect is not a push from matter, for the greater can never come from the less. It is a gift from spirit, and that spirit is God.

The objection involves a vicious circle. The intellect is said to have been formed in the course of evolution by the necessity of handling the practical. But how could man conceive of handling the practical unless he had an intellect? The necessity of the practical is thus made the origin of the intellect, and the intellect in its turn the origin of the practical.

The true notion of the intellect and its relation to the practical has been stated by St. Thomas in these words: "What is accidental to the nature of the object of a power does not differentiate that power; for it is accidental to a thing coloured to be man, to be great or small; hence all such things are apprehended by the same power of sight. Now, to *a thing apprehended by the intellect, it is accidental whether it be directed to operation or not.*"[419] Such a conception of the intellect is at the pole's end from the conception that intellect began with tool-making, and justifies our contention that modern anti-intellectualism is not a criticism of a faculty, but a state of mind of the last century.

Another error at the base of modern thought, to which we have already made reference, is that of the confusion of reason and the intelligence.

Reason is not identical with the intelligence in all respects.[420] A well-defined distinction between the two is the basis of the Scholastic system. The confusion of the two, and at certain times their identification, is the source of the modern error of anti-intellectualism. "Scientism" of the nineteenth century deified reason. The thinkers of the twentieth century identified that abuse of reason with the intelligence. In other words, they called reason the intelligence.

---

[419] I q. 79 art. 11 c.

[420] *Cf.* Part II. chap. I; I q. 99 art. 8; *De Veritate*, q. 15 art. 1; 3 d. 3 q. 4 art. 1 ad 5.

The criticism of "Scientism" which they made was not one of an abuse of reason, which it should have been, but a complete and total rejection of the intelligence; and with the passing of the quantitative, rationalistic and mechanical formulae of the exaggerated Scientists, intelligence passed away.

In the search for a new way of knowing, and particularly, a new way of knowing so far as the things of religion are concerned, a distinction must be made between *ideal* and *fact*. The *ideal* which modern philosophy adopts in rejecting Scientific Intellectualism is that of directness and immediacy in knowledge—and to this ideal the intelligence, in the Scholastic sense of the term, corresponds. But Scholasticism is either not known or is ignored; hence the defective substitutes for the intelligence of the Scholastics.

In fact, the new knowledge by sympathetic intuition and its other forms does not attain the ideal of the intelligence, but really sinks back into a lower form—a knowledge by sense experience. It is at this point that modern philosophy is reposing at this moment.

If there had been one leader of modern thought during this period who was clear-visioned enough to see the distinction between the abuse of a thing and its legitimate use, and between the reason and the intelligence, we might today be enjoying the fruits of a philosophy whose basis would be the intellectual intuition of the Angelic Doctor instead of the sentimental and affective knowledge which can give us nothing better than an evolving God.

Modern philosophy has severely condemned reason, or analysis, as it is sometimes called in modern terminology. It is rejected because it is imperfect, being a mere mechanical instrument without any real value for life in its continuity and in its evolution.

In declaring the imperfection of reason, modern philosophy has emphasized a truth of common-sense philosophy. Throughout the philosophy of the Angelic Doctor there is nothing more clearly manifest than his insistence on the imperfection of reason. The answer to the question, Why do we abstract? why do we make judgments by composition and division? is the same as the answer to the question, Why do we reason? We reason, St. Thomas answers, because of the "weakness of the intellectual light in us."[421]

If our knowledge were by infused ideas and not from the sensible universe, we should have no need of abstraction. If we saw everything that is realizable in an idea as an angel does, we should have no need of sense knowledge. We should merely *see* intellectually, as we see corporally.

Furthermore, if our intelligence could see in an idea all the possible predicates of that idea as does an angel or God, we should have no need of judgment by predication.

In like manner, if our intelligence were sufficiently strong to see all the possible conclusions in a principle, we should have no need of reason, as at present we have no need of reason to see the truth of principles which are immediately evident.[422]

Reason, then, is a necessary result of our present condition. As we are not born men, but children, so intellectually we are not born with all the conclusions contained in a given principle, but must grow up to them gradually by a certain *movement.*[423] As in judgments there is a comparison of subject and predicate, so in reason there must be a comparison of conclusion and principle. Such a process implies a movement, and such precisely is the nature of reason.[424]

The modern objection against the imperfection is really a Thomistic truism![425] "Reason is the imperfection of the intelligence." "Certitudo rationis est ex intellectu; sed necessitas rationis est ex defectu intellectus."[426]

---

[421] "Quod contingit ex debilitate luminis intellectualis in nobis."—I q. 58 art. 4 c.

[422] "Si enim intellectus statim in ipso principio videret conclusionis veritatem, numquam intelligeret discurrendo vel ratiocinando."—I q. 58 art. 4 c.

[423] "Sic ergo patet, quod ex eodem provenit, quod intellectus noster, intelligit discurrendo et componendo et dividendo; ex hoc scilicet, quod non statim in prima apprehensione alicujus primi apprehensi potest inspicere quidquid in eo virtute continetur. Quod contingit ex debilitate luminis intellectualis in nobis."—Ibid.

[424] "Discursus quemdam motum nominat."—I q. 58 art. 3 ad 1.

[425] "Sed ad imperfectionem pertinet discursus intellectus."—*De Veritate*, q. 2 art. 1 ad 4.

[426] II-II q. 49 art. 5 ad 2. "Defectus quidam intellectus est ratio."—*C. G.*, lib. 1 c. 57. "Ex imperfectione intellectualis naturae provenit ratiocinativa cognitio."—Ibid. John of Saint Thomas says reason is defective both according to its succession and according to its causality *(Phil. Nat.*, t. 3 q. 56 art. 4). "*Ex imperfectione, intellectualis naturae* provenit

But because reason is an imperfection, it does not follow that we can dispense with it. It is an imperfection which attaches itself to our nature. It is a *necessary imperfection.* "Necessitas rationis ex defectu intellectus." It is the penalty of being a man and of having an intelligence whose light is not equal to that of the intelligence of the angels. In denying its necessity, modern philosophy has been false to one of its basic principles—the principle of evolution or movement. Reason is rejected because, as we are told, it is unsuited for life in its continuity and progress. This is the very reason the Angelic Doctor gives for its necessity. Under the penalty of having no progress and continuity in nature, we must have reason. Evolution demands continuity. There must be a *rapprochement* between the various orders; and what is the highest yet evolved must in some way possess continuity with the order from which it has been evolved, as Professor Alexander has shown in his work, *Space, Time and Deity.* But if there is no reason, there is no continuity between the mere materials of sense knowledge and conclusions which are contained potentially in them. Once the reason is introduced as the *natura intellectualis obumbrata* a continuity is established not only with the order below man but also with the order above him.[427]

Instead, then, of being unsuited for life in its continuity, reason is the very condition of our vision of this continuity. Without it there is a hiatus which renders unintelligible any evolutionary conception of the universe. Furthermore, reason is movement. Why should a philosophy of movement reject it? Thus at one time it deifies movement, and at another rejects reason because it cannot grasp movement. A philosophy of movement is, like a child, extremely difficult to satisfy.

Reason is a movement. It is a progress from a principle to conclusion. Being movement, it must have a point of departure and a point of arrival. Without a point of departure and without a point of arrival there is no movement. At both extremes there is something which is not movement. From these extremes the

ratiocinativa cognitio."—*C. G.*, lib. 1 c. 57. "Defectus quidam intellectus est ratio."—Ibid.

[427] "Natura inferior secundum supremum sui attingit infimum naturae superioris; et ideo natura animae in sui supremo attingit infimum naturae angelicae et ideo aliquo modo participat intellectualitatem in suo summo. Ratio enim nihil est nisi natura intellectualis obumbrata; unde inquirendo cognoscit et sub continuo tempore quod intellectus *statim* et plena luce con fertur."—3 d. q. 4 art. 1 ad 4.

reasoning process draws its validity and its value. "Certitudo rationis est ex intellectu." At the extremes stands an intellectual intuition, an immediate and direct perception of a truth. At one extreme is the intellectual seizure of a principle, which is known immediately, as the eye sees and immediately knows colour. At the other extreme is the apprehension of a conclusion.

Aristotle has told us in his *Perihermenias* that reason is dependent on two anterior operations of the mind—abstraction and judgment—which depend one upon the other. Here we must revert to what has been said of ideas, namely, that they attain reality. They have a real value because they attain reality in its very essence without distorting it in any way, merely giving to the physical existence an intentional or mental existence. The judgment which is made up of these ideas attains reality in like manner. The same must now be said of the reasoning process. If it is made up of judgments which are judgments of reality and not mere mental creations of a blind workman at his loom, then its conclusions are of real value. If the scientist reasons about quantity, his conclusions apply to quantity as it is; if the biologist reasons about life in its biological manifestations, his conclusions possess a real value for that life; if the metaphysician reasons about the world, his conclusions apply to a real world and are not merely subjective ideas.

If the metaphysician reasons about God, religion means something more for him than a "relation between our upper and our lower self." It means a relation with a real Being upon whom we are absolutely dependent. That article of the *Summa* which treats of the value of the idea is of first importance in philosophy, and rightly deserves to be called "the cornerstone of philosophical reconstruction."

Professor Taylor has seen its importance, as he so well testified during the Thomistic sexcentenary celebration. He writes:

"This at least is clear, that a theory of perception and perceptual knowledge which is to meet the requirements of modern science will have to be something in its general characters very much like that of St. Thomas. It will have to combine, as he, at any rate, meant to combine, the two complementary positions that our knowledge of the world around our bodies is mediated in fact by highly complicated processes of a special kind, and that as knowledge it *is direct*, *unmediated* apprehension not of ideas or images but of actual physical reality. *No one, so far as I know, among great modern philosophers has ever seen as clearly as St. Thomas that the problem is precisely not to sacrifice one of the true positions to the other.*"[428]

In conclusion, it is worth noting that very serious consequences follow from the modern anti-intellectualist doctrines. The modern position denies a speculative value to the intelligence. It also denies that God is the Alpha and the Principle of all things.

But from this double denial there flows a double consequence. First, if the intelligence is destined merely for matter and for the practical, is organic and not spiritual, why are things intelligible? Why can things be known? Why are things known? Modern philosophy cannot answer this question.

Secondly, if God is not the Principle of things, but merely the outcome of the world's evolution, then what ultimate explanation is there of intelligibility in things?

I. What is the proximate reason of *intelligibility? Why can things be known?* Is it not because their nature is *separable from matter?* "Anything whatsoever is knowable inasmuch as it is separable from matter."[429] The animal never knows a thing in its *ratio*, because it never knows it apart from *this individual.* So true is it that intelligibility varies with separability from matter, that the moment you reach a point where there are things without matter, the intellect and that which is known are one and the same.[430]

What, then, is the conclusion? If forms *de se* are communicable—that is, separable from matter—and separability from matter constitutes intelligibility, then material things are

[428] A. E. TAYLOR, M.A., *Saint Thomas as a Philosopher*, Aquinas Sexcentenary Lectures (Oxford, 1924), p. 31. The intelligence from a psychological point of view is studied in the work of Professor C. SPEARMAN of London University: *The Nature of Intelligence and the Principles of Cognition.* We have dismissed this work by placing ourselves at the metaphysical point of view.

[429] "Unaquaeque res in tantum est intelligibilis inquantum est separabilis a materia."—JOHN OF SAINT THOMAS, *Logica*, t. 1 p. 2 q. 27 art. 1; and *Philosophic Naturalis*, t. 3 p. 3 q. 10 art. 2.

[430] "Idem est intellectus et quod intelligitur"—I q. 55 art. 1 ad 2, and I q. 87 art. 1 ad 3.

intelligible in potency.[431] They are not intelligible in act, because *de facto* forms are individualized in matter. "It is not because the *form* or the nature of *man* is individualized in this particular man, that it is unintelligible; it is because it is associated with matter."[432] Natural *knowable* things antedate our knowledge and constitute its measure.[433] If the intelligibility in potency were not already in our sense knowledge, it would not be possible for us ever to know the thing.[434] We do not put intelligibility into things except artificially; we discover it.[435]

The condition of intelligibility is separability from matter. Things can be known because the form of things is capable of existing apart from such and such individual matter. What is the condition of *intelligence?* If separability constitutes the *power to be known*, what *constitutes the power to know?* It is *separation from matter.* The condition of the act of intellectual knowledge is *separation from matter*, as the condition of knowability is the separability from matter. Matter is the reason of impenetrability. Knowledge demands penetration; an assimilation of the *other.* To receive the *other* while remaining oneself is possible only to a spiritual faculty which is not determined to the *hic et nunc.*[436] Knowledge implies, therefore, the reception of the form without the matter. But can a form exist without matter? Is there anything intrinsically impossible about such a condition? The answer of the Angelic Doctor is to be found in a work of his youth, *De Ente et Essentia.*

---

431 "Res quae sunt extra animam sunt intelligibiles in potentia."—*De Veritate*, q. 10 art. 6; I q. 79 art. 3 ad 1; I d. 35 q. 11 art. 11 ad 3.

432 "Singulare non repugnat intelligibilitati inquantum est singulare, sed inquantum est materiale, quia nihil intelligitur nisi immaterialiter; id quod repugnat intelligibilitati est materialitas."—*C. G.*, lib. 2 c. 75.

433 "Scibilia naturalia sunt priora quam scientia nostra et mensura ejus."—I q. 14 art. 8 ad 3.

434 "Si autem ita esset quoad sensus apprehenderet solum id quod est particularitatis, et nullo modo cum hoc apprehenderet universale in particulari, non esset possibile quod ex apprehensione sensus causaretur in nobis cognitio universalis."—2 *Post. Analy.*, lect. 20.

"Intentio universalitatis non est nisi in singularibus."—I q. 85 art. 2 ad 2.

"Natura speciei nunquam est nisi in his individuis."—*C. G.*, lib. 2 c. 75.

435 This is not the ultimate reason why things are intelligible. See following.

"A forma quae est in anima nostra procedit forma quae est in materia in artificialibus; in naturalibus autem est e contrario."—*Metaphysics*, lib. 7 lect. 6.

436 "Angelus autem cum sit immaterialis est quaedam forma subsistens et per hoc intelligibilis in actu."—I q. 56 art. 1 c.

"Ipsa immaterialitas substantiae intelligentis creatae non est ejus intellectus, *sed ex immaterialitate habet virtutem ad intelligendum.*"—I q. 56 art. 1.

"It is impossible," he writes, "that there should be any matter without form, but it is not impossible that there should be form without matter. Form, as form, does not depend on matter. If one thing is the cause of another thing, the cause can exist without the thing caused, but not *vice versa.* The form is the cause (formal) of the composite. 'Forma dat esse materiae.' It can therefore exist apart from matter."[437]

In order, therefore, that knowability be reduced to knowledge, the nature of the individual thing given through sense knowledge must be revealed without its individual notes, which constitute the very *reason of its unknowability*. The intelligible in potency can become the intelligible in act only by a denudation of its matter.[438] It is not yet intellectual nourishment any more than the plant is ready-made nourishment for the animal. The nutritive elements of the plant are only in potency for the animal; in order that the animal may utilize them its nutritive faculty must be active.[439] In like manner, in order that we may grasp the intelligible in potency we must have an intelligence in act. What the enzymes of the stomach juices are in the digestive order, the power of the active intellect is in the intellectual order. "The necessity of positing an active intellect is due to the fact that the nature of material things which we know does not exist outside the soul immaterially and inteligibly in act, but is there intelligible in potency only. Hence it is fitting that there should be some power which makes these natures intelligible in act. This power in us is called the 'active intellect.'[440] By this power of extraction the *principium essendi* becomes the *principium cognoscendi*, and these

[437] "Immaterialitas alicujus rei est ratio quod sit cognoscitiva; et secundum modum immaterialitatis est modus cognitionis."—*De Anima*, lib. 3 c. 8.

[438] "Oportet quod intelligibile in potentia fiat intelligibile in actu per hoc quod ejus species denudatur ab omnibus apenditiis materiae."—1 d. 35 q. 1 art. 1 ad 3, and 2 d. q. 1 art. 1 c., and 1 d. 8 q. 5 art. 2 c.

[439] "All sensible things are in act outside the senses, hence the senses are merely passive in face of their reception."—I q. 79 art. 3 ad 1.

"Man comes to the knowledge of sensible colour through two things: (1) visible object, (2) a light by which it is seen. So also in intellectual knowledge two things are required, namely: (1) the intelligible things, (2) the light by which it is seen. This light is the Active Intellect."—2 d. 9 q. 1 art. 2 ad 4.

[440] I q. 54 art. 4. "Such an intellect was unnecessary for Plato, for whom the universals (direct) are in act outside the mind."—*De Spirit. Creat.*, art. 4.

are identical, so far as the thing known is concerned; for a thing is knowable by the principle."[441]

II. *Ultimate explanation of intelligibility.*—In answer to the question, Why are things intelligible in potency? St. Thomas gives this solution. In all things not generated by mere chance the form of a thing is always the end of the generation. The plant generates a plant, not a horse; the animal generates an animal like unto itself, not a vegetable. But the form cannot be the end of the process of generation unless the likeness of the form is in some way in the generator.

Now, in nature there are two kinds of generation in the broad sense of the term. There is first the generation which operates in virtue of a blind necessity of nature or by instinct, and there is another which operates in virtue of the intelligence. An example of the first is all biological generation in the lower orders; an example of the second is the form of a house, which exists in the mind of the architect before the house is built. In the first there is an assimilation of the effect to the form; in the second the form which is conceived in the mind is reproduced in the real order. The architect seeks to make the house like the form which is in his mind.

Since the world was made, not by chance, but by God, who is Intelligence itself, as we shall prove, it is necessary that there should be in the Divine Mind a form according to which the world is made. And this is the reason of the idea. "Et in hoc consistit ratio ideae."[442]

This idea which exists in the mind of God, and to which all things are likened, is nothing else than the Essence of God.[443]

---

[441] "Illud quod est principium essendi est etiam principium cognoscendi ex parte rei cognitae, quia per sua principia res cognoscibilis est, sed illud quo cognoscitur ex parte cognoscentis est similitudo rei vel principiorum ejus quae non est principium essendi ipsius rei nisi forte in practica cognitione."—*De Veritate*, q. 2 art. 3 ad 8. Thus, St. Thomas escapes Idealism.

[442] I q. 15 art. 1. Creatures proceed from God in virtue of this double similitude.

"Aut quantum ad id quod habet in natura sua, sicut home generat hominem; aut quantum ad id quod habet in intellectu suo, sicut artificiatum. Utroque modo procedit creatura a Deo in similitudinem ejus. Primo modo, quia ab ente sunt entia, et vivo viventia; secundo modo quia procedunt a rationibus aeternis."—2 d. 16 q. 1 art. 2 ad 2.

[443] "Deus secundum essentiam suam est similitudo omnium rerum. Unde idea in Deo nihil est aliud quam Dei essentia."—I q. 15 art. 1 ad 3.

God knows His Essence perfectly. He knows it in every way in which it is knowable and in all its perfections. He knows His Essence not only as it is in itself, and in its necessity and eternity, but also in its *participability*; that is, all the possible ways in which created beings may participate in His Being—the stone by existence, the plant by life, the animal by consciousness, man and angel by intelligence. All of these possible participations He possesses within Himself from all eternity, as the artist, in a feeble way, possesses within himself the form of the statue which he intends to chisel. No creature, therefore, possesses being or any other perfection except in so far as it is an imitation or a copy of or a participation in the Being and the attributes of God, just as no statue exists in the world which does not imitate in some way the design and the formal idea of the artist who conceived it.[444]

Although these exemplar ideas which exist in the mind of God, and according to which the whole universe has been made, are multiple in relation to the things themselves, they really are not distinct from the Divine Essence, inasmuch as the Divine Essence, because of its infinity, may be imitated in innumerable ways.[445]

The meaning of idea is *form* in the Greek. Ideas are therefore the forms of things existing outside the things themselves. Now, the form existing outside the thing itself may be considered in one of two ways: as *exemplar*—that is, as the principle of the making of the thing; or as *type*—that is, as principle of its cognition, inasmuch as the forms are said to be knowable in the one knowing. As *exemplars* they pertain to the practical intellect, and as *type* or *ratio* they belong to the speculative intellect as well as to the practical.[446] The Second Person of the Blessed Trinity,

[444] "Ipse enim essentiam suam perfecte cognoscit, unde cognoscit eam secundum omnem modum quo cognoscibilis est. Potest autem cognosci non solum secundum quod in se est, sed secundum quod est participabilis secundum aliquem modum similitudinis a creaturis."—I q. 15 art. 2 c.

[445] "Quae quidem, licet multiplicentur secundum respectum ad res, tamen non sunt realiter aliud a divina essentia, prout ejus similitudo a diversis participari potest diversimode. Sic igitur Deus ipse est Primum Exemplar Omnium."—I q. 44 art. 3.

[446] "*Idea* enim graece, latine *forma* dicitur. Unde per ideas intelliguntur formae aliarum rerum, praeter ipsas res existentes. Forma autem alicujus rei praeter ipsam existens, ad duo esse potest; vel ut sit exemplar ejus cujus dicitur forma, vel ut sit secundum principium cognitionis ipsius, secundum quod formae cognoscibilium dicuntur esse in cognoscente."—I q. 15 art. 1 c.

in the language of theology, is the *exemplar* and *type* or *ratio* of all things. *He is therefore the source of all art and all science; for what is art but a participation in the Exemplary Cause, and what is science but the participation in the Formal Cause?* It is here that the transcendentals, beauty and truth, find their perfection; it is here, too, that all art and all science must look, if they would know their source.

Since the world has been made by God, who is Intelligence itself, the Exemplary and the Formal Cause of all creation, *the world is intelligible—that is, it has been made intelligibly.* We do not put intelligibility into the universe; we discover it. As the statue is the imitation of the idea in the mind of the artist, so each creature is an image of an idea existing in the Divine Mind. Boethius therefore correctly says that "all forms which are in matter can be called images, inasmuch as they come from those forms which are without matter."[447] Everything, from the stone to an angel, is the realization of an idea. Eternal ideas realized in the angels make of each one a distinct species, because there is no matter to individualize them. Eternal ideas realized in the mineral, plant, animal and man, make of each an individual, owing to the matter which is associated with the nature of each, and which is the principle of their multiplication. It cannot, therefore, be argued that everything which is intelligible must be in matter; for it is *only accidental to the object to be separated from the knower in the ontological order.* This follows from the principle that knowledge ultimately comes from above and not from below. There can never be an object which an idea has not preceded, but there can be ideas which have not been materialized.[448] "The idea outside of God and outside of us is thing; the thing in God and in us is idea."[449] This is also the ultimate reason why God and not man is the measure of things. "Natural things are midway between the knowledge of God and our knowledge; for we receive knowledge from natural things, of which God is the cause by His knowledge. Hence, as the natural objects of knowledge are prior to our

"Et secundum quod est principium factionis rerum *exemplar* dici potest, et ad practicam cognitionem pertinet. Secundum autem quod principium cognoscitivum est proprie dicitur *ratio*, et potest etiam ad scientiam speculativam pertinere."—I q. 15 art. 3 c. *Metaphysics*, lib. 5 lect. 2.

[447] 2 d. 16 q. 1 art. 2 ad 2.

[448] CAJETAN in I q. 14 art. 1.

[449] A. D. SERTILLANGES, *Mélanges Thomistes*, p. 182.

knowledge, and are its measure, so the knowledge of God is prior to natural things, and is their measure; as, for instance, a house is midway between the knowledge of the builder who made it and the knowledge of the one who derives it from the house already built."[450] We receive our knowledge from natural things, of which things God by His knowledge is Cause.[451] In each thing, therefore, there is the *ratio*, the principle of its intelligibility. But this principle of intelligibility is there only in potency. Coming from the mind of God into matter, it has lost its character of universality, necessity and transcendence, which makes it the direct and immediate object of the intelligence. It has fallen into extent, number, movement and contingency. In order that "it may revive in the mind with its proper characteristics, it is necessary that the reality, coming into our mind by sense perception in some way, make a return to its source, disincarnate itself from matter, and go in the opposite way from that which *individuation* by matter imposed on it. The individuation, realized by the generation of a being, is as an *attraction* of the idea in matter ('agens facit formam esse in materiam'). In order to know, there must be a contrary action, an *extraction* or abstraction."[452] Such is the profound and ultimate reason of abstraction—namely, to render ideas intelligible in act, as they are in the mind of God. It is the Divine Plan of bringing all things back to God who is the Source, the Alpha and the Omega of all things. "Divine wisdom is the reason of all things."[453]

In conclusion, then, it may be truly said that the intelligence, instead of being a barrier to philosophical progress, is really the only royal road to wisdom. It alone reveals the wonderful coordination of matter and spirit; the descent of all things from God by creation, and their ascent through the intellectual knowledge of man. Only a philosophy which upholds a spiritual faculty can explain even the possibility of knowledge, as only such

---

[450] I q. 14 art. 8 ad 3.

[451] "Species intelligibiles, quas participat noster intellectus, reducuntur, sicut in primam causam, in aliquod principium per suam essentiam intelligibile, scilicet in Deum. *Sed ab illo* principio procedunt mediantibus formis rerum sensibilium et materialium, a quibus scientiam colligimus, ut Dionysius dicit" (*Div. Nom.*, c. 7)—I q. 84 art. 4 ad 1.

I q. 15 art 3; Quod 7 q. 1 art. 3; *De Spirit. Creat.*, art. 10.

[452] A. D. SERTILLANGES, *St. Thomas* (3rd edition, 1922), vol. ii. p. 165.

[453] I q. 44 art. 3 c.

a philosophy can account for real progress in perfection among created beings. The philosophy of St. Thomas gives an answer to the intelligibility of the universe, both on the part of the object and on the part of the subject. On the part of the object, because forms are *de se* communicable; on the part of the subject, because the intellect is spiritual. For those who would go still deeper into the reason of intelligibility it gives the more ultimate answer that things are intelligible on the part of the object, because they have been made intelligible by God; and they are intelligible on the part of the subject, thanks to the light of the active intellect given by God, which reveals the ideas according to which all things were made.

But according to the modern notion, separation from matter is impossible, either because the intellect is represented as organic, or because ideas are merely the composition of material images. Possessing no faculty for transcending matter, man is therefore incapable of ever arriving at the intelligibility in things.

Furthermore, since it denies God as the Principle and Final Cause of the universe, it cannot say that things have been made intelligibly. If the world has not been made according to the ideas of a Perfect Intelligence, there is no ultimate reason why we should find, in the last analysis, a rational universe.

Denial of the intelligence means denial of intelligibility. Is it any wonder, then, that Dr. Schiller, who denies a value to the intelligence, should see nothing more in metaphysics than "an idiosyncrasy," or that Mr. Baillie should say that "not reasonableness but dramatic completeness" is the chief unifying power in man's life?[454]

[454] *Cf.* Part I. chap. II.

CHAPTER IV:

EVOLUTION AND THE FIRST PRINCIPLES OF THE INTELLIGENCE

Necessity of First Principles

EVERY faculty has a formal object to which it is ordained by nature; this formal object is natural to the faculty. It is natural for the eye to see colour; it is natural for the ear to hear sound; it is natural for the intellect to apprehend *being*.

But these faculties which attain their natural objects are not static, dead and inert. They are alive and vital. They function; they move. Movement is the law of the universe, as modern philosophy tells us, and this we accept as our starting point. It is another way of saying that all created things are composed of act and potency.

But nothing moves unless it is moved by another. This principle in like manner is common to both modern and traditional philosophy. It is the dictate of common sense. At first sight it would seem that modern philosophy is opposed to this principle, and this is true if the principle is made ultimate, for the source of all things is movement. But in its remote applications the principle holds true, inasmuch as modern philosophy explains the *particular movements* in the universe by a Mover—which is either an Urge, a Divinal Imagining, a Desire, an "Lan Vital" or the like. Everything that moves in the universe is moved by this principle. The "Élan Vital" is creative; Desire is creative; Divinal Imagining is a kind of spontaneous generation;

Space-Time is creative. They are all the source of every particular movement found in the universe.

It is not true to say that a philosophy of becoming excuses us from the necessity of positing a first principle. On the contrary, it is the very reason for so doing. Something must account for the movement. Whether it be God, or Space-Time, or Divine Imaginal or "Elan Vital," does not matter at this point. The fact is, man is moved by some mover, and the very fact of his being moved constitutes his "first principle."[455]

The necessity of first principles in the rational order is not something "invented" by common-sense philosophy because of its intellectual character. Rather, first principles are the dictates of nature and common sense; they are necessary for the very same reason that first principles are necessary in every order within the whole hierarchy of the visible universe.

Nature of First Principles

There is a wide breach between theory and practice. Ovid has given the universal experience of this fact a poetical turn in his "... Aliudque cupido, mens aliud suadet; video meliora proboque, deteriora sequor." St. Paul has expressed the same idea: "I do not the good which I will; but the evil which I hate, that I do."[456]

What is true in the moral order is true in the speculative order. There is often a wide breach between what a philosopher teaches and the principles upon which he acts in his ordinary life. In the face of such divergencies between theory and practice, common sense is never long in making a decision. One *fact* is often the refutation of a whole philosophy. Berkeley, the English Empirical Idealist, refuted his whole philosophy by dodging a runaway horse. Diogenes answered Zeno's philosophical arguments about the impossibility of movement by walking. Henry More answered Descartes' philosophical argument of the

[455] The strict metaphysical argument for the necessity of first principles is drawn from the impossibility of going back infinitely in the reasoning process. See *Metaphysics*, lib. 4 lect. 6.

[456] Rom. vii. 15.

reciprocity of movement—that it is indifferent to say that we move to our destination or our destination moves towards us—by asking Descartes the reason of fatigue after running towards his destination. Schopenhauer nullified his philosophy of cosmic suicide by dying a natural death. Mr. Chesterton upsets the extreme determinist philosopher by asking him why he says "thank you" for the mustard. And M. Bergson, the inspiration of modern philosophy, after writing three volumes on the philosophy of becoming, finally confesses that the Aristotelian doctrine is really "the natural metaphysics of the human mind," which, however, he condemns.

These judgments passed on philosophical theories, as well as a host of other judgments which we make in the course of the day, are judgments of *common sense. Common sense* is a term we have been employing throughout to characterize the philosophy of Aristotle and St. Thomas and their successors. The time has now come to give the term a definite meaning. *The natural, spontaneous, primitive, infallible judgments of the human reason constitute common sense.*[457] These judgments are not reflective judgments; they are immediate. They extend themselves to three kinds of natural certitude: first, the data of sensible experience (for example, a square has four sides); secondly, to intellectual principles evident of themselves (for example, the whole is greater than any of its parts); thirdly, conclusions which are proximately related to these intellectual principles which are self-evident. From two equal quantities take away two equal amounts, and there still remain two equal quantities.

These certitudes are natural; they spring from the natural working of the human intelligence. They are never learned, they are never taught, they are never forgotten. In practice they are admitted by every one, though in the last twenty years modern philosophy has denied their value. "Inasmuch as they spring from the nature of man, they should be found among all men—that is, they are *common* to all men. This is why it is said that they

[457] Boethius calls the proposition which each one approves on hearing it, the *common* conception.

"Communis animi conceptio est enuntiatio quam quisque probat auditam."—*Lib. de Hebdomadis*—initium.

arise out of common appreciation, or consent, or instinct, or the *common sense* of humanity."[458]

For the majority of men these certitudes remain implicit and confused. They form the hidden foundation for the philosophy of every one. Every man is a philosopher inasmuch as he has these certitudes, particularly the certitude of self-evident principles. It was in virtue of these certitudes, which arise spontaneously, that Berkeley refuted his own philosophy, that Diogenes refuted Zeno, More refuted Descartes, and M. Bergson testified to the unnaturalness of his philosophy of becoming. There is, then, a relation between the certitudes of common sense and philosophy. This relation remains to be determined.

There are three answers to the problem of the relation of common sense and philosophy. One is the answer of the Scottish School. Reid and Stewart, at the close of the eighteenth and the beginning of the nineteenth century, having seen the ravages of scepticism wrought by Hume, endeavoured to restore philosophy to a solid foundation. They admitted that the certitudes of common sense were valid; but common sense was either an instinct or an authority, which served as a foundation of philosophy.

Another answer to the problem of the relation of common sense and philosophy is that of sentimentalism and intuitionism. Lord Balfour in his *Foundations of Belief*, and W. H. Matlock in his *Is Life Worth Living?*, place the foundations of philosophy in a faith dictated by the need of our noblest inspirations.[459] James, M. Bergson, Bradley, Professor Pringle-Pattison, Dr. Schiller and the generality of modern philosophers agree in basing these certitudes on some vision of the practical or on an intuition. This second group of philosophers, who have been classed under the title intuitional or sentimental, differ from the Scottish School in denying any value to common sense as the basis for philosophy.

Between these two extremes—the one admitting the validity of these certitudes of common sense, but making common sense a blind authority or instinct, and the more modern school which

---

[458] JACQUES MARITAIN, *Éléments de Philosophie*, p. 88; *Cf.* pp. 87-94.

[459] For a criticism of these notions, see Cardinal MERCIER, *Critériologie générale* (9th edition, 1918), p. 179 ff.

denies all value to the certitudes of common sense—stands the philosophy of Aristotle and St. Thomas. On the one hand, it opposes itself to the Scottish School by denying that philosophy is founded on the *authority* of common sense; and on the other hand, it opposes itself to modern philosophy, which denies all value to common sense. Positively, its position is that philosophy is derived from common sense, *regarded as the natural intelligence of first principles.* One of the elements of common sense is the knowledge of first and immediately evident and naturally known principles; *e.g.* the whole is greater than any of its parts. "If therefore philosophy finds its principles already proclaimed by common sense, let it be well understood that it is not because they are proclaimed by common sense; it is not because they are based on *the authority of common sense taken as the general consent or the common instinct of humanity*; but it is because they are proclaimed by the absolute and unique authority of the *evidence* which it has for principles."[460]

Philosophy is superior to common sense in its mode of knowing; for common sense is simply the raw material from which the whole edifice of philosophy is built. As regards the object of knowledge, however, common sense is, in its technical meaning, superior to philosophy and to all the sciences; for the latter are based on the natural evidence of first principles.

Modern philosophy, in breaking with common sense, may justifiably be contrasted with common-sense philosophy, as has been done throughout the whole of this work. In opposing itself to common sense it takes its stand against the immediate judgments of all mankind. Its doctrines make loose speculation for the class-room, but for life they are unsuited—yet this is their greatest boast. The naïve, the mysterious, the original and not the reasonable, has become the standard by which they are judged. Catchwords and not ideas have gained such an importance that we find verified the words of Stevenson: "Not by bread alone doth man live, but principally by catchwords." As a German writer has put it: "We are very resourceful in coining marketable

[460] JACQUES MARITAIN, *Éléments de Philosophie*, p. 90.

and attractive formulae, but idle in creating fully developed systems and views of the world."[461]

Professor Ralph Barton Perry is no less disheartened at the divorce from common sense. He writes that "we suffer from a new kind of credulity. It was once complained that men are too easily inclined to believe what their fathers believed; that men lacked originality, independence. But there is now reason to fear that men may too easily believe what no one has ever believed before. Men with settled convictions may become as rare as were free-thinkers in an earlier time. And the consequences must be scarcely less detrimental to social welfare than the consequences of the earlier complacency and narrow-mindedness."[462] And Professor Radhakrishnan adds: "At the present day philosophy has become fundamentally plebeian or democratic. Its one self-chosen aim is to arrange the life of the ordinary man. If he requires a God, philosophy will supply him with one; if a ghost, it will also be supplied. This prejudice of the plain man is the seed of the plant of this new philosophy."[463]

It may even be added that modern philosophy in recent years has been playing so fast and loose with common sense, "believing what no one else ever believed before," that the time will soon come when a modern philosopher who returns to common sense will be hailed as one of the most original thinkers of all time. It will be a repetition of the story of the man who went out in a boat, and on returning "discovered England."

But this boasted originality which comes from playing fast and loose with common sense is really not original at all. Philosophical errors are reducible in principle to exaggeration or defect. This is a corollary of the principle that being and truth are convertible. Nothing which is, is essentially false. These two possible errors into which thought may fall, namely, exaggeration and defect, have already been exhausted. They were exhausted in great part before the advent of Aristotle, and in their entirety before the birth of Christ. The Greeks had their James and Dr. Schiller in Protagoras; they had their Bradley in Parmenides; they

---

[461] LUDWIG STEIN, *Die philosophischen Strömungen der Gegenwart*, p. 7.

[462] *Present Philosophical Tendencies* (1912), p. 20.

[463] *The Reign of Religion in Contemporary Philosophy*, p. 31 *Cf.* F. C. S. SCHILLER, "Novelty," *Proceedings of the Aristotelian Society* (1921-2) p. 1.

had their M. Bergson and M. Le Roy and Professor Alexander and the whole School of Becoming in Heraclitus. They had their Dynamists and their Atomists. In a word, they saw all philosophy from its highest reaches in Aristotle to its shallows in the Sceptics. All modern aberrations were foreshadowed in the Greeks.

The Origin of First Principles

Traditional philosophy begins with common sense. Its basis is the certitudes of the immediately evident principles which are apprehended by the light of intelligence from the most simple and evident facts about us.

The problem before us now is to give a reflective and philosophical explanation of the first principles. Following in the footsteps of Aristotle, as he approaches the problem in the fourth book of his *Metaphysics*, the first problem we have to deal with is the conditions of a first principle. Aristotle enumerates three conditions.

First, the first principle ought to be one about which it is impossible to be mistaken. Men are mistaken only about those things of which they are ignorant. In order, therefore, not to be deceived, the first principle ought to be so evident as to admit of no error.

The second condition is that it be not a supposition.

The third condition is that it be *naturally known*—that is to say, it must not be reached by demonstration.[464]

The first two conditions admit of little confusion, but the same cannot be said of the third. There are two possible errors to be avoided. First, that the first principles are innate and born with us. The second, that they are the result of demonstration. In recent times certain philosophers who have given themselves over to a superficial reading of the Angelic Doctor have concluded that he identifies that which is naturally known with

[464] *Cf.* Commentary on this book by St. Thomas, lect. 6: "Manifestum est ergo quod certissimum principium sive firmissimum, tamen debet esse, ut circa id non possit errari, et quod non sit suppositum, et quod adveniat naturaliter."

what is *innate*. The reason for this confusion is that St. Thomas, in speaking of the first principles as being naturally known, calls them *innata*, *semina*, *rationes seminales*, *indita*, *naturaliter nata* and the like.[465]

Before passing to the explanation which St. Thomas gives of these terms, it is well worth while to read the opinion of Aristotle regarding *innate* first principles, in the sense that we are born with them. In the last chapter of the second book of his *Posterior Analytics*, the philosopher[466] tells us that "to suppose these treasures are innate is really absurd. If they were innate, it would follow that, possessing certain knowledge more exact than the demonstrations, we should not be conscious of them."

But the other extreme is also false, namely, to say that we derive them from demonstration. For if we had no previous knowledge, how could we draw an existing from a non-existing knowledge?[467]

If, then, the habit of first principles does not exist in us as determined and complete, and if "they are not acquired by demonstration, as the sciences are generated in us from pre-existing principles,"[468] how may they be said to be natural?

"There are in me certain natural habits, which exist partly by nature and partly through an exterior principle."[469]

The habit of first principles is exactly of this kind.

---

[465] "Primum principium quorum cognitio est nobis innata."—*De Veritate*, q. 10 art. 6 ad 6.

"Prae-existunt in nobis quaedam scientiarum *semina*—ex istis autem principiis universalibus omnia Principia sequuntur, sicut ex quibusdam *rationibus seminalibus*."—*De Veritate*, q. 11 art. 1; I d. 17 q. 1 art. 3.

"Principia ei naturaliter *indita*."—I-II q. 90 art. 3 ad 2.

"Lumen naturaliter *inditum*."—*Lib. Boet. Trinitat.*, q. 1 art. 3.

"Naturaliter *nata*."—I d. 17 q. 1 art. 3.

St. Thomas explains his meaning of *innata*: "Quaedam statim a principio naturaliter homini innotescunt absque studia et investigatione: et hujusmodi sunt prima principia; haec naturaliter homini nata sunt."—*De Virtutibus in Communi*, q. 1 art. 8.

[466] St. Thomas seldom calls Aristotle by his name, but gives him the glorious and exclusive title which testifies his great devotion to him—"The philosopher."

[467] "Omnis doctrine et omnis disciplina a praeexistenti fit cognitione."—*Post. Analy.*, lib. 1 lect. 1.

[468] *Post. Analy.*, lib. 2 lect. 20.

[469] "Sunt ergo in hominibus aliqui habitus naturales, tamquam partim a natura existentes; et partim ab exteriori principio Intellectus principiorum dicitur esse habitus naturalis."—I-II q. 51 art. 1.

"There therefore pre-exist in us certain seeds of sciences, namely, the first conceptions of the intellect, which are known immediately by the light of the active intellect working on the species abstracted from sensible matter." *And because the sense element is not the sole constituent of first principles, they have a value which may and does transcend sense.*[470]

"Immediately upon knowing what is a *whole* and what is a *part*, the intelligence knows that the whole is greater than the part. But what the *whole* is, and what the *part* is, the intelligence cannot know except by intelligible species abstracted from sensible matter."[471] Just as to expand and to grow are natural acts of the soul, not arbitrarily, but on condition of receiving food, so the habitual knowledge of first principles is in the soul, on condition that its terms come from without.[472]

These first principles which are known *quoad nos* immediately on the knowledge of the terms have been called *Dignitates* by the Scholastics, following the usage of Boethius.[473] The term was applied on account of the excellence of the proposition, inasmuch as it manifested certitudes to all other things.[474] They are *Dignitates* because they are learned from no teacher, but from the natural intelligence of the terms; they are true, not on account of anything else, but merely on account of their own evidence. The sun is manifested by no other light than itself, yet in the light of the sun all things else are manifested; so in the light of the first principles which are manifest of themselves all other things are revealed. Just as the eye sees the visible things merely on

[470] *De Magistro*, art. 1. "Cognitio principiorum accipitur a sensu, et tamen lumen quo principia cognoscuntur est innatum."—*De Trinitate*, q. 3 art. 1 ad 4. *Metaphysics*, lib. 4 lect. 6.

[471] I-II q. 51 art. 1. "Ipsa principia immediata non per aliquod medium extrinsecum cognoscuntur sed per cognitionem propriam terminorum ... quia in talibus propositionibus ut supra dictum est praedicatum est in ratione subjecti."—*Post. Analy.*, lib. 1 lect. 7. *De Veritate*, q. 8 art. 15 c.

[472] CAJETAN in I-II q. 51 art. 1. Sylvester Fer. in *C. G.*, lib. 1 c. 2 no. ii.

[473] "Quaedam sunt dignitates, vel propositiones per se notae communiter omnibus."—I-II q. 94 art. 2. *Metaphysics*, lib. 3 lect. 5.

[474] "Et in talibus utimur nomine praedicto, scilicet Dignitatis vel maximae propositionis, propter hujusmodi principiorum certitudinem ad manifestandum alia."—*Post. Analy.*, lib. 1 lect. 5.

condition of turning itself upon them, so the intelligence sees the first principles on condition of turning its light on the terms.[475]

First principles, then, are not of psychological origin, nor the fruit of a subjective interpretation of mental data, nor the urge of the will. Their sole explanation is in the intellect as a faculty, which belongs to man in virtue of his human nature.[476] Experience gives the matter. Abstraction is the necessary condition, and the objective and immediate evidence the formal reason of the consent.[477]

Which is the First Principle?

The conditions which Aristotle laid down for a first principle were threefold: it must admit of no error, it must not be conditional, and it must be naturally known. It remains now to determine which principle fulfils these three conditions.

Everything is intelligible only in function of being. In the ontological order, *being is first*, and without being nothing is known.

A judgment is the composition and division of concepts. The first judgment in the ontological order, in the sense of being the most fundamental, must be a judgment of affirmation, and the

[475] "Dicamus igitur primo, quod *Dignitas* est, ut dicit Boetius, propositio quam propter sui evidentiam quisque probat auditam ... Quia sicut extra, quaedam visibilia sunt non ad lucem alienam super se cadentem, sed sua propria luce manifesta sunt, sicut sol, sub cujus luce omnia alia videntur ab intellectu, quorum luce omnia alia manifestantur, et haec apud se habet intellectus et sunt in ipso sicut prima instrumenta, per quae accipit omnia aliarum scientiarum. In omnibus scibilibus nihil accipit quod est contra illa, et per singularem intellectum accipit illam, nullo alio indigens, nisi quod extendat intellectum ad illa, sicut visus accipit per se visibilia, nullo indigens nisi quod convertat visum ad ea."—ALBERTUS MAGNUS, *Post. Analy.*, lib. 1 tract. 3 c. 2.

The first principles may be divided into two classes: first, the complex; and secondly, the non-complex. Such Dignitates belong to the first, as "the whole is greater than any of its parts," or "things which are equal to the same thing are equal to each other." Such propositions belong to the *order of generation.* The second class, the *non-complex*, is the first principle underlying all others in the ontological order, and which serves as the premise of the first syllogism. It is with the non-complex that we concern ourselves from this point on: "Prima principia ... sive sint complexa, ut dignitates, sive incomplexa, sicut ratio entis."—*De Veritate*, q. 11 art. 1 c.

[476] "Intellectus principiorum consequitur ipsam naturam humanam."—II-II q. 5 art. 4 ad 3.

[477] T. RICHARD, *Philosophie du Raisonnement* (1918), p. 175.

second a negation; for there is no modality more ultimate than that of affirmation or negation.[478] The supreme judgment will therefore be: *Being is, non-Being is not.* This principle of identity is not purely tautological, as Kant believed.

The Angelic Doctor sums up these fundamental modalities in these words: "That which first falls in our apprehension is being, and in function of being all things are understood. Hence the first undemonstrable first principle, which is that we cannot affirm and deny a thing at the same time, is founded upon the reason of being and non-being, and upon this principle all others are founded."[479] In the logical order, this principle states the impossibility of affirming and denying the same attribute of a subject at the same time and under the same formal relation. In the real order, it states the impossibility of a thing being and not being at the same time and under the same formal relation.[480]

---

[478] "Aliqua dicuntur addere supra ens, in quantum exprimunt ipsius modum qui nomine ipsius entis non exprimitur."—*De Veritate*, q. 1 art. 1.

"Identitas est unitas vel unio; aut ex quo illa quae dicuntur idem, sunt plura secundum esse, et tamen dicuntur idem in quantum aliquo uno conveniunt, aut quia unum sunt secundum esse, sed intellectus utitur eo ut pluribus ad hoc quod relationem intelligat, sicut cum *dicitur aliquid esse idem sibi ipsi.* Tunc enim intellectu utitur eo quod est unum secundum rem ut duobus."—*Metaphysics*, lib.5 lect. 11.

[479] I-II q. 94 art. 2. "In principiis per se notis, ordo quidam invenitur, ut quaedam in aliis implicite contineantur, sicut omnia principia reducuntur ad hoc, sicut ad primum, impossibile est simul affirmare et negare."—II-II q. 1 art. 7.

"Nec aliquid hac operatione potest mente concipi, nisi intelligatur ens. Et quia hoc principium, impossibile est esse et non esse simul, dependet ex intellectu entis ... ideo hoc etiam principium *est naturaliter primum in secunda operatione intellectus*, scilicet componentis et dividentis."—*Metaphysics*, lib. 4 lect. 6.

[480] The principle of contradiction is the first principle in the speculative order. In the practical order, it is *good must be done and evil avoided*, and this is the natural foundation of moral science (I-II q. 94 art. 2). See this first principle worked out in a critical study of Sociological Morality by Monseigneur S. DEPLOIGE, LL.D., Ph.D., *Le Conflit de la Morale et de la Sociologie*, 3rd edition, 1923.

It must be noted from the outset that the *time element* does not enter into the principle of contradiction. There are many who express it as the impossibility of being and not being at *the same time*. Aristotle takes the precaution of adding the words, "the same subject considered under the same relation."

Cardinal Mercier shows textually that the Greek word (ἁμα), which is translated usually as "at the same time," really means "at once or together" *(a la fois, ensemble)*. It is the relation of the subject and the predicate (which are concepts of the intellect, and not images of the sense) which is the basis of the principle. The principle of contradiction, then, is not subject to evolution; it is beyond time, and consequently beyond evolution. "Universalia sunt aeterna, inquantum ab omni tempore."—*Métaphysique générale*, pp. 265-266.

"Impossibile eidem simul inesse et non inesse idem, sed addendum est, *et secundum idem.*"—*Metaphysics*, lib. 4 lect. 6.

The principle is valid for both orders, the logical and the real. Ideas attain things, in the sense already defined. There is no question of a separation of the two orders. Furthermore, to reduce the being to a subjective form of the mind, and the principle of contradiction to a merely simple logical law, and not an ontological one, is to identify two notions which are manifestly distinct: the *impossible* (or the unrealizable) and the *inconceivable.* It also means to doubt the extra-mental possibility of the absurd. He who doubts the ontological value of the notion of *being* and of the principle of contradiction ought to say: "A square circle is *inconceivable*, but it is not *unrealizable* outside the mind."[481] This first principle is valid in both orders because being is valid and necessary in both orders. Being is the condition of its own negation, as it is the condition of its own destruction. Being identifies itself with all there is, there being no differences other than being.[482]

No speculative principle of any science extends beyond the range of these first principles, because on these principles all knowledge virtually depends. [483]

The first principle of thought is the foundation of all our intellectual constructions. There is no certitude in the last analysis unless they can be resolved back to the first principles of thought.[484] Only on condition that the first principles are firm and stable will the conclusions be firm and stable,[485] and the nearer our conclusions are to the first principles the more certain they are, just as the nearer a body is to the sun the more it participates in its light.[486]

---

[481] GARRIGOU-LAGRANGE, *Dieu : son Existence et sa Nature*, p. 125.

[482] *Cf.* Cardinal MERCIER, *Métaphysique générale*, p. 263. In the order of *reduction* the principle of contradiction is said to be the first principle.

Cf. Post. Analy., lib. 1 lect. 29.

[483] I-II q. 3 art. 6. "Insunt enim nobis naturaliter quaedam principia prima complexa omnibus nota, ex quibus ratio procedit ad cognoscendum in actu conclusiones quae in praedictis principiis potentialiter continentur, sive per inventionem propriam, sive per doctrinam alienam, sive per revelationem divinam in quibus omnibus modis cognoscendis homo juvatur ex principiis naturaliter cognitis."—Quod. 8 q. 2 art. 3 c. *De Veritate*, q. 10 art. 13; I-II q. 91 art. 2; q. 112 art. 5.

[484] "Nullius scientiae certitudo potest esse nisi per resolutionem in prima sui principia."—1 d. 35 q. 1 art 3 ad 2.

[485] "Non enim potest esse aliqua firmitas vel certitudo in his quae sunt a principiis, nisi principia essent firmiter stabilita."—*De Veritate*, q. 16 art. 2.

[486] "Quanto medium demonstrationis est propinquius prime principio, tanto

This intimate connection between the first principles and knowledge of any kind is repeated throughout the works of the Angelic Doctor. The relation between the two is not accidental but essential. If some one should err regarding the principle that the whole is greater than any of its parts, geometry would be impossible, because it is often necessary to have recourse to this principle in some of the succeeding operations.[487] But if this is true for geometry, it is much more true of the principles which underlie all knowledge, for ultimately we accept conclusions because of the principles.[488] So thoroughly do the first principles of thought, and in particular the principle of contradiction, penetrate our conclusions, that given any conclusion of any human science whatsoever, and an intellect capable of tracing premisses, we could eventually trace the given conclusion to the first principle which prompted it. It is merely a question of finding a first mover in the rational order. We cannot go back infinitely; otherwise we should never have the present movement. We must eventually come to some active principle which sets all the others in movement, and this is the principle of contradiction. St. Thomas sums up this doctrine admirably in his commentary on Aristotle in these words: "Nothing can be known by the intellect except in function of being. Since, therefore, this principle—it is impossible for a thing to be and not be under the same relation—depends on the knowledge of being—just as this principle, the whole is greater than any of its parts, depends on a knowledge of the whole and of the part—it is said to be naturally the first principle of the second operation of the intelligence, namely, judgment. No other judgment is intelligible except in virtue of this judgment. Just as the whole and the part are not known except in function of being, so in like manner this principle, the whole is greater than any of its parts, is known only in virtue of the above-mentioned principle."[489]

---

demonstratio est potior (*Post. Analy.*, lib. 1 lect. 38) ... sicut intensio lucidi attenditur per accessum ad aliquid summe lucidem cui quanto aliquis magis appropinquat, tanto est magis lucidum."—I-II q. 22 art. 2 ad 1.

[487] "Si quis errat circa hoc principium, tutus majus est sua parte, non posset habere scientiam geometricam, quia oportet multum recedere a veritate in sequentibus."—I-II q. 65 art. 1 ad 4.

[488] "Sed conclusiones scimus et eis credimus propter principia."—Ibid.

[489] "In prima quidem operatione est aliquod primum, quod cadit in conceptione intellectus, scilicet hoc quod dico ens. Et quia hoc principium, impossibile est esse et non

This first principle fulfils the three conditions which Aristotle laid down for a first principle. It admits of no error; it is not conditional nor hypothetical, and it is naturally known, once the terms of the proposition are known. This first principle is the "urge," or the motive-force of human reasoning. What the determination of form and end is for plants, what instinct is for animals, this and more the first principle is for man. There are no breaks in nature. That water-tight compartments in an intelligible universe are quite impossible, we concede even with emphasis. The acts of reason are like the acts of nature. Art imitates nature so far as it possibly can.

In certain things nature acts from necessity, and never fails in that particular activity. The bird builds a nest, the bee makes honey—all from the necessity of instinct. Now, if the acts of reason imitate nature, there must be a certain analogical necessity in the intelligence. This necessity is found in the mind's assent to first principles, in which there can never be a defect of truth, and by which the certitude of knowledge is acquired.[490] In this sense we are determined. There is no liberty regarding first principles, as there is no liberty for an acorn not to become an oak. Our assent to first principles is necessary and spontaneous.[491]

Fundamentally, there are only two errors possible regarding the nature of first principles. These errors arise from a denial of one of the essential elements of knowledge.

---

esse simul, dependet ex intellectu entis, sicut hoc principium omne totum est majus sua parte, ex intellectu totius et partis; ideo hoc etiam principium est naturaliter primum in secunda operatione intellectus, scilicet componentis et dividentis. Nec aliquis potest secundum hanc operationem intellectus aliquid intelligere, nisi hoc principio intellecto. Sicut enim totum et partes non intelliguntur nisi intellecto ente, ita nec hoc principium omne totum est majus sua parte, nisi intellecto praedicto principio firmissime."—*Metaphysics*, lib. 4 lect. 6.

[490] "Attendendum est autem, quod actus rationis sunt similes quantum ad aliquid actibus naturae, unde et ars imitatur naturam inquantum potest ... In quibusdam enim natura de necessitate agit, ita quod non est deficere ... Est enim aliquis rationis processus necessitatem inducens, in quo non est possibile esse veritatis defectum, et per hujus rationis processum scientiae certitudo acquiri tur."—*Post. Analy.*, lib. 1 lect. 1.

[491] "Prima principia intelligibilia quibus ex necessitate intellectus assentit."—*Perihermenias*, lib. 1 lect. 14.

"Principia quae quidem homo non habet necesse addiscere aut invenire, ne oportet in infinitum procedere; sed eorum notitiam naturaliter *habet*."—*De Trinitate Boethi*, q. 6 art. 4 c.

In Greek philosophy the two errors are represented by Parmenides on the one hand, and Heraclitus on the other. Parmenides denied the data given by the senses. In denying this, he denied multiplicity and becoming. He reduced the real to the rational, being to mind, the concrete to the abstract, and the transcendence of God into immanence of the spirit. The modern followers of Parmenides are the Italian idealists.[492]

Heraclitus, on the other hand, fell into pure empiricism. The only reality, therefore, is that which is revealed by the senses, namely, becoming. He reduced the rational to the real, the spirit to the sensible, and God to the world. The modern followers are the philosophers of becoming.[493]

The two errors of Greek thought, one of which is acosmic, the other atheistic, are both half-truths, one refusing to open its eyes upon the world of sensible movement, the other refusing to reflect upon the world which it sees.

The truth is to be found in the philosophy of Aristotle and St. Thomas and the tradition of common sense. With Heraclitus, it admits the reality of becoming. With Parmenides, it admits the primacy of being over becoming. "Becoming is too genuinely real to be called nothing, as Parmenides did; yet it is not real enough to be called being, as Heraclitus did. It is therefore between being and nothing. It is a potency."[494]

But why is modern philosophy so adverse to these first principles of the intelligence?

The general reason given is this: the first principles of thought are intelligible only on the condition of a static universe. For their right understanding there must be substances which remain

---

[492] GENTILE, "Niente è reale fuori del pensiero," *Teoria generale dello spirito*, p. 254. Idealism is "una concezione che risolve il mondo nell' atto spirituale ed atto del pensiero, unificando l'infinità varieta naturale ed humana in una assoluta unita, in cui l' umano è divino ed il divino è umano."—Ibid., p. 271.

[493] "There are no things; there are only actions. Things and states are but views taken of becoming by the mind."—*L'Évolution Créatrice*, p. 270.

[494] C. JOURNET, "L'Existence de Dieu," *Revue des Jeunes*. "La philosophie a pour principes formels les premiers principes saisis dans la notion de l'être et dont la lumière intelligible fait toute sa force (*versus* Positivistes) et d'autre part elle a pour matière l'expérience et les faits (*versus* l'Intellectualisme Pur); les faits les plus simples et les plus évidents sur lesquels elle se fonde pour s'élever aux causes ou aux raisons qui en donnet le pourquoi suprême."—JACQUES MARITAIN, *L'Introduction à la Philosophie*, vol. i. p. 94.

fixed throughout the flux of things. But there are not things, there are only actions. What we call a thing is merely the solidification of the flow of things wrought by our intelligence.[495] In pure change there is a change without a thing that changes. Movement has no necessity of a mover. It is in vain that one seeks in change the things that change. It is only provisorily and to satisfy our imagination that we seek for the thing that moves.[496] In fact, *nothing is, everything becomes.* "There is no difference between a glass of water, sugar, and the process of dissolution of the sugar in the water."[497] Briefly, existence is becoming.[498] This notion that everything is becoming and that nothing endures is difficult to grasp, as we find nothing like it in nature. Professor Aliotta, in order to help our imagination, has represented the Eternal Devenir as a flowing river without bed, without shores, without mouth and without source. Another figure which may enable us to grasp the idea has been given by the former disciple of the French Heraclitus. Imagine, he says, a snowball rolling down a mountain side, gradually gaining in size as it descends. Now make abstraction from the mountain and the snow; "abstract everything but pure rolling, and you have an idea of the substance of things."[499]

The obvious conclusion is that if nothing endures and everything becomes, the first principles of thought are meaningless. This is precisely the conclusion of the majority of modern thinkers. James was so impressed by the Bergsonian Devenir, which, he says, made him bolder in his anti-intellectualism, that he finally came to give up logic, fairly and squarely. Dr. Schiller treats first principles as pure conventionalities; M. Le Roy, as mental creations which we may leap over;[500] and Mr. Holmes writes that "for him who looks at things from the standpoint of the idea of evolution they are as so much 'hot air.'"[501] The only determinant, therefore, of any

[495] "Il n'y a pas de choses, il n'y a que des actions."—*L'Evolution Créatrice*, p. 270. "La chose résulte d'une solidification opérée par notre entendement."—Ibid.

[496] "En vain on cherche sous le changement la chose qui change; c'est toujours provisoirement et pour satisfaire notre imagination."—Ibid., p. 325.

[497] Ibid., p 10.

[498] "Le changement c'est la substance," Ibid., p. 26.

[499] JACQUES MARITAIN, *La Philosophie Bergsonienne*, p. 27.

[500] *Revue de Métaphysique et de Morale* (Juillet 1907), pp. 480-88.

[501] EDMOND G. HOLMES, M.A., "The Idea of Evolution and the Idea of God,"

ontological position is "in the end purely a matter of one's personal taste at any given time."[502]

The basis of the argument is the "lyricism of science." Biology proves evolution. Physics proves relativism. Therefore philosophical conclusions are relative and evolving. There are no necessary principles. Evolution is a presupposition for philosophy. It is thought to be that which no living man should question. But grant that it is a presupposition. Is it valid? If we can answer this question, we have the solution, not only of the modern objection to the first principles, but also of Freudian interpretations of mystic states, Einsteinian interpretations of knowledge, psychological interpretations of moral judgments, and naturalistic interpretations of the supernatural.

The validity of the presupposition will be judged in the light of the answer to this question.

Grant that evolution is a scientifically established fact. Does it follow that philosophical principles and the subject-matter of higher sciences are evolving?

We may here take occasion to correct a false impression about the attitude of Neo-Scholasticism towards modern evolution. Common-sense philosophy has never seen anything intrinsically impossible about it. In fact, many of the early fathers saw in it something very beautiful, as may be found in St. Augustine and the Alexandrine School with their doctrine of the *rationes seminales*. There is nothing in evolution which shocks the Scholastic. It seems very much in accordance with the Scholastic principle that things gradually attain their perfection. Nothing is further from the truth than the words of a recent writer in the *Hibbert Journal*: "Scholastic Logic has no use for the idea of evolution, and the idea of evolution has no use for Scholastic Logic."[503] The long list of modern Scholastics who have at their head such men as Wassman and Mendel is a sufficient answer to such an ill-

---

Hibbert Journal, vol. xxi. No. 3 (January 1923), p. 235.

[502] C. J. DUCASSE, "A Defence of Ontological Liberalism," *The Journal of Philosophy*, vol. xxi. No. 13 (19th June 1924), p. 337. *Cf.* CHARLES A. BECKWITH, *The Idea of God* (1923), pp. 5-38; BERTRAND RUSSELL, "Essence of Religion," *Hibbert Journal*, vol. ix. No. 41, p. 50; H. A. YOUTZ, *Enlarging Conception of God*, p. 28.

[503] EDMOND G. HOLMES, "The Idea of Evolution and the Idea of God," *Hibbert Journal*, vol. xxi. No. 2 (January 1923), p. 235.

founded statement. It is true that Scholasticism is opposed to a certain form of evolution, and that form sets out as its basic principle that the ontological greater comes from that which is ontologically less. But the whole world of common sense is opposed such a crudity, and science itself finds no interest in it.

To return to the point. Suppose we grant that science has proved evolution. Does it follow that first principles are evolving, and that contradictories may be true and swallowed up one in the other? This is the assumption of modern philosophy and the great point at issue. As regards the fact of movement and becoming there can be no doubt. M. Bergson and St. Thomas are in agreement. There is only a difference of terminology. The former writes: "Speculation must begin with the fact of movement."[504] The latter: "He who is ignorant of movement is ignorant of nature."[505] How is it, then, that they arrive at totally different conclusions? It is a result of their different attitude toward the intelligence.

M. Bergson and writers of the day believe that the assimilation of the object known is according to the *nature of the thing known.* St. Thomas, on the contrary, believes that the assimilation is according to the nature of the *knower.*[506] The modern mind rests in the sense knowledge of the thing, and hence sees only the movement; the intellectual mind transcends the *sense-data*, sees the *ratio or the law of the movement.* This latter explanation alone is in accord with the nature of things. The nutritive process of the animal life never takes place until the plant life has been assimilated and adapted to the animal nature. The cognitive life begins only when sense knowledge has been assimilated according to the intellectual life of man. Assimilation, it has been shown, always takes place according to the nature of the one

[504] "C'est du mouvement que la spéculation devrait partir," *L'Évolution Créatrice*, p. 342.

[505] "Ignorato motu, ignoratur natura" (*Physics*, lib. 3 lect. 1). He speaks even of the fluidity of things: "Dicitur autem creatures fluvius, quia fluit semper de esse ad non esse per corruptionem, et de non esse ad esse per generationem" (*Sermones Festivi*, 61).

[506] See the modern objection concerning the variability of our knowledge as stated in *De Veritate*, q. 2 art. 13. God knows things; but things are variable, therefore the knowledge of God is variable.

The answer of the Angelic Doctor is the one given above: "Quod assimilatio scientis ad scitum non est secundum conformitatem naturae, sed secundum repraesentationem; *unde non oportet quod rerum variabilium sit scientia variabilis.*"—Ibid, ad 1; *Cf.* ad 3.

assimilating, and never exclusively according to the nature of the thing assimilated. Knowledge, being an assimilation, follows exactly the same process if the universe is continuous, and this contemporaries profess to believe.

But this brings us back to the modern criticism of the intelligence. Does not the intelligence distort reality if it does not see it as it is? It does distort reality if it does not see it as it is in its nature, but otherwise not. He who knows the *ratio* of a thing knows the thing better than he who knows only juxtaposed notes. Sense knowledge reveals the staff bent in the water. Intellectual knowledge knows the *reason* why it appears bent. Sense knowledge sees the sun rise and set; intellectual knowledge knows the *reason* of such a popular belief. The intelligence penetrates into the reason and into the nature of things, and in doing so does not distort the sensible reality, but renders it intelligible. This is precisely what it does in the case of movement. Sense reveals the flux of things. The intelligence sees the *reason* of the flux.[507] The sense sees the dilation of iron by heat, or the "fact;" the intellect sees the "that on account of which."

Because then, there is evolution in the sensible universe, it does not follow that first principles are evolving. "Contingent things can be considered in two ways: either as contingent, or as containing some element of necessity, since *every contingent thing has in it something necessary*: for example, that Socrates runs, is in itself contingent; but the relation of running to motion is necessary, for it is necessary that Socrates should move if he runs. Now, contingency arises from matter; for contingency is of that which may either be or not be. But potentiality belongs to matter: whereas necessity results from the nature of form, because whatever flows from form belongs of necessity to the informed subject. But matter is the individualizing principle: whereas the universal comes from the abstraction of the form from the particular matter. Moreover, it was laid down (article 1) that the

[507] "Scire simpliciter est cognoscere causam propter quam res est et non potent aliter se habere."—*Post. Analy.*, lib. 1 lect. 4. *Metaphysics*, lib. 2 lect. 4.

"Forma rei intellectae est in intellectu universaliter et immaterialiter et immobiliter."—I q. 84 art. 1.

Material plurality means nothing. It is vanity to know individuals for the mere sake of knowing them (Introd. to *De Coelo*). The intellectual element is necessary to seize the *bond* or the *ratio of the facts*.

intellect of itself and directly has the universal for its object, while the object of the sense is singular, which in a certain way is the indirect object of the intellect, as we have seen above (*Ibid.*). Therefore the contingent, considered as such, is known directly by the sense and indirectly by the intellect; while the *universal and necessary principles of contingent things are known only by the intellect.* Hence, if we consider the objects of science in their universal principles, then all science is of necessary things. But if we consider the things themselves, thus some sciences are of necessary things, some of contingent things."[508]

What applies to contingent things applies for exactly the same reason to movement and to evolution. "*Every movement presupposes something immutable*; for when a change of quality occurs, the substance remains unmoved; and when there is a change of substantial form, matter remains unmoved. *Moreover, the various conditions of movable things are themselves immutable*; for instance, though Socrates be not always sitting, yet it is an unchangeable truth that whenever he does sit he remains in one place. For this reason there *is nothing to hinder our having an immutable science of movable or evolving things.*"[509]

In all things of this world there is necessity, both absolute and conditional. The first kind of necessity is found in the order of being, which is, strictly speaking, the field of metaphysics or the science of *being* as *being*. The second kind of necessity is in the order of essential principles, and the third in the order of properties flowing from these principles.[510] Some of these kinds of necessities may not always exist, so far as their time element is concerned, but they are eternal in relation to their causes.[511] And not only are there immutable relations linked to causes, but also

---

[508] I q. 86 art. 3 c.

[509] I q. 84 art. 1 ad 3. *Cf.* CAJETAN in I q. 86 art. 4 x.

[510] "Diversimode autem ex diversis causis necessitas sumitur in rebus creatis ... Uno quidem modo per ordinem ad esse ejus cujus sunt ... alio vero modo ex principiis essentialibus ... tertio modo per ordinem principiorum essentialium ad proprietates."—*C. G.*, lib. 2 c. 30.

St. Thomas has a long commentary on the necessity in generated things in *Physics*, lib. 1 lect 15, Sylvester Ferrariensis on necessity in both transitive and immanent action (*C. G.*, lib. 2 c. 30).

[511] "Quaedam non sunt semper secundum tempus, sunt autem semper per comparationem ad causam."—*Post. Analy.*, lib. 1 lect. 16.

to antecedents, to ends, and immutable relations of parts and wholes and of substances and accidents.[512]

Furthermore, has not evolution its laws? Do not these laws preside throughout the whole evolutionary process? At least, the law of evolution must be constant, otherwise there would be no evolution. Does not this law hold good under given conditions? Is not evolution an evolution of conditions, but not of laws? Cannot philosophy study these laws in their fixity and permanence? *The law of evolution*, as it is called, does not mean that the law is evolving. In a word, nothing seems to render certain immutable things necessary more than a universe in which there is a flux. "Evolution supposes that a reality, while remaining itself in a certain fashion, becomes another thing. It postulates the analogy of being. If all is in all, if being is identical with itself, becoming is impossible."[513]

In conclusion, evolution in the empirical order does not mean that the fundamental laws of being—that is, of thought and reality—are evolving. Grant that evolution is scientifically demonstrated; then, instead of denying necessary laws, it presupposes them and is intelligible only in virtue of them.

The error is to remain in sense knowledge. As if writing for the philosophy of today, St. Thomas says: "Because they observed that all bodies are mobile, and considered them ever to be in a state of flux, they were of the opinion that we can have no certain knowledge of the true nature of things. For what is in a continual state of flux cannot be grasped with any degree of certitude, for it passes away ere the mind can form a judgment thereon ..." This reads as if St. Thomas had the works of Professor Alexander and M. Bergson before his eyes.

The solution is to transcend phenomena and work with the intellect, which seizes the *intelligibility of evolution*. "The intellect, according to its own mode, receives, under conditions of immateriality and immobility, the species of material and mobile bodies: for the received is in the receiver according to the mode of the receiver. *We must therefore conclude, that through the intellect the*

[512] I q. 21 art. 1 ad 3.

[513] N. BALTHASAR, *L'Être et les Principes métaphysiques*, p. 7. *Cf.* T. RICHARD, *Philosophie du Raisonnement*, p. 237.

soul knows bodies by knowledge which is immaterial, universal and necessary."[514]

There is yet another objection to this fundamental law drawn from the idea of *nothing.* It runs as follows: "Absolute Being, according to the law of contradiction, must have as its contradictory Absolute not-Being, Absolute Nothingness. Is this a reasonable or even a possible conception? Is Absolute Nothingness a concept which the mind can bring itself to entertain? ... If they were mutually exclusive they would be mutually destructive; for if Absolute not-Being were a valid concept, Absolute Nothingness would be an entity, and we should have to predicate existence of that which is *ex hypothesi* the negation of all existence. In other words, we should have to admit that there was *such a thing as nothing.*"[515]

Notice that the principle of contradiction is used to show that there is no principle of contradiction. Can there be any greater or stronger argument than this for the statement that the principle of contradiction is the basic law of thought and reality?

The argument of Mr. Holmes has as its inspiration twenty-five pages of M. Bergson in which he seeks to prove that the idea of nothing is a pseudo-idea,[516] because it is neither an image, nor a positive idea nor a negative idea. He thus hopes to escape the problem of existence which implied a nothingness or a non-being.

Apart from more or less important misunderstandings of the real nature of the law of contradiction, and granting with Mr. Holmes that it is extremely difficult for us to *imagine* a nothingness, we pass to consider the backbone of the argument. What is the idea of non-being which is implied by the principle of contradiction? It certainly is the negation of the content of the idea of being. But does the negation of the content of the idea of being imply the affirmation of a substantial reality? In mathematics the negation of 3, which is −3, does not imply another reality. The idea of non-being or nothingness, then, is not an "entity," as Mr. Holmes supposes, and hence there can be

[514] I q. 84 art. 1 c.

[515] EDMOND G. HOLMES, *Dying Lights and Dawning*, pp. 61-2.

[516] *L'Évolution Créatice*, pp. 298-323.

no necessity to admit "such a thing as nothing." A negative judgment supposes a positive judgment, but it supposes only that. It is absurd to ask that another positive judgment supplant the one which was denied. To say that "this man has no children" does not mean that he has something else besides children.[517]

Mr. Holmes has this to say of St. Thomas: "The standing still of the sun and the moon at the bidding of Joshua was a trivial miracle compared with the standing still of human thought at the precise points which it reached in the respective minds of Aristotle and St. Thomas."[518]

But if thought stood still at those points, and if the philosophy of St. Thomas has nothing "in common with modern developments," how explain the fact that the modern misconceptions of the first principles of thought have their solution in the *Summa Theologica*? Can any one doubt that this reply of St. Thomas to another is the answer to the objection just given: *not-being has nothing in itself whereby it can be known; yet it is known in so far as the intellect renders it knowable?*" St. Thomas thus admits the psychological bent of the mind to conceive "nothing" as "something;" but, on the other hand, he does not allow that bent to throw him into a confusion worse confounded by identifying a negation with a something. The answer of the Angelic Doctor is simply this: *thinking an object existent* does not equal *thinking that an object exists.* The ideal and the real are distinct. The nought of thought is not the nought of reality. The whole argument would never have arisen had philosophers considered mathematical zero. This is played with in equations, which help in the solution of physical problems. What is done by the mathematician with "zero" may surely be done by the metaphysician with non-being!

From a consideration of the presupposition of modern philosophy we pass on to a more direct consideration of its major proposition, in virtue of which it denies the absolute nature of the first principles of thought. It must first be noted that a direct refutation of a philosophy which denies the first principles is impossible. The reason is that there is no other prior proposition

[517] JACQUES MARITAIN, *La Philosophie Bergsonienne* (1914), pp. 366, 367.
[518] *Op. cit.*, p. 50.

in knowledge from which an inference may be made.[519] The refutation must therefore be effected indirectly. Because the refutation of necessity is indirect, Aristotle, and after him St. Thomas, believe that those who hold pertinaciously to such opinions cannot readily be dispossessed of them.[520]

If the major proposition of the modern philosophy is true, namely, if "there is only change and nothing which changes," if "change has no need of a support," and if "movement does not imply a movable thing,"[521] then certain consequences follow which by their absurdity nullify it.

(1) If everything is movement, and there is nothing which underlies the movement, how explain our abiding consciousness of ourselves? We do not pass away with our thoughts any more than the bed of the river passes away with the flowing water. We distinguish ourselves from our thoughts; we regard them merely as transient events throughout the permanent duration of our life. There are no thoughts without a thinker, no dreams without a dreamer, no volitions without a will. A new mental attitude or a new thought does not make a new thinker, any more than a new suit of clothes makes a new man. The important distinction between an accident and a substance must not be lost sight of, under penalty of dissolving the universe into an irrational chaos. In the face of this objection some moderns have attempted to explain the permanence of consciousness by the metaphor of a melody. A melody is nothing but a succession of harmonious sounds. This is quite true, but we must not forget that every melody implies an abiding something which retains the successive

[519] "Quod autem non possit simpliciter demonstrari, probat ex hoc, quod non contingit facere syllogismum ad hoc principium demonstrandum ex aliquo principio magis noto; quod oportet si contingeret illud principium simpliciter demonstrare."—*Metaphysics*, lib. 11 lect. 5.

[520] "Si qui incidunt in praedictas opiniones non propter aliquam rationem, ita quod ex pertinacia non concedant aliquid neque inquirant rationem eorum quae dicuntur, sed pertinaciter inhaerent his, quae opinabantur, non facile est eis solvere hujusmodi opinionem."—*Metaphysics*, lib. 11 lect. 6.

[521] "Il y a des changements, mais il n'y a pas de choses qui changent; le changement n'a pas besoin d'un support ... le mouvement n'implique pas un mobile."—*Conférence d'Oxford*, p. 24.

Cf. *L'Évolution Créatrice*, pp. 12, 139, 203, 260, 279, 395, 398, etc. *Cf.* S. ALEXANDER, *op. cit.*

notes. We would never know there was a melody, unless we could retain the notes.

(2) If there is nothing that remains throughout movement, how can we distinguish the point of departure from the point of arrival? And if there is no distinction between the two, why should there be movement? The thing is already there.[522] Since one thing cannot become another for the very reason that there are no things, then there can never be movement. There is nothing into which things could transform themselves. Hence, to say everything evolves is to say that nothing evolves.

(3) If there is no enduring substance, then the least change is a change of entire being, and there are only continual creations which succeed one another. The past, as such, continues in fact to exist by continuous creation, and you have the absurd conclusion that *that which is no more, is.* It is truly indeed "the philosophy of nothing which changes."[523]

(4) Motion can never be an end in itself. We tend to "something;" we never tend to a tendency. The object of the will, for example, cannot be the act of willing, because the object of the will is some definite end, as the object of vision is colour. As it is impossible that the first thing visible should be the act of vision, because every act of vision is of some visible object, so it is impossible that the act of willing should be the end of the will.[524] Every being of its nature tends formally to one thing: the eye to colour, the ear to sound, the intellect to truth. For this reason it is impossible that anything should tend to motion as motion, because motion is disparate. To say that motion, which

---

[522] "Si enim idem foret esse in termino ad quem, et non esse, nulla ratio esset quare moveretur ad terminum ad quem aliquid quod nondum est in illo, quia jam esset ibi."—*Metaphysics*, lib. 11 lect. 6.

Evolution is possible only on condition of the analogy of being. The Non-being of Becoming, as Evolution, is not absolute, but *relative.* It implies a reality—the potency of Being.

Cf. N. BALTHASAR, *op. cit.*, p. 8.

[523] JACQUES MARITAIN, *La Philosophie Bergsonienne* (Paris, 1914), p. 132. *Cf.* The four arguments against the Heracleitan philosophy in *Metaphysics*, lib. 11 lect. 6. St. Thomas asks the question of a philosopher who believes "everything becomes:" "Why take the food a doctor orders?" If there is no *fixed nature* in food, why take this particular food which the doctor commands, any more than any other?

[524] I-II q. 1 art. 1 ad 2.

is disparate, has as its end a unity, is to say that motion is at once disparate and a unity.[525]

Substance is a primordial determination of being, and is required to furnish the reason of the being of movement or juxtaposed notes. And substance is not like the core of an apple hidden away from the surface; it is not extent, as M. Bergson imagines, for extent is an *accident.* Movement is possible only on condition of substance. Denying substance, modern thinkers must therefore logically deny movement.

Among the particular arguments against first principles, perhaps none is more common than that based on the immutability of essences. In the words of one of the modern philosophers it may be stated as follows: "The Law of Identity owes its importance to its connexion with the doctrine of essences, in virtue of which it is the parent of all *a priori* propositions ... This law affirms that every being is or contains its own nature or essence. The doctrine of essences is the outcome of a purely static view of the world of our experience. The classes into which things seem to be divided are supposed to have been what they are today ever since the world began ... But *what if* the nature of a being is to become what it is not, to transform nature, to transcend itself?"[526] In such a case there is nothing left of identity.

This argument is of great historical interest. It is nothing more than a repetition of a thirteenth-century fictitious objection which St. Thomas urged against his own doctrine to make it clearer.[527] The modern version of it is much less forceful, being purely hypothetical. Apart from this consideration, what is to be said regarding the transformation of species? Can they transform? To transform may mean one of two things. It may

---

525 Movement cannot ever be on account of movement. "Cum enim natura semper in unum tendat determinate, non se habens ad multa, impossibile est quod aliqua natura inclinet ad motum secundum seipsum, *eo quod in quolibet motu* difformitas quaedam est in quantum non eodem modo se habet *quod movetur*; *uniformitas mobilis est contra motus rationem.* Unde natura numquam inclinat ad motum propter movere, sed propter aliquid determinatum."—*De Pot.*, q. 5 art. 5.

526 EDMOND G. HOLMES, M.A., "The Idea of Evolution and the Idea of God," *Hibbert Journal*, vol. xxi. No. 2 (January 1923), p. 240. Italics are ours. *Cf. Dying Lights and Dawning*, same author, p. 73.

527 I q. 84 art. 1 obj. 3.

mean that the essence is, *per se*, the term of the motion, or merely that something joined with the essence is the term of the motion.[528] In the first case the species is entirely lost. In the second kind of transformation the species remains, just as we remain man amid all the vicissitudes, physical and psychological, of our earthly existence. In both of these transformations there is something which remains; otherwise we should never know there was a change. In the accidental transformation the substance remains immutable; in the substantial transformation the prime matter remains immutable.[529] Neither of these transformations offers any difficulty to the principle of identity. In both cases each thing is its nature. If the nature remains, as in accidental transformation, it is still identical to itself. If the nature is completely lost, it ceases to be *that thing* and it becomes *that other thing*, in which case the intellect knows it as such. When Scholastics say that essences change, they merely mean that, if A substantially changes, it ceases to be *that thing*; just as, if you add or substract, *e.g* 3, from a given number, you change the number. If a cow should evolve into a horse, it is no longer a cow, but a horse. The intellect is measured by things; it draws its knowledge from reality, and thus even with a transformation of species it knows things as *they are*. *Veritas est adaequatio rei et intellectus.*

The basis of the foregoing objection is made to serve as an argument against the principle of contradiction. After quoting the principle of contradiction as it was correctly presented in a manual of Scholastic Logic,[530] a writer in the *Hibbert Journal* says: "So far, so good. But what if the idea of Being, as the one idea that underlies all others, were to be superseded by the idea of becoming—the idea of an eternal procession of Being out of

---

[528] "Dicitur enim aliquid secundum essentiam suam moveri dupliciter. Vel quia essentia est per se terminus motus ... et sic moveri per essentiam est essentiam amittere et corrumpi; vel quia est motus secundum aliquid conjunctum essentiae, quod est per se terminus motus."—1 d. 17 q. 2 art. 1 ad 3.

Cf. De Veritate, q. 1 art. 6.

[529] "Cum enim transmutatio fit secundum qualitatem, remanet substantia immobilis; et cum *transmutatur forma substantialis* remanet materia immobilis."—I q. 84 art. 1 ad 3.

"Creaturae corruptibiles, in perpetuum manent secundum materiam, sed *mutantur secundum formam substantialem*. Creaturae vero incorruptibiles permanent quidem secundum substantiam, sed sunt mutabiles secundum alia, puta secundum locum ut corpora coelestia, vel secundum affectiones ut creaturae spirituales."—I-II q. 52 art. 1.

[530] R. F. CLARKE, S.J., "Stonyhurst Series."

non-Being. In that case, what would happen to the law of contradiction?"[531] We are tempted to ask, "But what if it would not?" We pass on to the source of this writer, namely, M. Bergson, in the hope of finding some justification for the argument. In this latter author we read: "There is more in a movement than in the successive positions attributed to the moving thing, more in the becoming than in the forms traversed little by little, more in the evolution of a form than in the forms realized one after another."[532] Being and non-Being melt, therefore, into *becoming*; and the law of contradiction ceases to be a law of thought.

This argument draws its strength from an ambiguity. To say "there is more in movement than in the immobile," and more in the becoming than the mere being of a thing, may be regarded from one of two points of view. It may be considered, first of all, from the point of view of the senses, and secondly, from the point of view of the intelligence. In the sense order the *immobile* equals repose and inertia. A being which moves is more perfect than a being which does not move. Under this consideration it is true to say that there is "more in the movement than in the immobile." But in the intellectual order the *immobile* equals perfection and stability, as contrasted with repose and inertia. It is that which *is*, compared with that which is *to become*; it is the *possessing* of a perfection in contrast with the *acquiring* of a perfection. In the sensible order the immobile needs completion; in the intellectual order the immobile already possesses it.[533] Hence it is untrue to say that in the intellectual order the movement is more than the immobile. The man who already possesses a fortune is worth more than Mr. Micawber who is continually "waiting for something to turn up." Constancy of the

---

[531] EDMOND G. HOLMES, "The Idea of Evolution and the Idea of God," *Hibbert Journal*, vol. xxi. No. 2 (January 1923), p. 236.

[532] "Il y a plus dans un mouvement que dans les positions successives attribuées au mobile, plus dans l'évolution de la forme que dans les formes réalisées l'une après l'autre ... Au fond de la philosophie antique gît nécessairement ce postulat: il y a plus dans l'immobile que dans le mouvement."—*L'Évolution Créatrice*, p. 341.

[533] "Contemplation, for example, is not a movement, but an operation."—I-II q. 35 art. 5.

"Pleasure without movement is more intense than pleasure with movement, because movement is in the order of becoming and the other in the perfect state."—*Ethics*, lib. 7 lect. 14.

will is higher than the inconstancy of the imagination. *Becoming* is an imperfection. It is a state in which one is in potency to a perfection which is not yet possessed. To carry the principle to its highest reaches, God is in perfect possession of perfections and is not in the process of attaining them, as Professor Alexander and the modern school in general believe. God possesses the plenitude. It is only imperfect beings such as ourselves who are the *viatores* on the road to our proportionate perfection.

No thesis in the philosophy of St. Thomas is clearer than that which asserts that all knowledge rests upon a single first principle. To it all other principles of thought may be reduced. Upon it all depend for their validity. Without it there can be no certitude, but only opinion.[534] Whether we choose to express this absolute, first principle in the form of an affirmation—the principle of identity—or in the form of a negation—the principle of contradiction—it matters not. The point is, that unless our knowledge hangs upon this basic principle, it is devoid of certainty. Wherefore, causality—efficient, formal, material or final—must attach itself in some manner to the principle of identity. In the Thomistic view, the connection is immediate. Its very immediateness gives to the notion of causality the absolute necessity and complete universality of the ultimate principle.

He who denies causality must ultimately deny the principle of identity and the principle of contradiction—and this is mental suicide.[535] It is to assert that that which has not in itself and by itself its reason of being, is its own reason of being; or, in other words, is and is not, under the same formal consideration.

Causality is a conclusion drawn from the principle of identity. It is intelligible only in function of being. The finite which is not being, but *of being*, is not being but by being which is being, as one is one. Finite being acts only in the order of *such a* being; God acts in the order of being as being. Causality, then, is an affair of the intelligence, and not of the sensation, or will or psychical experience.

---

[534] I-II q. 94 art. 2; *C. G.*, lib. 2 c. 83; *Post. Analy.*, lib. 2 lect. 20; 1 d. 35 q. 1 art. 3 ad 2.

[535] "Quia etsi non possunt demonstrari simpliciter, tum Philosophus primus tentat monstrare eo modo quo est possibile, scilicet, contradicendo negantibus ea, per ea quae oportet ab eis concedi, non per ea quae sunt magis nota."—*Post. Analy.*, lib. 1 lect. 20.

Sir Henry Jones sees no more than the empirical in causality precisely because he allows Hume to do his thinking for him at this point. "Causality," he writes, "is a hypothesis or conjectured relation. No one has ever actually perceived a cause. According to Hume we can perceive only sequence; if the sequence is unvaried and we expect it to be invariable, we call it a 'cause.'"[536]

Experience teaches us nothing regarding the necessity of the relations of succession. It tells us that which happens, but not that which ought to happen.[537]

To define causality as an extension of the internal experience of the will to all the objects of our experience is also to miss the whole point at issue. Dr. Beibitz says: Genetic psychology leaves us in no doubt as to the origin of the category of causality.[538] To this we answer that genetic psychology can teach us nothing about the origin of causality. To say it does is to confuse the consciousness of a cause with a cause. It merely gives a cause *for us*, not a *cause in itself.* Geometry is little interested in the formation of spatial images; so, too, metaphysics is little interested in the psychological origin of necessary principles. The sensible data is merely the condition of intellectual knowledge.

But this notion has been abandoned by some modern thinkers. Now they say that the popular conception of causation as production by the exercise of the will "has had to be supplemented by the scientific conception of the equation of causation as the inter-determination of phenomena."[539] But the inter-determination of phenomena is the statement of a fact, and not the reason of a fact. It is merely the result of a generalization of experience, and nothing more. It is a contradiction to define causality by such a formula. Phenomena in themselves are undetermined and unrelated. Causality is the inter-determination of phenomena, according to the definition, or the inter-determination of the undetermined, or the relation of the unrelated, which is a contradiction.[540]

---

536 *A Faith that Enquires*, p. 94.

537 N. BALTHASAR, *op. cit.*, p. 34.

538 *Op. cit.*, p. 60.

539 EDMOND G. HOLMES, M.A., "The Idea of Evolution and the Idea of God," *Hibbert Journal*, vol. xxi. No. 2 (January 1923), p. 238.

540 Mr. Broad defines causality as follows: "to every true proposition that asserts the

It is not the will, it is not the senses, it is not an internal experience which discovers the efficient cause as the actualizing principle of the effect. The intelligence alone sees the reason of being.[541] If sense sees the change and the succession, the intellect sees the reason of it. It does not make the least particle of difference, then, from what kind of sensation we draw our notion of cause through intellectual abstraction. *Its value is not dertermined by its sensible origin, but in function of being.* It is the object of the intelligence, not inasmuch as it is human—that is, as having the essence of material things for its proportionate object—but as having *being* for its formal and adequate object.

The first principles of causality, then, and all the ultimate principles of thought are *not laws* of the *idea* of being; they are *laws of being.* We know *cause*, and not the *idea of a cause.* Before knowing ideas we know things. The idea of a cause presupposes a cause. It is only by reflection that we attain the idea of cause.

The difficulty remains always the same. It is a failure to distinguish between the sense and the intellect. Having rejected the God-like faculty of the intelligence, which certain thinkers of the last century identified with reasoning, modern thought finds itself incapable of ever getting out of the multiple, the relative, the becoming, the imperfect. Sense knowledge manifests becoming; therefore everything becomes. Such is the argument. So impressed has it become with the evidence of becoming, that it makes a god of it. One wonders if the worship paid to it will someday carry its followers to the same extreme to which it carried the followers of Heraclitus. Aristotle tells us in his *Metaphysics* that Cratylus, a disciple of Heraclitus, was so enamoured of becoming that he concluded it was wrong even to say a word—*so he moved only his finger.* He did this because he believed that the truth of the thing which he wished to enunciate

---

happening of an event at a time, there is a set of relevant true propositions such that, relative to the whole of them, the probability of the event happening is one" (*Perception, Physics and Reality* [1914], p. 154). Causality is thus reduced to mental propositions, and seems to have no reference to the real other than that which the mind gives it.

Cf. L. MORGAN, *Emergent Evolution*, pp. 288-90

[541] This is the first kind of necessity, says St. Thomas, viz. the necessity of being: "Ex his autem principiis, secundum quod sunt essendi principia, tripliciter sumitur necessitas absoluta in rebus. Uno quidem modo per ordinem ad esse ejus cujus sunt."—*C. G.*, lib. 2 c. 30.

had passed before the words were finished. He could move his finger in a quicker time than he could say the words, and was thus more united with the universal flux of things.[542]

Those who have more idealistic tendencies have recourse to another objection against the principle of contradiction. The author of *The Idea of God*,[543] for example, in objecting to the proofs for the existence of God, has recourse to Hegel. "Hegel has proved there is no such thing as pure being," therefore the proofs for the existence of God cannot be based on the notion of being. The law of contradiction, on this logic, is merely the law of superior reason, but not the law of all reality.[544] The argument of Hegel is well known, and can be reduced to this simple form: "Pure being is pure indetermination; but pure indetermination is pure non-being; therefore pure being is pure non-being. Pure being does not exist."

The use of the phrase "pure indetermination" in two different senses has won many followers for Hegel, who were unable to detect the fallacy contained therein. In the first proposition, pure indetermination designates the negation of any *specific* or *generic* determination. Pure being is not *this kind of being.* In the second proposition, pure indetermination means the negation of *all being* and not a specific or generic kind of being. Pure being, then, is not the simple equivalent of non-being.[545]

The above objections make sufficiently clear a point upon which we have already insisted, namely, the proper relation between the rational and the real. The real has priority over the rational; being has priority over *becoming.* "Cognitio autem est posterior quam esse."[546] This is the Intellectualism of common-sense philosophy. The principle of identity and the principle of contradiction being laws of being, are also laws of thought. In its construction it excludes neither the sensible fact of becoming nor the intellectual abstraction of the priority of being over *becoming.*

---

[542] Book 4. *Cf.* lect. 12 of ST. THOMAS.

[543] C. A. BECKWITH, *loc. cit.*

[544] The principle of contradiction is the "loi suprême du discours et non de la pensée en général; il n'a prise que sur la statique, sur le morcelé sur l'immobile, bref, sur les choses douées d'une identité."—LE ROY, *Revue de Métaphysique et de Morale* (1905), p. 200.

[545] P. GARRIGOU-LAGRANGE, art. "Dieu" in the *Dictionnaire apologétique de la Foi Catholique* (Paris, Beauchesne, 1910), pp. 998, fasc. iv.

[546] *De Veritate*, q. 21 art. 3 c.

Becoming in the intellectual order is an imperfection. To say, then, that there is more in movement than in the immobile in the intellectual order, is to say that there is more in the acquiring of a thing than in the possession of it; there is more in being on the way to Rome than residence in Rome itself. Stripped of all the metaphors of boiling teapots, gushing fountains, speeding trains, and translated into simple language, it means that the *part is greater than the whole, or that the greater can come from the less.* More will be said on this point when we touch upon the evolving "God."

Another problem now offers itself before we pass to the proof for the existence of a transcendent being through the application of the above-mentioned principles. Can these principles raise us above the phenomena to God? What are our propositions about God worth? Can we validly conclude that God is, by application of these principles to the visible things of the world? Is God a reality, or is God a symbol?

The answer of modern thought to these questions is quite clear. Professor Pringle-Pattison has very well stated it in these words: "The point is, modern philosophy is but little interested in God as the object of knowledge, but greatly interested in Him as the object of experience."[547] Prescinding entirely from any intellectual approach, and resting solely in the way of religious experience, philosophers deny any interest in God as God, but profess great interest in Him inasmuch as He has a value for our lives. This is what we have characterized as the third note of modern religious experience, viz. God is to be designated merely intrinsically and in function of our own experiences instead of by the object which determines the knowledge.[548]

God, then, may be either of two things for the modern philosopher.

First, He may be merely a symbol. He may be nothing more than the projection of our own affections, the creation of our desire, the generation of our imagination or society divinized, or the sum of our ideals. In this case, in the words of Bertrand Russell, "Man worships at the shrine his own hands have made."

---

[547] *Op. cit.*, p. 334.

[548] *Cf.* Part I. chap. IV.

Secondly, God may be more than a mere symbol. He may be a reality, a "larger self from whom saving experiences come." But in this case, as in the first, He is still to be designated in the light of our experiences and with special regard to values for our own lives. Terms which we apply to things about us will therefore name Him *without any correction* whatsoever. He may be, therefore, "the President of a Great Commonwealth," "the Great Toiler," "the Idealized Common Will," "the Democrat," in opposition to "the bickering monopolist who will have no other gods but Me," as Mr. Wells puts it. Or He may be graced more properly as Space-Time, Divinal Imaginal and the like.

Whatever God be, either that of a pure Symbol or a Reality, He is never known apart from relation to our lives in the sense that He is never transcendent to them. It is the "voice of human experience within us, judging and condemning all gods that stand athwart the pathway," that determines and designates God. In fact, so dependent is He upon us, that even though He be real we must be said "to help to sustain the nature of God" in the sense that "God Himself is involved in our acts and in their issues."

There is a double presupposition at the basis of the modern contention that we cannot designate God properly as object, but merely symbolically or metaphorically. The first presupposition is that we do not know reality. Hence God is taken to be a symbol for reality. The second presupposition is that mind is the measure of reality, and hence God is to be measured in terms of the needs of the individual, the needs of the age, of values for our lives and in function of evolution.[549] Both of these presuppositions are false. The first, because ideas are not pictures or substitutes. They are transparent. Their term is the real, not the mental.[550] The second is false because the greater is never to be subordinated to the less. No faculty measures its object. The eye does not determine the colour of its object; the ear does not determine its sound; and neither does the intelligence determine its object, which is God in this particular case. To say our mind

[549] See Part I. chap. IV. pp. 41-46.

[550] "The *stone* is that which is known, not the *idea* of the stone except by reflex abstraction, otherwise knowledge would not be of things but ideas."—I q. 76 art. 2 ad 4. "The idea is only secondarily known; that which is first known is the thing of which the idea is the similitude."—I q. 75 art. 2 c.

is the measure of God is to make the means determine the end, the object determine the faculty, the determinable determine the determined, the less determine the greater.

But how can we designate God?

Every being is one, good and true. These are transcendental properties of being.

Although the notions of cause, intelligence and will are not transcendentals in the strict sense of the term, because they are to be found only in certain genera or species, nevertheless they have an immediate relation to them. Causality has a relation to being, of which it is the actualization or realization; intelligence has a relation to being, of which it is the knowledge; will has a relation to being, of which it is the appetite. Inasmuch as they are defined in relation to being, they may be less properly called transcendentals, because under this consideration they rise above genus and species.[551] These transcendental notions, along with certain others—for example, life and justice—are *notions which in their formal aspect imply no imperfection whatsoever*, although the finite mode of being which they have in creatures is imperfect. Being, for example, cannot be restricted to any genus or species; neither can goodness, nor truth nor unity. Everything that is possesses these properties, and none to the exclusion of the others. They transcend all the categories and yet are found in all of them. Other notions which do not enjoy the same transcendence are not free from imperfection in their formal aspect. *Reason*, for example, in its formal aspect is an imperfection, because it designates a progress toward a term and not the possession or the intuition of it.[552]

[551] "Omne enim ens est adaequatum intellectui divino, et potest sibi adaequare intellectum humanum et e converso."—*De Veritate*, q. 1 art. 2 ad 1.

"If the human intellect were blotted out, things would still be true in relation to the Divine intellect. But if both the human intelligence and the Divine intelligence were blotted out, which of course is impossible, there would be no more truth."—*De Veritate*, q. 1 art. 2 c.

Cf. GARRIGOU-LAGRANGE, art. "Dieu," *Dictionnaire apologétique de la Foi Catholique.*

[552] "Quaedam vero nomina significant ipsas perfectiones absolute, absque hoc quod aliquis modus participandi claudatur in eorum significatione, ut ens, bonum, vivens, et hujusmodi; et talia proprie dicuntur Deo."—I q. 13 art. 3 ad 1.

For the same reason, because we find "littleness" in the world we do not predicate it of God as a certain atheist has mockingly contended we should. "Littleness" pertains to imperfection; goodness, truth, justice, mercy do not. See *De Veritate*, q. 2 art. 2 ad 8.

So thoroughly do these absolute perfections, being, goodness and truth, rise above all imperfection, all genus and all species, that, so far as the *thing itself* is concerned which these names signify, they *more properly belong to God than they do to creatures*, and should be first predicated of Him rather than of creatures.[553] If, now, it can be proved that God exists, there is a way of designating Him which far exceeds that of modern philosophy, namely, by relation to our emotions and the needs of the age and in function of evolution. If, furthermore, it can be proved that God exists, then there are certain predicates which of themselves imply no imperfection, and which may be used to designate Him properly. We are thus a long way from defining Him as a symbol or in function of the subject experienced.

But how apply these simple perfections to God? Certainly not by a pure verbal arbitrariness which is solely equivocation, for such is merely a play on words.[554] Neither do these names apply univocally, since such predication supposes participation in a common notion. The attributes of God and of creatures have not the same definition.[555]

---

[553] Although as regards their mode of signification the converse is true. "Quantum igitur ad id, quod significant hujusmodi nomina, proprie competunt Deo, et magis proprie, quam ipsis creaturis, et per prius dicuntur de eo. Quantum vero ad modum significandi non proprie dicuntur de Deo; habent enim modum significandi qui creaturis competit" (I q. 13 art. 3 c). *Cf.* St. Thomas's refutation of Rabbi Moyses (Maimonides), and compare it with the modern agnostic notions regarding the ontological value of first principles and the applicability of names to God (*De Pot.*, q. 7 art. 5). We do not say God is good because there are good things in the world: rather we say there are good things in the world because God is good.

[554] "Nec tamen potest dici quod omnino aequivoce praedicatur quidquid de Deo et creatura dicitur, quia si non esset aliqua convenientia creaturae ad Deum secundum rem, sua essentia non esset creaturarum similitudo; et ita cognoscendo essentiam suam non cognosceret creaturas ... ex aequivocis non differt quodcumque nomen imponatur ex quo nulla rei convenientia attenditur."—*De Veritate*, q. 2 art. 11 c.

"Creatura enim non habet esse nisi secundum quod a primo ente descendit; unde nec nominator ens nisi inquantum ens primum imitatur."—*Sent. Prol.*, q. 1 art. 2 ad 1.

[555] "Creatura autem quantumcumque imitator Deum, non potest pertingere ad hoc ut eadem ratione aliquid sibi conveniat et Deo; illa enim quae secundum eamdem rationem sunt in diversis, sunt eis communia secundum rationem substantiae sive quidditatis, sed sunt distincta secundum esse. Quidquid autem est in Deo, hoc est suum proprium esse; sicut enim essentia in eo idem est quod esse, ita scientia idem est quod scientem esse in eo; unde cum esse quod est proprium unius rei non potest alteri communicari, impossibile est quod creatura pertingat ad eamdem rationem habendi aliquid quod habet Deus, sicut impossibile est quod ad idem esse perveniat."—Ibid.

But if the names cannot be predicated univocally or with pure equivocation, how are they to be predicated? Analogically—that is, by a certain proportion.[556] This kind of proportion, more properly called proportionality, "is the relation between two things which have not a direct relation, in virtue of which one of them is to the other what the second is to a fourth. Thus the number six has a similitude with the number four in that the first is the double of three, as the second is the double of two."[557] This kind of analogy can therefore be predicated of God and of creatures.[558] Here is the Thomistic answer to the difficulty that there is no proportion between the finite and the infinite or between creatures and God: "*If there is no proportion between the finite and the infinite, it does not follow that there is no proportionality, since what the finite is to the finite, the infinite is to the infinite, and thus it is that the similitude between God and creatures must be understood, namely, that God is in the same relation to that which concerns Himself as the creature is in relation to that which concerns itself.*[559]

Keeping in mind the analogy of proportionality, such as the prince is to his people as the pilot is to his ship,[560] let us return now to our transcendental notions. These notions, which in their formal aspect imply no imperfection whatsoever, are to be applied to the whole range of being according to the particular mode of its being. The substance is *being* according to its manner

[556] What follows does not profess to be a treatment of the subject of analogy. Here, as elsewhere, we do not attempt to give the speculative Thomistic position, but merely to indicate the broad lines of solution. This analogy cannot be that of attribution, in virtue of which the same predicate is attributed to two subjects, because both have an identical relation with a third term. Such an analogy supposes a third term anterior to two others. If this analogy were true, there would be a reality anterior logically to God and to creatures which would be diversely participated in by both. Neither can the analogy be that of a direct and reciprocal relation, "because no creature has such a relation to God that this relation can serve to determine the perfection of God."—*De Veritate*, q. 2 art. 11. *Cf.* I q. 13 art. 5.

[557] "Convenientia etiam quandoque attenditur duorum ad invicem inter quae non sit proportio sed magis similitudo duarum ad invicem proportionum, sicut senarius convenit cum quaternario ex hoc quod senarius est duplum ternarii, ita quaternarius binarii."—*De Veritate*, q. 2 art. 11.

[558] Ibid. Hence both substance and accident may be called "being," according to an analogy of proportionality; for the substance is to its being as accident is to its being.

[559] "Similiter finitum et infinitum, quamvis non possint esse proportionata, possunt tamen esse proportionabilia; quia sicut infinitum est aequale infinito, ita finitum finito; et per hunc modum est similitudo inter creaturam et Deum; quia sicut se habet ad ea quae ei competunt, ita creatura ad sua propria."—*De Veritate*, q. 23 art. 7 ad 9.

[560] Ibid.

of being (*in se*), as accident is to its manner of being (*in alio*). This fruit is *good* according to its manner of being (as regards its taste), as this man is good according to his mode of being (morally). The same is to be said of "the true," of cause, of intelligence and will. Now, if we can prove God to be existent, these transcendental notions should be applied to Him according to His mode of being. There is nothing repugnant in using them to express analogically the sovereignly Perfect Being, once His existence is proved. God will be Intelligence according to His manner of being; Good according to His manner of being; Cause according to His manner of being; Intelligence according to His manner of being.

This analogical predication in virtue of which the *created mode* of these absolute perfections is denied of God, and the *formal reason* of the perfections is predicated of Him, is the solution of the so-called antinomies. The imperfections which attach themselves to the finite mode of being are purified in applying them to God, in order that they may correspond with His manner of being. Because cause in its finite mode of being is an accident of a being, it does not follow that it is necessarily true of God's manner of being. Quality of subject and object which flows from our finite and potential mode of being is not predicable in exactly the same way of infinite being.[561]

Add to this a further principle which is implicitly admitted by modern philosophy, namely, every being acts according to its nature. *Omne agens agit simile sibi.*[562] Every effect resembles in some way its cause. To cause, means to actualize, to realize, to determine; and since no cause can determine except according to the determination which is in it, it necessarily follows that there

[561] "Possunt hujusmodi nomina et affirmari de Deo et negari: affirmari quidem propter nominis rationem, negari vero propter modum significandi" (*C. G.*, lib.1 c. 30). For solution of antinomies see the second part of GARRIGOU-LAGRANGE'S art. "Dieu," which is given over to their refutation. Analogy removes God from a genus. "Quod autem Deus non sit in genere per reductionem, ut principium, manifestum est ex eo, quod principium, quod reducitur in aliquod genus, non se extendit ultra genus illud; sicut punctum non est principium nisi quantitatis continuae et unitas quantitatis discretae. Deus autem est principium totius esse, unde non continetur in aliquo genere, sicut principium."—I q. 3 art. 5 c.

[562] The source of all things is Becoming or Space-Time, and all things that have evolved from this original "stuff" participate in its nature.

must be some analogy between the two.[563] If the agent is in the same species as its effect, there will be similitude of form between the maker and the thing made—as, for example, man generates man. But if the agent is not contained in any genus, there will not be a similitude according to species or genus, but merely that of analogy.[564] This is the positive foundation of analogy, from which it follows that there can be no impossibility in applying analogical notions to God.

In the course, then, of the demonstration of God's nature, the mean term is analogous. Such a demonstration does not imply four terms, because in the major and the minor the mean term has exactly the same extension.[565] In general, we can affirm three things of Him: first, that the visible things of the world require a First Cause which exists *per se*; secondly, that all the perfection which is in the effect ought to pre-exist in the cause; and thirdly, according to His Divine mode of being.[566] The perfections we attribute to God vary according to the communicability or non-communicability of the Divine attributes. James makes the mistake of accepting only the moral attributes, and rejects as useless the metaphysical attributes. He forgets that there are two general kinds of perfections in God: the perfections which are communicable to creatures, such as goodness and wisdom and mercy; and secondly, the incommunicable perfections, such as infinity and deity. According to the first kind of perfections, creatures are more like to God as they more nearly approach the formal reason of these perfections. But according to the second kind of perfections, creatures are more like to God according as they separate themselves further from the opposites. A thing, for example, is more like Deity as it recedes from *non-being*. The metaphysical attributes, then, are just as essential for knowing and designating God as are the moral attributes. They are not

[563] GARRIGOU-LAGRANGE, art. "Dieu," *Dictionnaire apologétique de la Foi Catholique*. N. BALTHASAR, *op. cit.*, pp. 47-95. Dr. LUDWIG FAULHARBER, *Die "drei Wege" der Gotteserkenntnis und der wissenschaftliche Gottesbegriff* (1923), pp. 70-79.

[564] I q.4 art. 3.

[565] "Quidquid convenit uni, convenit etiam alteri proportionaliter: et quidquid negatur de una, negatur proportionaliter de alia: quia quidquid convenit simili in eo quod simile, convenit etiam illi, cujus est simile, proportionalitate semper servata."—CAJETAN, *De Nominum Analogia*, cap. 10.

Cf. JOHN OF SAINT THOMAS, q. 13 art. 5.

[566] I q. 12 art. 12.

Scholastic constructions. They are based on the incommunicability of the Deity, as the moral attributes are based on His communicability.[567]

The complete and full knowledge of the Essence of God is reserved for faith and vision.[568] We multiply terms in order to clarify our knowledge of God. This is due to the fact that knowledge is primarily from above and not from below. Objects which are below us we can designate more simply than they are in themselves; but things which are above us, angels and God, we must designate less simply.[569]

Though we cannot know God as He is in Himself, we have a knowledge which is more than a symbol or a series of metaphors. Such designations as Space-Time, Divinal, Imaginal, Duration, Great Toiler, President of the Cosmic Commonwealth, and the like, imply imperfections in their formal aspect, and give us no knowledge whatever of God. On the contrary, they reduce Him to a state equal to or less than man. Thus, professing to make God more known and closer to us, they make Him less known and less human. As far as value for our lives is concerned, what thing could be less adapted to help our struggling selves than a bit of Space-Time?

It cannot be too often repeated: We are not the measure of God; God is our measure. Objects measure our knowledge; we do not measure them.[570] It is not our privilege to measure out the kind of God we shall have, any more than it is within our

---

[567] CAJETAN in I q. 55 art. 3, VI.

[568] "Intellectus autem noster totum Deum intelligere potest, sed non totaliter totum, quia necessarium est ut de ipso aut totum intelligatur aut nihil, cum in eo non sit pars et totum; sed dico, non totaliter, quia non perfecte cognoscit ipsum, secundum quod ipse est in sus natura cognoscibilis."—*De Veritate*, q. 2 art. 1 ad 3.

[569] "Sed si esset aliqua res perfecte repraesentans Deum, non esset nisi una tantum, quia uno modo repraesentaret, et secundum unam formam; et ideo non est nisi unus Filius, qui est perfecta imago Patris."—*De Veritate*, q. 1 art. 1 c.

"Ratio nostra connaturale habet secundum statum viae accipere cum tempore, propter hoc quod ejus cognitio oritur a sensibilibus, quae in tempore sunt, ideo non potest formare enuntiationes, nisi per verba temporalia."—1 d. 8 q. 2 art. 3 c.

Cf. Ibid., art. 1 ad 2; I q. 13 art. 12 ad 3; I q. 54 art. 2; I q. 82 art. 3.

"Quanto intellectus est perfectior tanto est similior Deo, non solum in hoc quod limpidius cognoscit sed etiam in hoc quod per pausiores species cognoscit."—CAJETAN in I q. 55 ad 3, VI.

[570] "In sentiendo et sciendo mensuramus per res quae extra nos sunt."—*Metaphysics*, lib. 10 lect. 2. "Ratio humana secundum se non est regula rerum."—I-II q. 91 art. 3 ad 2; I q. 21 art. 2 c; I q. 16 art. 1; I-II q. 93 art. 1 ad 3.

power to measure out the kind of object which will determine our vision as vision. When philosophy reaches a point where it insists that we need a new idea of God, it is time for us to make a philosophical examination of conscience. When man takes upon himself to measure God according to his own experiences and his own utility, he has by that very fact constituted himself as God. If there is any fitting to be done, it is we who are to fit ourselves to God, and not God to ourselves. Our finite experience as finite experience is a very poor criterion of God. It is not God who is intelligible in function of our experience; it is our experience which is intelligible in function of God. God has no value as an object of experience before He is an object of knowledge.[571]

[571] "Illud quod est in aliquo non sequitur illud in quo est nisi causatur ex principiis ejus; unde lux quae causatur in aere ab extrinseco, scilicet ex sole sequitur motionem solis magis quam rerum. Similiter etiam virtus quae est in anima causatur a rebus, *non sequitur aestimationem* animae, sed existentia in rebus."—*De Veritate*, q. 1 art. 2 ad 3.

CHAPTER V:

THE VALUE OF THE NON-INTELLECTUAL APPROACH TO GOD

CONTEMPORARY thought is quite unanimous on the point that God is not reached by a rational or discursive process. None are found "so intellectually poor to do reverence to the proofs for the existence of God." Apart from the general prejudice against an intellectualist philosophy, one of the principal objections against the proofs is their abstract nature, or what Professor Schiller and Professor Beckwith have erroneously called their *a priori* nature. They are too dry, too Scholastic, too rational.

This criticism must, in great part, be conceded to be true. There is perhaps nothing colder in the whole realm of philosophy than the *Responded dicendum* of the *Summa.* There is not throughout this whole work a single appeal to emotion such as one finds, for example, in St. Augustine. The five ways of proving the existence of God make but little appeal to the heart, and are sorry rhetoric for the multitude.

But much of the objection against the Scholastic position would disappear if a distinction were kept in mind. Is the proof of the existence of God, as given in a Scholastic manual or in the *Summa*, the exact representation of the way in which men arrive at the knowledge of God, or is it a fuller and more explicit statement? Is it for scientific or for popular consumption? Is it the result of immediate or of reflex knowledge?

To answer these questions by affirming the second alternative is to halve the objections. Because the chemist knows oil of vitriol by its formula, there is no reason why the man in the street should complain that science is destructive. Scientific language is adapted to science; the five ways of proving the existence of God are adapted to philosophy. By the same logic by which we reject the proofs because of their dry, abstract nature, we should reject the science of chemistry because it symbolizes the very water we drink at the dinner-table. The proofs in the Summa are the result of reflex knowledge. Thanks to his spiritual soul, man reflects on himself. He can know a thing, and know that he knows a thing. But he knows the thing before examining his knowledge of it. He knows directly and spontaneously before knowing reflectively.

The distinction is not between two different kinds of knowledge: there is here merely a distinction of degree. Really, the proofs which the plain man gives are in principle the same as those of the Angelic Doctor. The difference lies in their manner of expression. The five arguments in the Summa are the result of reflection; they are the explicit, definite and clear exposition of the spontaneous proofs of the ordinary person.

Thus the criticism of the proofs by an appeal to their abstract nature is irrelevant. In the supposed revolt against all this abstractness "religious experience" is said to be free from rigid formalism. Its value remains to be determined. From the outset, however, it is well to remember that "religious experience" is only a new name for old ways of thinking.

It has by no means sprung from modern philosophy alone. During the Patristic period it was known as *cognitio naturalis inserta, innata* and the like.[572] During the Scholastic period it was known

[572] Not in the sense that the knowledge of God was innate, but that the faculty of religious experience by which God was attained was innate and capable of attaining God.

"Deus magnus, Deus bonus, et quod Deus dederet, omnium vox est. Judicem quoque contestatur illum, Deus videt et Deo commendo, et Deus mihi reddet et *testimonium animae naturaliter christianae*. Denique praenuntians haec non ad Capitolium, sed ad coelum respicit."—TERTULLIAN, *Apol. ad Gent.*, c. 17.

"Inserta est mentibus hominum veri bonique cupiditio."—BOETHIUS, *De Consolatione Phil.*, lib. 3 p. 2, LX.-LXI.

The method of the Fathers in dealing with the idolaters was not so to prove to them the existence of God as if they knew not God, but rather to purify their notion of God. The existence of God is a heritage of reason and not of faith. Even the pagans can know God.

Cf. ST. THOMAS, I q. 13 art. 10 ad 5; q. 12 art. 12; *De Veritate*, q. 22 art. 2 ad 1.

Cf. ST. ATHANASIUS, *Oratio contra Gentes*, n. 27, 42. *P. G.*, t. 25 cols.54, 86. ST. AUGUSTINE, *De Civitate Dei*, lib.11 c. 55, 2. *P.L.*,t. 32 col. 81. ST. JOHN DAMASCENE, *De Fide Orthodoxa*, lib1 c 3. *P. G.*, t. 94 col. 796.

as confused or common knowledge. *Confused knowledge*, for the Scholastic, is that by which something is known without analysis or the discernment of its parts or its predicates. Thus it is not sufficient to distinguish one object from other objects. *Distinct knowledge*, on the other hand, is that by which something is known through the analysis or the discernment of its parts or predicates. It therefore serves to differentiate one object from another.[573]

Religious experience is thus really to be identified at its best with the "confused knowledge" of the Scholastics. Now, "confused knowledge" is at least of two kinds. In its operations it may prescind altogether from reason and base itself upon the inclination of nature in the search for goodness;[574] or it may be intellectual—a kind of immediate inference or brush with reality which is not further specified nor clarified.[575]

Now, the first of these two kinds of confused knowledge bears a close resemblance to the modern "religious experience" in its non-rational character. The second has only this in common with crude religious experience, that both profess to be

Cf. CICERO, *De Natura Deorum*, 2: "Quid enim potest esse tam apertum tamque perspicuum cum coelum suspeximus, celestiaque contemplati sumus, quam esse aliquod Numen praestantissimae mentis, quo haec regantur?" Compare these words with those of the Psalmist: " Coeli enarrant gloriam Dei, et opera ejus annuntiant firmamentum" (Psalm xviii.).

[573] "Cognitio, sive in sensu, sive in intellectu, alia est confusa, alia distincta. Cognitio confusa est qua attingitur aliquid non resolvendo nec discernendo ejus partes, seu praedicata, aut attributa. Distincta est e converso, qua cognoscitur aliquid resolvendo, seu discernendo partes ejus, aut praedicata. Et omnis confusio dicit ordinem ad plura; vel actualiter in se inclusa, quia ex illis actu constat, vel potentialiter subjecta, quia sub se continentur; unde oritur quod alia est cognitio confusa actualis, scilicet respectu eorum quae actu conveniunt rei, alia confusa potentialis, scilicet respectu eorum, quae sunt objecta, et quasi in ejus potentia continetur, et similiter distingui potest e converso cognitio distincta."—JOHN OF ST. THOMAS, t. 2 p. I q. 1 art. 3.

ST. THOMAS, I q. 14 art. 6; q. 85 art 3 and ad 3; q. 85 art.4 ad 3; q. 85 art. 8; q. 86 art. 2. *C. G.*, lib. 3 c. 38 and 39.

[574] "Inclinationes enim naturales maxime cognosci possunt in his quae naturaliter aguntur absque rationis deliberatione."—*C. G.*, lib.3 c. 38.

"Omnia cognoscentia cognoscunt implicite Deum in qualibet cognitione ... nihil est cognoscibile nisi per similitudinem primae veritatis."—*De Veritate*, q. 22 art. 2 ad 1.

"Verum enim est bonum intellectus, ad quid naturaliter ordinatur, unde sicut res ratione carentur moventur ad suos fines absque ratione, ita interdum intellectus hominis quadam naturali inclinatione tendit in veritatem, licet rationem veritatis non percipiat."—*Phy.*, lib. 1 lect. 10.

[575] "Est enim quaedam communis ex confusa Dei cognitio, quae quasi omnibus adest ... quia naturali ratione *statim* homo in aliqualem Dei cognitionem pervenire potest."—*C. G.*, lib. 3 c. 38.

immediate. But how both differ from the modern notion will be made clear later.

The first kind of "confused knowledge," it has been said, is founded on the inclinations of nature. St. Thomas states his doctrine as follows: "Every creature, whether rational or irrational, or even inanimate, loves God above all things according to the kind of love which can properly belong to it."[576] Hence, it applies not only to man and to angels, but even to the lower creatures according as they love sensibly or naturally.[577] By natural love is here understood the inclination of a being towards its end. In every tendency, in every inclination, in every urge, it is God who is sought, whether it be the stone obeying the law of gravitation or the Seraphim burning in adoration.[578] The principle underlying the doctrine is simply this: the whole is greater and more powerful than any of its parts. In other words, the motive force of all our actions is the whole. Every action is just a part-vision of the whole.

We indeliberately expose our arm to ward off a blow, in order to save the whole body. The citizen exposes his life for the good of the state.[579] Now, as God is the common good of the whole universe, it follows that every creature implicitly desires and tends toward Him in every act.[580] The particular good is sought because it participates in the Divine likeness.

In the lower orders this natural love of God, based on the tendency toward the common good, is not voluntary or affective. It is natural, however. The young ravens, for example, may truly be said to call upon God on account of their natural desire for

---

[576] I-II q. 109 art. 3.

[577] "Diligere Deum super omnia plus quam seipsum, est naturale non solum angelo et homini, sed etiam cuilibet creaturae, secundum quod potest amare aut sensibiliter aut naturaliter."—*Quod.*, q. 1 art. 8.

[578] I q. 60 art. 1 ad 3; I-II q. 28 art. 4; 2 d. I q. 2 art. 1. *C. G.*, lib. 3 c. 24.

[579] "Naturaliter pars se exponit ad conservationem totius: sicut manus exponitur ictui absque deliberatione ad conservationem totius corporis. Et quia ratio imitatur naturam hujusmodi inclinationem invenimus in virtutibus politicis. Est enim virtuosi civis, ut se exponat mortis periculo pro totius rei publicae conservatione."—I q. 60 art. 5.

[580] "Quia igitur bonum universale est ipse Deus, et sub hoc bono continetur etiam angelus et homo et omnis creatura, quia omnis creatura naturaliter secundum id quod est, Dei est, sequitur, quod naturali dilectione etiam angelus et homo plus, et principalius diligat Deum, quam seipsum. Alioquin, si naturaliter plus seipsum diligeret, quam Deum, sequeretur, quod naturalis dilectio esset perversa, et quod non perficeretur per caritatem sed destrueretur."—I q. 60 art. 5.

the Divine Goodness according to their mode of being.[581] They desire God implicitatly, without knowing Him, or perhaps more correctly *interpretative.*

What is true of the lower orders is true equally of man. He may act consciously in view of the whole. In desiring existence he is desiring that which resembles God, and therefore is implicitly desiring God.[582] In desiring even a sensible good he is desiring God in some way. In fact, he cannot do otherwise. His will has a certain determination about it. It is free in its *exercise* but determined in its *specification.* It is never determined to choose *this particular good,* but it is determined to choose *the good.*[583]

In seeking evil, even, he does so *sub specie boni.* By the very fact that we are on the quest of perfection we are seeking God. If we may anticipate a reason for this, it is that we are made in the image and likeness of God. But unlike inorganic things we are both living and conscious. We are like artists constantly retouching our portraits to make them better correspond to the original exemplar. In the words of St. Augustine, we are frightened when we fail to imitate the original, we burn with the success of our imitation.[584] God, then, is very close to us. In a

[581] "Pulli corvorum dicuntur invocare Deum, propter naturale desiderium quo omnia suo modo desiderant consequi bonitatem divinam; sic etiam bruta animalia dicuntur Deo obedire propter naturalem instinctum quo a Deo moventur."—II-II q. 83 art. 10 ad 3.

Cf. CH. V. V. HERIS, "L'Amour naturel de Dieu," *Mélanges Thomistes. Cf.* also Dr. P. M. HALLFELL, "Die Gottsehnsucht der Seele" in *Studia Friburgensia* (October 1923) *Divus Thomas.* In the above sense animals have a "religious sense," as K. B. BANSFIELD insists in his work *On Values,* p. 44 *Cf. De Veritate,* q. 22 art. 2 ad 5.

"Aliae creaturae participant divinam similitudinem, et sic ipsum Deum appetunt."—*C. G.,* lib. 3 c. 38.

"Omnia appetunt bonum; sed non omnia cognoscunt verum."—*De Veritate,* q. 21 art. 3.

"Unaquaeque res habeat connaturalitatem ad id quod est sibi conveniens secundum suam naturam."—I-II q. 26 art. 1 ad 3.

[582] "In quantum aliqua desiderant esse, desiderant Dei similitudinem et Deum implicite."—*De Veritate,* q. 22 art. 2 ad 2.

"Omnia appetunt Deum ut finem appetendo quodcumque bonum, sive appetitu intelligibili, sive sensibili, sive naturali, qui est sine cognitione; quia nihil habet rationem boni et appetibilis boni nisi secundum quod participat Dei similitudinem."—I q. 44 art.4 ad 3.

[583] I-II q. 10 art. 2; I q. 82 art. 1 ad 2; I-II q. 5 art. 8.

[584] "Res omnes creatae sunt quaedam imagines primi agentis, scilicet Dei agens enim agit simile sibi; perfectio enim imaginis est ut repraesentet suum exemplar per similitudinem ad ipsum, ad hoc enim imago constituitur. Sunt igitur res omnes propter divinam similitudinem consequendam sicut propter ultimum finem."—*C. G.,* lib. 3 c. 19.

Confessions, lib. 11 c. 9.

certain sense God is innate, not of course by His nature, but by His likeness, because all is desired after the likeness of the Divine Goodness and all is known after the likeness of Divine Truth.[585]

But man, in virtue of his spiritual soul, becomes attached to God by even stronger bonds. The capacity to know, it will be recalled, increases with freedom from matter. But the soul of man, being spiritual, is free from all matter. It can therefore know all things, however imperfectly. It follows, then, that the soul is in essential relation to God because it can attain the universal reason of all being and the goodness of being.[586]

But though the mind is capable of conceiving being in all its latitude, it actually finds itself in the order of the finite, the phenomenal and the material. There is no creature which it sees, or knows or loves which exhausts its capacity for being, truth, goodness and beauty. It is characterized by a "radical resistance to limitation."[587]

Experience of the world leaves our hunger unassuaged. As the Angelic Doctor has put it, nothing finite can give rest to the urge of the intellect. In presence of something finite it pushes out beyond. Every desire, unless it be spiritual, can be enjoyed in its plenitude in this life. Hence the natural tendency to transcend phenomena to give rest to our spiritual yearnings.[588] The mind

---

[585] "(Innatum) non quidem ipsum prout consideratur in sua natura, sed in sui similitudinem, quia nihil desideratur, nisi inquantum habet similitudinem ipsius, et etiam cognoscitur."—3 *Sent.*, q. 1 art. 2 ad 1.

"Ejus cognitio nobis innata dicitur esse, inquantum per principia nobis innata de facili percipere possumus Deum esse."—*De Trinitate Boetii*, q. 1 art. 3 ad 6. *Cf. C. G.*, lib. 1 c. 2; *De Veritate*, q. 22 art.1 ad 1; *De Mente*, art. 12.

[586] "Sola autem natura rationalis habet immediatum ordinem ad Deum, quia caeterae creaturae non attingunt ad aliquid universale, sed solum ad aliquid particulare ...: natura autem rationalis, inquantum cognoscit universalem boni et entis rationem, habet immediatum ordinem ad universale essendi principium; perfectio ergo rationalis creaturae non solum consistit in eo, quod ei competit secundum suam naturam, sed in eo etiam, quod ei attribuitur ex quadam supernaturali participatione divinae bonitatis."—II-II q. 2 art. 3 c.

"Ex hoc quod substantia aliqua est intellectualis comprehensiva est totius entis."—*C. G.*, lib. 2 c. 96. Cajetan, commenting on this text, says that this immediate order of the rational creature to God is in virtue of the fact that God is its mover, its end, and its object—II-II q. 2 art. 3 c. 5.

"Unumquodque ordinatur in finem sibi convenientem secundum rationem suae formae."—*C. G.*, lib. 3 c. 151.

[587] Sir HENRY JONES, *A Faith that Enquires* (1922), p. 51.

[588] *C. G.*, lib. 3 c. 50.

sees the disproportion between its capacity and its realization. Vaguely and confusedly, but necessarily, it sees its adequate object as possible. It knows, in some way, that created being does not exhaust its possibilities, and so it moves onward to its real object. Prior to any act of reason men know happiness and seek their many visions of the good. Confusedly, implicitly, however dimly in so doing, they seek after God the Supreme Good, and thus have a knowledge of God, not as He is in Himself but *in confuso*.[589]

There is a more definite kind of religious experience in Thomistic thought than the above-mentioned. It is a reasoning process, it is true, but of a very desultory and spontaneous kind. It is the reasoning attendant upon the application of the first principles of knowledge to the things of the universe. It is a congenital and natural knowledge, and just as universal in its extent as the desire for happiness. By it all men can easily come to a knowledge of the existence of God.[590] It is a kind of knowledge that is independent of social environment, and it functions without any education or aid of authority. It is even more readily attainable than the knowledge of worldly sciences: "For if they were able to know so much as to make a judgment of the world, how did they not *more easily find out* the Lord thereof?"[591] It is a logical conclusion, so spontaneous in its character that it happens almost in spite of ourselves.

In the last chapter it was stated that there are certain conclusions which attach themselves immediately to the first principle of the speculative and the practical intellect, such as causality and finality.[592] They are the common heritage of all men without exception. Their expression may be crude, and is so with the generality of mankind, but this in no way affects their

---

[589] JOHN OF SAINT THOMAS, *Cursus Theologicus*, vol. i. p. 1 disp. 3 art. 1 n. 9.

"The soul does not desire God as He is in Himself. It would have to know Him first. But it desires God *in confuso*."—*De Veritate*, q. 10 art. 12 ad 7.

[590] "Cognitio existendi Deum dicitur omnibus naturaliter inserta, quia omnibus naturaliter insertum est aliquid unde potest pervenire ad cognoscendum Deum esse."—*De Veritate*, q. 10 art. 12 ad 1.

[591] Wisdom xiii. 9.

[592] "Ex istis autem principiis universalibus omnia principia sequuntur sicut ex quibusdam rationibus seminalibus."—*De Veritate*, q. 2 art. 1.

necessity or universality. The "why" of the child is his own simple way of expressing the principle of sufficient reason.[593]

These first principles, striking the visible things of the world, are immediately reflected back to some First Principle. As an object may be seen reflected in a mirror, so, too, God may be seen reflected in the mirror of the universe by the light of these first principles.[594] Or the universe maybe looked upon as on a book in which we read our knowledge of God.[595] Immediately on intellectually perceiving that the world is moved, the intelligence by a sort of "reflex action" infers the existence of a Mover. From the laws which govern it, or from the laws which govern mankind, the reason infers the existence of a Legislator. From the beauty of the universe it infers the existence of a Supreme Archetypal Beauty.[596] From the order of the universe the mind concludes to some Governor. From any of the transcendentals it is reflected back to a cause or archetype of these transcendentals. As St. Thomas has put it, by natural reason man immediately comes to some knowledge of God. Seeing that natural things change in an orderly fashion, and knowing that there can never be order without some one who orders, he perceives that there must be some governor of the general order of things.[597]

The result of this confused and immediate knowledge, as St. Thomas calls it, is a series of predicates, there being no fixed formula to which the confused knowledge attaches itself. God may be designated as the Being of all Beings, the First Mover, the Lawgiver, the Authority of the Moral Law, the Supreme Good, Truth or Beauty. But in every case it is a predicate which is

---

593 "Naturaliter ex necessitate inhaeret principiis et conclusionibus habentibus necessarium cum illis."—I q. 82 art. 2. *C. G.*, lib. 3 c. 50.

594 I q. 85 art. 8 ad 1.

595 "Visibiles creaturae in quibus sicut in quodam libro, Dei cognitio legeretur."—*Com. in Rom.*, c. 1 lect. 6.

596 "Omne quod est in aliquo genere oportet reduci ad primum illius generis, sicut omne calidum ad calidum ignis."—*De Veritate*, q. 3 art. 7, *Sed Contra.*

597 "Naturali ratione statim homo in aliqualem Dei cognitionem pervenire potest; videntes enim homines res naturales secundum ordinem certum currere; quum ordinatio absque ordinatore non sit, percipiunt ut in pluribus aliquem esse ordinatorem rerum quas videmus."—*C. G.*, lib. 3 c. 38.

This knowledge St. Thomas expressly calls confused knowledge. In another place he calls it a "kind of confused estimation" ("Cognitio Dei qua communiter ab omnibus vel pluribus cognoscitur secundum quamdam aestimationem confusam"—*C. G.*, lib. 3 c. 48).

convertible with God. It is to the application of these first principles, to the visible things of the world, that the historian of religion must go if he would give an ultimate explanation of the universal cult of God. Because of their fundamental nature and the easy and even spontaneous response which they evoke, St. Paul considered the failure of the pagan Romans to know God to be inexcusable. For the invisible things of Him from the creation of the world are clearly seen, being understood by the things that are made; His eternal power also and divinity; so that they are inexcusable (Romans i. 20).

The knowledge which is given is not proper to a Christian any more than to a pagan. It is universal.[598] This confused knowledge of which we are now speaking is imperfect, but, small though it be, "*even the least knowledge which we can have of God is worth more than all the knowledge we can have of creatures.*"[599]

Much that has been written about instinct, desire and the like can be accepted if understood as identical with confused knowledge. Professor Alexander, for example, insists that we have an appetite for God, just as we have an appetite for food.

The Angelic Doctor might well have been quoted in support of this position when he writes in *De Malo*: "Man desires Divine similitude by a natural appetite."[600] The Manchester Professor at times describes the confused knowledge in such terms as these, which are perfectly acceptable: "When we ask how we come by the nature of God, we must answer that, as with love and hate and appetite and aversion, it is because the world provokes in us a certain response ... which makes us aware, in no matter how primitive a form, of God."[601] The same approval is to be given

---

[598] "Ipsam naturam Dei prout in se est, neque catholicus, neque paganus cognoscit; sed uterque cognoscit eam secundum aliquam rationem causalitatis vel excellentiae vel remotionis. Et secundum hoc in eadem significatione accipere potest gentilis hoc nomen *Deus* cum dicit: Idolum est Deus, in qua accipit ipsum catholicus dicens: Idolum non est Deus."—I q. 13 art. 10 ad 5.

[599] "Nec obstat quod materialia a nobis perfectius cognoscuntur quam Deus; quia minima cognitio quae de Deo haberi potest, superat omnem cognitionem quae de creatura habetur. Nobilitas enim scientiae ex nobilitate sciti dependet."—*De Veritate*, q. 10 art. 8 ad 3.

[600] "Homo quolibet naturali appetitu appetit divinam similitudinem inquantum omne bonum naturaliter desideratum est quaedam similitudo divinae bonitatis."—*De Malo*, q. 8 art. 2.

[601] *Space, Time and Deity*, vol. ii. p. 374 and pp. 382-5.

to the following explanations of Professor Beckwith and Professor Spalding in the above sense. When Professor Beckwith says, for example, "Belief in God is not innate, but the tendency to such belief is constant and the inexpugnable structure of our consciousness,"[602] he is unconsciously giving the translation of a response in the Commentary on the *Sentences* of Peter Lombard.[603] Professor Spalding, even more than the others, gives an excellent description of this confused notion as a desire which "pushes the soul on until it comes to perfect existence. Thus when God is attained no desire can exceed a desire of Him."[604]

The Scholastic, who insists that the primary element in religious experience is intellectual, is immediately met with the objection that the intellect never works alone. "Modern philosophy," Mr. Davidson has told us, "affected in part by biology, has worked out the fruitful notion of mind as an organic unity, and consequently has insisted on the fact that the intellect or reason does not stand alone, but is in most intimate relation with feeling and willing."[605] The objection falls into line with the general attack on Scholasticism as the solidifier of the real.

"Modern philosophy, affected in part by biology," in insisting on the unity of mind has merely rediscovered that which has been generally admitted through the centuries. St. Thomas, for example, makes it quite clear in his treatise on *Mind* that the act of knowing, strictly so called, is not of the intelligence, but of the soul."[606] The Mind means something much more than the Reason. "It embraces the memory, the intelligence and the will; in a word, all the potencies which in their acts are free from material conditions."[607]

---

602 C. A. BECKWITH, *The Idea of God*, p. 112.

603 *Sent.*, q. 1 art. 2 ad 1.

604 K. J. SPALDING, *Desire and Reason*, p. 211.

605 WILLIAM M. DAVISON, *Recent Theistic Discussion* (1921), *loc. cit.*

Dean Inge, too, insists on the "high reason" which means to "include the will and the feelings disciplined under the guidance of the intellect" (*Personal Idealism and Mysticism* [2nd edition, 1913], p. 5).

606 "Intelligere proprie loquendo non est intellectus, sed animae per intellectum, sicut non calefacere est caloris, sed ignis per calorem."—*De Veritate*, q. 10 art. 9 ad 3.

607 "Et ideo mens potest comprehendere voluntatem et intellectum, absque eo quod sit animae essentiae, inquantum scilicet nominat quoddam genus potentiarum animae, et sub mente intelligitur comprehendi omnes illas potentias quae in suis actibus omnino a

Closely associated with this intellectual element in religious experience is a second, the affective. They have a repercussion one upon the other. Hence, when the intelligence attains its object even confusedly, the soul responds affectively. In a certain sense there is no knowledge of the real without some affective process, because man seeks the truth with his whole soul.

The above brief analysis of the elements of Scholastic religious experience will be more clearly thrown into relief in contrasting them with three possible errors which may arise.

The first is to make the affective state primitive in religious experience and the cause of the intellectual state.

The second is to make this type of experience the criterion of the primitive data concerning God.

The third is to make the reflex intellectual knowledge merely secondary and accidental in the development of our knowledge of God.

The intellectual element is not primitive in the modern account of religious experience; that which gives us God is, according to it, some "experience," some "sthenic affection," "instinct," "imagination" or "faith-state." In a word, it is by emotion that we mount up to the all-inclusive reality. "The emotional attitude is non-intellectual and carries its own assurance in its own state, or its warmth in the complete satisfaction which the emotion supplies."[608] The knowledge of God is the result of this emotion. It is the affective state which begets God. By an extension of principle, such theories as those of Desire and Hypothesis may be grouped under this class, since something non-intellectual is the *fons et origo* of the certitude.

Apart from the Agnostic and Pantheistic prejudice which often underlies these theories, they are for other reasons philosophically untenable. In opposition to the errors stated above we may lay down three principles:

materia et conditionibus materiae recedunt."—*De Veritate*, q. 10 art. 1.

"Mens omnis tria continet."—Ibid., ad 3.

Cf. This quotation of the Angelic Doctor with that of Dean Inge, for the sake of noting the striking similarity. See also W. R. THOMSON, *The Christian Idea of God*, p. 165.

[608] J. B. BAILLIE, *Studies in Human Nature*, p. 165.

(1) The affective religious state presupposes the intellectual coefficient.

(2) Religious experience is not a criterion of the primitive data about God, whether those data are an affective state, or a hypothesis, or a faith-state.

(3) Intellectual elaboration is necessary and essential.

(1) Affective Religious State Presupposes the Intellectual Coefficient

Some elements of religious experience, in the broad sense of the term, have been traced through all the hierarchies of creation. All creatures, from the stone to the angel, fundamentally tend toward God, however indirectly. In seeking their end they are seeking God. But this tendency, or inclination, or desire, or movement presupposes throughout the whole extent of these orders a cognitive *state*. If the knowledge does not exist in the thing itself, it must exist in some one outside itself who gave it its nature. The arrow does not know its mark, nor does it tend to its mark unless some one directs it. The orders of being below man do not know their end; they are directed to it by God.[609]

In the animal there is a natural movement to its end, which is due to sense knowledge. In man the movement is due to his intellectual knowledge.[610] Man cannot will anything, love anything, tend toward anything, have a "faith state" toward anything, unless he knows the thing. With even far greater force than in the lower kingdoms the law applies: knowledge underlies every movement.

609 "Amor naturalis, qui est in omnibus rebus causatur ex aliqua cognitione, non quidem in ipsis rebus naturalibus existente, sed in eo qui naturam instituit."—I-II q. 27 art. 2 ad 3.

"Res enim naturales appetunt quod eis convenit secundum suam naturam non per apprehensionem propriam, sed per apprehensionem instituentis naturam."—I-II q. 26 art. 1.

Hence, to say "instinct leads, intelligence does but follow" (*Varieties of Religious Experience*, pp. 74, 436, 501) is a contradiction. Instinct implies intelligence, if not in the animal, at least in some one else.

610 I q. 3 art. 1 ad 2.

The affective state in its turn presupposes knowledge. In its nature it is a reaction. It presupposes something which causes the reaction—that is, an object presented either by the senses or by the intellect. The affective state, therefore, begins only when the intellectual operation is terminated.[611] It is borne toward the object of knowledge in order to hold it, as it were, in such a way as to render unnecessary the retracing of the steps by which the knowledge was gained. An affective state of a son for his mother, for example, dispenses him from reviewing the intellectual procedure which begot that affection.[612] In this sense it may be said that the habits of the affective part of man act as a remote principle of knowledge, inasmuch as they elicit acts by which the intellect knows them.[613] But to subvert this order and to make antecedent what by its nature is consequent, is to destroy the very nature of the thing. Emotion never creates but presupposes knowledge. Solomon has lived immortally for refusing to admit that emotion could create truth. The guilty woman who appeared before him showed far more emotion than the innocent mother. The guilty woman tried to make emotion create the truth; the innocent woman allowed truth to create emotion. And the truth made her free.[614] There is a sentiment in religion, it is quite true.

---

611 "Intellectus autem est prior affectu."—*De Veritate*, q. 10 art. 5.

"Ubi terminator operatio intellectus, ibi incipit operatio affectus."—Ibid. q. 10 art. 11 ad 6; I q. 87 art. 4; I-II q. 32 art. 1. *C. G.*, lib. 3 c. 57. *De Veritate*, q. 22 art. 1 ad 5 and ad 7; q. 10 art. 12 ad 5.

Knowledge implies immanent assimilation of the object known to the knowing subject. The affective state, on the contrary, implies the inclination or affection to the thing as it is in itself. Affection, therefore, by itself can never be a means of knowledge; secondly, in order to function it must know the object to which it tends.

"Per vim appetitivam anima habet ordinem ad ipsas res, prout in seipsis sunt: ... Vis autem apprehensiva non trahitur ad rem, secundum quod in seipsa est sed cognoscit eam secundum intentionem rei quam in se habet vel recipit secundum proprium modum."—I-II q. 22 art. 2.

612 *De Veritate*, q. 10 art. 11 ad 6.

613 "Tertius modus est eorum quae pertinent ad partem affectivam, quorum ratio cognoscendi non est in intellectu, sed in affectu, et ideo non per sui praesentiam, quae in affectu, sed per ejus notitiam vel rationem, quae est in intellectu cognoscuntur, sicut per immediatum principium, quamvis etiam habitus affectivae partis per sui praesentiam sint quoddam remotum principium cognitionis inquantum eliciunt actus in quibus intellectus eos cognoscit; ut sic etiam possit dici quodammodo, quod per sui praesentiam cognoscuntur."—*De Veritate*, q. 10 art. 9 ad 1.

Compare the following words of GEORGE PLIMPTON ADAMS: "What I am saying is that there are circumstances in which feeling and sympathy and love are vehicles of knowledge."—*Idealism of the Modern Age* (1919), p. 226.

614 *Cf.* H. PINARD, art. "L'Expérience Religieuse," *Dict. de la Foi Catholique* (Vacant-

But because there is sentiment, it does not follow that the sentiment is primitive or that everything is sentiment. The affective state merely tells the direction. It does not tell what directs it. "Feeling is important for religious belief, not in supplying its content, or in supplanting its content, but in lending it strength."[615]

We may set the point at issue in the form of a question. It is argued that the "affective state" puts me in contact with Him "from whom saving experiences come;" or again, that we have an instinct or a desire for God. But we must ask: Why this instinct? Why this desire? Why does the affective state put me in contact with the "invisible God?" Why, in a word, is God the object of these states, or identified with them? Why is this object not evil, cosmic suicide or what you will? Why does God answer the need of these faculties more than the stars or the moon? Is it not because there is a certain proportionality between my intellect and the object, as there is between the eye and a thing seen? Is it not

---

Adam, Paris, 1923).

[615] PRATT, *Religious Consciousness*, p. 215. There is a text in St. Thomas which has sometimes been interpreted as an affective knowledge preceding the intellectual, by those who like to have the authority of such a philosopher for their doctrines. It may be said that there are two ways of having correctness of judgment: first, by the perfect use of reason; and secondly, in virtue of a certain connaturality with things which we must actually judge. In the matter of chastity, to judge by the rational method is the work of the man who knows moral principles. But to judge by connaturality is the work of him who has the habit of chastity (II-II q. 45 art. 2 c.). Elsewhere, just as the man by the natural light of the intelligence gives his assent to principles, so the virtuous by the habit of virtue judges correctly of that which belongs to virtue (II-II q. 2 art. 3 ad 2). These texts in no way militate against the intellectual theory of St. Thomas, for two reasons: "Virtue once acquired—that is, according to Thomistic principles—and the appetites once formed to act of themselves as reason ordains, there is no longer a need of a reflection which returns to first principles for each particular act; man has only to cast an interior bird's-eye view over his *tendencies* to *see* how they react, the present circumstances being given. Thus the habit once fixed, and known, *we judge with more or less greater facility the specification of the act.* Thus a Londoner, incapable of establishing a logical classification of the cases when he ought to say *shall* and *will*, answers correctly and without hesitation on all concrete examples. A rapid inference takes place between the action and the enunciation founded upon the connection, known beforehand, of the act and the habitual term. Furthermore, the opposition between chastity known by the rational method and known by connaturality is not an opposition between the intellect and an affective state, but between a logical or rational method and an intellectual method. The one is abstract and conceptual, the other is concrete and intuitive in the Thomistic sense. *Est enim aliquid scientia melius, scilicet intellectus*" (PIERRE ROUSSELOT, *L'Intellectualisme de St. Thomas* [2nd edition], p. 72). *Cf.* JAQUES MARITAIN, *Réflexions sur l'Intelligence*, pp. 114, 115.

Cajetan reminds us that here St. Thomas is speaking of supernatural virtues and habits, and not of natural ones (in II-II q. 45 art. 2).

because, in a certain way, we are predetermined by nature to depend upon God by a real relation, and God is predetermined to us by a logical relation? In other words, is it not because we were made for God, and hence only God can satisfy us? Furthermore, is not this power on the part of the object to satisfy us independent of our tendencies? The coloured object which in point of fact satisfies the eye is independent of the tendency of the eye to see. By the very fact that the object calls the tendency into act, it does not depend for existence on the tendency.[616] So, too, by the very fact that God calls forth the tendency, the need, the desire, He does not depend on it. No faculty creates its own object.[617]

If there is a proportionality between ourselves and God, and this proportionality is independent of our making, some faculty is needed which can embrace an object of knowledge proportional to both in some analogical fashion. Now, no object is wide enough to include the two, except *being*; for in *being*, as particular determinations, are contained the good, the true, the beautiful—in a word, anything that can satisfy a desire or an inclination. Inasmuch as the intellect is commensurate with being, it follows that all proportionality between God and man must be reduced to this faculty. Religious experience, then, as confused intellectual knowledge, puts us in contact with God, because it can grasp all being. No other faculty has an object with the same broad inclusiveness. Indeed, the very fact that the affective state is a function of the material side of us excludes such contact as a direct and primitive form of knowledge.

From a denial of the priority of the intellectual element over the affective, certain consequences follow which render the *modern theory* of religious experience untenable.

Whence comes the affective state, the sentiment of God, or the "sense of something there"? From ourselves? If so, we are God. From experience? If so, it has no greater value than any

---

[616] F. A. BLANCHE, O.P., 197, "Un Essai de Synthèse pragmatiste," *Revue des Sciences Philosophiques et Théologiques* (1907), p. 447.

[617] Professor ALEXANDER in his *Space, Time and Deity* says that instinct does not create, it discovers God. But does not discovery presuppose existence? Columbus would never have discovered America if it had not existed; neither will instinct discover God unless He exists. The problem ultimately is, why does instinct recognize its own object more than another object? The intellect alone can give the answer.

organic state. But experience can only approve or disapprove the reality of an object: it cannot produce or create an object. It is an adjective flung at a substantive. Does it come from God?

The affective state is organic. It is therefore personal and incommunicable, as are all affective states. But if it is personal and incommunicable, there follow two results. First, God will vary from person to person because no affective state is the same in two persons.[618] Secondly, God will vary from experience to experience in the same person. When man is in a passion, something will seem good to him which does not seem so when he is not in a passion.[619] As taste depends upon a certain disposition of the tongue, so will God follow the disposition of the "experiencer."[620] It is precisely because the affective states vary from one philosopher to another that we have so many different gods in modern philosophy. Mr. Fawcett, for example, comes into contact with a Divinal Imaginal,[621] Professor Alexander with a *nisus*, Mr. Holmes with a President of a Cosmic Commonwealth, James with a "God in the dust," and Mr. Wells with a "youth in the morning sun." There are as many Gods as there are philosophers.

Sir Henry Jones, speaking of this, pertinently remarks: "No ultimate law or principle can be operative *only* occasionally. To maintain that God is Good now and then, and present and operative here and there, or that order rules the universe at times and in certain spots, while elsewhere contingencies are rampant and particulars run amok—all that seems to me as foolish as to say that 2 x 2 is 4 now and then on certain days and in certain

[618] "Si sit dolor intensus, impeditur homo ne tunc aliquid addiscere possit. Et tantum potest intendi quod nec etiam instante dolore, potest homo aliquid considerare etiam quod prius scivit."—I-II q. 37 art. 1.

[619] "Unde secundum quod homo est in passione aliqua, videtur sibi aliquid conveniens, quod non videtur ei extra passionem existenti."—I-II q. 9 art. 2.

P. T. YOUNG, "An Experimental Study of Mixed Feelings," *American Journal of Psychology* (1918), vol. 29, pp. 237-71. The author refers to five or six reports of experiences on the affective processes to show how all are unanimous in finding marked individual differences.

[620] "Dispositionem linguae sequitur judicium gustus."—I-II q. 7 art. 1.

[621] "Cum igitur homo cessat ab usu intellectualis habitus, insurgunt *imaginationes extraneae* et quandoque ad contrarium ducentes."—I-II q. 53 art. 3.

"Intemperatus ... totaliter sequitur concupiscentiam, et ideo etiam ipse utitur syllogismo trium propositionum."—*De Malo*, q. 3 art. 9 ad 7.

places. Both the theory and the practice of religion demand for its sovereign authority an unlimited domain."[622]

Then, too, with the same person God will vary from one experience to another. Professor Leuba assures us that "the validity of the religious states of consciousness is precisely the same as any other state of consciousness; they are absolutely undeniable, *only as long as they are considered merely as the experience of the subject*, and no longer."[623] The affective state which gives us contact with God in climbing the Alps will not be that which we feel in a shipwreck, and will not give us the same kind of God. God will vary with our joys and our sorrows, our laughs and our tears, our fortunes and our misfortunes. There will be as many Gods as there are "varieties of religious experience." In every case we shall be "worshipping at the shrine our own hands have made." God will become nothing more than the "God we can use;" which is equivalent to saying there will be no God but ourselves. Such a God would be absolutely worthless as the foundation of any religion. He would be nothing more than a mere justification of our own mode of living. Instead of making our lives conform to dogmas, this view would make dogmas conform to our lives.[624]

But make the foundation of our belief in God intellectual, and it is immediately removed from the vicissitudes of the affective life; God then becomes something more than a "variant." He becomes a constant. Hence it is that the God as well as the Credo of an Intellectualist are true independently of his affective states. God will have the same objective validity for us, whether we are contemplating a sunset or suffering in anguish. He will be above the needs of the age and the progress of biology, as every cause is above its effect. He will be the God who is the same

[622] *A Faith that Enquires*, p. 42

[623] *Psychological Study of Religion* (1913), p. 237.

[624] The affective approach makes each man the measure of the God in whom he will believe. It is this that explains the rather blasphemous judgments sometimes passed on God. James, for example, in his *Pluralistic Universe* writes: "The prince of darkness may be a gentleman, as we are told he is; but whatever the God of heaven and earth is, he surely can be no gentleman" (72). The same is true of Wells, who writes: "If I thought there was an omnipotent God who looked down on battles and death and all the waste and horror of the war—able to prevent these things, doing them to amuse Himself, I think I should spit in His empty face" (*Mr. Britling Sees it Through*, p. 397). See E. H. REEMAN, p. 20: "I would not have use for such a God anyway."

yesterday, today and for ever, in contrast with the modern "God" found by an affective state, who will vary from forest to forest and from horizon to horizon.

In conclusion, it may be said that the origin of the modern insistence on the affective state lies in the failure to distinguish confused from reflex knowledge. It is quite true that an affective state often precedes reflex knowledge; but it is never true that it precedes all knowledge. What modern philosophers call *contact with God* is really only a *conclusion from first principles* drawn from the visible things of the universe. God is not the phenomenon which we perceive; rather He is the Ultimate Cause which produces it. In a word, the whole modern position falls into an inconsistency. On the one hand, it declares it to be impossible for the intelligence to surpass experience and to reach God; on the other hand, it declares experience to be the royal route to Him. Certainly, if the organic and affective part of us, by which we are like unto animals, can attain God, then the intellectual part of us, by which we are like unto God, *can* attain Him.

The doctrine which has just been exposed is the Thomistic statement of the primary importance of the intellect in the quest for God. As time goes on, thinkers are more and more coming back to the Thomistic notion. Mr. Flower of Oxford has admirably stated the argument in these words: "To be reasonable is therefore as primary a duty in religion as to be passionate, emotional or impulsive. It is not enough to 'feel good' ... to enjoy the aesthetic and emotional satisfactions and thrills which some forms of religion set themselves out to secure ... Any belief that stimulates an instinctive tendency will, it is true, do for this. But for those to whom religion means something that does not make them 'feel good,' but be and do good, it is essential to have beliefs which represent the nearest approach to truth we can make, which are, so to speak, outstretched hands grasping the reality of God and bringing to our life and its opportunities the wider vision of a divine purpose to be fulfilled."[625] "Emotion is apt to be misleading, not because the thing in which we believe is also an object of desire, but because wanting it is apt to affect our mental processes and prevent us from looking at facts just as they

[625] J. CYRIL FLOWER, M.A., *Psychological Studies of Religious Questions* (1924), pp. 12, 13.

are ... The source of the trouble is not that we reason in terms of emotional objects, but that we reason in emotional ways and so cannot get objects into their true perspective."[626] "To appeal to the emotions on questions where only reason and evidence are really relevant is to build upon sand."[627]

(2) Experience cannot be the Criterion of the Primitive Data about God, whether those Data are given by an Affective State, of "Faith," or as a Hypothesis

Religious experience demands interpretation. There are to be certain standards by which it is to be judged. Among these are the needs of the individual, the needs of the age, or both, in the light of the theory of evolution. "The practical idea which has to do with life as it launches itself on the great venture of living" is the greatest of these determinants.[628] Its conclusion is that "the gods we stand by are the gods we need and can use."[629] But all these standards by which "religious experience" is to be judged imply an act of the intelligence. Every judgment of value is intellectual. It supposes the non-empirical and the transcendental. The very assertion that there will be no intellectual dogmas to judge religion is in itself an intellectual dogma. There is no dogma in the whole of the intellectual order more rigid than the dogma that we need no dogma. In denying its necessity we are asserting it.

The empirical test, in itself, is not in the intellectual order, it is true, but the reason for which we choose to use the empirical test is of the intellectual order. Evolution in itself is of the empirical order, but the reason for making that a test of a religious experience falls within the scope of the intellect.

---

[626] ARTHUR KENYON ROGERS, *What is Truth?* (1923), pp. 16, 17.

[627] PRATT, *Religious Consciousness*, p. 183. *Cf.* ARMSTONG, "Is Faith a Form of Feeling?" *Harvard Theological Review*, No. 4, p. 79.

[628] W. R. THOMSON, *The Christian Idea of God*, p. 165.

[629] W. JAMES, *Varieties of Religious experiences*, p. 331.

Apart from this, there are certain inconsistencies in the modern criterion which cannot be explained away. For example, to make God depend on the particular value He may have for our lives is to subvert the relation between the end and the means. Health is not desirable on account of the medicine, otherwise medicine is more desirable than health.

Health is the end. Medicine is the means to the end.[630] In like manner, God is not desirable because He may be of some use in our lives. He is not a means "to the richer, fuller and more satisfying life." He is the end of life, or rather He is Life. Nothing has any value for us unless it has a value in itself. God does not exist because He is useful for our lives. He is useful because He exists. His value for us is a consequence of His existence; His existence is not a consequence of His value. God is not good because He has a value for our lives; He has a value for our lives because He is Good. *Operatio sequitur esse.* To make our experience, in its finite mode of being, the determinant of either the existence of God or His attributes is to suppose that God has no value whatever except in relation to our puny selves, and that apart from this value for us He is not worth knowing.

It is very true to say that "the tree shall be known by its fruits," but this must not make us oblivious of that which underlies this judgment, namely, the tree explains the fruits.

"The utility of a religious doctrine," as M. Michelet has put it, "can put in relief its superiority, but this utility finds its sufficient *reason* in the superiority of the doctrine."[631] There will be no fruits unless the tree exists; neither will there be any fruits of the idea of God unless God exists. To say, then, that the questions, "Does God exist? How does He exist? What is He?" are so many irrelevant questions,[632] is to say the absurd.

There must be at the outset some intellectual data, even though that data be known only *in confuso.* This has been sufficiently insisted on to allow us to pass on to the value of experience. God must be tested in the crucible of experience, is

[630] "Si dicatur, quod sanitas est desiderabilis propter medicinam, non ideo sequitur, quod medicina sit magis desiderabilis: quia sanitas est in ordine finium, medicina autem in ordine causarum efficientium."—I q. 87 art. 2 ad 3.

[631] *Dieu et l'Agnosticisme contemporain* (Paris, 1920), p. 100.

[632] J. LEUBA, "The Contents of Universal Consciousness," *Monist*, xi. p. 536

the assertion of modern philosophy. If He "dignifies human character, adds reach and sanity to man's aims, elevates and secures the life of man and makes for peace and mutual helpfulness among the nations,"[633] then the proof of His existence is strong.

Let us suppose that experiences concerning God are multiplied indefinitely. Even suppose that all these experiences are spiritual. Represent the experience or the fact by SV, signifying Spiritual Value. Represent multiplication of this test indefinitely by SV ∞. At the end of all my experiences, numerous, varied and multiplied as they may be, what have I? I merely have made *experiments* without gaining an increase in knowledge. To affirm a constant character of a common subject is mere repetition. There is arithmetical universality; there is a multiplication of facts; experience abounds, but there is no knowledge. The unity of a proposition depends on the unity of a thing designated. In the whole series of facts a different thing is designated inasmuch as there is a plurality of objects accidentally juxtaposed. The only way by which a unity within all these facts can be found is to reduce them to their specific unity by a dose of intellectual abstraction.[634] It is a fact, for example, that hydrochloric acid decomposes into chlorine and hydrogen. This is a fact which may be multiplied indefinitely. But that which is not a *fact* but a *law*, and which is the work of the intelligence, is that hydrochloric acid is not homogeneous as are its constituents. Here there is more than a mere sign representing a group of similar things; it is a law of facts which ultimately has its foundation in one of the principles of being.

To apply this to the problem in point: experience as experience does not in the least affect our knowledge of God. A thousand facts are no richer than ten facts, as long as they are juxtaposed. Neither do multiplied spiritual experiences about God give us any knowledge of God. The intelligence must intervene with certain principles which will render these experiences intelligible. Our conclusion, then, is that a philosophy of experience without the work of intelligence is

[633] Sir HENRY JONES, *op. cit.*

[634] J. MARECHAL, *Études sur la Psychologie des Mystiques* (1924), t. 1, p. 7.

unintelligible. As a famous French scientist has well said: "On dit souvent qu'il faut expérimenter son idée préconçue. Cela n'est pas possible; non seulement ce serait rendre toute expérience stérile, mais on le voudrait qu'on ne le pourrait pas."[635]

Grant, now, that the modern philosopher becomes intellectual to the point of accepting the necessity of an intellectual abstraction. The question now is: Will experience verify our preconceived ideas? Will results make the idea true? Because result is the term toward which the idea leads us, will they constitute its truth? In other words, what is the value of modern *faith*?

Is the judgment about God "a candidate for the truth"? In a word, are there "cases where faith creates its own justification"?[636] As an illustration of this principle, the interesting example which James gave will be recalled: "Our faith beforehand," he writes "in an uncertified result is the only thing that makes the result come true." If we have faith that we can jump the mountain abyss, we can make that "universe" true by our faith, as we make it untrue by our mistrust.

There is much bad logic hidden behind the example. Examples cover a multitude of sins. The example proves the contrary of what James intented to prove. The object of our faith or hypothesis is God. This corresponds to the other side of the abyss in the example given. Now, does the fact that I succeed in making the jump in the least affect the other side of the abyss? Certainly not. It is existent anterior to my faith, as it is existent posterior to it, being in truth quiet independent to it. My faith does not in the least verify its existence, as my failure to attain does not in the least destroy its existence.

My judgement of the object remains intact. What will be new will be my attitude of mind toward that relation. What it consider as hypothetical it now considers as perfectly well founded. The relation between the judgment and the object has remained immutable though our mind has a different view of it.[637]

---

[635] L. POINCARÉ, *Science et Hypothèse*, p. 50.

[636] W. JAMES, *The Will to Believe*, p. 97.

[637] F. A. BLANCHE, "Pragmatisme," *Dict. Apologétique de la Foi Catholique*, col. 157.

The judgment which we make about God in confused intellectual knowledge remains unchanged. The verification which follows adds nothing to the context of knowledge. Just as the other side of the abyss continues to exist whether I succeed in making the leap or not, so God's existence remains unaffected by my mental attitude. The proposition which is at the base of this faith and of the *als ob* philosophy is that there is a direct and general influence of the ideas on things. It is true that the ideas have influence on the things indirectly. Our mental attitude or outlook does affect the things themselves, very much as smoked glasses affect the object of our vision. Hence the importance which St. Thomas attaches to the moral preparation as necessary for the perception of certain truths.[638] But at the same time there is danger of exaggeration. James is guilty of it in the example. It makes a condition a cause, and a quality a substance. If our mind had the power of modifying the real in virtue of that which it awakens, our physical activity would be useless, or at least it would play merely a secondary role in the transformation which we impose on things in order that they may satisfy us. It is a fact beyond all dispute that to conceive or to will energetically does not make things correspond to our thoughts and desires. Hunger has never been satisfied by an idea of bread.[639]

If ideas reveal reality, there is no need of verifying them. Hence the great importance which Thomistic realism lays upon the doctrine that by ideas we do not rest in photographs, but attain to the very things themselves. That which we know is the object, not the idea of the object. It is only by a reflex act that we know the idea. When two concepts united by the verb *to be* imply one another reciprocally, *e.g.* "a thing cannot be and not be viewed under the same formal aspect," we have no need to go to experience to know that this is true of the reality. Only where this necessary

---

[638] 4 d. 33 q. art. 3.

[639] II-II q. 46 art. 2.

In an excellent article on Pragmatism, F. A. Blanche shows how this notion of ideas determining reality runs counter to the very principles of the philosophy of evolution. According to this philosophy the world was undetermined. Without any transcendent cause, which it denies (and which consequently renders evolution absurd), mind is said to have evolved. Ideas now determine reality. Hence from the undetermined has come the determined (col. 159).

connection between the subject and the predicate is lacking is there need to go to experience.

The philosophy which makes the idea of God true if the consequences are good confuses the true and the good. The error is not that the truth is made to consist in the nature of such and such a consequence, but rather that the good is presented as the mark of the true or as the constituent of the true. In the good the dispositions of the subject enter in as an essential element. It is good to sit near a fire when the weather is cold, but not when it is warm.[640] The same cannot be said of the true. It is independent of the dispositions of the subject. Furthermore, by the good we are drawn to the thing; by truth the thing is drawn toward us. By the appetitive faculties the soul is related to things as they are in themselves.[641] The good supposes the true, as desire supposes knowledge, and as an inclination supposes a reason for the tendency. *The idea of God's existence is not true because it succeeds practically; it succeeds practically because He exists.*

Hypothesis and Fiction or "Als Ob"

What, then, is to be thought of that theory according to which God is the "most reasonable and probable hypothesis"? One cannot but admire the sincerity and the good intention with which Sir Henry Jones and others have set about the task of reconstituting some belief in God. But the intention of the writer must not blind us to those features which render *A Faith that Enquires* an erroneous substitute for the common-sense notion.

First, in answer to the question, What is the origin of hypothesis?, this author writes: "The idea of God comes as a possible or probable and convincing explanation of the universe and man's life and destiny."[642] "We approach the facts of life with a preconception, favourable or unfavourable, of the

[640] "Adveniente frigore, incipit esse bonum sedere ad ignem, quod prius non erat."—I q. 19 art. 7.

[641] "Magis autem trahitur anima ad rem per vim appetitivam, quam per vim apprehensivam; nam per vim appetitivam anima habet ordinem ad ipsas res, prout in seipsis sunt ... vis autem apprehensiva non trahitur ad rem, secundum quod in seipsa est; sed cognoscit eam secundum intentionem rei, quam in se habet vel recipit secundum proprium modum."—I-II q. 22 art. 2 c.

[642] *A Faith that Enquires*, p. 228.

existence of God, which is the result, not so much of external observation, as of reflection upon our own nature and needs."[643] These preconceptions are the result of "gifts that come to man by inheritance, as potencies in his very structure at birth; the treasure of slowly accumulated traditions and habits of living into which he enters, little by little, day by day, as a member of society."[644] Here there is a confusion of the origin of hypothesis and the origin of first principles. Such a knowledge of God is really the confused knowledge of the Scholastics. It is true that we do approach the facts of life with a certain preconception which is the result of potencies in our structure at birth, which are in perfect accordance with our nature and our needs. But what are these but the knowledge of principles, which are naturally known and indemonstrable,[645] which lie in potency in the soul and flash in the act of knowledge once the terms become known?[646] They are the "seeds" of all consequent knowledge.[647] These principles belong to our nature from a certain preconception, if you will, of our needs, our end and our destiny. In virtue of them "man has a natural inclination to know the truth of God."[648] They are the "first movers" of our intellectual life, and their natural term is their knowledge and love of God.

But they are far from being hypothesis. They are not conditional. They are not tentative explanations of things. They are necessary and absolute. They admit of no exception, as they admit of no demonstration. They are perceived by an intuition once the terms are understood this point has been insisted on in previous chapters, and it suffices here to recall it. Sir Henry Jones has vaguely seen that some movement is necessary at the beginning and throughout the whole of our intellectual principles

---

[643] p. 212. "There is only one way of knowing. It consists in finding a place for new phenomena within our system of experience" (p. 79).

[644] p. 93.

[645] "Sicut enim in speculativis ... ita etiam in operativis sunt quaedam principia naturaliter cognita quasi indemonstrabilia principia."—*Eth.*, lib. 5 lect 12.

[646] "Ita in anima humana est quidam habitus naturalis principiorum primorum."—*De Veritate*, q. 16 art. 1

[647] "In ratione hominis insunt naturaliter quaedam principia naturaliter cognita tam scibilium quam agendorum, quae sunt quaedam seminalia intellectualium virtutum et moralium."—I-II q. 63 art. 1.

[648] "Inest homini inclinatio ab bonum secundum naturam rationis quae est sibi propria, sicut homo habet naturalem inclinationem ad hoc quod veritatem cognoscat de Deo."—I-II q. 94 art. 2.

for mere "accumulated traditions and habits of living." He has divined their origin in saying "they are born from the intercourse of mind and objects," but he errs in calling them "mere subject of proof."[649] Had he thoroughly seen the necessity contained in the first principles of both the speculative and the practical intellect, he never would have descended into hypotheses in his treatment of God, as he never would have set up out of the world-process the kind of God he actually proposed. Then his foundations of knowledge (p. 346) instead of being hypotheses would have been *necessities.*

Furthermore, it would have been well, at the outset of any work which treats God as a hypothesis, to inquire the meaning of the very term hypothesis and its conditions. Why is a hypothesis possible? Is it not for a formal and a material reason? First, the failure of the mind to attach a given judgment about things or a group of facts to some necessary and certain principle;[650] for example, "the dream is the disguised realization of an unfulfilled desire." This judgment has no evident connection with a certain fixed and necessary principle, and consequently has that element of possibility about it which makes it apt to be a hypothesis.

The second reason for a hypothesis is the mutability and the potency of material things.[651] The material principle in reality is determinable, and precisely because it is infinitely determinable there is a possibility of an infinity of individuals in the same genus, and a possibility of multiplied tests in the same genus.[652] The more you have of matter, the more you have of the indefinite.[653] The first element represents the formal aspect of hypothesis, and the second the material. One is in relation to

[649] *Op. cit.*, pp. 94, 100, 101.

"Ille qui quaerit scientiam non omnio ignorat, sed secundum aliquid eam praecognoscit, vel in universali vel in aliquo ejus effectu, vel per hoc quod audit eam laudari ut Augustinus dicit 10 *De Trinitate*; sic enim eam cognoscere non est eam habere, sed cognoscere eam perfecte."—I-II q. 27 art. 2 ad 1.

[650] "Si autem aliquis alicui proponat ea quae in principiis per se notis non includuntur, vel in aliud non manifestantur, non faciet in eo scientiam, sed forte opinionem vel fidem."—*De Veritate*, q. 2 art. 1.

[651] "Incertitudo causatur propter transmutabilitatem materiae sensibils."—*Post. Analy.*, lib. 1 lect. 14.

[652] "Infinitum congruit materiae quae est individuationis principium."—Ibid.

[653] "Quanto magis proceditur versus particularia, tanto magis itur versus infinitum."—Ibid. "Contingentia in rebus sensibilibus est conditio consequens materiam individuantem sensibilia."—CAJETAN in I q. 86 art. 4, X.

knowledge and the other in relation to matter. But God, as the object of knowledge, falls under neither of these elements. He does not fall under the first, because the proof for His existence has immediate connection with the necessary principles of the mind, *e.g.* the principle of identity. He does not fall under the second, because He is not matter. Any test made on matter will be about our subjective attitude toward God. It will in no way be a test about His objective existence. Matter does not make Him intelligible. Rather He makes matter intelligible. The very conditions, then, which render a hypothesis possible make it at the same time impossible to apply it to God. God and hypothesis are travelling in opposite directions, and it is impossible that one should ever fall under the other. And what is true of hypothesis in this matter is true of Professor Vaihinger's *Als Ob.*

It may now be asked, why have the philosophers seen fit to throw God into experience to test Him as "any other scientific hypothesis"? In this matter it is important to get to the foundation of things. What is the basis of the distinction of higher sciences? Sir Henry Jones has rightly insisted on the fact that "the matter of a system of knowledge determines the method of enquiry."[654] "The method which can be fruitfully employed depends upon the aspect of reality, or the matter which is investigated."[655] In other words, sciences vary according to the abstraction brought to bear upon them. "Every science has its particular point of view and purpose."[656] This is perfectly good Aristotelianism.

Now, if the degree of abstraction determines the science, and there are three supreme grades of abstraction, it follows that there will be three supreme sciences. The first degree of abstraction is that of quantity in movement, which gives the science of physics.[657] The second degree of abstraction is from movement. The objects considered are *immobilia*, which, though not separated from matter according to being, are separate according to

[654] *Op. cit.*, p. 36.

[655] p. 49.

[656] p. 32.

[657] "Physica enim est circa inseparabilia et mobilia."—*Metaphysics*, lib. 6 lect. 1.

"Physics ... deals with quantities. Of qualitative differences it offers no explanation."—SIR HENRY JONES, p. 32.

reason.[658] This gives the science of mathematics. These two abstractions Sir Henry recognizes, but unfortunately recognizes them as ultimate. There is, however, yet another degree of abstraction, which abstracts from all formal quality and quantity and existence, except being, and "this most honourable science is concerned with the most honourable genus of beings, in which are contained divine things."[659]

Sir Henry stops with the second degree of abstraction. Instead of mounting up to the third, where he would find even a greater necessity than in physics or mathematics, he descends into the empirical order, wherein he finds a proof of necessity wherever there is systematic coherence and existential interdependence.[660] In this precisely consists the fallacy. The philosophy of God's existence belongs to the third degree of abstraction. He is *Being.* Now, if the degree of abstraction determines the method,[661] and God is discovered and treated by the third degree of abstraction, which is metaphysical, it follows that He will not be studied by a method dependent on psychological states. God is not tested in the "spiritual laboratory of the universe."[662] God will for ever remain outside the realm of experience as experience, just as the truth of the multiplication table will remain outside Freudian interpretation of dreams. To say that God must be tested "like the test of an invention, and in no wise like the argument for or against the theory" (p. 86), is to miss the whole point at issue. Why can an invention be tested by the way "it works"? Because both in its *nature* and in its *mode of operation* it is entirely in the order of experiment. But God is not in the order of experiment either in His nature or in His mode of operation.

---

658 "Mathematica quaedam circa immobilia, quae tamen non sunt separata a materia secundum esse, sed solum secundum rationem."—*Metaphysics*, Ibid.

659 "Sed prima scientia est circa separabilia secundum esse, et quae sunt omnino immobilia ... Honorabilissima scientia est circa honorabilissimum genus entium in quo continetur res divinas ... ista scientia est circa res divinas; et ideo dicitur theologia, quasi sermo de divinis."—*Metaphysics*, Ibid.

660 p. 33.

661 This Sir Henry Jones concedes, p. 49.

662 To say we verify the hypothesis by experience is a contradiction. God is known only by an abstraction from experience. To turn about and say that the abstraction must be tested by experience means that our mind must immediately place itself outside the conditions where it placed itself by abstraction. T. RICHARD, *Philosophie du Raisonnement* (Paris, 1918), p. 90.

What makes the test possible for an invention is the very thing that makes it impossible with God. God is shown to be by the intellectual and not by the empirical order. He must therefore be the object of *intellectual* and not *empirical* investigation.

Furthermore, before an invention can be tested it must exist. So, too, before God can be tested He must exist. Experiences and tests, then, can bear only upon His *utility* for us, and not upon His *existence.* Throughout the whole philosophy of faith or hypothesis there is this fundamental confusion between the existence of a thing and its utility.

Sir Henry Jones says that the denial of God's existence will have far-reaching "consequences which are recognized as too insane to be entertained."[663] This indeed is true, for God cannot be denied without ultimately denying the principle of contradiction. To do this argues insanity, if you will, but it is the insanity not of an empirical, experimental world, but of the world of necessary truths. Our knowledge of God comes from experience, but the reason of our adhesion is not experience alone. In a word, the whole philosophy of "hypothesis" falls into a vicious circle. On the one hand, it says that principles must be tested by experience, and at the same time it tests experience by principles. The facts have no value unless considered in the light of the general ideas of being, cause and effect, finality, reason of being, and the like. They have no value except in virtue of principles. The only way out of the vicious circle is to admit with genuine intellectualist philosophy that we adhere to certain principles not only because of the testimony of experience, but by reason of their intellectual content. The modern philosophy of "faith" and "hypothesis" reveals a sincerity of intention among its adherents, as it also reveals the chaos among modern minds which results from the rejection of intelligence.

The fallacy of the German school is that it forgets that, before we can have belief in God, we must have a reason for that belief. Before we can live *as if* God existed, we must have a reason for this hypothesis of His existence. What is the foundation of the supposition, or the fiction, as the German school calls it, if it is not something intellectual? Fiction proceeds "as if the thing

[663] p. 346.

existed." In other words, it is a kind of mental hypnotism by which we make the imaginary real. The philosophy of the *Als Ob* does not sound so bad when it keeps to Kantian terms; but bring it down to the field of reality, without changing its principles, and it refutes itself. Living *as if* we had our three meals a day will never fill an empty stomach. Living *as if* we were rich will soon drive us into the poorhouse. Living *as if* there was a God will never give us God. It may eventually affect our mental attitude, as we have already pointed out; but if God is no more than this mental attitude, then there is no God but ourselves.

Hypotheses and fictions have their place, but their place is not in the problem of God. A bird in the hand is worth two in the bush. Reason does not warrant, nor does prudence dictate, our abandoning genuine intellectual principles for mere suppositions.

(3) Reflex Intellectual Knowledge is Essential in the Development of Religious Experience

Modern philosophy has not gone to the extreme of denying every intellectual development of religious experience. Many writers agree that some "elaboration of reflection"[664] is necessary to "bring such immediate knowledge to greater conceptual clearness."[665] We must, in the words of Professor Hoernlé, "make plain what in a sense is there and possessed by us all the time."[666]

But what part does the intelligence play? Is the "building out, performed by the intellect,"[667] accidental and secondary? The answer to the question is shown by one general opposition to all dogma. The reflective element is merely a "surface exhibition,"[668] a sort of philosophical luxury. Scholastic thought, on the contrary, regards it as an essential, an integral part of our

[664] *Space, Time and Deity*, pp. 378, 375, 377 of vol. II.
[665] LINDSAY, *Great Philosophical Problems*, p. 225.
[666] *Matter, Life, Mind and God*, *loc. cit.*
[667] *Varieties of Religious Experience*, p. 431.
[668] Ibid., pp. 74, 436, 501.

knowledge of God. The reason is that to know God by a confused knowledge is not to know Him as distinct from other objects of knowledge. Knowledge properly so called is not confused, rather it is distinct.[669]

That God is involved in every act of knowledge is true, but He is involved only implicitly. The confused notion of being, for example, which the intelligence has in its ontological infancy is by no means identical with God.[670] God is implicitly in every desire and in all love, but only in His likeness and not in His essence.[671] If we should restrict our desires always to confused knowledge without making them reflexly definite, they would be in vain. Hence the necessity of drawing them out of their confused state.[672] Simply because we have a natural desire to such happiness, we are not dispensed from seeking God by intellectual investigation.[673] The same may be said for the "instinct" of God of which Professor Alexander speaks. Instinct for food is for food in general, not for caviare. The particular determination of the instinct functions through sense knowledge. So, too, simply because we have an "instinct" for God in the above-defined sense, it does not follow that that undetermined pabulum which satisfies our soul's hunger is God. "In what the particular determination consists—that is, whether it be in virtue, or knowledge, or pleasure, or anything of the kind nature has not determined."[674] To call any of these things God, or to make of Him a creation of Space-Time, or a bud from the Divinal Imaginal, is not to know Him at all. "He who errs about God does not know God. If any one believes God to be a body, he

---

[669] "Habere propriam cognitionem de rebus est cognoscere res non solum in communi, sed secundum quod sunt ad invicem distinctae."—I q. 14 art. 6, Sed Contra.

[670] "In statu viae, in quo per species a rebus abstractas intelligimus ei cognoscimus ens commune sufficienter, non autem ens increatum."—*De Veritate*, q. 10 art. 2 ad 10; art. 12 ad 3.

[671] "Summum bonum desideratur dupliciter; uno modo in sui essentia, et sic non omnia desiderant summum bonum; alio modo in sui similitudine et sic omnia desiderant summum bonum, quia nihil est desiderabile nisi in quantum in eo similitudo summi boni invenitur (Dei)."—*De Veritate*, q. 10 art. 12 ad 5.

[672] "Si intellectus naturalis creaturae non possit pertingere ad primam causam rerum, remanebit inane desiderium naturae."—*C. G.*, lib. 3 c. 50.

[673] *De Veritate*, q. 22 art. 5 ad 11.

[674] *De Veritate*, q. 22 art. 7; q. 10 art. 9 ad 1.

does not know God, but knows something else in the place of God."[675]

The confused knowledge of God effected by the use of first principles in the visible things of the world is no richer in its content than the foregoing. It will be recalled that the Angelic Doctor, in illustrating immediate religious experience, used the example of a man who, on seeing the order of the world, concluded some governor thereof. Later on he adds: "But who or what this governor of nature is, whether he be unique or not, we do not know immediately by confused knowledge. It is much like our concluding a soul as the cause of man's operations, when we see him moving and doing things. But what the soul is, whether it be a body, and how it affects its operations, we do not know."[676] Dr. Tudor Jones in this connection writes: "We have a certain knowledge of the doings of people without ever having even formed logical constructions concerning these doings. In the same way, the normal human mind has a certain idea that there must be at the back of the universe a reality corresponding in some way at least with what exists and happens in the world. The idea of God in this sense has been the possession of man at all times in the history of the race."[677] All confused knowledge of whatsoever kind sins against this one point—to wit, it can never clearly distinguish its object from other things. Though it is natural for us to know God by a confused knowledge, we cannot conclude that we know God as He is, any more than "when we know some one is coming over the hill in the distance we can conclude that it is Peter, although it may be Peter who is coming."[678] When, therefore, James says that from the point of view of religious experience polytheism is as satisfying as

---

[675] *C. G.*, lib. 3 c. 118.

[676] "Quis autem vel qualis, vel si unus tantum est ordinator naturae, nondum statim ex hac communi consideratione habetur, sicut quum videmus hominem moveri et alia opera agere, percipimus in eo quamdam causam harum operationum quae aliis rebus non inest, et hanc causam animam nominamus, nondum tamen scientes quid sit anima, si est corpus, vel qualiter operationes praedictas efficiat."—*C. G.*, 3 c. 38.

[677] *Metaphysics of Life and Death* (1923), pp. 160, 161.

[678] "Non recte sumitur conclusio nisi per resolutionem in prima principia, ita appetitus creaturae rationalis non est rectus nisi per *appetitum explicitum* ipsius Dei actu vel habitu."—*De Veritate*, q. 22 art. 2 c.

"Sed hoc non est simpliciter cognoscere Deum esse, sicut cognoscere venientem, non est cognoscere Petrum, quamvis sit Petrus veniens."—I q. 2 art. 1 ad 1.

monotheism, he is in some accord with St. Thomas, who says that from confused knowledge we do not know whether the governor of the world is one or many.[679] But the mistake of James was to consider any further precision and determination of the confused notion by the intellect as something merely accidental. Make the intellectual element accidental and secondary, and you have religious experience opening the door to Divinal Imaginals and Presidents of Cosmic Commonwealths. All such perversions in the doctrine of the nature of God find their way between the confused and the reflex or distinct knowledge. There need be no perversion of the rudimentary knowledge of God, nor perversion of the reflex knowledge if it develops along the line of the first principles. The origin of the modern idea of God is thus a distortion of the elementary knowledge of God. Instead of elaborating the elementary knowledge of God by the use of intellectual principles, it perverts them. Make the confused knowledge ultimate and independent of intellectual analysis, and you pave the way to relativism and atheism. The confused knowledge of God is only an undeveloped knowledge of God.[680] The intellectual elaboration does for this confused knowledge what St. Paul did for the Athenians, one of whose altars he found inscribed, "To the unknown God." Both make known what men are worshipping without knowing it.

Religious experience gives only the groundwork of knowledge. To say that the intelligence, which determines this knowledge and defines it, is secondary and accidental, is to say that that which *determines* is subservient to that which is *determinable.* The potter then becomes the servant of his clay, and the sculptor of his marble. This is but another way of putting the principle which

---

[679] "Sed hoc proprie non est cognoscere quod Deus existit sub conceptu proprio Dei."—JOHN OF SAINT THOMAS, *Cursus Theologicus*, vol. i. q. 2 part 1 dist. 3 part 3 art. 1 n. ix.

The following excerpt from W. L. DAVIDSON shows the confusion between the two orders: "Just as in the case of hunger, on the lower or animal side of our nature, hunger as a want obviously could not originate save in a living organism whose very existence depends on its being nourished by food, and therefore presupposes the real existence of its object, food; so, in the higher or spiritual side of our being, the actual fact of our need of God, laid deep in the human constitution, implies that God *is*, as both originating and as satisfying it."—*Op. cit.*, pp. 29-30.

[680] *C. G.*, lib. 3 c. 38.

lies at the base of the whole philosophy of becoming: *the part is greater than the whole.* Such is the strange fortune of this form of Rationalism. Only a century ago Rationalism gloried in having liberated the intelligence from extrinsic control. Now it has denied the rights of reason entirely and falls down before the altar of sentiment. In pulling the mitre from intellectual man it has pulled the head off with it. We are no longer men, but animals. We "feel" our way instead of knowing it.

While the intellectual must precede the affective, there is a danger of confounding what is intellectual with intuition, in the modern sense of the term. This point has already been touched on, in considering the intellect. Here it is reintroduced with some new considerations. Intuition, as a mode of knowledge, has been contrasted with the intellect, which is said to distort reality. It is said to reveal life "in its flow and before it takes the bend." But does not this theory of intuition offer serious difficulties, which render it unacceptable? First of all, it seems illogical that a philosophical system which insists so much on unity and inveighs against splitting up reality should at the very outset juxtapose two modes of knowledge, namely, intelligence and intuition. It immediately breaks up the unity of thought at the same moment that it cries out against its adversaries for so doing. It places in juxtaposition what should never be so placed. Intuition and intelligence, if properly understood and not distorted, are not different. The intelligence may even be shown in a special sense to be an intuitive faculty.[681] The more perfect the intelligence, the more perfect the intuition. The intuition of the human intelligence is meagre when compared with an angel's, as is an angel's when compared with God's. God's Intelligence is Pure Intuition.[682] Now, the intimate vision of the nature of things—*intus legere—does not by itself demand abstraction.* "It is merely by the accident of knowledge that the universal is abstracted from the particular."[683] There is, too, a vicious circle, in that the necessity of Bergsonian intuition must always be proved by reason, and the

[681] "Intelligere autem dicit nihil aliud quam simplicem intuitum intellectus, in id quod sibi est praesens intelligibile."—I d. 3 q. 4 art. 5.

[682] "Perfectius (res) cognoscitur per Verbum quam per seipsam etiam in quantum est talis."—*De Veritate*, q. 8 art. 16 ad 2.

[683] I q. 55 art. 3 ad 1.

fallacious character of reason in turn by intuition. Otherwise there would only be confusion. "How can we place ourselves in the moving currents of other objects, as M. Bergson would have us do, by intuition? To know reality, its concrete duration must interpenetrate the being of the knower. There is, however, the possibility that when it comes to consciousness it may get fused with his own duration in one blended whole. In that case, if we say that we know the object, we may either be drawing upon our own imagination or relying upon the intellect. If we draw upon imagination we are opening the floodgates to every form of mysticism, emotionalism and sentimentalism. Then the only chance of agreement among different intuitions seems to be chance. If two people have the same vision they may agree, but their experience will not be authoritative for the others. It is only if we make intuition intellectual that there is any chance of communicating our intuitions to others."[684]

Summarizing briefly, we see that the fundamental difference between religious experience of the present day and that of the *philosophia perennis* is that in the modern view there are only two elements, whereas in the Scholastic system there are three. For the modern thinker the first element is some affective state; the second element is the intellectual development of that experience which is accidental and unnecessary. For the older philosophy the first element is intellectual. It is either an implicit knowledge of God indirectly based on the inclinations of nature, or else an immediate knowledge by inference. Immediately upon this first element, which gives confused knowledge, there follows an affective state, which constitutes the second element. Finally, the intelligence again comes into play to make the implicit knowledge explicit and distinct in the literal metaphysical sense.

These differences may be even more fundamentally analysed. They pivot upon philosophies which are anti-intellectual and intellectual. All other differences are merely accidental. The battle must ultimately be fought between the followers of Aristotle, for whom the intelligence is "Divine," and the followers of James and M. Bergson, for whom it is a "beast" and

---

[684] S. RADHAKRISHNAN, M.A., *The Reign of Religion in Contemporary Philosophy* (1920), p. 190.

the "original sin of thought." Knowledge of God is more than feeling or instinct. "Intelligence at the helm is worth a whole cargo of instincts."[685] "It is not instinct that makes us religious; it is we who give religious significance and value to instinct. And this requires clear, honest and strenuous thinking. If we would be religious it is not enough to stand by while the waves of emotional energy break upon the shore of our souls; we must learn to launch the frail barque of intelligent purpose on that stormy ocean, and by skill and insight make its boisterous energies convey us to the far and unknown shores of spiritual growth and discovery."[686]

It is worth observing that much of the modern doctrine of religious experience is founded on a confusion of the natural and the supernatural order. This, of course, modern philosophy does more or less wittingly. Professor Hoernlé has said: "Modern philosophy of religion does not assume as its basis this distinction between revelation and reason. Hence it does not attempt to prove, if 'proof' is the proper word ... the existence of God without appeal to religious experience. And, whilst appealing to this experience, and indeed regarding it as the only really relevant evidence, it also enlarges the scope of it far beyond 'revelation,' so as to include, in effect, all that is valuable in the old appeal to 'reason.'"[687]

The confusion is the result of a long evolution of thought which does not need more than a brief recall. The fundamental cause of the changed doctrine of our relation to God is a changed notion of human nature. Until the fifteenth century, human nature was considered perfectible by a gratuitous gift of God. Grace was not the destruction of nature; it was its perfection. From that time began a war against all *extrinsic* authority, either in the form of the church as with Luther, or of the speculative intelligence as with Kant, or of government as with Rousseau. The biological hypothesis of evolution was taken over, and was held by many to imply that for the perfectibility of human nature

[685] JOHN LAIRD, *A Study in Realism*, quoted in Flower.

[686] J. CYRIL FLOWER, M.A., *Psychological Studies of Religious Questions* (1924), p. 15.

[687] *Matter, Life, Mind and God*, p. 191. The psychology of religious experience, in which genuine mystical states of saints are put side by side with subconscious experiences of converted drug addicts, is a manifestation of the same tendency to dissolve one order into the other.

by a gift of God was substituted perfectibility through the natural laws of progress and becoming. In other words, until the fifteenth century, nature and grace were regarded as *superposed*, one being the perfection of the other.[688] Then came the new notion, one of *juxtaposition* of nature and grace. A philosophy and a theology began in which nature was separated from grace, which was regarded as a sort of cloak thrown over corrupted nature. Descartes carried on the separation by making an inseparable distance between subject and object, and Kant between moral and objective knowledge, metaphysics and science. Such a juxtaposition, which never should have been admitted, continued until biology offered the wearied philosophers an apparent solution, viz. *the identification of what is juxtaposed.* It is in this stage that we are now living. Evolution introduced flux into existence, and pantheism further introduced a flux in the conception of value. Nature and grace were fused into one, knower and known united in an ineffable intuition of becoming, God and the universe dissolved into one organic unity. Technically, this all means that the measure became itself a thing measured.

Modern religious experience, modern gods, modern notions of religion are born of this identification of juxtaposed elements. Faith is no longer a gift of God, and the "perfection of the intellect," as the Angelic Doctor calls it. In the words of one of its modern exponents, it is neither a substitute for reason nor an addition to it. "Faith is nothing more than reason grown courageous ... reason raised to its highest power, expanded to its widest vision."[689] We admit and state that there is progress and continuity in the universe; there is evolution, if you will, but *continuity* is not *confusion.* Continuity is possible only on condition that there be no confusion.

Modern philosophy must be given credit for its happy reaction against *a priori* systems which were nothing more than mere phantasy, or the wild upstart of some "imaginal." For the latter it has substituted a philosophy of religion which is intimately intermingled with life and action, and in doing so has

---

688 "Fides est perfectio intellectus."—II-II q. 4 art. 4.

689 L. P. JACKS, D.D., *Religious Perplexities*, pp. 64-5. *Cf.* Sir HENRY JONES, *A Faith that Enquires*, p. 77.

given both new meanings. But it has erred by being too simple. It has taken a detail to explain the whole. Affective states and pragmatic judgments do very well as secondary considerations, but not as primary. An affective philosophy is necessarily relative and contingent. It is private interpretation of God. It is a way of knowing which has never been adequately described, which is strictly incommunicable, which by some of its exponents has not been adequately known or felt. *Perhaps a not irrelevant fact is that he who wrote most about it, and is recognized as the spokesman of religious experience, has never experienced it himself.* We refer to William James, who said, "I have no living sense of commerce with God."[690]

[690] In a letter to James Leuba from Cambridge, April 17, 1904, W. James wrote: "I have no living sense of commerce with God." In a questionnaire sent out by Professor Pratt on the subject of religious belief, James was asked this question: "Have you experienced His (God's) presence?" The answer of James was "No" (*Letters of William James*, vol. ii. pp. 211 and 213).

"Much interest in the subject of religious mysticism has been shown in philosophical systems of late years. Most of the writings I have seen have treated the subject from the outside, for *I know of no one who has spoken as having the direct authority of experience* in favour of his views."—*Journal of Philosophy and Psychology and Scientific Methods* (1910), vol. vii. p. 85; republished in *Collected Essays and Reviews* (1920).

CHAPTER VI:

IS GOD ORGANIC WITH THE WORLD?

INASMUCH as the purpose of this work is to examine the conclusions reached by modern philosophers about natural theology, we omit the Scholastic arguments for the existence of God. The problem is not much, Does God exist? As, What is His nature, and *how* do we know that He exists? Hence the long treatment that we have given to the subject of religious experience. The ridicule heaped on the proof of the existence of God has little or no logical background. It is stated merely to prepare the way negatively for the non-intellectual substitutes.[691]

But before passing onto the problem of this chapter, it may be well to note the comprehension and the extent of the five ways of proving the existence of God as given by St. Thomas. The five ways are based on five notes of the universe: movement, dependency, contingency, composition and ordered multiplicity. The first three notes are dynamic, the last two are static.

But these five notes of visible universe are the notes of the modern God. (1) He is mobile, inasmuch as "He is a process form stage to stage and from perfection to perfection."[692] (2) He is dependent, for "He buds off from Divine Imaginal," or from Space-Time, or from our consciousness.[693] (3) He is contingent,

---

[691] For an excellent exposition of the five ways of proving the existence of God, and the best we know of, see GARRIGOU-LAGRANGE, *Dieu: son Existence et sa Nature*, pp. 226-342. How distant these five ways are from the three ways which Kant criticized can be recognized at a glance. See also GEORGE HAYWARD JOYCE, M.A (Oriel), *Principles of Natural Theology*, pp. 56-198.

[692] Sir HENRY JONES, *op. cit.*, pp. 356-360. S. ALEXANDER, *Space, Time and Deity*, vol ii. pp. 353, 365; "Some Explanations," *Mind* (October 1921), p. 428. H. G. WELLS, *God the Invisible King*, p. 67. F. JOHNSON, *God in Evolution* (passim). H. A. YOUTZ, *Enlarging Conception of God*, p. 46.

[693] D. W. FAWCETT, "Imaginism and the World Process," *Mind* (April 1922), p. 168.

for without our help He would for ever remain unachieved.[694] (4) He is imperfect and composite, being a "variable quality, and as the world grows in time, deity changes with it."[695] (5) He is ordered multiplicity, for "He faces the blackness of the Unknown and the blind joys and confusions and cruelties of life."[696]

The modern God, like the visible universe, possesses five common notes, three of the dynamic order and two of the static. But if the universe, being mutable and complex, demands a cause because the mutable and the complex is the undetermined determined, and the undetermined determined as ultimate is a contradiction,—so, too, does the modern God demand a cause for exactly the same reason. In other words, the modern God needs a God. Thus, from mutability we argue back to a First Mover, from dependency to an Efficient Cause, from contingency to a Necessary Being, from graded perfections to Perfect Being, and from ordered complexity to a Supreme Intelligence. Each of these conclusions corresponds to a nominal definition of God, to whom these five predicates belong without interesting themselves in the question how they belong to God.[697] Hence it is that the five ways do not find their complete development and perfection until the following question of the *Summa*, where St. Thomas treats the problem of the identity of essence and existence in God.[698] God is First Cause and

F. B. RUSSELL, "Free Man's Worship," in *Philosophical Essays*, *loc. cit.* H. A. OVERSTREET, "God and the Common Will," *Hibbert Journal*, vol xiii. No. 1 (1914), p. 155. BERNARD BOSANQUET, *Individuality and Destiny*, p. 250. S. ALEXANDER, *op. cit.*, vol ii. p. 399.

694 A. C. MCGIFFERT, "Christianity and Democracy," *Harvard Theological Review*, vol. xiii. p. 49. D. W. FACCETT, *Divinal Imagining*, p. 221. E. H. REEMAN, *Do we need a New Idea of God?* pp. 24-28. *G. H.* HOWISON, *God in Evolution*, p. 422.

695 S. ALEXANDER, *op. cit.*, vol. ii. pp. 348-53. Sir HENRY JONES, *op. cit.*, p. 359. W. E. HOCKING, *Human Nature and its Re-making*, p. 393. A. SETH PRINGLE-PATTISON, *op. cit.*, p. 432; supplementary notes, pp. 220-55.

696 H. G. WELLS, *God the Invisible King*, p. 114; *Mr. Britling Sees It Through*, p. 397. J. WARD, *Pluralism and Theism*, pp. 315, 478. F. H. JOHNSON, *op. cit.*, p. 87. S. ALEXANDER, *op. cit.*, vol ii. pp. 384, 421.

697 "Quaedam praedicta inveniri in rerum natura, quae secundum veritatem sunt propria Dei; non curando quomodo vel qualiter sint."—CAJETAN in I q. 2 art. 3, III.

698 *Cf.* JOHN OF SAINT THOMAS, I q. 2 disp. 3 art. 2 n. 1. I q. 13 art. 7 ad 1. CAJETAN, *loc. cit.*

"*Deum esse* scientifice non scit, qui Deum esse *ipsum esse* non didicit."—DEL PRADO, *De Veritate Fundamentali* (1911), p. 347.

Before passing on to the question of whether or not God is organic with the world, we may note the value of Being as a designation of God. Being when applied to God does not mean Undetermined Being, which stands as the first abstraction in the ontological

Necessary Being in virtue of the identity of His essence and existence. All things else in the world are composed of the determined and undetermined, the conditioned and the unconditioned, of act and potency, of essence and existence. In virtue of this composition they change, they evolve, they die—evolution without composition is impossible.[699] God is Pure Being, Pure Determination, Subsisting Being. He neither gives existence to Himself nor receives it from another. He *has* no being; He *is*. There can be no such thing in Him, then, as Deity and Goodness, as Professor Alexander believes.[700]

---

order. Here it means Subsisting Being; Being sovereignly determined, which admits of no further determinations.

But does Élan Vital, or President of a Cosmic Commonweath, Invisible King, give us more information about God than Being? Why use Being as a term that designates the Divine nature? Certaintly for this reason, if for no other: God Himself has so designed Himself—*I am who am.* Commenting on this text, the Angelic Doctor gives his reason for the pre-eminence of Being:—

"First, because of its signification. For it does not signify form, but simple existence itself. Hence, since the existence of God is His essence itself, which can be said of no other (q. 3 art. 4), it is clear that among other names this one specially denominates God, for everything is denominated by its form.

"Secondly, on account of its universality. For all other names are either less universal, or, if convertible with it, add something above it at least in idea, hence in a certain way they inform and determine it. Now, our intellect cannot know the essence of God itself in this life, as it is in itself; but whatever mode it applies in determining what it understands about God, it falls short of the mode of what God is in Himself. Therefore the less determinate the names are, and the more universal and absolute they are, the more properly are they applied to God. Hence Damascene says (*De Fide Orthod.*, I.) that He who IS *is the principal of all names applied to God; for, comprehending all in itself, it contains existence itself as an infinite and indeterminate sea of substance.*"—I q. 13 art. 11; I d. 8 q. 1 art. 1.

[699] Composition of any kind demands a cause. "Licit habitudo ad causam non intret definitionem entis quod est causatum, tamen sequitur ad ea qua sunt de ejus ratione, quia *ex hoc quod aliquid per participationem est ens sequitur quod sit causatum ab alio.* Unde hujusmodi ens non potest esse quin sit causatum; sicut nec homo quin sit risibile. Sed quia esse causatum non est de ratione entis simpliciter, propter hoc invenitur aliquod ens increatum."—I q. 44 art. 1 ad 1.

"Compositum est participatum, non principium."—JOHN OF SAINT THOMAS, *Phil. Nat.*, t. 3, p. 1., q. 9 art. 2.

[700] Professor Alexander's theory finds its critical examination in that article of the *Summa* where St. Thomas speaks of the simplicity of God. "Nothing composite," he says, "can be predicated of any single one of its parts. And this is evident in a whole made up of dissimilar parts, for no part of a man is a man, nor any of the parts of a foot a foot. But in wholes made up of similar parts, although something which is predicated of a whole may be predicated of a part (as a part of the air is air, and a part of water is water), nevertheless certain things are predicable of the whole which cannot be predicated of any of the parts: for instance, if the whole of the water is two cubits, no part of it can be two cubits. Thus in every composite there is something which is not in itself. But, even if this could be said of whatever has a form, viz. that it has something which is not in itself, as in a white object there is something which does not belong to the essence of white, nevertheless in the

But it may be asked: Will not God demand a cause as well as the universe or the modern God? There are some modern thinkers who are inclined to think so. Professor Pringle-Pattison, for example, writes: "Historically, the idea of God as a purely transcendent Being ... a Cause or Author of the universe, entirely distinct from an effect which is spoken of metaphorically as 'the work of His hands,' carries us back to a primitive stage of pictorial thought like that of the Zulus, mentioned by Tylor, who trace their ancestry back to Unkulunkulu, the Old-old-one, who created the world. It meets us with something of a sublime simplicity in the opening words of Genesis: 'In the beginning God created the heaven and the earth.' Such a statement yields a temporary satisfaction to the craving for causal explanation, though it is not necessary to go beyond the child's question, 'Who made God?' to become aware of its metaphysical insufficiency. As has been not unjustly said, 'Contentment with regress to a God-creator or some similar notion is the true mark of speculative indolence.'"[701]

It is quite evident that there is here a confusion of two questions, one of which is legitimate and the other absurd. The two problems, Why has the world a cause?, and, Why has God no cause?, are distinct. The error is to roll the two problems into one and posit the pseudo-problem, Why is there being?[702] To identify the Being of God and the being common to all things, is to suppose Pantheism at the outset. It is absurd, Aristotle says, to ask the question, Why is man a man?; but it is not absurd to ask the question, Why does man eat? It is also absurd to ask the question, Why is the Being of God Being?, inasmuch as it is His essence to exist.

But it is not illegitimate to ask why such a thing *has* being. In one case the essence of a being is its existence, in the other it is not. It is not our essence to exist; therefore we may validly ask the whence of our existence. In God the two are identical, hence the question cannot be asked.[703] "To demand, then, a cause for

form itself there is nothing besides itself. And so, since God is absolute form, or rather absolute being, He can be in no way composite."—I q. 3 art. 7; also art. 8.

701 *The Idea of God*, p. 289. VON HARTMAN, *Philosophy of the Unconscious*, vol. ii. p. 196 (English translation).

702 J. MARITAIN, *La Philosophie Bergsonienne*, p. 261.

703 "Oportet ergo quod illud cujus esse est aliud ab essentia sua, habeat esse causatum

the First Cause, is merely to demand that that which is first shall at the same time be second. It is to insist that the great Cause of all shall at the same time not be the cause at all, though being an effect."[704]

This brings us more into the heart of the modern problems. It is quite clear that contemporary philosophy is inclining more and more to the notion of a God who is organic with the world. There are three reasons commonly advanced in support of this position: first, God and the universe are both in movement; secondly, the only distinction between the two is that of "consciousness" or "value or quality," but in no case is it an ontological separateness; thirdly, creation, in the modern sense of the term, implies that God is organic with the world.

I. Common-sense philosophy in face of the first argument answers that every movement, even though it be the movement of a modern God, demands a Mover distinct from it.

What is revealed by sensible experience? It is movement, evolution, becoming, change. "It is certain, as the senses testify, that there is movement in the world." God, too, according to modern philosophy, is in movement being, as He is, "a process from stage tó stage—that is, from perfection to perfection."[705] The movement here referred to may be substantial or accidental, spiritual or physical, qualitative or local, and may with equal force be applied to a stone, a plant, an animal, man, will, intelligence, spirit, or even the modern God of becoming.

"But everything which is moved is moved by another." This principle, so clear to the intelligence and so confirmed by sense experience, has its foundation the principle that "every thing has its reason of being, either in itself or in another." What is movement but a passage from potency to act, or, in modern language, from the undetermined to the determined? The wood, says St. Thomas, is in potency to heat before it comes in contact with fire. The fire changes this potency *into heat in act*, or it changes the wood from an *undetermined to a determined state.* To

ab alio. Hoc autem non potest dici de Deo quia dicimus Deum esse primam causam efficientem."—I q. 3 art. 4.

[704] FRANK BALLARD, M.A., D.D., *Christian Theism Justified*, p. 24.

[705] Sir HENRY JONES, *A Faith that Enquires*, pp. 356 and 360.

deny that movement has need of a cause or of a mover, is to say that the same thing is at once and under the same formal relation the undetermined and the determined or mover and moved. This is impossible, as the undetermined determined is a contradiction.

It is equally beside the mark to say that "movement has no need of a thing which moves."[706] Pure movement without a thing which moves is impossible, as is a thought without a thinker, or a volition without a will. There is never a landslide without land, nor a snowstorm without snow, nor a headache without a head. To say there can be "movement without a thing that moves" is to say that that which is in progress to a thing is the thing itself.

Movement as movement can never be ultimate, either in the universe or in God. Movement implies duality, dissociation and composition. By the very fact that a thing moves, it changes, for there is succession.[707] What a thing is *now*, cannot be what it was at first. If nature tends to unity, and if movement is duality, then movement can never be the end of nature. To make God this movement does not solve the difficulty; for to say that that which is determined to unity (unity of process) is by its nature duality (duality of movement) is a contradiction.[708] It is for this reason that St. Thomas says it is impossible that the will be the first thing

[706] "Le mouvement n'implique pas un mobile."—H. BERGSON, *Perception du Changement*, p. 24. S. ALEXANDER, *op. cit.*, vol. i. p. 329.

[707] "Motus autem secundum suam rationem est hujusmodi, quod enim movetur inquantum hujusmodi dissimiliter se habet nunc et prius."—*C. G.*, lib. 3 c. 23. *Comp. Theol.*, c. 107.

"Ea enim quae sunt composita sunt mutabilia et ita pluribus modis se possunt habere quae autem pluribus modis habere se possunt, possunt se habere aliter et aliter, quod est contra rationem necessari.—Nam necessarium est, quod est impossibile aliter se habere. Unde oportet quod primum necessarium, non aliter et aliter se habeat, res per consequens nec pluribus modis. Et ita oportet ipsum esse simplex."—*Metaphysics*, lib. 5, lect. 6.

"Omne quod non potest esse nisi concurrentibus pluribus est compositum." *C. G.*, lib. 1 c. 22. *De Spirit. Creat.*, q. 1 art. 1.

Motion is different from the thing in movement. "Actus autem, ille qui mensuratur tempore, *differt ab eo* cujus est actus a *secundum rem* quia mobile non est motus, et secundum rationem successionis, quia mobile non habet substantiam de numero successivorum sed permanentium."—I d. 19 q. 2 art. 2; d. 5 q. 2 art. 2.

[708] "Cum enim natura semper in unum tendat determinate, non se habens ad multa, impossibile est quod aliqua natura inclinet ad motum secundum se ipsum; eo quod in quolibet motu difformitas quaedam est, in quantum non eodem modo se habet quod movetur; uniformitas vero mobilis est contra motus rationem. Unde natura numquam inclinat ad motum propter movere, sed propter aliquid determinatum quod ex motu consequitur."—*De Pot.*, q. 5 art. 5.

willed, or that the first thing visible be the act of vision.[709] Movement of itself can never be an end, because it is a tendency to an end. Running a race can never be identified with victory.[710]

Evolution is intelligible only in terms of being. To evolve is to be in *becoming*. To act is to be in *existence*. Since nothing can be the cause of itself, and movement has not in itself the reason of its being, it must have its cause in another. The sense, then, of the principle, "everything which is moved is moved by another," is not *negative*; it does not mean that nothing which is moved is ever moved by itself; we must understand it as affirming that everything which cannot move itself totally and with perfect sufficiency must be moved by another.[711] Nor is this principle founded on a mechanical conception of the universe, as M. Bergson and Dr. Schiller and their followers believe. On the contrary, the foundation of the whole argument rests upon the vision of a dynamic universe. The more that modern philosophy insists on movement and evolution and becoming, the stronger the argument, because to insist upon movement is to emphasize insufficiency. "The basis of the argument is not a spatial image, but rests on the very notion of becoming rendered intelligible in function, not of corporeal being, but of being which is the object of the intelligence."[712]

There is to be added to the above principle, that there is movement in the universe, and everything which is in the universe is moved by another, another principle, namely, *an infinite regress is impossible* in the series of motors actually or essentially subordinated. "If that by which a thing is moved is moved in its turn, and that in its turn by another, there cannot be

[709] "Impossibile est autem quod primum visibile sit ipsum videre; quia omne videre est alicujus objectum visibilis; ita impossibile est, quod primum appetibile, quod est finis, sit ipsum velle."—I-II q. 1 art. 1 ad 2.

[710] "Motus enim, ex ipsa ratione repugnat ne possit poni finis, eo quod motus est in aliud tendens; unde non habet rationem finis, sed magis ejus quod est ad finem."—*De Pot.*, q. 5 art. 5.

[711] "In hoc sensu, bene penetranti terminos est manifestum quod omne quod movetur, hoc est intrinsece aliter et aliter se habet, nunc eodem carendo, non est sibi tota causa habendi hoc intrinsecum esse."—SYLVESTER MAURUS, *Metaphysicae*, t. 3 q. 8 ad 1.

"Omne movens, seipsum componitur ex duobus quorum alterum est movens et non motum. Sed animal est movens seipsum; movens autem corpus anima igitur est movens non motum."—*C. G.*, lib. 2 c. 65; 1 d. 8 q. 3 art. 1 ad 3.

[712] GARRIGOU-LAGRANGE, *Dieu: son Existence et sa Nature*, p. 259.

infinite *regress*, because *then there would never be a first mover*, because secondary movers are moved by some first mover, just as the staff is not moved except by the hand. It is therefore necessary to come to some first mover, which is moved by no one, and by this every one understands God."

Note that in this proof there is no question of an infinite multitude of movers in the past, for this is not at all impossible provided that the actual presence of all these causes is not required in order that the last of them may act. An artist, for example, in the making of a work of art, may use an infinity of hammers, each one of which breaks after the others, because the preceding hammer is not necessary in order that the present one shall act. So, too, man may generate man even though the father or grandfather is no longer living, because neither of them is necessary for the present act.[713] There is therefore no contradiction in an infinity of accidentally subordinated movers in the past. This present argument is independent of this consideration. It reposes on the fact that an existing movement cannot have its sufficient reason in a series where these are only movers which themselves are moved. The essential subordination of infinite uncaused causes is contradictory.

Multiply the number of movers as much as you will, you never get beyond the fact that all these movers are but instruments.[714] They can always be considered as making one. There is in my series only three terms: "at the summit, the source, the activity; in the middle, the intermediaries, unique or multiple; and finally, the results which this activity produces. Multiply Intermediary causes into infinity, and you complicate the instrument, but you do not fabricate a cause; you elongate the canal, but do not make a

[713] "Sed per accidens, in infinitum procedere in causis agentibus non reputatur impossibile, ut puta, si omnes causae, quae in infinitum multiplicantur, non teneant ordinem, nisi unius causae, sed earum multiplicatio sit per accidens; sicut artifex agit multis martellis per accidens, quia unus post unum frangitur. Accidit ergo huic matello, quod agit post actionem alterius martelli. Et similiter accidit huic homini, inquantum generat, quod sit generatus ab alio: generat enim, inquantum homo et non inquantum est filius alterius hominis. Omnes enim homines generantes habent gradum unum in causis efficientibus, scilicet gradum particularis generantis. Unde non est impossibile, quod homo generatur ab homine in infinitum; esset autem impossibile, si generatio hujus hominis dependeret ab hoc homine, et a corpore elementari, et a sole, et sic in infinitum."—I q. 46 art. 2 ad 7.

[714] "Sed si in infinitum procedatur in moventibus et motis, omnia erunt quasi instrumentaliter mota, quia ponentur sicut moventia mota."—*Physics*, 7.

source. To say that the intermediaries, if sufficiently multiplied, will serve as a cause, is like saying that a brush will paint by itself if the handle is long enough."[715] Addition of instruments does not diminish the reason of insufficiency, because the reason of insufficiency is in each of the movers. Ten thousand idiots never make one intelligent man.

This argument is independent of the philosophical consideration of the eternity of the world. Eternity as such is only a chronological attribute, and can never be made equal to a reason of being. If the world is eternal,[716] it is eternally insufficient in terms of existence. If the world has always existed, then God has always caused its existence.

The argument of St. Thomas does not ask *where* the world came from. It asks something much more fundamental, namely, *Who* moves it?

It is worth noting, too, that in considering the impossibility of an infinite regress among the causes either accidentally or essentially subordinated, there is no question of going back over each of the individuals in the series until you come to the First Mover. The intelligence neither goes back over the whole series, nor does it consider the elements of the series from the point of view of time. It considers them rather from the point of view of *dependence.* The intelligence seizes the *ratio* of movement, and from a present movement immediately recognizes that there can be no infinite series in the causes which depend actually one on the other. The proof of the existence of God can be made from *this* movement; it is not necessary to know the history of the world to prove His existence. There are ultimately only three terms, it has been said: the source, the intermediaries and the term. It is these the intellect considers from the point of view of existence and nature, and not from their phenomenal order. If, then, everything which is moved is moved by another, and infinite regress in the series of movers is impossible, because in such a case there would never be the present movement, "it follows that there must be a First Mover Who is moved by no

---

[715] A. D. SERTILLANGES, *Les Sources de la Croyance de Dieu* (5th edition, 1908), p. 65.

[716] Revelation teaches us it is not eternal. The question here, then, is purely speculative.

one, and this every one calls God." He must therefore be *outside the series*, and a Mover in whom there is no shadow of change. The modern, because it is an evolving God, demands a Mover who is immobile—not immobile with the immobility of inertia, but immobile by pure and supreme activity.[717] Being the Immobile Mover, He is *distinct* from the world. There is in Him no composition or diversity which belongs to the diversity of movement.

Rerum Deus tenax vigor
Immotus in te permanens
Lucis diurnae tempora
Successibus determinans.

II. The identity of essence and existence in God has already been mentioned. The problem of the relation between God and the world is elucidated mainly by the use of this principle. This principle, which has been called the "fundamental truth of Christian philosophy," has been neglected by certain modern philosophers, with unfortunate results for theodicy. Its importance may be well seen if we turn to the theodicy of Professor Seth Pringle-Pattison. The theory of this learned professor is the most sane proposed in any of the Gifford Lectures in recent years. There has been a sincere attempt to escape much of the contemporary misunderstanding and to make God a "self-communicating Love" and creation an "eternal act" which finds itself consummated in the divine sonship of man."[718] Even the Incarnation is introduced as the full complement of God as self-communicating love, and as the supreme and triumphant reconciliation of immanence and transcendence in God.

But, at the same time, we have classified the God of his theory under the modern God of becoming, though we admit that there is less of becoming in it than in the God whose nature is expounded by Professor Alexander. "The traditional notion of God," he writes, "must be profoundly transformed."[719] But what does this mean? It means that "as soon as we begin to treat God

[717] See Part II chap. VII.
[718] *Op. cit.*, p. 432; supplementary notes, p. 412.
[719] vol. i. p. 405.

and man as two independent facts, we lose our hold upon the experienced fact, *which is the existence of the one in the other and through the other.*"[720] We are here approaching an extremely intimate union of the two. But if God and the world are organic, and the world is evolving, then God in some way is evolving. Hence God is not perfect in the traditional sense. That this interpretation is correct is clear from these words: "But if we revise our idea of perfection—if we keep in view the conclusions to which we were led in the two preceding lectures, and definitely *abandon the conception of God as a changeless and self-sufficient unit*—the movement to the finite, and the realization of the infinite in the finite, must be taken as the fundamental character of the Divine life."[721] Putting this into metaphysical language, we get this conclusion: "In the present connection it may be sufficient to suggest that transcendence which must be retained, and which is intelligible, refers to a distinction of value or of quality, *not to the ontological separateness* of one being from another."[722]

It is at this point that Thomistic metaphysics must break away from any theory which denies "ontological separateness of God and the world," or which asserts, as Professor Morgan does, that "we are in a measure one with Him in substance."[723] The position of St. Thomas, in contrast with this, is that it is metaphysically impossible that God and the universe can be in any way organic one to the other, or that the only difference which separates them can be one of "value" or "quality." Experience reveals to our intelligence a double principle. First, every effect resembles its cause inasmuch as a cause acts according to its nature.[724] Man resembles man because by generation man acts according to his nature. There is no difficulty on this point. This is the foundation of analogy. But there is yet another aspect which, though often neglected, is no less important. It is this: *every effect differs from its cause inasmuch as no*

---

[720] p. 254; italics are the author's.

[721] p. 340; italics ours.

[722] p. 255. A dinstiction between the experience of the two, however, is insisted upon (p. 314). *Cf.* CARR, *Theory of Monads*, p. 112. Dr. Carr admits that in God essence and existence are identical, but does not carry the distinction between the two into creatures.

[723] *Emergent Evolution*, p. 301.

[724] "De natura agentis est ut agens sibi simile agat, quum unumquodque agat secundum quod actu est."—*C. G.*, lib. 1 c. 29.

cause can communicate its identity; if it could, it would be different for the very same reason that it is the same, which is not possible. Because the effect does not completely equal the cause, there will be a certain dissimilarity between them. The heat of the sun is possessed by objects of the earth, but not in the same way that the sun possesses it. The cause will always be the *reason producing*, while the effect will be the *reason produced*.[725]

Hence in every effect there is something by which it resembles the cause and something by which it differs from it. In the statue which the sculptor chisels there will be the idea of Apollo which is in the artist; but there will also be something which is not in the artist, namely, the marble. In creation the same is true, *mutatis mutandis*. The universe, which is the effect, will be like its Cause inasmuch as it will possess a similitude of being.[726] The similarity will not be essential but causal.[727]

But the world will also be different from God inasmuch as He draws it out of nothing.[728] As it was in the Creator's power to

725 "Unumquodque nobilius invenitur in causa quam in effectu" (*C. G.*, lib. 1 c. 23). "In causa enim agente habet rationem producentis, in effectu autem habet rationem producti. Modo nobilius est producere quam produci. Ideo nobilius est esse in causa ut causa est, quam esse in effectu ut effectus est" (SYLVESTER FERRARIENSIS, lib. 1 c. 23 n. vii.). *Cf. De Malo*, q. 4 art. 1 ad 15, art. 3 ad 5; 4 d. q. 1 art. 4 d. q 1 ad 3; *C. G.*, lib. 1 c. 28 and c. 29. This last chapter gives the fundamental reason why we know God by affirmation, negation and eminence. We affirm certain attributes because effects resemble the cause; we deny others because they differ, and we use eminence to affirm the perfect way in which they exist in God. This is why, for example, we do not predicate finity of God, although we do predicate truth and goodness. *Cf. De Veritate*, q. 2 art. 2 ad 8. The similarity and dissimilarity of effect and cause are also the basis of the distinction between the communicable and the incommunicable attributes of God. A creature is more perfect as it approaches the communicable attributes, because it mounts in the order of being. Thus the higher the intelligence, the more perfect the creature. The contrary is true of the incommunicable attributes. The more a creature departs from the opposite of an incommunicable attribute, the higher it will be. The more a creature departs from non-being, the nearer it is to deity. *Cf.* CAJETAN in I q. 55 art 3 vi.

726 "Licet causa prima, quae Deus, est non intret essentiam rerum creaturam tamen esse, quod rebus inest, non potest intelligi nisi ut deductum ab esse divino; sicut nec proprius effectus potest intelligi nisi ut deductum a causa propria."—*De Pot.*, q. 3 art. 5 ad 1. "Ipsa autem natura vel essentia divina est ejus esse; natura autem vel essentia cujus libet rei creatae non est suum esse, sed esse, participans ab alio."—*De Veritate*, q. 21 art. 5.

727 "Deus est esse omnium non essentiale ... Divinum esse producit esse creaturae in similitudine sui imperfecta, et ideo esse divinum dicitur esse omnium rerum a quo omne esse creatur effective et causaliter manat."—I d. 8 q. 1 art. 2 c.; *C. G.*, lib. 1 c. 6.

728 "Sola relatio ad causam efficientem non facit in simplicibus compositionem, sed hoc quod relinquitur in eis ex tali exitu in esse. Quod per simile videri potest. Quod enim per generationem exit in esse ex materia, quae est in potentia et sub privatione; et licet per generationem non sit potentia in materia, quae fuit ad illam formam quae per

produce creatures before they existed in themselves, so likewise it is in the Creator's power, when they exist, to bring them to nothing. In this way, therefore, by the power of another, namely, of God, they are mutable, inasmuch as they are producible from nothing by Him, and are by Him reducible from existence to non-existence.[729] Drawn from nothing, they must necessarily be contingent. They will thus always differ in nature from Pure Being who made them. Furthermore, at the same time that God gives existence He gives that which measures existence.[730] The measure of existence is the essence, which constitutes its limit as the marble limits the idea of the sculptor.[731] It follows, then, that the effect will of necessity always be of a different nature from the cause, for the cause can never reproduce its identity. The only other possibility would be to say that God is the essence or form or matter of all things, as David of Dinant "has so foolishly said." But this is impossible, because God would then be maker and made, dependent and independent under the same formal consideration, even in the case of eternal creation.[732] Every creature, then, necessarily proceeds from God in diversity of nature. Drawn from nothing, it will always be sealed with its mark. Being diverse in nature from things, *God is for ever outside the order all created things.*[733] He will be related to creatures only logically, while creatures will be related to Him really. As a science cannot exist without its object, neither can we exist

---

generationem accepta est, tamen remanet potentia ad formam aliam ex hoc ipso quod res exit in esse post nihil, *remanet potentia tendendi in nihil nisi contineatur ab alio.*"—ALBERTUS MAGNUS, 4 *Sent.* 1 d. 8 art. 24 (Vives edition), t. 25, p. 252.

"Efficiens vero et forma effecti idem sunt specie in quantum omne agens agit simile sibi, sed non idem numero quia non potest idem esse faciens et factum."—*De Veritate*, q. 21 art. 4.

Cf. De Pot., q. 3 art. 7 ad 21.

[729] I q. 9 art. 2 c.

[730] "Deus simul dans esse, producit id quod esse recipit; et sic non oportet quod agat ex aliquo praeexistenti."—*De Pot.*, q. 3 art. 1 ad 17, q. 3 art. 5 ad 2.

[731] This does not mean that creation is the "building up of a composite thing from pre-existing principles, but it means that the composite is created so that it is brought into being at the same time with all its principles"—I q. 45 art. 4 ad 2. "Antequam esse habeat, nihil est"—*De Pot.*, q. 3 art. 5 ad 2.

[732] "Non tamen oportet effectum esse simplicem sicut causam; quia nec in universalitate nec in simplicitate oportet effectum causae aequare."—*De Pot.*, q. 3 art. 7 ad 21.

[733] "Cum creatura procedat a Deo in diversitate naturae, Deus est extra ordinem totius creaturae, nec ex ejus habitudo ad creaturas."—I q. 28 art. 1 ad 3.

without God; but as an object can exist without a science, so can God exist without us.

God and creatures will be diverse in nature. "In all things other than God there are to be found two real elements, the first of which (essence) in relation to the second (existence) is a *real potentiality*, and the second of which (existence) in relation to the first (essence) is a *real act.* From this real composition in *linea entis* results, formally constituted, *being* by participation. On the other hand, from the Absolute identity of essence and existence one necessarily concludes to Pure Act in *linea entis*, and herein one discovers the true notion of *being* by essence."[734]

Here, then, is the fundamental reason for the distinction and the separation and the diversity of God and the world. In God essence and existence are identical. In creatures they are not. There is therefore an "ontological separateness" between God and the world; there is more than a mere difference of value or quality or consciousness.

If there were not "ontological separateness," and if the existence of one were involved in the other, even as Professor Morgan seems to mean in his *Emergent Evolution*, then there would be no reason for one being distinct from the other. There would be unity without reason for unity, and distinction without reason for distinction. To make God and the world ontologically one, makes both God and the world unintelligible, denies both a reason of being, and asserts the unconditional unity of the diverse, which is a contradiction. There are many other ways in which God and the universe may be related than by denying transcendence in the traditional sense.

Furthermore, as the moving thing can never be identified with the mover under the same formal relation, as the composite can never be identified with the simple, neither can the universe be identified with God or made organic with God or evolving with Him; neither can it be said, as Viscount Haldane believes, "that Man and God are not numerically distinct subjects in knowledge. They are the one foundational mind, disclosing itself in different degrees or logical shapes in the progress of reality, but as identical

[734] A. WHITACRE, *Veritas: The Theology of St. Thomas Aquinas* (Aquinas Sexcentenary Lectures, Oxford, 1924), p. 28.

through divergences of form."[735] God and the universe never mix, nor fuse, whether it be in a "foundational mind" or an "organic universe." There can be no identification of being between God and creatures. God and creatures are not *diversified by differences added to both*, but rather by differences in themselves. Hence, strictly speaking, God and creatures are not *different*; they are *diverse*. The diverse is absolute, the different is relative.[736] There is no communication of substance by the act of creation. As the seal does not communicate its substance to the wax in making the impression, so neither does God communicate His substance in making the universe.[737] There is more than a "mere quality or value" separating the two. Later on we shall see whether this ontological separateness justifies the modern criticism that on this view God "is too aloof from the world's need." The possibility of an eternal creation does not dispense from the necessity of diversity of nature between God and the universe. When it is said the world is made from nothing, the temporal or material element does not enter into consideration. It is rather the order of nature, inasmuch as one being depends on another being. Considered in itself, the universe has only non-being, since its whole being depends on God. In this sense, whether the world is eternal from the point of view of time does not affect the composition which will necessarily be in all things made by God. Even though the world were eternal, says St. Thomas, it would still be true to say that it is *ex nihilo*, because the being which it has depends on God.[738]

[735] *The Reign of Relativity* (1921), p. 398.

[736] *C. G.*, lib. 1 c. 117; *Metaphysics*, lib. 10 lect. 4; d. 4 q. 1 art. 3 ad 2.

[737] "Deus cum sit una singularis simplex omnino et incommutabilis substantia spiritualis, praedicandus est re et essentia a mundo distinctus."—*Council of Vatican*, sess. 3 c 1.

"Nihil de substantia ejus egreditur."—*Div. Nom.*, c. II.

"Creaturae vero non procedunt a Deo tanquam consubstantiales ei, unde non dicitur esse de ipso, sed ex ipso."—*Comm. ad Epis.*, 2 *Cor.*

[738] "Cum autem dicitur esse ex nihilo, remanet ordo affirmativus ad nihil. Sed aliquid habet ordinem ad nihil dupliciter, scilicet ordinem temporis, et ordinem naturae. Ordinem tempore ex eo quod prius fuit non ens, et postea ens, et hoc nulli alterno convenit. Ordinem naturae, quando aliquid habet esse dependens ab alio, hoc enim et parte sui non habet nisi non esse, cum totum esse suum ab altero dependeat; et quod est alicui ex se ipso naturaliter procedit id quod est ei ab aeterno. Et ideo supposito quod coelum et hujusmodi, fuerit ab aeterno, adhuc tamen est verum dicere quod est ex nihilo, sicut probat Avicenna."—I d. 5 q. 2 art. 2.

III. This brings us to the third modern argument, which maintains that God is organic with the world. It is based on the notion of creation. Here, as elsewhere, we do not propose to give a complete Scholastic exposition, but merely to indicate the general lines of solution suggested by modern criticism. The traditional notion of creation meets with general ridicule. Professor Pringle-Pattison classes it "in the same circle of ideas as the waving of a magician's wand," and by the use of the same magic wand discards the doctrine as worthy of "no place in serious thinking or in genuine religion."[739] James classes it as "the product of childish fancy," and as lacking "sweep and infinity enough to meet the requirements of even the illiterate natives of India ... The vaster vistas which scientific evolutionism has opened," he says, "and the rising title of social democratic ideals, have changed the type of our imagination, and the older monarchical theism is obsolete or obsolescent. The place of the Divine in the world must be organic and intimate. An external creator and his institutions may still be verbally confessed at church in formulas that linger by their mere inertia, but the life is out of them; we avoid dwelling on them, the sincere heart of us is elsewhere."[740] Like other terms in philosophy, creation has changed its meaning. With M. Bergson it means "novelty;"[741] with Howison it simply means "the eternal fact that God is a complete moral agent, that His essence is just a perfect conscience,"[742] or else the moral recognition of God by the republic of spirits.[743] For Professor Ward it means "internal limitation;"[744] while it assumes almost the meaning of "created" with Professor Alexander. God in the sense of the universe tending toward deity is "creative only of deity. God, then, like all other beings in the universe—for Space-Time itself is not in the

---

[739] *Op. cit.*, p. 303.

[740] *Pluralistic Universe*, pp. 29, 119.

[741] *L'Évolution Créatrice.*

[742] *Limits of Evolution*, Introd., pp. xii-xvii.

[743] p. 355. Howison denies God as Efficient Cause, because every self is by the very nature of its selfhood a *causa sui.* Dr. Schiller is seduced by the same contradictory argument: "Egos are uncreated and uncaused; only the phenomenal selves which are manifestations of the ultimate and eternal ego change" (*Riddles of the Sphinx*, p. 354 ff.). Pringle-Pattison overleaps this contradiction by identifying origin and development (*op. cit.*, p. 317).

[744] *Pluralism and Theism*, p. 243.

universe, whereas God, since His deity is a part of the universe, is in it—is in the strictest sense not a *creator, but a creature.* I need hardly say I do not mean that He is a creature of our imagination or of our thought. He is the infinite creature of the universe of Space-Time."[745] Although the term *creation* has, for these philosophers, lost its old meaning, it has not lost its use.[746] The most generally accepted interpretation in these days, and certainly the sanest, is that of Professor Pringle-Pattison. There are moments when it approaches the traditional notion, and we would often interpret him in that sense were it not for the ridicule he directs against it, thus forbidding such an interpretation. In an effort to escape a false statement of the problem by Janet,[747] namely, that there is a moment when God alone was, and then a next moment when God and the world were, he makes God and the world eternal. We create a difficulty for ourselves, he says, "by substantiating God as a solitary unit apart from the universe in which He expresses Himself."[748] "This solitary, ante-mundane Figure is a residuum of a primitive and pictorial fashion of thinking. Creation must be regarded as an eternal act, an act grounded in the Divine nature, and therefore, if we are to use the language of time, coeval with the Divine existence."[749] There is no priority of the infinite over the finite.[750] "Creation is an eternal act or process which must be ultimately understood not as the making of something out of nothing, but as a self-revelation of the Divine in and to finite spirits."[751]

Apart from individual differences among philosophers, creation *ex nihilo* is rejected because of a confusion, into which they have fallen, and the clarifying of this confusion is the answer to their positive doctrines.

The confusion results from *spatially imagining* creation instead of *intelligibly understanding* it. Two quite distinct and separate problems are rolled into one. The comprehension of the notion

---

[745] *Space, Time and Deity*, vol. ii. p. 398. *Cf.* H. OVERSTREET, *God as the Common Will*, p. 155.

[746] A. SETH PRINGLE-PATTISON, *The Idea of God*, p. 414.

[747] *Final Causes* (Eng. trans.), p. 447.

[748] *Op. cit.*, p. 310.

[749] pp. 304-5.

[750] p. 316.

[751] Ibid., supplementary notes, p. 432; *Cf* pp. 308, 315.

of creation depends on their distinctness. One is a *chronological* problem, the other is *ontological.*

The chronological problem is concerned with the time element. The Pluralists along with Professor Pringle-Pattison insist on the eternity of the universe, there being "no priority of the infinite over the finite." As far as reason is concerned, this notion is in perfect accord with St. Thomas.

There is no metaphysical necessity for the *commencement of the world. Reason* alone cannot prove that the world had to have a beginning, nor can it prove that it could not have had a beginning. "It cannot be demonstrated that man, or heaven, or a stone did not always exist. Likewise, neither can it be demonstrated on the part of the efficient cause which acts by will. For the will of God cannot be investigated by reason ... But the Divine will can be manifested by *revelation*, on which faith rests. Hence, that the world began to exist is an *object of faith*, but *not of demonstration or science. And it is useful to consider this, lest any one presuming to demonstrate what is of faith should bring forward reasons which are not cogent, so as to give occasion to unbelievers to laugh, thinking that on such grounds we believe things that are of faith.*"[752]

So far as reason is concerned, the world need not necessarily have a beginning; time might go on for ever as far as human science is concerned; there might be a kind of eternal flux and flow of universal nature. In this sense, and from the point of view of reason, a philosopher may see no reason for denying the eternity of the universe, and thus consider God and the world existing co-eternally.[753]

But for Christians this conception is untenable. We know by revelation that the world is finite in duration in the past. This is a

[752] I q. 46 art. 2 c.

[753] The theory of the Scottish professor will even find some approbation in the *Summa.* St. Thomas writes: "The efficient cause, which acts by motion, of necessity precedes its effect in time, because the effect is only in the end of action, and every agent must be the principle of action. But if the action is instantaneous and not successive, it is not necessary for the maker to be prior to the thing made in duration, as appears in the case of illumination. Hence they say that it does not follow necessarily, if God is the active cause of the world, that He should be prior to the world in duration; because creation, by which He produced the world, is not a successive change, as was said above (q. 45 art. 2)—I q. 46 art. 2 ad 1.

fact, but an indemonstrable fact; it is a knowledge, but an incommunicable knowledge—as certain as it is incommunicable.

It is at this point that the position of Professor Pringle-Pattison appears illogical. Throughout his work there is a splendid attempt to reveal the Love of God as communicating Himself to us, and a recognition of the Incarnation as the sublime reconciliation of the transcendence and immanence of God. Scripture is quoted, and Christian thought prevails throughout. But if revelation is worthy of credence in the case of the Incarnation, it is worthy of credence in the case of creation. There seems to be no valid reason for accepting it in one case and denying it in the other.

So much for the chronological problem, which is purely accessory. The ontological problem is much more important. Here we prescind from the time-element. The problem is now transcendental and not one of duration. Whether the world existed eternally or not does not affect this problem. If it existed eternally, it is eternally insufficient. Neither does the hypothesis of evolution affect the problem in any way, as James and his disciples would have us believe. The idea of evolution answers the question of the temporal relations of beings one to the other. What temporal bonds are between them? How do they succeed? Are they causes, effects, conditions, of such and such a kind? The idea of creation refers to something entirely different, as it is the question of the transcendent relation between being as such and its First Cause. Evolution is a problem of the before and after; creation is a problem of the above. *Evolution is concerned with relations in a circle; creation is a tangential problem.*[754]

Whether being is evolving or not, whether it is perpetual or not, it still must have a source. As it is the most universal effect, it must have the most universal cause.[755] If being is not evolving, but is perpetual, then there must be a source for being. If there is evolution, there is a double reason for the existence of God,

---

[754] A. SENTILLANGE, "L'Idée de Création," *Annales de l'Institut Supérieur de Philosophie de Louvain* (1920), pp. 567-8. This is a clear, simple and timely treatment of the subject. We acknowledge indebtedness to it in treating of this particular matter.

[755] "Necesse est dicere omne ens quod quodcumque est, a Deo esse ... Necesse est igitur omnia, quae diversificantur secundum diversam participationem essendi, ut sint perfectius, vel minus perfecte, causari ab uno primo ente, quod perfectissime est."—I q. 44 art. 1 c.

because God must be postulated, first, as the source of being as such (God Creator); secondly, as source of being inasmuch as it is in evolution (God First Mover); and thirdly, as cause of the order according to which the world evolves—that is, the intelligibility which it expresses and the ends which it realizes (God, Word; God, Alpha and Omega; God, Beginning and End).[756] The vaster vistas which scientific evolution have opened in no way affect creation, any more than the invention of machinery affected the necessity of manufacture. The *how* of a process never dispenses with the explanation of the *why*. It does little credit to a philosopher to say that contentment with the regress to a God-Creator, or some similar notion, is the true mark of speculative indolence.[757]

Apart from this, creation has been brought into disrepute among philosophers by their spatially imagining a sort of nothing from which the world is made, and conceiving the creative act as a becoming, or a movement or a change. It is quite true that we often imagine creation as two moments—one in which there was God, and the second in which there was the world.[758] Explaining what he believes to be the traditional notion, a contemporary writes: "God is conceived as a pre-existent, self-centred Person to whom, in His untroubled eternity, the idea of such a creation occurs, one might almost say, as an after-thought. The inspiration is forthwith put into execution; the world is created by the word of His power. A universe is summoned into existence and stands somehow there, as shapes and figures might appear at a sorcerer's word of command, or as temples and towers rise like an exhalation before the eyes of a dreamer."[759] This is a fine example of creation spatially imagined, in which there are two moments, before and after; and two terms, a *terminus a quo* and a *terminus ad quem*.

Creation is not made up of two moments, one of labour and the next of rest. *Creation is not change*; *it is a relation*. St. Thomas, speaking on this point, says: "Creation is not change, except

[756] A. SENTILLANGE, *op. cit.*, p. 569.

[757] VON HARTMANN, *Philosophy of the Unconscious*, vol. iii. p. 196 (English trans.). Quoted approvingly by A. SETH PRINGLE-PATTISON, *op. cit.*, p. 299.

[758] "Imaginamur unum tempus commune dum mundus non erat, et postquam mundus in esse productus est."—*De Pot.*, q. 3 art. 2 c.

[759] A. SETH PRINGLE-PATTISON, *op. cit.*, p. 302.

according to a mode of understanding. For change means that something should be different now from what it was previously. But in creation, *by which the whole substance of the thing is produced*, the same thing can be taken as different now and before only according to our way of understanding, so that a thing is understood first as not existing at all, and afterwards as existing. But as action and passion coincide as to the substance of motion, and differ only according to diverse relations (*Phys.*, iii. tex. 20, 21), it must follow that, when motion is withdrawn, only diverse relations remain in the Creator and in the creature."

In things which are made without movement, as in creation, to become, and to be already made, are simultaneous. In these things that which is being made, is; but when we speak of its being made we mean that it is produced by another. Hence, since creation is without movement, a thing is being created and is already created at the same time.[760] There is then no passage from nothing to being, as if nothing were a "stuff," or an abyss, first, because nothing cannot be the subject of a phenomenon, and, secondly, because being nothing it cannot first be nothing and then something.[761] Creation is intelligible only as a relation—real in us, and logical in God.[762] Creation of the world by God means the world has its reason of being in God, it depends on God, in its entirety, which includes the duration which is its measure. Or, more briefly, creation is the dependence of finite being on its First Cause.[763]

This absolute dependence of created being on God is the evidence of the omnipotent power of God. Power, says St. Thomas, is not to be judged uniquely by *what* is made, but also by

---

[760] I q. 45 art. 2 ad 2 and ad 3. "In omni motu successivo est aliquid medium inter ejus extrema; quia medium est ad quod continue motum prius venit, quam ad ultimum; inter esse autem, et non esse quae sunt quasi extrema creationis, non potest esse, aliquid medium; igitur non est ibi aliqua successio."—*C. G.*, lib. 2 c. 19.

Cf. De Pot., q. 3 art. 2 c, art. 4 ad 4.

[761] *Cf.* I q. 45 art. 1 c. and ad 3.

"Cum fit aliquid ex nihilo; non esse sive nihil, non se habet per modum patientis nisi per accidens, sed *magis per modum oppositi ad id quod fit per actionem.*"—*De Pot.*, q. 3 art. 1 ad 4.

[762] "The creature is the term of creation as signifying a change, but is the subject of creation, taken as a real relation, and is prior to it in being, as the subject is to the accident. Nevertheless, creation has a certain aspect of priority on the part of the object to which it is directed, which is the beginning of the creature."—I q. 45 art. 3 ad 3.

[763] "Creatis nihil est aliud realiter quam relatio quaedam ad Deum cum novitate essendi."—*De Pot.*, q. 3 art. 4, c.

how a thing is made. The greater the heat, the more it heats and the more quickly it heats. The creation of some finite effect would not show forth the omnipotent power of God, but the creation *ex nihilo* does. However small a being is, and however finite it is, to create it from nothing requires an infinite power, which can belong only to an infinitely perfect Being.[764] In creating there is no addition made to the infinity of God's Being, because it is not in the same order as the Being of God. Being in an inferior order is possible, because of the analogy of *being*. Nor is there any more being in the world after creation than before. Suppose that there was only one man in the world who had knowledge. Knowledge would be quantitatively and qualitatively one in such a case. Now suppose that learned man should teach a populated world. What would be the result? Knowledge would increase quantitatively; instead of there being one man who knows, there would be millions. But qualitatively the knowledge would remain the same. There would be no more knowledge qualitatively in the world than before.

This comparison is feeble, but it helps to illustrate the point in question. Creation is an increase of being *extensively* but not *intensively*. There are more beings in the world after creation than before, but there is no more *being*; there are more good things, but the good is not multiplied. Creation introduced the word "have" into the world to denote participation. Before creation there was no such thing as "having;" there was only *being*.

[764] "Virtus facientis non solum consideratur ex substantia facti, sed etiam ex modo faciendi. Major enim calor non solum magis sed etiam citius calefacit. Quamvis igitur creare aliquem effectum finitum non demonstret potentiam infinitam; tamen creare ipsum ex nihilo demonstrat potentiam infinitam. Quod ex praedictis patet. Si enim tanto major virtus requiritur in agente, quanto potentia est magis remota ab actu oportet, quod virtus agentis ex nulla praesupposita potentia, quale est agens creans, sit infinita; quia nulla proportio est nullius potentiae ad aliquam potentiam, quam praesupponit virtus agentis naturalis, sicut non entis ad ens."—I q. 45 art. 5 ad 3.

There is no question here of bridging an infinite distance strictly so called, because strict infinite distance supposes two real terms and a real infinity between them. In creation there is no real infinity between positive terms. Hence, the infinite distance between being and non-being in the act of creation is only an infinite distance in the wide sense of the term, which signifies real opposition between being and nothing, which distance can be bridged by God.

"Objectio illa procedit ex falsa imaginatione ac si aliquod infinitum medium inter nihilum et ens. Quod patet esse falsum. Procedit autem falsa haec imaginatio ex eo, quod creatio significatur ut quaedam mutatio inter duos terminus existens."—I. q. 45 art. 2 ad 4.

Cf. De Pot., q. 3 art. 1 ad 3.

The misunderstanding on this point usually arises from a spatial conception, according to which God is understood mathematically. The being of God is not *quantitative*; it is Divine. Being Divine, it possesses the fullness of perfection, and nothing can be added to it. What is created is related to the uncreated as a point to a line, there being no proportion between one and the other. A line added to a point does not make it greater, nor does a created good increase the goodness of God.[765] The finite, therefore, being placed outside the infinite as an *extensive* increase of being, offers no contradiction, and in fact is in perfect accord with the Perfection of God; for it allows Him causality, without which He would not be perfect.

But to place the finite in the infinite, then God is both finite and infinite, and "this is not a mystery as is creation, but the absurd."[766] Neither can it be said that the creative act implies a change in the Divine will, simply because at a given moment God became a creator in time. By His *power* God was never a creator in time, because the power is identical with Him from all eternity. The Divine will is not like our will, which needs external help and other faculties to make it efficacious. There is a change, but the change is in *creatures* and not in God. Creation is an eternal act which terminates at its object when God wills it.[767] If there is anything new in God, it is only a logical relation, and even that is from our point of view.

St. Thomas, on this point, touches the root of the problem in saying that "the will does not act according to the *mode of its being*, but according to the *mode of its resolution*." The Divine will embraces not only what the effect will be, but when it will be.[768]

---

[765] "Bonum creatum se habet ad bonum increatum sicut punctum ad lineam, cum nulla sit proportio unius ad alteram, unde sicut linea additum punctum non facit maius, ita nec bonum creatum additum ... bono increato fecit melius."—3 d. 1 q. 2 art. 3 ad 1.

[766] GARRIGOU-LAGRANGE, *De Revelatione*, vol. i. p. 267.

[767] "Novitas divini effectus non demonstrat novitatem actionis in Deo cum actio sua sit sua essentia."—*C. G.*, lib. 2 c. 35.

[768] "Effectus autem ab intellectu et voluntate sequitur secundum determinationem intellectus et imperium voluntatis. Sicut autem per intellectum determinatur rei factio, et quaecumque alia conditio, ita et praescribitur ei tempus; non solum enim ars determinat ut hoc tale sit, sed ut tunc sit, sicut medicus, ut tunc potio detur; unde si ejus velle per se esset efficax ad effectum producendum, sequeretur de novo effectus ab antiqua voluntate, nulla actione de novo existente. Nihil prohibet igitur dicere actionem Dei ab aeterno fuisse, effectum autem non ab aeterno, sed tunc cum ab aeterno disposuit."—*C. G.*, lib. 2 c. 35.

A king, for example, decides to make war within a year. When a year comes, the war is carried on without the least change in the will of the king, his resolution remaining the same as during the preceding year. There is a change, but the change is wholly on the part of the soldiers. St. Augustine has used another figure to show that the newness of Divine effect does not imply newness of action in God.

Without any change the sun illumines the earth, heats it, nourishes, hardens some things, softens others, dries up others, raises vapours and vegetation, and strengthens the feeble. All the change is on the part of its *terminating object*; it is not in the nature of the sun.[769] If there is no change in God, there is certainly no necessity that He should create one kind of world more than another. He is not bound to create the best possible world, as Leibnitz contended; for otherwise He would lack a sufficient reason. The sufficient reason for an act of the will is to be found, not in the object absolutely considered, but in consideration of the end in view. The present world, then, is the best world possible for the end God had in view in creating it.

But if creation depends on the will of God, if it adds no new perfection to God, and if God is not organic with the world, is God for that very reason static and aloof from the world's needs? It is this question that we shall briefly consider in the next chapter.

[769] Enarratio Psal. 72.

CHAPTER VII:

GOD IS PERFECT

MODERN philosophy has rejected the traditional notion of God for a twofold reason. It represents God, first, as static; and secondly, as aloof from the world's needs and desires.[770] In one case its complaint is against God considered in Himself, and in the other against the relation of the universe to Him. The substitute notion is that of an "evolving God," or of God as a "perfect process."

In answer to these objections we assert two positive principles: first, God is Life; secondly, God is in the world intimately.

I. God is Life

The main outline of that which modern philosophers have written against the static notion of God, the common-sense philosopher accepts. If God were static and lifeless He would be no God. The desire for a new notion of God has arisen from the false belief that perfection is necessarily static. Sir Henry Jones, for example, speaks of "that helplessness which a fixed and static perfection implies, that eternally immobile substance with which theology in the past has identified its perfect God." But the history of *philosophia perennis* as well as of theology fails to reveal any period when a perfect God was identified with a static God. The modern philosopher is the first to suggest such an equation.

Life is activity. In the organic order it is a process. This is obvious. "We are in some way and in some degree new beings every day, for the past constantly enters into us and becomes a

[770] *Cf.* Part I. chap. V.

part of us. The instant that process stops, death ensues. Death is the stopping of a process."[771]

But activity is twofold—and this is the point where modern philosophy falls into a snare. It may be either transitive or immanent. The first implies an imperfection; the second is less imperfect. The activity of the first passes beyond itself; the activity of the second remains within itself as its own perfection. The imperfection of life is characterized by its degree of transitive activity, just as its perfection is characterized by its degree of immanence.[772] Life is characteristically immanent activity, and the highest kind of immanent activity that we know is intellectual. Intellectuality follows immateriality. But God is Pure Spirit and Pure Intelligence. He is therefore Pure Life.[773] In Him intelligence, the principle of life, and the act of the intelligence which is the manifestation of life, are identical. This point was earlier explained more in detail. The conclusion that God is Life results from the application of the definition of life, viz. immanent activity, to all the orders of the universe. Philosophy itself, then, without revelation, can prove that God is Life. But revelation can make more definite our knowledge of the operation of this Life of God. If we appeal to revelation, it is just for two reasons, namely, to show against Sir Henry that "*theology* in the past" has not identified perfection and the static, and also to show the beautiful continuity and progress of all orders, *e.g.* between reason and revelation. Metaphysical and theological continuity, it will be noted, far exceeds biological continuity.

Not content with the mere statement that God is Life and that His activity is immanent, the Angelic Doctor draws from the revealed Word of God those notions which permit him to describe the great and tremendous mystery of the Sacred Trinity. If life is immanent activity, and God is Life, then there is

---

[771] Ibid., p. 359

[772] *Cf.* Part II chapter II.

[773] "Illud igitur cujus sua natura, est ejus ipsum intelligere, et cut id, quod naturaliter habet, non determinatur ab alio, hoc est quod obtinet summum gradum vitae. Tale autem est Deus. Unde in Deo maxime est vita. Unde philosophus in 12 *Meta.* ostenso, quod Deus sit intelligens, concludit, quod habeat vitam perfectissimam, et sempiternam, quia intellectus ejus est perfectissimus, et semper in actu."—I q. 18 art. 3 c.

"Vivere Dei est ejus intelligere."—*C. G.*, lib. 1 c. 98.

immanent activity in God.[774] This activity in a perfect being can be only twofold, namely, that of the intelligence and that of the will.[775]

God thinks. This thought is immanent in Himself and equal to Himself. Being a Perfect Thought, it is unique. It is not multiple as ours, in which one thought succeeds another, but it is perfect, and the complete and total reflection of Himself. This Thought of God—the fruit of His Intelligence, the "splendour and the glory of His substance"—is His Verbum, the Word. This Verbum is the one of whom St. John speaks in his Gospel: "In the beginning was the Word ... The Word became flesh—Jesus Christ our Lord."

Being necessarily loves its own perfection. The Word is the Perfection of the Father.[776] The Father, therefore, loves the Word, His Son. All love has two terms: he who loves and he who is loved. I love and I am loved. Between us there is something: it is not my love; it is not His love; it is our love. We have no word to express perfectly this act of God's will (for love is properly of the will), as there is nothing exactly like it in all creation. It is best expressed as a breath of love, as a sigh of love, which does not pass away as our love, but which subsists; and this subsisting love is the Holy Spirit.

One in Nature, three in Persons, really distinct one from the other in virtue of the relations which separate them, yet all consubstantial in the one nature: such is the Blessed Trinity.

All other life is but a participation of that Life; and all activity is but a participation of that Activity. The nearer beings approach God by their likeness, the more immanent activity they possess;

---

[774] *C. G.*, lib. 2 c. 23.

[775] "Feeling, although it seems to be an operation in the one feeling, is outside the intellectual nature, and is not totally removed from that genus of actions which are *ad extra*. Feeling is perfected by sensible action in the sense. It follows, therefore, that no other procession can be in God than that of the Verbum and Love, one proper to intelligence, the other to will."—I q. 27 art. 5; *C. G.*, lib. 2 c. 23.

The creative act, which is terminatively an action *ad extra*, does not interest us at this moment. Suffice it to note at this point that even the creative act is formally immanent. See preceding chapter.

[776] The procession of the Word from the principle is by an act of *intellectual generation*. God being fecund, and the source of all fecundity in consequence of this spiritual act of *generation*, is rightly described as Father inasmuch as He is the principle; and as Son inasmuch as the Son is the term of this intellectual fecundity.

just as the more they recede from Him, the less do they show that activity.

But while, on the one hand, modern philosophy cries out with great insistence against a static God and pleads for a God with life, it renders life almost an impossibility in God. What is life for the modern thinker? It is the activity by which a being progresses from perfection to perfection. God is then made an evolving God for whom perfections increase as the process of the universe increases. He therefore has not all the perfections at present, but perhaps He will acquire them in countless ages. But activity of this kind, as we have already seen, is a sign of imperfect life. The *having* is always more than the *acquiring*, and *being* more than the *becoming*. Now, to make change the very *ratio* of God is to *make that which constitutes the imperfection of life the very life of God.* Such a philosophy is a deification of the imperfect. Indeed, we see that there is an ironic turn in the wheel of fate. The notion of this philosophy of God is too charged with imperfection and with transitive change. It tends to be too lifeless, and finally too static!

How little the modern philosopher understands perfection when he bemoans a God "existing in solitary bliss," as does Professor Pringle-Pattison, or when he speaks of "that helplessness which a fixed and static perfection implies," as does Sir Henry Jones! Why bemoan the fact that there is no change in God? He has no need of change. Possession and repose never cry out for change, and much less does perfection.

There is a certain immutability and fixity which belongs to the "surfeited," the narrow-minded, the narrow-hearted. Such immutability is an imperfection, and this we concede to modern thinkers. It is the immutability of the *dilettante*, who in the words of Pascal delights more in the search for truth than in truth itself: he has not the force to stop and contemplate truth when he possesses it, for he has fear of its exigencies.

But this immutability of the mediocre, this changelessness of the surfeited, is *not the immutability of God.* There is another kind of immutability which comes from the good of the perfection which one already possesses,[777] and the value of an end attained. In creatures, and from the point of view of the will, this superior

[777] GARRIGOU-LAGRANGE, *Sens Commun* (3rd edition), pp. 59-60.

immutability is that by which sanctity is defined.[778] In God this changelessness is "the Thought of the Thought" always actual, or the Act of Love of the Good eternally subsistent.[779]

God is changeless because He is perfect and eternally active in the activity of His Divine perfection; not inconstant through mediocrity, but constant in perfection; not helpless with the helplessness of the indigent, but omnipotent with the richness of perfection; not "existing in solitary bliss," but complete with the perfect possession of the good and the true; not static in His nature, because active; not dynamic in His nature, because perfect; immutable, moving all things; eternally active, eternally in rest; bountiful, and losing nothing—the Perfect God, to whom be honour and glory for ever.

II. The Universe is Intimately Related to God

The second objection of modern philosophy is that God is too commonly presented as "aloof from the world's process," and "aloof from human needs." Religious thinking, it is said, must "rid itself of a transcendence which seeks to magnify God's greatness by separating Him from the world."[780] He must be a "God in the dirt," and intensely interested in the dust of our human lives.

Again, the traditional common-sense philosophy agrees with the complaint. It is just as averse to a God "aloof from the world" as any modern philosophy. The dissatisfaction with the transcendent God is in reality directed against Deism, but not against genuine Christian thought. According to Deism, God is represented as making the world and for ever after remaining disinterested. For the *philosophia perennis*, on the contrary, the whole universe is intimately related to God by bonds which have

[778] II-II q. 81 art. 8.

[779] I q. 9 art. 1. "Intellectus autem non perficitur per motum, sed per hoc quod est extra motum existens ... Modus igitur substantiae intelligentis est, quod esse suum sit *supra motum* et per consequens supra tempos."—*C. G.*, lib. 2 c. 55.

[780] *Cf.* Part I. chap. V.

as their extremes the beginning of the universe as well as its final end, and all the intermediate bonds. God is not "aloof from the world," in any sense of the term, in the traditional notion. This is perfectly apparent from a consideration of these points: First, Why did God make the world? Secondly, What was His plan? Thirdly, What is the relation of existence to Him? Fourthly, What is the end of the movement of all created things? The first and last questions refer to God as the Final Cause of all things; the second to God as Exemplary Cause, and the third to God as Efficient Cause.

I. Why has the universe come into being? It has come into being because of the goodness of God. Everything which is good diffuesses itself.[781]

The plant is good, it diffuses itself in its flower; the animal is good, it diffuses itself in its kind; man is good, he diffuses himself in thought and in action and in the world. But God is perfect and the transcendent Good. He diffuses Himself in an eminent way. And because He is transcendent, this diffusion is intrinsic which is the Sacred Trinity. The extrinsic diffusion, which is creation, is dependent on His will. By it He communicates His Goodness to others. All those who give their goodness to others do so for one of three reasons. First, by the direction of a superior force: here the good is given of necessity. Secondly, on account of some anticipated interest: here it is given for utility. Thirdly, by a benevolent inclination: here it is the effect of goodness. It is not of necessity that God has brought creatures into existence because He has no power which dominates Him; it is not for utility, for He is God and has no need of creatures. It is therefore because of His Goodness that He brings them into existence.[782] The Goodness of God is thus the final reason for the creation of the universe. "This goodness is manifested in creation, but it is even more deeply manifested in the fact that

---

781 "Bonum est diffusivum sui secundum quod dicitur quid finis movet efficientem."—1 d. 34 q. 2 art. 1 ad 4; I q. 5 art. 4 ad 2.

Even though the world were eternal this principle would still be true, for the world would have an eternal dependence of being on God on account of His Goodness.

782 "Ad divinam bonitatem pertinet ut, sicut produxit res in esse, ita etiam eas ad finem perducat."—I q. 103 art. 1 c.

"Causa productionis rerum in esse est divina bonitas."—*De Veritate*, q. 5 art. 8 c.

God needs no things, because He possesses in Himself the plenitude of all perfection."[783]

It was not because of *appetitum finis* that He made the things; it was *propter amorem finis.*[784] This notion of the nearness of God and the motive of love in creation immediately takes us far from the modern objection that God is aloof from the world.

II. According to what plan did God create the universe? Before the world was created, *all things existed as "rationes aeternae" in the mind of God.* "Being in God from all eternity, He knew them in their nature and loved them for that very reason."[785] There are few thoughts in common-sense philosophy more pregnant than this. It not only carries with it the refutation of the false notion that "God is aloof from the world's needs," but asserts His love for it from all eternity.[786] The love of God for man did not commence with the creation of man, as His knowledge of the nature of man did not commence with the existence of man. God loves man, as well as all other creatures, with an eternal love. It is, then, with justice that St. Bernard says, "Man is eternal because he is eternally loved."[787]

---

[783] "Quamvis bonitas Dei manifestetur in hoc quod esse communicavit rebus per creationem, tamen perfectio bonitatis ostenditur in hoc quod rebus conditis Deus non eget, sed in seipso sufficientiam habet."—2 d. 15 q. 3 art. 3 ad 2. *Metaphysics*, lib. 5 lect. 18.

"Non quidem ut ipsi bonitatem acquirat, sed ut bonitatem aliis communicet."—4 d. 46 q. 1 art. 1 c.

[784] Ibid. The Justice of God was not less revealed in creation, inasmuch as justice determined the quality of the communications. Goodness and justice differ by a logical reason in creation. Goodness pertains to the very perfection of the Divine Nature inasmuch as it is Final Cause. Justice pertains to the act of communication. Furthermore, goodness looks to the communication in general, justice to its equality and its determinations.

"Bonum respicit essentiam; justitia actum; bonum generale est et justitia specialis."—4 d. 46 q. 1 art. 1 c.

De Pot., q. 3 art. 15; I q. 103 art. 2 ad 3. *Metaphysics*, lib. 12 lect. 9.

Mercy, too, was manifested in the creation of being from non-being. "Et secundum hoc etiam salvatur ibi ratio justitiae, inquantum res esse producitur, secundum quod convenit divinae sapientiae et bonitati; et etiam salvatur quodammodo ratio misericordiae inquantum res de non esse in esse mutatur."—I q. 21 art. 4 ad 4.

[785] "Licet creaturae ab aeterno non fuerint nisi in Deo, tamen per hoc quod ab aeterno in Deo fuerunt ab aeterno cognovit res in propriis naturis et ab eadem ratione amavit."—I q. 20 art. 2 ad 2.

[786] "Deus absit ut temporaliter aliquem diligat, quasi nova dilectione quae in illo ante non erat, apud quem ne praeterita transierunt et futura jam facta sunt."—ST. AUGUSTINE, *De Trinitate*, lib. 5 c. 16-17.

[787] "Homo ab aeterno (est), tanquam ab aeterno dilectus."—*Sermon* 71 *Cant.*

And if we would go still deeper and ask why God's plan called for such a multiplicity of creatures, we can only suggest the answer of His Divine Excellence. Divine Goodness cannot be manifested in one way or in only one creature, just as a thought cannot be expressed in a single word. Hence the diversity of creatures forming the diverse orders of *esse, vivere, sentire, et intelligere*, in which are manifested in a multiplied way the perfections of God.[788] It need hardly be remarked that the various participations in Divine Goodness in creatures are a participation in the Divine Essence. There is nothing of the substance of God in creatures; it is His likeness which is in them: just as it is not the stone in its individual materiality which is in our intelligence; it is its likeness.[789]

III. But if the universe is related to God by His Goodness, which is the reason of creation, and by His love of it from all eternity, it is no less intimately related with Him by the very act of creation itself. It was this lesson that St. Paul gave to the Areopagites: "God is not far from any one of us, for in Him we live and move and have our being."[790] The same truth finds its echo in the doctrine of the Angelic Doctor: "God is in all things intimately." "Deus est in omnibus rebus et intime."[791] He is not in all things as part of their substance, nor as an accidental element, but as an agent is present in the subject on which it operates.[792]

---

[788] "Finis omnium divinorum operum est manifestatio divinae bonitatis. Tanta est autem divinae bonitatis excellentia, quod non potest uno modo, nec in una creatura sufficienter manifestari. Et ideo diversas creaturas condidit in quibus diversimodo manifestatur."—ST. THOMAS in *Com. Ep. ad Romi.*, lect. 4 c. 9.

[789] "Deus est in omnibus, sed in quibusdam per participationem suae bonitatis ut in lapide, et aliis hujusmodi; et talia non sunt Deus, sed habent in se aliquid Dei, non ejus substantiam sed similitudinem ejus bonitatis."—ST. THOMAS in *Epis. ad Col.*, lect. 2 c. 2.

"Quia vero omnem creatam substantiam a perfectione divinae bonitatis deficere necesse est, ut perfectius divinae bonitatis similitudo rebus communicaretur, oportuit esse diversitatem in rebus, ut quod perfecte ab uno aliquo repraesentari non potest, per diversa diversimodo perfectiori modo repraesentaretur; nam et homo, cum mentis conceptum uno vocali verbo videt sufficienter exprimi non posse, verba diversimode multiplicat ad exprimendam per diversa suae mentis conceptionem."—*C. G.*, lib. 3 c. 97.

[790] Acts xvii. 27-8.

[791] I q. 8 art. 1.

[792] "Deus est in omnibus rebus, non quidem sicut pars essentiae, vel sicut accidens, sed sicut agens adest ei in quod agit. Oportet enim omne agens conjungi ei in quod immediate agit, et sua virtute illud contingere: undo in vii. *Phys.* probatur quod motum et movens oportet esse simul."—I q. 8 art. 1 c.

"Since the Essence of God is Being, the effect of God's act is being, just as the effect of fire is heat. This effect God causes in all things when they begin to be, and continues to conserve them in being, just as light caused in the air by the sun remains there as long as the air is illumined. As long as things have being, God will be present in them according to the mode in which they have being. Since being is that which is most profoundly intimately in a thing, God is therefore present in all things intimately as their efficient cause."[793]

"While above all things by the excellence of His nature, He is in all things as the efficient cause of their being."[794]

But if God is intimately in things in virtue of His causality, He is no less intimately in them in virtue of that same power by which He conserves them in being. Creatures are so dependent on Divine conservation, that, were God not to sustain their being for a moment, they would fall into nothingness.[795] Before things were, God could communicate being, and thus make them. After they were made, He could withdraw being from them and they would cease to exist.[796] All movement comes from God, inasmuch as effects are more properly due to the first cause than to the second cause.[797] "God is the ultimate cause of any action whatsoever, inasmuch as (1) He gives its subject the power of acting, (2) He conserves it in being, and (3) He applies it to action. In sum, He operates *immediately in every operating thing*, without in any way excluding the operation of the will or of nature."[798]

---

[793] Ibid.

[794] "Deus est supra omnia per excellentiam suae naturae, et tamen est in omnibus rebus ut *causans omnium esse*."—I q. 8 art. 1 ad 1.

[795] "Ex hoc modo omnes creaturae indigent divina conservatione. Dependet enim esse cuiuslibet creaturae a Deo, ita quod nec ad momentum subsistere possent, sed in nihilum redigerentur, nisi operatione divinae virtutis conservarentur in esse."—I q. 104 art. 1.

[796] "Antequam res essent, potuit eis non communicare esse, et sic eas non facere, ita postquam jam factae sunt, potest eis non influere esse, et sic esse desineret. Quod est eas in nihilum redigere."—I q. 104 art. 3 c.

[797] "Quia causa prima magis influit in effectum quam secunda."—*De Pot.*, q. 3 art. 8 ad 15.

[798] "Deus est causa actionis cujus libet in quantum dat virtutem agendi, et inquantum conservat eam, et inquantum applicat actioni, et in quantum ejus virtute omnis alia virtus agit. Et cum conjuxerimus his, quod Deus sit sua virtus, eo quod sit intra rem quamlibet, non sicut pars essentiae, sed sicut tenens rem in esse, sequetur quod ipse in quolibet operante immediate operetur, non exclusa operatione voluntatis et naturae."—*De Pot.*, q. 3 art. 7.

This conservative activity of God is in no way different from His creative activity. Creation involves the relation of the being of all things with their source. Conservation involves no new relation; it denotes the temporal condition of the effect.[799]

It may be objected against the doctrine of the conservation of being by God, that experience reveals the fact that many effects continue to exist long after their cause has ceased to exist. A house, for example, does not fall into nothingness when the architect dies. This is quite true, because the architect is merely the cause of the *becoming* of the house, but not the cause of its *being*. God is not the cause of the *becoming* of the universe merely, but is the cause of its *being*; and just as the air ceases to be illumined when the sun sets, so the universe would cease to exist if God were not to sustain it in being.[800]

God is in no sense like an artist who touches his work only with the intermediary of an instrument, and who, though present to his work at one moment, can retire from it altogether without compromising its existence. Rather He is so intimately present to His works that without His continued creation or conservation they would cease to exist. But how can God be present in all things, He who is spiritual and pure act? He is present in a threefold way: by His *power*, by His *presence*, and by His *essence*. He is present everywhere by His *power*, because all things are subject to His sovereign empire, just as a monarch, although confined to the limits of his palace, is present throughout his empire by his authority. He is everywhere by His *presence*, because He knows all and sees all. He is everywhere by His *essence*, inasmuch as He is present to all things as the cause of their being.[801] Because in God substance and action are one and indivisible in the Divine

[799] "Deus non alia operatione producit res in esse et eas in esse conservat. Ipsum enim esse rerum permanentium non est divisibile nisi per accidens, prout alicui motui subjacet, secundum se autem est in instanti. Unde operatio Dei, quae est per se causa quod res sit non est alia secundum quod facit principium essendi et essendi continuationem."—*De Pot.*, q. 5 art. 2 ad 2.

"Conservatio rei non est nisi continuatio esse ipsius."—*C. G.*, lib. 3 c. 65.

[800] "Sicut igitur fieri rei non potest remanere cessante actione agentis quod est causa effectus secundum fieri, ita nec esse rei potest remanere, cessante actione agentis quod est causa effectus, non solum secundum fieri, sed etiam secundum esse."—I q. 104 art. 1; *De Pot.*, q. 5 art. 2 ad 6.

[801] BARTHÉLEMY FROGET, *De l'Habitation du Saint-Esprit* (4th edition), part I.

simplicity, it follows that He is present wherever He operates—that is, in all things and in all places.[802]

In a word, He is present everywhere, not by extension but by His power.[803] It is not in virtue of His own essence that He is everywhere, but only in virtue of His causality. Where He is not there is nothing. The Psalmist has beautifully testified to this universal presence of God in all creation:

'Whither shall I fly from Thy Spirit?
Or whither shall I flee from Thy face?
If I ascend into heaven, Thou art there;
If I descend into hell, Thou art present.
If I take my wings early in the morning,
And dwell in the uppermost parts of the sea;
Even there also shall Thy Hand lead me;
And Thy right Hand shall hold me.
And I said, perhaps darkness shall cover me;
And night shall be my light in my pleasures.
But darkness shall not be dark to Thee,
And night shall be as the light of the day;
The darkness thereof and the light thereof are alike to Thee.
For Thou hast possessed my reins;

---

[802] "Sic ergo est in omnibus per potentiam, inquantum omnia ejus potestati subduntur. Est per praesentiam in omnibus, inquantum omnia nuda sunt et aperta oculis ejus. Est in omnibus per essentiam, inquantum adest omnibus ut causa essendi."—I q. 8 art. 3. I d. 37 q. 1 art. 2.

[803] "Dei proprium est ubique esse; quia cum sit universale agens, ejus virtus attingit omnia entia, unde est in omnibus rebus."—I q. 112 art. 1.

"Non est aestimandum quod sic in rebus quasi in rebus mixtis ... sed in operibus per modum causae agentis."—*C. G.*, lib. 3 c. 68.

"Neque enim mole, sed virtute magnus est Deus."—ST. AUGUSTINE, *Epis.* III.

"Non determinatur (Deus) ad locum, vel magnum, vel parvum, ex necessitate suae essentiae, quasi oporteat eum esse in aliquo loco, quum ipse fuerit ab aeterna ante omnem locum; sed immensitate suae virtutis attingit omnia quae sunt in loco, quum sit universalis causa essendi. Sic igitur ipse totus est ubicumque, quia per simplicem suam virtutem universa attingit."—*C. G.*, lib. 3 c. 68.

Thou hast possessed me from my mother's womb.'[804]

IV. There is yet another title by which the world and God are in intimate relation, namely, that God is the end toward which all creation moves. The end of everything is its perfection. *This is the reason of all movement and all process.* Things move because they tend toward a perfection which they do not now actually possess.[805]

But if the end of a thing is its perfection, the perfection of everything is its good. No one tends to an end unless it is good. This is merely a corollary of the principle and of the fact that every being seeks to conserve its own existence. The Supreme Good will be then the Supreme End of all things. And since God is the Supreme Good of all things, He is therefore the End of all things.[806] Toward Him all things tend, not that they may evolve Him as their term, which is the modern notion, or that they may add some perfection to God, but rather that they may in their own nature and degree be like to Him as their end.[807]

This tendency to participate in His perfection[808] the Angelic Doctor illustrates by a subtle comparison. He compares the Creator and the creature to an agent and a subject of the action.

---

[804] Psalm 138.

[805] "Illud autem ad quod aliquid tendit quum extra ipsum fuerit, et in quo quiescit quum ipsum habuerit, est finis ejus. Unumquodque autem, si perfectione propria careat, in ipsam movetur, quantum in se est; si vere eam habeat in ipso quiescit. Finis igitur uniuscujusque rei est ejus perfectio. Perfectio autem cujuslibet est bonum ipsius. Unumquodque igitur ordinatur in bonum sicut in finem."—*C. G.*, lib. 3 c. 16.

[806] "Quod est maximum in unoquoque genere causa est omnium illorum quae sunt extra illius generis; sicut ignis, qui est calidissimus, est causa caliditatis in aliis corporibus. Summum igitur bonum quod est Deus, est causa bonitatis in omnibus bonis. Ergo et est causa cujuslibet finis quod sit finis, quum quidquid est finis sit hujusmodi inquantum est bonum. Propter quod autem est unumquodque, et illud magis. Deus igitur maxime est omnium rerum finis."—*C. G.*, lib. 3 c. 17.

[807] "Relinquitur igitur quod Deus sit finis rerum, non sicut aliquid constitutum, aut aliquid effectum a rebus, neque ita quod aliquid ei a rebus acquiratur, sed hoc solo modo quia ipse rebus acquiritur ... Res igitur non ordinantur in Deum sicut in finem cui aliquid acquiratur, sed ut ab ipso ipsummet suo modo consequantur, quum ipsemet sit finis."—*C. G.*, lib. 3 c. 18.

"Totum universum cum singulis suis partibus ordinatur in Deum, sicut in finem et inquantum in eis per quamdam imitationem divina bonitas repraesentatur ad gloriam Dei; quamvis creaturae rationales speciali quodam modo supra hoc habeant finem Deum, quem attingere possunt sua operatione, cognoscendo et amando, et sic patet quod Divina bonitas est finis omnium corporalium."—I q. 65 art. 2.

[808] It does not mean absorption in the Divine Essence.

One gives, the other receives, but it is the same thing which one gives and which the other receives. Their end is therefore the same, but from different points of view. The First Cause intends to communicate His Goodness, and every creature intends to attain His likeness. By tending to its own perfection it tends toward the perfection to which it has a distant resemblance.[809]

But there is another and a higher way in which certain creatures tend to grow like to God. They may tend toward God not merely in seeking their own perfection, but in communicating it to others. Thus there may be the double ground of likeness—one of being, the other of causality. The reason of this is that an effect resembles its cause. The animal, for example, when it is generated, receives from its parent its nutritive power (assimilation of being), and also its generative power (assimilation of causality). Every effect thus tends to be like its cause in a double way. First, in seeking the perfection of its own being, it tends to God who is its perfection. Secondly, in communicating its causality to others, it tends to the likeness of God, who has communicated His causality because of His Goodness.[810]

The assimilation is not always the same in all creatures, being more intimate in some than in others. Rational creatures, for example, attain their ultimate end by knowing and loving God. God is known by the intelligence as its objective perfection. Irrational creatures attain their end only inasmuch as they are like to God in possessing being, life and knowledge.[811]

---

[809] "Unumquodque autem tendens in suam perfectionem tendit in divinam similitudinem."— *C. G.*, lib. 3 c. 21.

[810] "Item, ejusdem rationis est quod effectus tendat in similitudinem agentis, et quod agens assimilet sibi effectum. Tendit igitur effectus in finem in quem dirigitur ab agente. Agens autem intendit sibi assimilare sibi patiens, non solum quantum ad esse ipsius, sed etiam quantum ad causalitatem; sicut enim ab agente conferuntur effectui naturali principia per quae subsistit, ita principia per quae aliorum sit causa; sicut enim animal, dum generatur, accipit a generante virtutem nutritivam, ita etiam nutritivam generativam. Effectus igitur tendit in similitudinem agentis, ut ostensum est, non solum quantum ad speciem ejus, sed etiam quantum ad hoc quod sit aliorum causa. Sic autem tendunt res in similitudinem Dei sicut effectus in similitudinem agentis. Intendunt igitur res naturaliter assimilari Deo in hoc quod sunt causae aliorum."—*C. G.*, lib. 3 c. 21.

[811] "Si autem loquamur de ultimo fine hominis quantum ad consecutionem finis, sic in hoc fine hominis non communicant creaturae irrationales: nam homo, et aliae rationales creaturae consequuntur ultimum finem cognoscendo et amando Deum, quod non competit aliis creaturis quae adipiscuntur ultimum finem, inquantum participant aliquam similitudinem Dei, secundum quod sunt, vel vivunt, vel etiam cognoscunt."—I-II q. 1 art. 8.

Thus God, who is the principle of all creation, is necessarily its end. The end of the Perfect Being can never be anything but His principle. All things thus constitute a circle: their final reason of creation was the Goodness of God, as their final destiny is participation according to their mode of being in the Divine Goodness. The reason of this order, by which all things are directed towards their end, is Divine Providence. Because God is Being, and because everything that is is a participation in that Being, there is nothing that falls outside the reign of God. All that is knowable falls under His intelligence; all that is desirable is embraced in His Will; all that is being falls under His active power. Being the cause of all things by His intelligence, He has necessarily the knowledge of the order according to which all things are related to the end. He thus orders all, and this ordinance constitutes Divine Providence.[812]

This is not the place to give a detailed analysis of these points, but merely to sketch in general the intimate way in which God is in the universe.[813] Suffice it, then, to summarize briefly what has gone before. God is the efficient, the final and the exemplary cause of all things in the universe.[814] He is the Cause of all being, the Exemplar of all being and the End of all being. Thus it is that, from the point of view of the creature, *everything has being in virtue of God as Efficient Cause, everything is good in virtue of God as Final Cause, and everything is true in virtue of God as Exemplary Cause.* The transcendentals consequently attach themselves to God in virtue of the real relation between creature and God. *Ex Ipso, per Ipsum, et in Ipso. From Him*, because of His Creative Power; *by Him*, inasmuch as He made all things according to His Wisdom; and *in Him*, inasmuch as all things are conserved in His Goodness.

Cf. C. G., lib. 3 c. 25 and 27; *De Veritate*, q. 5 art. 6 ad 4, and q. 20 art. 4 c. *Quod.*, q. 10 art. 17; *C. G.*, lib. 3 c. 17, lib. 4 c. 32.

812 "Causalitas autem Dei, qui est primum agens, se extendit usque ad omnia entia ... Unde necesse est omnia quae habent quocumque modo esse, ordinata esse a Deo in finem secundum illud Apostoli, ad Rom. xiii. *quae a Deo sunt ordinata sunt.* Cum ergo nihil aliud Dei providentia quam ratio ordinis rerum in finem, ut dictum est, necesse est omnia, inquantum participant esse, intantum subdi divinae providentiae."—I q. 22 art. 2 c. *Perihermenias*, lib. 1 lect. 14.

813 The full development of these points may be found in any manual of Scholastic Theodicy.

814 Not material cause, because matter is a subject which receives the effect of action. "Materia quidem non est principium actionis, sed se habet ut subjectum recipiens actionis effectum."—I q. 105 art. 5 c.

These three, Power, Wisdom and Goodness—*Ens*, *Bonum* and *Verum*—Efficient, Exemplary and Final Cause of all creation, are the vestiges in creation of that Divine Family of the Godhead: three Persons in God, the Father, the Son and the Holy Ghost. The Father by appropriation is the Power, the Son or the Verbum by appropriation is Wisdom, and the Holy Ghost by appropriation is the Good.[815] Such are the unity and coherence of common-sense metaphysics that revelation is its crown and glory, instead of being a check and an opposition. All things lead to God, as all things come from God. There is nothing intelligible without Him, as there is nothing unintelligible with Him. He is the Alpha and the Omega, the beginning and the end of all things.

Professor Pringle-Pattison, then, in attacking transcendence as he understands it, is stating a position which is quite acceptable to us, because for him transcendence means disinterestedness. "Theories of sheer transcendence of the Divine," he says, "defeat their own object, because the very exaltation of the Divine into an inaccessible Beyond confers a spurious independence of self-existence upon the finite."[816] But for traditional thought God is not exalted into an inaccessible Beyond, for He is "intimately in all things," as St. Thomas puts it. This being so, He is not, as Sir Henry Jones believes, a God "who sits aloof from the world-process, eternally contemplating His own perfections."[817]

Can God be said to be "aloof from the universe" when from all eternity He loved the Eternal Archetypal ideas according to which it would be fashioned? Can God be said to be "aloof from the universe" when He is the very cause of its being? Can He be said to be "aloof from human desires" who conserves beings in existence in order that they may reach the fullness of their perfection? Can He be truly said to be "too far removed from

[815] "Omnia sunt ex Ipso, scilicet Deo, sicut ex prima operatrice potentia Omnia autem sunt per Ipsum, inquantum omnia facet per sapientiam. Omnia sunt in ipso sicut in bonitate conservante. Haec autem tria, scilicet potentia, sapientia et bonitas communia sunt tribus personis ... sed tamen potentia quae habet rationem principii, appropriatur Patri, qui est principium totius Divinitatis. Sapientia Filio, qui procedit ut Verbum, quod nihil aliud est quam sapientia genita; bonitas appropriatur Spiritui Sancto, qui procedit ut amor, cujus objectum est bonitas."—ST. THOMAS, *Commen. Epis. ad Roman.*, c. 11 lect. 4.

[816] *Op. cit.*, p. 254.

[817] p. 360.

the universe" when, without His sustaining power for even a single moment, the universe would lapse back into the nothingness from which it came? Is He a "separated and disinterested God" who is in all things by His presence, His essence and His power? One line of St. Thomas would have saved some of the modern philosophers from such a faulty notion: "Deus est in omnibus, et intime ut causans esse omnium."[818] He is in the universe as the Power that brought it into being, as the Power which conserves it and as the Goodness which prompted it and towards which it moves.

Modern thought is asserting no new ideal in its desire to have God interested in "the dust of human lives." Traditional thought is just as interested in this point. It, too, wants a God who is the motive force of all our actions, the hidden Truth of our intellectual quest, the hidden Good in every volition and the hidden Love in every affection. It, too, wants a God to whom the universe can look with assurance that He is the satisfaction of every ideal, and that no man's desire shall be in vain, nor any human value without foundation.

But just precisely *because it does want a God who is interested in us, it shrinks from identifying Him with the world, or making him evolve with the world, or even appear at the end of the world's evolution.* If He were more in the universe than He is, He would not be God, but the universe. He would be lost in confusion with it. And this is precisely the objection to the modern notion—it makes God "too aloof from human needs and human desires." It makes Him aloof because it makes "the world too much with Him." Make Him one with the universe, or organic with it, deny ontological separateness, and He has no more relation to our needs and desires than the universe with which He is in process. If He is to help the universe, He must not be in it. If the universe, *per impossibile*, helps Him, He is of little help to it. In time of sore need our poorest consolation is our own self. It is too much with us. So, too, with the universe. If God is too much bound up with it and unintelligible apart from it, then He can be of no service to it. In such a sense intimacy is aloofness.

[818] I q. 8 art. 1.

Because the universe is evolving, because it is spending its energy and being spent, because it is multiple and composite, common-sense philosophy looks forward to something that is not identified with or dependent on it. Intimately in things God must be, but He must be distinct from them. God is intimately in us, even in the natural order, because He is above us. Distinctness and separation from God do not mean independence of Him. To make God helpful to the world, modern thought identifies Him with the world and thus makes Him helpless. Common-sense thought, on the contrary, to make God helpful to us, recognizes Him as distinct from the world and thus makes Him helpful. That poverty-stricken notion of God, whose sole right to adoration and love is the fact that some future day He will be greater and better than He is today, is of little consolation to our day and age. When men need God most, they are doing their best to get along without Him. If philosophy is sincere in its aim to make God intimate and helpful in this world of ours, it can do nothing better than meditate over and over again that sublime thought of the Angelic Doctor: "God loved us before He made us."

Since the traditional notion of God is one of life and intimate being in the universe, there is no necessity for any substitutes such as the evolving God. Make God evolve in any way whatsoever—make Him a process or a nisus or organic with the universe, or a God dying a thousand deaths daily and rising again—and you deny the most evident characteristic of movement itself.

If God is a movement, an urge or a *nisus*, He should follow its law. But what is its law? In a general sense, it is that there must be some relation between movement and perfection. "Changelessness is a ruinous condition," as Sir Henry Jones has rightly said.[819] But what is this relation? For the modern thinker it is, the greater the movement the more perfect the nature. For St. Thomas it is just the contrary: the greater the movement the more imperfect the nature. For the former, perfection increases in *direct* ratio with movement. For the Angelic Doctor, perfection

[819] *Loc. cit.*

increases in *indirect* ratio with movement.[820] Movement is an imperfection because it is the tendency of a being towards a term which it does not now actually possess. Multiplied movements towards a term are evidence of multiplied imperfection. Hence it is that the nature becomes more perfect as the necessity of movement decreases.[821] A perfect God, then, can never be in movement.

St. Thomas explains his principle by the disposition to health that may reside in various individuals. "We observe that, as the Philosopher says (*De Coelo*, ii. 12), the lowest order of things cannot acquire perfect goodness, but they acquire a certain imperfect goodness, by few movements; and those which belong to a higher order acquire perfect goodness by many movements; and those yet higher acquire perfect goodness by few movements; and the highest perfection is found in those things which acquire perfect goodness without any movement whatever. Thus he is least of all disposed to health who can acquire only imperfect health by means of few remedies; better disposed is he who can acquire perfect health by means of many remedies; and better still he who can by few remedies; best of all is he who has perfect health without any remedies."[822]

There are four grades of beings to which this principle is applied. The first grade attains only an imperfect good, the others a perfect good. All creatures below man attain an imperfect good with movements decreasing in number as the good becomes less imperfect.

Once we come to man, the consideration is no longer of an imperfect but of a perfect good. Being endowed with an intellectual nature, which is capable of transcending the particular good revealed by the senses, the final end of human activity is the contemplation of truth and the attainment of perfect happiness in God Himself.

---

[820] This principle of St. Thomas is the inverse of the principle, the higher the nature the more immanent the activity. Here he speaks of transitive activity—movement and not immanent activity. Modern philosophy having lost the distinction between immanent and transitive activity, identifies movement with operation, whereas the two are quite distinct.

[821] "Quanto a pluralitate receditur tanto perfectior gradus."—I q. 77 art. 2; I-II q. 5 art. 7.

[822] I q. 77 art. 2 c.

Being lowest in the order of intellectual beings, man attains his end only by multiplied movement. His intellectual light being dim, he is under the penalty of abstracting his ideas from sense knowledge. Add to this movement a second, of the intellectual order, namely, judgment—the combination of these ideas. Finally, there is a third movement—that of reason, by which the intelligence mounts from a known to an unknown object, as from the undetermined to the determined. The idea of God is not innate; His attributes are not known by an intuition; man must reason to attain the ultimate object of his intelligence. God is not grasped by a unique operation; multiplied movements are necessary, but in proportion as those movements become unified and continuous they possess more the nature of ultimate happiness. Hence it is that in the active life, which is interested particularly in things of the external order, there is less of the nature of beatitude than in the contemplative life, which is interested only in the contemplation of truth.[823]

The angelic order reveals a decreasing manifestation of movement. All nature is graduated according to its proximity to or its remoteness from its term. The nearer creatures are to God, the more perfectly they imitate Him; as the nearer an object is to the source of light, the more is it illumined. The angels, therefore, know God without abstracting an idea of God from the material universe. Their knowledge of God is the knowledge of infused species.[824] Even in the angelic order itself, the superior angels, being endowed with more universal ideas than inferior angels, have a greater knowledge with fewer movements than the lower angels with many movements.[825] The angelic intellectual light is strong enough to illumine details of knowledge which with its weaker intellectual light the human intelligence has to reach by additional movements. For the very same reason, the angel does not possess the imperfection of the movement of reason. Reason

[823] "Quanto operatio potest esse magis continua et una, tanto plus habet rationem beatitudinis. Et ideo in vita activa, quae circa multa occupatur, est minus de ratione beatitudinis quam in vita contemplativa, quae versatur circa unum, id est circa veritatis contemplationem."—I-II q. 3 art. 2 ad 4; I-II q. 5 art 7 c.

"Quanto creaturae magis appropinquant ad Deum qui est omnino immobilis, tanto magis sunt immobiles."—I q. 65 art. 1 ad 1.

[824] I q. 55 art. 2 c.

[825] I q. 55 art. 2 c.

implies that the knowledge of one thing is caused by the knowledge of another, but in the angels both of those are known by one and the same cognition.[826]

Up to this point the universe has been unfolding itself as a continuous regress from the plurality and the imperfection of movement. As we mount to more perfect creatures we find a decreasing movement. Experience and common sense are thus leading us to a conclusion which is the very contrary of modern philosophy. Instead of finding increased movement as we draw near God, we find decreased movement. "The nearer the creature approaches to God, the more motionless it is."[827] And the reason is to be found in the fact that it more nearly imitates its perfection, its cause and its end. In God, as we have shown, there is no movement. Wanting nothing to His own perfection, He does not tend to some end distinct from Himself, such as Deity, as Professor Alexander imagines. Neither does He identify Himself with a nisus which would be a contradiction. Though immobile, He is not lifeless; He is Life because He possesses perfect immanent activity. Source of all movement, He is outside all movement—a Being who is: "I am who am"—and not a thing that *becomes.*[828] He is a Being who is no less today than He will be tomorrow, a God who does not depend on Space-Time or Divinal Imaginals or "our life and blood," our "consciousness." He is rather the God on whom evolution depends, and without Him evolution is unintelligible. He is not a future God, but an Eternal God. *Tu autem idem semper es et anni tui non deficient.*

In making God equivalent to movement or process or nisus or evolution, modern philosophy identifies what is perfect with what is imperfect. If good health consists in freedom from sickness as its negative character, it is unwise to make good health equivalent to sickness. But this is the tendency of the modern notion. It makes the perfection of God consist in that which constitutes imperfection, namely, movement. It is a glorification of biology at the same time that it denies the most evident facts of biology.

---

[826] I q. 58 art. 3 c.
[827] I q. 65 art. 1 ad 1.
[828] I d. 8 q. 3 art. 1 c.

This brings us back to a point mentioned in the beginning of this work, namely, the lyricism of science. The modern God of evolution is nothing but the transfer, without correction, of biological categories to the spiritual world. Biology does reveal life as a continuity and a progress—but *only* organic life. Its laws are laws of *organisms* and not laws of *spirit*. The laws and methods of one science are not indifferently transferable to another. The predicates of an amoeba are not predicable of the Sphinx. If the subject-matter of one science differs from another, the formal method of study in two sciences will be different and their laws non-transferable. The laws of crystallography are not transferable to music; because there are only about ninety elements in chemistry, it does not follow that there are only ninety kinds of animals. The Weber-Fechner Law of Sensations is not applicable to the science of engineering. The principles of counterpoint are not applicable to psychology; and neither are the principles, laws and hypotheses of biology or physics applicable to the science of metaphysics. *Because organisms evolve, we are not justified in concluding that God evolves.* There is no more reason for applying biology to God than there is for applying music or chemistry or even mining engineering. The laws of biology are more universal than those of music, it is true, because life is more universal than the musical scale; but the laws of organisms are no more applicable to the non-organic than the laws of the musical are applicable to the non-musical, or the laws of the flesh to the spirit. Biological evolution explains merely the *how* or the *process*; it does not explain the *origin* or the *nature*. Modern philosophy identifies the two, and makes the nature of God consist in evolution. A feather dropped from a window *flutters*; that is *how* it falls. But no one has ever said that the nature of a feather was "fluttering" or a "perfect flutter." Neither can we identify the *progress* of organic life, which is its *how*, with its *nature* or the nature of God.

We pass from the world to God, not by way of Exemplarism but by way of Causality. Life is predicable of God before it is predicable of organisms. God is not evolving because animals evolve; animals evolve because they are organisms and composite. God is not a nisus because creatures are a nisus; creatures are a nisus because they tend to their perfection which is God. God is not intelligible in function of biology; biology is intelligible in function of God. The imperfect is intelligible only in virtue of the perfect. To reverse this process is to bring chaos into philosophy.

The God of Professor Alexander, for this reason, is in reality not God at all. He is not "all motion's source, but the outcome of motion." He is the mighty birth with which the womb of Time is big, and may be more justly described as our offspring and our achievement than as our Father and our Creator.[829] This process, which stands at the beginning of things in Professor Alexander's system, either has a cause or it has not. If it has a cause, it is intelligible. If it has not a cause, then the greater comes from the less—*and this is the basic principle of the modern philosophical notion of God.* According to Professor Alexander, the mineral comes from the non-mineral; the plant from the non-plant; the animal from the non-animal; mind from the non-mind; angel from the non-angel; and God from the non-God. And *all this in spite of the fact that many of these orders are travelling in different directions.* Minerals tend to simplicity because they are inorganic; life tends to complexity because it is organic; and yet, according to Professor Alexander, life comes from matter. Animal "mind" tends to the particular because it is sensible; the human mind tends toward the universal and necessary because it is spiritual; yet, according to his theory, the human mind comes from the animal "mind."[830]

Neither man nor angel is God, yet from man and angel God is born. The greater comes from the less, the superior from the inferior and the perfect from the imperfect. This passage from the undetermined to the determined has as its ultimate explanation motion, from which are analysed Space and Time. But motion is a combination of the undetermined and the determined; it is a composition of acquiring and having.[831] To

---

[829] *Cf.* Part I. chap. V.

[830] "What is the ground, we must ask, of his assurance that Space-Time itself, not only, as he puts it (vol. ii p. 413), by virtue of its own *nisus* elaborates *without thought* a hierarchy of ministration which, if it were produced by mind, would imply a vast and all-wise thought and providence, but is to be relied upon to continue this great work by producing in God's good time, and it must be added place (vol. ii p. 425), a quality worthy of the trust which is placed by the more developed religious mind in the Being thought of as possessing or embodying this quality."—C. C. WEBB, "Space, Time and Deity," *Church Quarterly Review*, no. 186 (January 1922), p. 355.

[831] "Space-Time holds everything together. But what holds Space-Time together? Can

make this ultimate is to say that the "undetermined determined" is the source of all the determinations of the universe—which is to deny the fundamental law of reality and thought.

In simple language, the acceptance of Professor Alexander's theory depends upon the refection of two elementary facts of experience and laws of being: first, that there can never be movement without a thing that moves; and secondly, that the greater can never come from the less. By the denial of the first principle he imagines a motion without a mover as the source of things, from which motion Space-Time is analysed. By the denial of the second, he imagines that Space-Time will go on producing higher and higher complexes with more wonderful qualities from something lower and lacking those qualities.[832]

The acceptance of those two principles is the necessary foundation of the modern notion of God. Common sense certainly cannot accept them; nor can the mind, if it will avoid intellectual suicide. Professor Santayana uttered a profound truth when he said: "I think that common sense, in a rough, dogged way, is technically sounder than the special schools of philosophy, each of which squints and overlooks half the facts and half the difficulties in its eagerness to find in some detail the key to the whole."[833] Why should there be any more reason to accept in philosophy, than in our daily life, the contradiction that the greater comes from the less? That this contradiction does not have the concrete absurd effects in philosophy that it would have in commerce or in banking or in architecture is no reason why it should be more acceptable in systematic thought. It is, after all, the abstract which makes the concrete absurd. And what abstract notion can have more far-reaching concrete effects than a notion

they be mutually assuming and supporting? The two do not logically assume and support one another: they have not their ground in one another; they cannot pass from one to the other; and you can very easily think away their correlation—that is as good as thinking away Space-Time. If they are mutually supporting in the sense that they prop each other up against otherwise inevitable collapse, are they trustworthy elements on which to build up the whole fabric of the world?"—MAY SINCLAIR, *The New Idealism*, p. 297.

[832] "Professor Alexander is prepared to accept—contrary to Aristotle's principle, that in the last resort Actuality must be prior to Potentiality—the emergence of a higher quality from a lower without the action upon the lower of something already possessing that higher quality."—C. C. WEBB, "Space, Time and Deity," *Church Quarterly Review*, No. 186 (January 1922), p. 354.

[833] *Scepticism and Animal Faith* (1923), Preface.

of God? If "Deity owes its being to pre-existing finites with their empirical qualities, and is their outcome," if "we also help to sustain the nature of God and are not merely His subjects," and if "God Himself is involved in our acts and their issues,"[834] then it is useless to speak of any other God than man. If Space-Time helps itself towards Deity, "why not in the beginning when Deity would do it some good?" asks the author of *The New Idealism.* "Because, Professor Alexander says, you can think away everything but Space-Time. So he thinks away everything and starts with bare Space-Time—well, not bare, packed with point-instants. If you ask him, What next? what can you get out of that? he says: Everything in time, if you give it time enough, and in space, if you give it space enough. Everything happens; and he is not obliged to account for its happening; he is not concerned with the implications of its happening ... If Space-Time can evolve a universe, why drag in God? And instead of dragging Him in at the end, since dragged in He must be, 'to satisfy the religious consciousness,' why not drag Him in at the beginning? ... So long as we are only bits of Space-Time, our backslidings will not so much matter. A bit of Space-Time bashing in its wife's head with the kitchen poker in a two-pair-back; a bit of Space-Time coming drunk out of the Bald-Faced Stag; a bit of Space-Time telling an improper story at its club, is not so shocking to the religious consciousness."[835]

---

[834] *Space, Time and Deity*, vol. ii. p. 398.

[835] MAY SINCLAIR, *The New Idealism*, pp. 297, 299, 305.

Professor Webb finds a similar difficulty in the theory of Professor Alexander. "The God of religious consciousness, however, is for Professor Alexander not any finite God or angel hereafter to be evolved, but the *nisus* of the universe towards the production of such higher beings, or, more strictly speaking, the universe itself with the *nisus.* The historic records of religion, however, scarcely confirm this view ... It certainly would seem more probable that the religious consciousness always demands that the object be conceived as a being, that in the words of Green 'is all that the human spirit (the highest kind of being that we know, as Professor Alexander would say, by 'enjoyment') is capable of becoming,' *than* that it is an emotion excited by the presence in the world of a *nisus* towards something which is not in being at all. And although, doubtless, expectations of a kingdom to come, a glory that shall be revealed, have played a great part in the history of religion, it cannot, I think, be denied that the consciousness of union with a Reality already and eternally perfect has been a not less important and a more universally present feature of religious life. It is hard, then, to agree with Professor Alexander in finding the object of religion in something which is neither real as yet, nor, if ever it becomes so, capable of satisfy the emotion which it, or rather the *nisus* towards it, has excited."—*Op. cit.*, pp. 350, 351, 352.

What is true of a God who issues from Space-Time is true of a God who buds off from a Divinal Imaginal, or is formed from the "cooperative contributions of all consciousness." If God comes from us in any way, or if He needs us in any way, He ceases to be God. Such a philosophy is the last step in deicide. Common sense demanding a *reason of being*, arrives at God who is the *Alpha* of all things. Common sense demanding the *intelligibility of action*, arrives at God as the *Omega* of all things. He is the Principle and the End, the *Alpha* and the *Omega* of all things. With the abandonment of genuine intellectualist philosophy the process of deicide set in. Deism made the first stroke: it left God the *Alpha*, but denied Him to be the *Omega*. The modern philosophy of "becoming" gave the last stroke, and denied that He was either the *Alpha* or the *Omega*. He was to be no more than a mere point in motion's tracks which just keeps ahead of us by one step, or else a mysterious something which changes its perfections as it grows from youth to manhood. The whole was no more than a deification of man, "who will have no other gods but me;" and a humanization of the Divine. The Absolutist denied morality to God to save His absoluteness; the Pragmatist denied absoluteness to save His morality; and the biological philosopher makes the supreme renunciation: He gives up God to save man.[836]

A detail of Professor Alexander's system enters into that of Sir Henry Jones in the notion that God is "moving from perfection to perfection." For a justification of this notion he asks: "At stage *A* may not *a* be perfection; and at stage *B* may not *b* acquire that character? ... What is admirable in a grown-up man can be repellent in a child."[837] The substance of this last line is to be found in a work of the thirteenth century. St. Thomas writes in the *Summa*: "A thing may be perfect according to time, though imperfect *simpliciter*, just as a child is not perfect *simpliciter*, but merely according to the condition of time."[838] There are therefore two kinds of perfections—and this is the point Sir

---

[836] MAY SINCLAIR, *The New Idealism*, p. 213.

[837] *Op. cit.*, p. 359.

[838] "Nihil prohibet aliquid non esse perfectum simpliciter, quod tamen est perfectum secundum tempus; sicut dicitur aliquid puer perfectus non simpliciter, sed secundum temporis conditionem."—I-II q. 98 art. 2 ad 1.

Henry Jones forgets—namely, a perfection *simpliciter* or absolutely considered, and a perfection according to the clock and the calendar.[839] Sir Henry Jones views the perfection of God according to the time element and not absolutely. Duration constitutes an imperfection. If Sir Henry Jones's God should die at stage *A* instead of being allowed to grow up to stage *B*, would we not say He had an imperfect life? If a child can die in its infancy, why not the modern God or Mr. Wells's God, "who is a beautiful youth, but hardly come to his strength"?[840]

There are two kinds of actualities: first, that which is essentially in time and is actual only for the moment; such is the concrete, which enchants us; it is actual only on condition of change: secondly, that which is above time and is actual without change; that which is actual without change is Divine, that which is actual in and through change is human.[841]

A perfect God evolving from one perfection to another is a contradiction. Sir Henry Jones calls God a "perfect process." If He is perfect, He cannot be a process; and if He is a process, He cannot be perfect. In every succession there is a double imperfection—the first in virtue of the division of movement, the second in virtue of the succession inasmuch as one part does not exist with the other part. If God is perfect, then He cannot be "moving from perfection to perfection."[842] Perfection, it must be

[839] "Perfectio dicitur aliquid dupliciter; uno modo, simpliciter, in quo scilicet nullus defectus invenitur, nec secundum suam naturam, nec per respectum ad aliquid aliud, et sic *solus Deus perfectus est* ... Alio modo potest dici aliquid perfectum secundum quid, puta, secundum suam naturam, aut statum aut tempus, et hoc modo homo virtuosus est perfectus; cujus tamen perfectio in comparatione ad Deum deficiens invenitur."—II-II q. 161 art. 1 ad 4.

[840] "Imperfectio esse potest considerari dupliciter: vel quantum ad durationem, et sic dicitur esse imperfectum, cui deest aliquid de spatio durationis debitae, sicut dicimus vitam hominis qui moritur in pueritia, imperfectam vitam."—1 d. 8 q. 2 art. 1 ad 3.

Mr. Chesterton writes as follows about Mr. Wells's *God, the Invisible King*: "He has selected a God who was really more like a daemon. He called his book, *God, the Invisible King*; but the curious point was that he specially insisted that his God differed from other people's God in the very fact that He was not a king. He was very particular in explaining that his deity did not rule in any almighty or infinite sense, but merely influenced like any wandering spirit. Nor was He particularly invisible, if there can be said to be any degrees in invisibility. Mr. Wells's Invisible God was really like Mr. Wells's Invisible Man. You almost felt he might appear at any moment, at any rate to His one devoted worshipper, and that, as if in old Greece, a glad cry might ring through the woods of Essex, the voice of Mr. Wells crying: 'We have seen, He hath seen us, a visible God'" (*New Jerusalem*, pp. 163-4).

[841] JACQUES MARITAIN, *Theonas*, p. 70.

[842] "In successivis est duplex imperfectio; una ratio divisionis; alia ratio successionis

recalled, "consists not in evolution but in the term of evolution."[843] Or more beautifully still, in the words of St. Augustine: "Perfectio non est in annis sed in animis."

The common-sense notion believes in a Perfect God and a perfectible universe. Because God is distinct from the world, and perfect and unchanging, it does not follow that there is no room for perfection in the universe. This has been too generally assumed as a starting-point by the modern philosophers of "becoming." There may be, and there is, progress towards perfection in the universe, but it is *in us and not in God.* It is only because God is not in progress that we can be in progress. If progress were the universal law, and applied radically to God and the universe, then not only the superstructure but even the foundations of things would crumble. If the law of progress means the constant change of foundations and principles admitted in the past, it equivalently states that the movement of humanity toward the best must accomplish itself by uninterrupted renovations, or, in other words, by destruction—which is manifestly untrue.[844]

Progress is necessarily conservative. To perfect we must conserve the gains of the past. More than that, the universe and the souls that are in it can progress only on condition that they have a Cause and an End of Progress. Without the first, they would never have begun to progress; without the second, they would never try to progress. In other words, God as the Cause and End, the Alpha and Omega of all things, is the necessary condition of all progress.

The law of progress which manifests itself in creatures and by which they attain their perfection is twofold. In order that an inferior nature may perfect itself, two things must concur: one which is proper to its own motion; the other which is proper to the motion of a creature above it.[845] The mineral finds its added

---

qua una pars non est cum alia parte; unde non habet esse nisi secundum aliquid sui. Ut autem excludatur omnis imperfectio a divino esse, oportet ipsum intelligere sine aliqua divisione partium perfectum."—1 d. 8 q. 2 art. 1 ad 4.

[843] "Perfectio autem non consistit in via, sed in termino viae."—2 d. 15 q. 3 art. 3 ad 3.

[844] JACQUES MARITAIN, *Theonas*, p. 131.

[845] "In omnibus naturis ordinatis invenitur, quod ad perfectionem naturae inferioris duo concurrunt: unum quidem, quod est secundum proprium motum: aliud autem, quod

perfection in the plant, the plant finds its added perfection in the animal, and the animal finds its added perfection in man. Man is the natural perfection of the universe, and all things exist on account of him.[846] In this whole process there is a double motion, one belonging to the perfectible nature, the other to the perfecting nature.[847] But progress towards perfection does not stop here. If it did, the lower order, in a certain sense, would have a higher perfection than man, inasmuch as it might be perfected by a higher order.

There are in God's plan of the universe three great orders: the order of *nature*, the order of *grace* and the order of *glory*.

Nature, too, has its perfection, and its perfection is the order of grace. But in order that this perfection may be effected, there must be a motion from the intellectual nature, which is that of belief, and a motion from a higher nature, which is the gift of supernatural participation in the Divine Goodness.[848] Nature does not absolutely require grace. But once nature does receive that participation in Divine nature, which is grace, it exceeds its own nature in a far greater way even than the mineral exceeds its nature in possessing existence in the mind of man.

The order of *grace* has its ultimate perfection in the reign of glory, which is that of the beatific vision of God. Grace is the germ of glory.

---

est secundum motum superioris naturae."—II-II q. 2 art. 3 c.

[846] "Sunt ergo elementa propter corpora mixta, haec vero propter viventia in quibus plantae sunt propter animalia, animalia propter hominem, homo enim est finis totius generationis."—*C. G.*, lib. 3 c. 20.

[847] The perfect precedes the imperfect in the order of nature and perfection; but the converse is true in the order of time and generation.—I q. 85 art. 3 ad 1; III q. 1 art. 5 ad 3 art. 6 c.; *De Malo*, q. 4 art. 3. *Metaphysics*, lib. 5 lect. 13.

[848] "Perfectio ergo rationalis creaturae non solum consistit in eo quod ei competit secundum suam naturam, sed in eo etiam, quod ei attribuitur ex quadam supernaturali participatione divinae bonitatis; unde et supra dictum est (I-II q. 3 art. 8), quod ultima beatitudo hominis consistit in quadam supernaturali Dei visione: ad quam quidem visionem homo pertingere non potest, nisi per modum addiscentis a Deo doctore, secundum illud Joann. 6, *Omnis, qui audivit a Patre, et didicit, venit ad me*; hujus autem disciplinae fit homo particeps non statim sed successive, secundum modum suae naturae: omnis autem talis addicens oportet quod credat, ad hoc quod ad perfectam scientiam perveniat; sicut etiam Phil. dicit (*Elench.*, lib. 1 c. 2) quod *oportet addiscentem credere*, unde ad hoc quod homo perveniat ad perfectam visionem beatitudinis, praeexigitur quod credat Deo, tamquam discipulus magistro docenti."—II-II q. 2 art. 3 c.

This takes us far beyond a philosophical notion of God, but it is worth while to introduce it at the close of this chapter, as evidence of the great progress and continuity that exists in the universe. If Scholastic thought has been accused of being the philosophy of the *static*, it is for no other reason than that it has never been understood. There is no system of thought which has so calm and keen a vision of progress and continuity in the universe. It is the philosophy of movement *par excellence*, for it alone gives intelligibility to movement. It is the philosophy of the *perfectible*, for it alone gives the reason of perfectibility—the tendency of all things toward their final end, which is God. Its laws of progress and perfection are not biological but transcendental. It interprets God, not in terms of organic life, but in terms of the *intelligence*, "which is the supreme and perfect kind of life," as the Angelic Doctor has so beautifully put it.[849] Nature for grace, grace for glory—there is its supreme synthesis. "All are yours, you are Christ's and Christ is God's."

[849] *C. G.*, lib. 4 c. 11.

CHAPTER VIII:

THE SPIRIT OF MODERN PHILOSOPHY

WE now pass to state our fundamental criticism of the whole spirit of contemporary philosophy on this subject in the light of the age-long traditional principles.

Our basic principles are extracted from the doctrines of Aristotle and St. Thomas—principles whose sole claim to be accepted are their accord with common sense, and not their authority.[850]

In the tenth book of Aristotle's *Metaphysics* and in the First Question of *De Veritate* we find the principles upon which the spirit of modern thought will be judged.

These principles are:—

1. The Divine Intellect is a measure, not a thing measured.
2. Natural things are both a measure and a thing measured.
3. The human intellect is a thing measured, not a measure.[851]

1. The term *measure* is a term strictly applicable to quantity; here it is applied in an analogical sense. God is the measure of all things in that He "has ordered all things in measure and number and weight."[852] The *measure* is the substance whose end is

---

[850] See Part. II. chap. IV.

[851] "Intellectus divinus est mensurans non mensuratus; res autem naturalis, mensurans et mensurata; sed intellectus noster est mensuratus, non mensurans quidem res naturales, sed artificiales tantum."—*De Veritate*, q. 1 art. 2.

"In sentiendo et sciendo mensuramur per res quae extra nos sunt."—*Comm. Met. Arist.*, lib. 10, lect. 2.

Cf. also I q. 21 art. 2 c.; q. 16 art. 1, and I-II q. 93 art. 1 ad 3: "Intellectus enim humanus est mensuratus a rebus, ut scilicet conceptus hominis non sit verus propter seipsum, sed dicitur verus ex hoc quod consonat rebus."

[852] Wisdom, xi. 21.

determined by its constitutive principles. The *number* is the species. To add or subtract from a number is to change it; to add or subtract a substantial element from a species is to destroy it, *e.g.* to add animality to mineral life. The *weight* is inclination and love. Love is to rational beings what the law of gravitation is to bodies. Matter is drawn to the centre of the earth; reason is drawn to its source—God;[853] *Amor meus pondus meum*, in the words of St. Augustine.

Yet God in turn is measured by no one. He is First Cause and Uncaused, and thus, having never received His existence from another, He has not been measured by another. He has set the bounds to all created being, yet no one has set bounds to His Being.

2. *Natural things are both a measure and a thing measured.*—They are first of all a measure; for they determine our knowledge. The object which I see determines my knowledge of that object.

Though natural things enjoy a reflected likeness of God they measure us proximately, as God measures us absolutely. They, however, bear the stamp of their imperfection, for they too are measured. God has made them, set limits to them, and given them their measure of existence.

3. *The human intellect is a thing measured, not a measure.*—It is measured first of all by God, who has given it its first principles of the speculative and the practical order. It is also measured by things. The intellect does not give truth and goodness to things; it discovers them in things. Only in the case of artificial things can man be said to be a measure, and to this extent He reflects the Creator Who made him. The architect is the measure of the house which he builds; the sculptor is the measure of the statue

---

[853] These three are also "vestigial" of the Trinity.

"Quaelibet enim creatura subsistit in suo esse, et habet formam per quam determinatur ad speciem, et habet ordinem ad aliquid aliud. Secundum igitur quod est quaedam substantia creata, repraesentat causam et principium, et sic demonstrat personam Patris, qui est principium, non de principio. Secundum autem quod habet quamdam formam et speciem, repraesentat Verbum secundum quod forma artificiati est ex conceptione artificis. Secundum autem quod habet ordinem, repraesentat Spiritum Sanctum, in quantum est amor; quia ordo effectus ad aliquid alterum est ex voluntate creantis ... Et ad haec etiam reducuntur illa tria numerus, pondus et mensura, quae ponuntur."—Sap. xi.; I q. 45 art. 7.

Cf. ST. AUGUSTINE, *Nat. Bon.*, cap. 3; *Cf.* I q. 5 art. 5.

which he chisels; in a greater way, God is the Cause and Measure of all things. So far as natural things are concerned—and this is our present interest—*man is not a measure; he is a thing measured.*

These three principles are at the basis of common-sense philosophy, and their proof, as we have shown, is ultimately reducible to the principle of contradiction. Not only philosophy but even religion itself reposes on these principles, for they determine the relations of God and man. To change them is to change the whole fabric of our thought and to substitute a series of relations which pervert the real order of things.

In face of these principles, the spirit of modern thought is clear. After reviewing that thought in its characteristic statements and conclusions we may now suggest its fundamental principles in terms of our own system. Possibly the philosophers who are thus criticized would be the first to say that our conclusions were not theirs, and that they were not aware of the attributed implications. This we state to be just. We, however, consider, after a careful survey, that the principles and implications lie deeply embedded in the nature, expression, and structure of their tenets.

What common-sense philosophy attributes to the human intellect, modern philosophy attributes to the Divine Intellect; and what common-sense philosophy attributes to the Divine Intellect, modern Philosophy attributes to the human intellect.

Putting their formula in the same terms as the common-sense formula, it reads as follows:—

The human intellect is a measure, not a thing measured.

The Divine Intellect is a thing measured, not a measure.

Its first principle, in other words, is the superiority of mind over being; its second principle is the superiority of man over God. One has as its consequence the divinization of man; the other, the humanization of God.

These two results are not diverse; they are reciprocal. One is the concave, the other the convex side of the same reality. The divinization of man means always the humanization of God.

This is true of nations and individuals. At that point in history of a people or the history of a soul when man stresses unduly his own powers and self-sufficiency, faith is lost in both gods and God.[854] John the Baptist, seized with the tremendous truth of this fact, cried out to his hearers beyond the Jordan: "I must decrease and He must increase."[855] As man takes on an added and undue gravity through an undue estimation of his worth, God naturally becomes less in His estimation. Humility, on the contrary, is not so much an emphasis upon one's own insufficiency as it is upon God's worth and power. God becomes greater in our eyes, according as we become less in our own. In either case, there is no change in God; the change is psychological and real—but in us.

The first perversion of a fundamental principle of the *philosophia perennis* is, that man is the measure of all things. This *anthropometrism and deification of man* finds concrete expression in two principles underlying modern thought, and asserting respectively:—

A. *The divinization of the human intelligence.*[856]

B. *The divinization of human nature.*

A. The Divinization of the Human Intelligence

The divinization of human intelligence is manifested in the boasted superiority of the human mind over being and truth.

Being and its transcendentals measure thought, this is the position of the perennial philosophy. Thought measures being and its transcendentals; this is the position of modern philosophy.

We turn then to show in contemporary thought mind is made the measure of being and truth.

---

[854] "Quanto enim aliquis magis afficitur ad Deum et ipsum cognoscit, tanto videt eum majorem; imo prope nihil in comparatione ad Deum."—*Comm. Ep. ad Ephes.*, cap. 5, lect. 7.

[855] John iii. 30.

[856] Divinization in ideal—not in fact.

I. Mind is the Measure of Being

For Aristotle and his followers mind is a *tabula rasa* upon which reality writes. Nothing is in the mind except that which was first in the sense and therefore in the objective reality. Mind is therefore not the measure of reality, so far as man is concerned. *Reality does not need to enter into a finite mind in order to exist.* Even when reality does measure mind, reality is in no way modified. Only the subjective reality is affected; not the objective. Hence there is no *real relation existing* between matter and mind, or being and mind. The only *real* relation exists between mind and matter, or mind and being, inasmuch as there is a causal dependence of the former on the latter. *Intellectus humanus est mensuratus, non mensurans.*

Modern thought, on the contrary, subverts this order of mind and being and makes mind a measure instead of the thing measured. Whether it be Idealism or Empiricism, both agree in this Kantian Copernican revolution: reality is to some extent the work of the mind. The planets of reality revolve about the world of self. Mind is the measure of reality. But how, on these theories, does mind measure reality? Either by the use of *a priori* forms native to the mind—and this is the Idealist's answer; or by practical forms arising from need and utility—and this is the Empirical answer. One is the modern interpretation of the First Critique of Kant, the other that of the Second Critique.[857]

Professor Ralph Barton Perry of Harvard has given the following principle as representative of idealism: "the assertion of the *priority of the cognitive consciousness*, the assertion that being is *dependent upon the knowing of it*, may be regarded as the cardinal principle of idealism."[858] What therefore is real, is real only in virtue of mind. That he has defined idealism well is evident from the words of the chief of the Engish Idealists: "We perceive, on reflection, that to be real, or even barely to exist, must be to fall within sentience. Sentient experience, in short, is reality, and what is not this is not real. We may say, in other words, that

---

[857] See LESLIE WALKER, M.A., *Theories of Knowledge*, for a full development of this point.

[858] *Present Philosophical Tendencies*, p. 107.

there is no real being or fact outside of that which is commonly called psychical experience. Feeling, thought and volition (any groups under which we class psychical phenomena) are all the material of existence, and there is no other material, actual or even possible."[859] This by no means implies pure solipsism, the author contends, for there is no such thing as a subject apart from reality. There is only one Reality, of which all things else are but appearances. Nothing exists independently of it. This system of mind which is and which measures reality is an Absolute—but it is not God. God is only an appearance of reality. "A God that can say to himself, I, as against you and me, is not in my judgment defensible as the last and complete truth of metaphysics."[860]

For the Empiricists of today mind, too, is the measure of reality; but instead of mind being a single whole, it is taken to mean the combined activities of many minds in the long course of evolution. There is "no ready-made world presented to us which we can suck in with passive receptivity," Professor Schiller tells us.[861] Reality "is *not* a 'fact' in its own right which pre-exists the cognitive functioning."[862] It is not something which measures our mind independently of any contribution which we may bring to it. We construct reality, instead of being constructed by it. Our needs, utilities and experience and conveniences are its determination and its measure. The *a priori* forms of the Idealist give way to the practical forms of action for the modern Empiricist. Professor James goes so far as to admit that these practical forms which measure reality may even antedate the appearance of real objects.

Though "the category of transcendental reality is now one of the foundations of our life," yet we can "speculatively imagine a state of pure experience before the hypothesis of permanent objects behind its flux had been formed."[863]

In just so far as reality depends upon it, mind may be said to be the measure and in some sense to be reality. If only that is real

[859] F. H. BRADLEY, *Appearance and Reality*, p. 144.
[860] F. H. BRADLEY, *Essays on Truth and Reality*, p. 432.
[861] *Personal Idealism*, chap. v.
[862] F. C. S. SCHILLER, *Studies in Humanism*, p. 426.
[863] WILLIAM JAMES, *The Meaning of Truth*, p. 63; *Cf.* p. 60.

which is in thought, and if it is meaningless to speak of anything outside thought,[864] then man has deified intelligence to the level of God's intelligence. A very happy reaction to this Protagorian philosophy has set in with Neo-Realism and Critical Realism.[865] Neither, however, has created sufficient metaphysics to merit discussion here. At present they confine themselves almost exclusively to the problem of sensible perception.[866]

2. *Mind as the Measure of Truth*

Common-sense philosophy has always maintained that truth, while involving mind of necessity, is not made or created by the mind. It in no way makes truth. It discovers truth; it does not manufacture it. Where is the ultimate source of that which it discovers? In the Mind of God. Truth resides, firstly, in the Divine Intelligence, which conceives eternally the ideas of its works. Secondly, it is found in things inasmuch as they are created in conformity with these Eternal Ideas. Thirdly, truth passes into human knowledge when it represents things as they are. Thus God measures truth just as things about us measure us.[867] "Thus we see that in the ontological order, in the order of real gradation and dependence among things, as distinct from the order of human experience, the reason why reality has ontological truth for the human mind is because it is essentially and antecedently in accord with the Divine mind, from which it derives its intelligibility."[868]

Modern philosophy has some accord with this traditional notion, at least at first sight. The source of truth for many is the *other*—but the *other* is not God. It is man, not as an individual, but as a stage in the evolutionary process. Ultimately, then, man has become the measure and the source of truth. This is true of

[864] M. POINCARÉ, *La Valeur de la Science*, p. 276.

[865] DRAKE, LOVEJOY, PRATT, ROGERS, SANTAYANA, SELLARS, STRONG, *Essays in Critical Realism*.

[866] R. KREMER, Ph.D., "Un nouvel Essai de Réalisme," *Revue Néo-Scolastique de Louvain* (August 1922), p. 332. *Cf.* also Dr. KREMER'S excellent work on *Néo-Réalisme Américain* (Louvain, 1921).

[867] *De Veritate*, q. 1 art. 2; I q. 14 art. 8 ad 3.

[868] P. COFFEY, Ph.D., *Ontology*, p. 161.

the generality of Pragmatic systems, and even of those Absolutist systems which admit evolution of mind and truth.[869]

(a) Man is the source of truth considered from the point of view of evolution. Truth has a biological, not a Divine source. Its source is not something transcendent to man; it *becomes* as man *becomes*. There is no such thing as a truth with a big "*T*." Truths "make themselves as we go." They are "so many new creations that add themselves as fast as history proceeds." Instead of being an "antecedent principle" that animates a process, truth is but an abstract name for its results.[870] The notion of a God as the source of truth is classed as a mere "idol of the tribe." Mach, Semmel, Avenarius and Professor Schiller insist particularly on this "man-made" attitude of truth. Just as our organs in the course of evolution acquire a certain fixity and stability and a certain biological immunity, so, too, do our truths. They are to be ultimately attributed to our ancestors. To speak of their source as residing outside the process of evolution is nonsense. "The world is essentially ὑλη. It is what we make it. It is fruitless to define it by what it originally was or by what it is apart from us."[871] Take man from out the evolutionary series, and truth automatically ceases to exist. Just as organic forms are born into the world, so is truth born with man. Suppress man, and you suppress truth. For St. Thomas it is the contrary: suppress man, truth will continue to exist; suppress angels, truth will continue to exist. But imagine that God were suppressed, then, he concludes, truth would no longer exist.[872] But, to this the modern will answer, this notion of Scholastic metaphysics was "expedient for centuries, but human experience has boiled over" its limits.[873]

(b) Less remotely, truth has been made by the experience of the individual, considered not as developing but as developed. "Human nature shapes all our questions, human satisfaction lurks in all our answers, all our formulas have a human twist."[874] But why have we come to recognize truths as man-made and not

---

[869] S. RADHAKRISHNAN, M.A., *The Reign of Religion in Contemporary Philosophy* (1920), p. 234.

[870] W. JAMES, *Pragmatism*, p. 242.

[871] F. C. S. SCHILLER, *Personal Idealism*, p. 60.

[872] *De Veritate*, q. 1 art. 2.

[873] *Pragmatism*, p. 223.

[874] Ibid., p. 242.

something coming from God? Professor James gives the answer: "The enormously rapid multiplication of theories in these latter days has well-nigh upset the notion of any one of them being a more literally objective kind of thing than another. There are so many geometries, so many logics, so many physical and chemical hypotheses, so many classifications, each one of them good for so much and yet not good for anything, that the notion that even the truest formula may be a human device, and not a literal transcript, has dawned upon us."[875] Being devices, then, their measure will be their utility ... their utility to us in handling the facts of experience. Subjective interests, our needs, our desires, will be at every step the measure of these "truths."[876] The measure will not be something objective; it will be that which satisfies us, or that which is expedient in the way of our thinking. If an idea "works," then it is true. "If theological ideas prove to have a value for concrete life, they will be true for pragmatism in the sense that they are good for so much."[877] "If the hypothesis of God works satisfactorily in the widest sense of the word—experience shows that it certainly does work—it is true."[878] If, therefore, at any time reason should come to prove the fallacy of some popular conclusion, and demonstrate conclusively that it was in contradiction to the fundamental laws of thought, Pragmatism would keep it as a valuable error or a "vital lie." Man, in the philosophical sense, is thus considered as an artist, measuring not only artificial things, but even the universe itself. The universe that we can know and use is moulded as potter's clay to the measure of the desires of man.

Modern absolutist systems do not adopt this anthropometrism with such boldness, at least the strictly philosophical part of it. But once the subject of God is introduced, man, either implicitly or explicitly, is made the measure. To judge or evaluate religion upon any other grounds than those of our own needs and desires is "dangerous" and mistaken.[879] But within the sphere of Absolutism it is difficult to

---

[875] *Meaning of Truth*, p. 242.
[876] F. C. S. SCHILLER, *Humanism*, p. 11.
[877] *Pragmatism*, p. 73.
[878] *Pragmatism*, p. 299.
[879] F. H. BRADLEY, *Essays on Truth and Reality*, p. 431.

see wherein it can find the *other* by which truth can be measured. There is only *one*, of which we are a part. On the common-sense view the *many* may be suppressed—world, men and angels—yet there will still be truth; on the Absolutist position, if you suppress the many—world, men and angels—you suppress the Absolute. Ultimately, then, on the Absolutist position, we are the measure.

B. *Divinization of Human Nature and the Humanization of God*

Traditionally there had been recognized a double perfection of human nature: one natural, the other supernatural. The natural perfection is the complete development of the natural powers in the knowledge of the highest truth, and in union through love with the highest good.[880] It is not the attainment of God *sub ratione Deitatis*; this is the object of the supernatural order. The supernatural perfection is effected through a gratuitous gift of grace by which we are made "partakers of the Divine nature," adopted sons of God and heirs of heaven. The supernatural order exceeds the powers, the nature, the capacity and the merits of the natural order. It is in the strictest sense a something not due to human nature—an *indebitum*.[881] There is greater difference between the state of a soul without grace and the state of a soul in grace, than a soul in grace on this earth and a soul enjoying the glory of heaven. Grace is such a precious gift that it is worth more than all creation. As we cannot know the intimate nature of Michael Angelo by looking at his statue of Moses, so, too, we cannot know the intimate nature of God by regarding His works—the visible universe. But thanks to this participation of the Divine nature, through the gratuitous gift of God, our nature becomes in an analogical sense *deified*, as St. Augustine has put it: "God became man in order that man might become God."

Now, this sharp distinction between the natural and the supernatural order, between knowledge by reason and knowledge by infused faith, between the natural perfection of our nature and

---

[880] JOS. SCHEEBEN, *Natur und Gnade* (München, 1922), p. 21

[881] I q. 13 art. 8 ad 2; q. 12 art.4 and 5; II-II q. 6 art. 1; I q. 1 art. 2 ad 1.

the supernatural perfection through grace, has been lost sight of in modern philosophy. The result has been that what really is a gift of God is now looked upon as natural to man, so that man, attributing to himself that Divine quality which makes him a partaker of the Divine nature, has divinized himself to just that extent.

According to the modern doctrines the mystical state is not due to any infusion of grace. It is properly a psychological state, "our soul being mysteriously one with a larger soul whose instruments we are."[882] Dean Inge rightly insists that to know God intimately we must become partakers of the Divine nature; but the source of this participation he attributes not to God, but to the "Divine spark already within us." "But though we are made in the image of God, our likeness to Him only exists potentially. The Divine spark already shines within us, but it has to be searched for in the innermost depths of our personality, and its light diffused over its whole being."[883] The foundation of mystical states being considered as natural and psychological, has given some the privilege to dispense with the Author of grace. "The indwelling Christ constituted the central doctrine of St. Paul, and can be apprehended and experienced by each one of us *now* without any historical difficulties, without any reference even to the historical Jesus."[884]

This intimate participation by the human nature in the Divine nature is yet more fully revealed in the various philosophies of "Becoming" in which man becomes identified with the life impulse which is God, or with the *élan vital*, or becomes continuous with God by a mystical interpenetration. God is not apart from man, but there is a presence of "one in and through the other." The Divine Imaginal reflects itself in us as well as in Him; for He, like us, is only a "child of the Divine Imaginal." God is above us, it is true, but not far above; He is just one stage above the stage yet evolved, and we shall in a future day attain the dignity and the level He now possesses.

---

[882] W. JAMES, *Pluralistic Universe*, pp. 307-8. *Cf.* B. RUSSELL, *Mysticism and Logic* (1918); W. KINGSLAND, *Our Infinite Life* (1922); J. LEUBA, *Psychological Study of Religion*, p. 242.

[883] Dean INGE, *Christian Mysticism* (London, 1922), p. 7. Mysticism is "the attempt to realize, in thought and feeling, the immanence of the temporal in the eternal, and of the eternal in the temporal" (p. 5).

[884] WILLIAM KINGSLAND, *Our Infinite Life* (1922), p. 173.

Modern philosophy has divinized the *power* of the human intelligence, making it the measure of Being and its transcendentals; it has also divinized the *mode* of this knowledge by making it like unto God's. It has divinized human nature by confusing a gift with a claim—that is, by turning the gift of grace and participation in the Divine nature into a claim and a *debitum* to human nature, and a natural consequence of its psychological structure.

This divinization of man has for its counterpart, as we hinted in the beginning of this chapter, the humanization of God. If we increase, God decreases in our estimation. Man has made himself like unto God; it now remains for God to be made like unto man by a misunderstanding of His nature. This is the negative side of the spirit of modern philosophy. It is that of the humanization of God.

This aspect of modern philosophy is best evidenced in the novel and original concept of *religion*.

For traditional philosophy and theology, religion is a term which has meaning only if a God or gods exist. This notion is not proper to Christianity; paganism implied it and Cicero defined it. There could no more be religion without God than there could be physics without bodies, or mathematics without numbers. The creature was considered as related to God as science to its object. The object is not relative to the science; it can exist without a science. Life would exist whether biology ever existed or not. So, too, God can exist without us. As the rays of the sun cease with the setting of the sun, so would our existence cease without the conservation of God. We are, therefore, dependent on God. This dependence begets religion. Religion is intelligible only in function of a God. Thus St. Thomas, quoting Cicero and St. Augustine, the pagan and the Christian, states religion to be a "relation to God, to whom we are bound as to an unfailing principle."[885]

But this notion has been changed. The idea of dependence on a Supreme Being has been lost. Instead of being rays that disappear with the setting sun, we are rays that survive in virtue

[885] "Religio proprie importat ordinem *ad Deum*; ipse enim est, cui principaliter alligari debemus tamquam indeficienti principio."—II-II q. 81 art. 1.

of our own sufficiency. Today, God is not conceived as the starting-point of religion; rather religion is the starting-point. Religion first, God afterwards. George Fonsegrive in his *L'Évolution des Idées dans la France contemporaine* characterizes this changed attitude in these words: "Nos contemporains paraissent aller de la religion à Dieu plutôt que de Dieu à la religion."[886] Professor Hoernlé in his study on contemporary metaphysics notes also that this new notion of the relation between God and religion is one of the characteristics of contemporary thought.[887] A German historian has been so struck by it as to give it special mention as a trait of modern thought.[888]

The modern conception of the relationship between God and religion can be understood only in the light of the new definition of religion. To retain the term "religion" in the traditional sense, and still to maintain that we proceed from religion to God, would result in "confusion worse confounded." Religion has lost the meaning which it has always possessed. Today it means a "relation" as of old, but not *necessarily* with God. God is no longer conceived as the starting-point of religion; rather, it is man. Man is the centre around which religion revolves, and not God. We are the highest examples of individuals, and therefore the solution of all riddles is to be found within us.[889] Religion is "the pure embodiment of the practical motive—that is, the highly interested desire for a plan of action which will secure the maximum of good fortune from the environment as a whole."[890] "Religion is a projection in the roaring loom of time of a concentration or unified complex of psychical values."[891] The term "god" or "God" is left entirely out of consideration; the "source" of the maximum of goodness is represented as the "environment" as a whole. Professor James has given a similar definition: Religion is "*the feelings, acts and experiences of individual men in their solitude, so far as they apprehend themselves to stand in relation to*

[886] p. 218.

[887] *Studies in Contemporary Metaphysics* (1920), p. 294.

[888] ERDMANN, *History of Philosophy*, vol. ii. p. 2; trans. by Hough.

[889] F. C. S. SCHILLER., *Riddles of the Sphinx*, p. 240.

[890] ALFRED HOERNLÉ, *Harvard Theological Review*, vol. xi. No. 2 (April 1918). R. P. PERRY, *Present Philosophical Tendencies*, p. 29.

[891] JOSEPH A. LEIGHTON, *Man and Cosmos* (1922), p. 545.

whatever they may consider the divine."[892] Lest we should be tempted to think that God is necessary for religion, and its starting-point, James goes on to explain what he means by the "divine." "We must interpret the term 'divine' very broadly, as denoting the object that is *god-like* whether it be a concrete deity or not."[893]

"Whether God exists or not, is not important to the nature of religion."[894] All the relations that religion implies may be found within man himself. The explanation which Mr. Bertrand Russell gives of it, and for which he won much praise from his contemporaries, is as follows: Religion consists in the transfer from the life of the finite self to that of the infinite, both of which are to be found in man. This transition comes "when all personal will seems to cease and the soul feels itself in passive submission to the universe. After passionate struggle for some particular good, there comes some inward or outward necessity to abandon the pursuit of the object which has absorbed all our desire, and no other desire is ready to replace the one that has been relinquished. Hence arises a state of suspension in the will, when the soul no longer seeks to impose itself upon the world, but is open to every impression that comes to it from the world. Thus from the moment of self-surrender, which to the finite self appears like death, a new life begins with a larger vision, a new happiness and wider hopes."

But is God required in order that the new "infinite life" be born in us? Mr. Russell answers in the negative: "To some men the belief in an all-wise God to whom submission is a duty" may make the surrender "easier." "But *it is not in its essence dependent upon this belief* or upon any other."[895]

Professor Pringle-Pattison in a commentary on this view of religion remarks: "Thus man creates God, all-powerful and all-good, the mystic unity of what is and what should be."[896] This is no exaggeration of the position of Mr. Russell; for the latter

[892] W. JAMES, *Varieties of Religious Experience*, p. 31.

[893] Ibid., p. 34.

[894] EUCKEN, *Truths of Religion*, p. 129.

[895] *Hibbert Journal*, "The Essence of Religion," vol. ix. No. 41 (October 1912), pp. 49-50.

[896] *Hibbert Journal*, vol. xii. (October 1913).

himself has told us: "Thus man worships at the shrine his own hands have built."[897]

Two entirely different notions of religion are bound to arise according as we take our point of departure from God or from man. Common-sense philosophy and theology made God the term of the relations of creatures to Him. Our very being, the conservation of our being—all is from Him. In the intellectual life the knowledge of certain conclusions, engendered by certain principles, would disappear if we forgot the principles, because it is these principles which are the superior cause, not only of the becoming but also of the being of the effect.[898] In a still deeper way do we depend upon God ... Religion, then, on the traditional notion, becomes the sum of man's duties to God—either in the natural or in the supernatural order. Religion is primarily and essentially man's *service of God.*

Contemporary thought, on the contrary, making religion start with self, makes it the sum of *God's duties to man.* If God is the source or the *ratio* of religion, then creatures are His servants; if self be the source of religion, then God is the servant of men.

If God is mere appearance in the Absolute, and will eventually be lost in it; if finite selves are eternal, and have a being independent of God; if God is a mere "child of the Imaginal," a creation of our desire, a being who learns from us how to be "more effectively faithful to His own greater tasks" and whose "very character depends on our acts," a mere *primus inter pares,* without foresight of good and evil, facing "the blackness of the unknown and the blind joys and confusions of life;" if God is merely the universe with a nisus towards deity; if He is the work of our conscience and we "worship at the shrine our own hands have built;" if God is the sum of all consciousness and appears at the term of evolution and not at its beginning; if He is so weak that He "draws strength and increase of being from us," and "owes His being to the pre-existing finites;" if we must change

[897] *Philosophical Essays*, chap. "The Free-Man's Worship" (1910).

"La religione è questo affissarsi dell' uomo nell' oggetto della sua coscienza e obliarsi."—C. GENTLE, *Discorsi di religione*, p. 79.

"La religione è ignoranza respetto alla scienza."—C. GENTLE, *Sommario de pedagogia*, ii. p. 212.

[898] I q. 104 art. 1.

our idea of God with every new scientific advance and change of government; if His "nature is sustained by us;" if He is a mere President of a Cosmic Commonwealth,—then all that common-sense had regarded as holy and sacred is vain and foolish, and God, instead of being the Lord and Creator of the Universe, the Supreme Goodness, Beauty and Truth, is merely the servant of man—and religion, whose real end is to express the dependence of man on God, now becomes the dependence of God on man, whether God be real or a mere creation of our conscience. We are no longer the "mere puppets" of God, as Dr. McGiffert reminds us,[899] but rather God-makers; hence all adoration is looked upon as childish and unworthy of God as well as of man. Professor James has told us that a God who can take "delight in toyshop furniture, tapers and tinsel costume and mumbling and mummery, and finding His glory enhanced thereby ... seems intolerably bald and chalky and bleak."[900] We are no longer the "subject of God," but His "intimate partner."[901] "It is, I believe, felt ... that we help to sustain the nature of God."[902] Man and God are business partners sharing one another's losses and profits. This whole modern conception is concisely summed up in the following sentence, which represents the priority of man over God in this business, of which God is really the silent partner: "We and God have business with each other."[903] To just this extent, God is humanized and reduced to the level of a mere man who enjoys priority, not in virtue of His intrinsic nature, but in virtue of convention or empty titles. Modern theology, taking over the philosophical notion of religion as the sum of God's duties to man, has worked it out in the Christian doctrines of the Incarnation and Redemption. Though such a discussion is outside the scope of this work, we can note it as another token of the humanization of God. The Incarnation is represented solely and exclusively as the evolution of God's love for man, of which the act of Redemption is the triumph. There is no question of justice nor genuine justification involved. Man has no debt which he owes to God. The whole idea may be represented by picturing

[899] A. C. MCGIFFERT, *Christianity and Democracy*, p. 36.
[900] *Varieties of Religious Experience*, p. 330.
[901] *Pluralistic Universe*, p. 27.
[902] S. ALEXANDER, *Space, Time and Deity*, vol. ii. p. 398.
[903] *Varieties of Religious Experience*, *loc. cit.*

a man sitting calmly on the wharf of a great sea. Suddenly up from behind him there rushes a friend who throws himself into the water and is drowned, just to convince the man on the wharf that he loved him. Such is the modern notion of the Incarnation and Redemption, viz. God throwing Himself into the sea of suffering and hardship to convince man of His love. The whole scene would have much more reason if the man on the wharf really fell into the water and his friend came to save him from drowning by giving His own life—and this is the traditional notion.[904]

"To put the situation bluntly, religion must be separated from the other-worldly pull of the traditional theologies and be sanely grounded in the outlook of modern knowledge. There is no need for a rabid antitheism. The truth is, rather, that mankind is outgrowing theism in a gentle and steady way until it ceases to have any clear meaning ... A humanist's religion can admit no cunning division into the things which are God's and the things which are Caesar's."[905] It would be quite as correct, then, to say that the highest term of religion is "humanity," and that Christianity is the "religion of humanity."[906] "The only possible service of God must consist in the service of men."[907]

Such is the spirit of modern philosophy—divinization of man and humanization of God. Stressing his own sufficiency, making himself the measure of Being and Truth, attributing to himself a divine knowledge and a participated Divine nature, man has pulled down God from the heavens and reduced Him to a mere shadow of Himself. In stressing his own insufficiency, John the Baptist stressed for his own mind the greatness of God. In stressing his own sufficiency, the modern philosopher stresses for his own mind the poverty of God. He takes an "irreligious humanity as a religion. It is actually much more difficult to worship a humanity that is not worshipping. A self-contained and self-centred humanity would chill us in the same way as a self-contained and self-centred human being. For the spiritual hungers of humanity are never merely hungers for humanity ...

---

[904] R. G. BANDAS, *The Master-Idea of Saint Paul's Epistles, or the Redemption*, pp. 268-85.
[905] R. M. SELLARS, *The Next Step in Religion* (1918), pp. 213-17.
[906] CHARLES A. ELLWOOD, Ph.D., *The Reconstruction in Religion* (1922), p. 183.
[907] Ibid., p. 162.

The child in the field, if left entirely to himself, does not wish to find the perfect parish ruled over by the perfect parish council. The child in the field wants to find fairyland; and that type of fancy must either be satisfied or thwarted, but it cannot be turned into something totally different ... In other words, it is impossible to turn all the eyes of that mutual admiration society inwards."[908] Putting the whole philosophy in a formula which expresses the perversion of the traditional notions, we have the following:—

Mind is confused with Being.

Grace is confused with Nature.

Man is confused with God.

Or, in one simple formula contrasted with the traditional notion, it may read:—

We take God's measure[909]—God takes our measure.[910]

There is "an alteration in the seat of authority." It is the transfer of the seat of authority from God to man, and a transfer of the measure from God to man. "The earth of things, long thrown into the shadow by the glories of the upper ether, must resume its rights."[911]

"In the beginning God made man to His own image and likeness."

In the twentieth century man makes God to his own image and likeness.

"Instaurare omnia in homine" is the motto of contemporary thought; with Swinburne it sings "Glory to man in the highest;" with Mr. Wells it pleads the cause of "the higher man of today," and predicts the day when "men will be like Gods;" it insists that "man must have a vote in the councils of the world."[912] With Mr. Fawcett it says that "each sentient is a prospective Demiurge."[913]

[908] FRANCIS DUDLEY, *Will Men be like Gods?*, introduction by G. K. Chesterton, pp. iv, v.

[909] *Pragmatism*, p. 98.

"The best in every case is to ask whether our ideas and practices really answer to our need, while to judge them from the *outside* by applying some other criterion is mistaken and dangerous."—BRADLEY, *Essays on Truth and Reality*, p. 431.

[910] *C. G.*, lib. 2, c. 12.

[911] *Pragmatism*, p. 123.

[912] MOORE, *Pragmatism and its Critics*, p. 415.

[913] *Divine Imagining*, p. 222. "Our nation has been founded upon what we might call

"The historic mission which it fulfils is to prepare the advent of a humanity sitting in the visible world as in the temple of God, and showing itself as if it were God Himself. It is this reign which it announces as the prophets announced the kingdom of God."[914] Yet there are many who, not lacking either wisdom or penetration, find such a "kingdom of God" no more than a travesty, and who, through their love of truth, cannot listen to these prophets. The wisdom of the ages and the epitome of our experience is given in the simple truth understood by the simple and forgotten by many a philosopher, that we are not "God-makers but God-made."

---

the American religion, has been baptized in the faith that a man needs no master to take care of him, and that ordinary men are very well able to take care of their own salvation by their own efforts."—JAMES, *Critique Philosophique*, t. 11, p. 139; quoted by WAHL, *Les Philosophes Pluralistes*.

[914] JACQUES MARITAIN, *Anti-Moderne*, p. 98.

It is interesting to note the attitude of the Angelic Doctor towards this process of divinization of man. "In another way," he writes, "one may desire to be like unto God in some respect which is not natural to one; as if one were to desire to create heaven and earth, which is proper to God; in which desire there would be sin. It was in this way that the devil desired to be like God. Not that he desired to resemble God by being subject to no one else absolutely; for so he would be desiring his own non-being, since no creature can exist except by holding its existence under God. But he desired resemblance to God in this respect—by desiring, as his last end of beatitude, something which he could attain by the virtue of his own nature, turning his appetite away from supernatural beatitude, which is attained by God's grace. Or, if he desired as his last end that likeness of God which is bestowed *by grace, he sought to have it by the power of his own nature*, and not from Divine assistance according to God's ordering."—I q. 63 art. 3. See also I-II q. 73 art. 5, and II-II q. 46 art. 1.

IVE Press